Gender and German Cinema

Gender and German Cinema

Feminist Interventions

VOLUME I:
GENDER AND REPRESENTATION IN NEW GERMAN CINEMA

edited by

Sandra Frieden
Richard W. McCormick
Vibeke R. Petersen
Laurie Melissa Vogelsang

BERG

Providence / Oxford

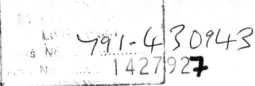

Published in 1993 by
Berg Publishers, Inc.
Editorial offices:
221 Waterman Street, Providence, RI 02906, U.S.A.
150 Cowley Road, Oxford OX4 1JJ, UK

© Sandra Frieden, Richard W. McCormick, Vibeke R. Petersen,
Laurie Melissa Vogelsang

**A CIP catalogue record for this book is available from the British
Library.**

Library of Congress Cataloging-in-Publication Data

Gender and German cinema : feminist interventions / edited by
    Sandra Frieden ... [et al.].
        p. cm.
    Filmography: v. 1, p.   ; v. 2, p.
    Includes bibliographical references and indexes.
    Contents: v. 1. Gender and representation in new German
    cinema — v. 2. German film history/German history on film.
        ISBN 0–85496–947–0 (cloth; v. 1) — ISBN 0–85496–243–3
    (pbk.; v. 1). — ISBN 0–85496–323–5 (cloth; v. 2). — ISBN
    0–85496–324–3 (pbk.; v. 2)
        1. Motion pictures—Germany—History. 2. Women in motion
    pictures. 3. Feminism and motion pictures—Germany.
    I. Frieden, Sandra G.
PN1993.5,G3G357   1993
791.43'652042—dc20   92–25618
                                                          CIP

Cover photo: Veruschka von Lehndorff as Dorian Gray in Ulrike
Ottinger's *The Mirror Image of Dorian Gray in the Yellow Press* (1984).
Photo courtesy of Ulrike Ottinger.

Printed in the United States by Edwards Brothers, Ann Arbor, MI.

Contents

Contents of Volume II:
German Film History/German History on Film

Acknowledgments

The editors would like to thank Helke Sander, Valie Export, Gabriele Weinberger, Renate Möhrmann, and Joyce Rheuban for their kind help in providing and/or obtaining photos for this volume. For computer help, we thank Bill Barthelmy, Karen Storz, and Leo Duroche. Angelika Rauch and Peter Mühle also provided much help in their functions as Research Assistants at the University of Minnesota, as did Thomas Stratmann and Tanya Reifenrath at the University of Houston. For moral support "when the details got too petty," we thank Karl Schaefer and Joan Clarkson; and for their tolerance, Blake, Cary and Kelly Frieden. Isa and Susana McCormick provided playful distraction. Robert Riddell, John Lowney, Ellen Maly, and Marion Berghahn at Berg Publishers were wonderfully supportive editors. The organization Women in German gave us the momentum to follow through on our original idea (and introduced us to each other), and we thank everyone who encouraged us.

We dedicate these volumes to the memory of Sydna (Bunny) Weiss and Sigrid Brauner, both of whom shared our joy in this project.

Foreword

Gender . . .

> "Until we understand the assumptions in which we are
> drenched we cannot know ourselves."
> — ADRIENNE RICH, *On Lies, Secrets and Silence*
> (New York: W.W. Norton, 1979), 35.

Our experience of the world, we understand Rich to say,
coheres as an immersion and a surfacing. Our assumptions
lie about us – some buoyant, others held in suspension, still others massive and unwieldy, submerged in the silence that Rich
would have us interrupt. Nothing is superfluous here, nothing
innocent. The assumptions in which we are drenched are not just
idle conjectures, suggestive speculations, working hypotheses.
Nor are they the ideas, objects, and people we only take for granted. In a more secret and profound way, these assumptions work
to appropriate, to seize, to dispossess us of our own presence. Sat-
urated with the collective dogmas of our histories, we see ourselves and the world only through the murky perspective of how-
things-have-always-been-and-are-supposed-to-be; contradictions
are lost in the undertow. Surfacing, then, to follow this metaphor,
means getting (at least) our heads above water. We need to see
the contradictions of our own experience: they validate our
uniqueness even as they intensify our fear of drowning. Indeed,
the point is not to get out of the water, but to learn to swim.

Our experience of the world, then, is cast in contradictions.
Once we surface, we begin to refract our assumptions through
the filter of our own experience (instead of the other way
around), seeking a reconciliation and a coherence that do not
obliterate contradictions, but rather illuminate them from
many sides. The particular interest of these two volumes is to
refract the history of German cinema, with all its contradictions, through the specific category "gender."

Why "gender"? Gender shapes our experience of the world – not exclusively, but profoundly, not uniformly, but persistently. With our birth into a gendered society, our perceptions of self and of others are defined within contexts of "masculine" and "feminine." While the socialization process assures that we all learn the meanings of strength and sensitivity, of dominance and dependency, of coercion and nurturance, this same process contorts us to impossible posturings of gender-appropriate behaviors. Human energy is thus harnessed in the service of gendered proprieties, from voice inflection to choice of profession. Gendered ways of being and gendered ways of seeing are imprinted to a depth we have only begun to explore.

Feminism, as both philosophy and politics, informs and reforms by exposing the contradictions and the consequences of gendered socialization. As a philosophy, feminism understands that societies ascribe to women *and* men supposedly "natural" characteristics – characteristics, in fact, to which societies subject their members from birth. It does not quite go without saying that most societies, at great cost to both women and men, assign inequitable importance and power to men, based on such characteristics. As a politics, feminism gives voice to the contradictions, works to question and change the value systems that perpetuate and cherish those traits understood as "masculine" over those understood as "feminine." Feminism, then, is quite meaningfully a *body* of thought aimed at change.

The products and the processes of cinematic production provide an illustrated study of gendered socialization. Feminists (among others, to be sure) see in film analysis the opportunity for a graphic accounting of existing social structures: not merely in historical representations of values and experience, but as the workings of contradictions and associations revealed in content, internal structure, and layers of social relations. Film, predominantly representational, provides illustrated social self-perceptions – social narratives of development cast to the judgments taught by culture. We can study cinematic reception as a cultural artifact: how a contextualized image elicits desired responses based on shared historical and cinematic-communicative experiences. Insofar as cinema depends on substantial financial resources, we may study the "rules" of its production and distribution in a given society – why some films (and some filmmakers) are highly visible, while others are in effect suppressed. Insofar as cinema is national and historical, we can study its function within a given society to (re-)produce or question the values and archetypes, the idols and idylls of the producing culture. Indeed, such studies of cinema's functioning within society have brought feminist cine-analysts to question the very forms and modes of cinematic communication, and in particular to investigate those cinematic issues which relate to cultural self-understanding and to feminism's project of change: what can cinema teach us about ourselves and about the processes, assumptions, contradictions, and limits of our socialization? How does cinema function within the experience of the individual and within society to perpetuate the status quo or to question it? Can film and the study of it be agents of social change?

Feminism(s)

Our mention of feminism is not coincidental. The category of "gender" is used here neither to disguise, nor to efface a feminist agenda. It is our goal in the two volumes of *Gender and German Cinema* to "intervene" in German film criticism by presenting a number of feminist discussions of German films – just as German feminist filmmakers have attempted to intervene in the course of German film history since the 1960s. This project arose from our frustration with publications that for the most part ignored films by women directors and feminist approaches to German film. At this point, Patrice Petro's excellent *Joyless Streets: Women and Melodramatic Representation in Weimar Germany*[1] is just about the only book-length analysis in English of German cinema that is explicitly feminist. Our volume includes discussions of German films from a number of historical periods, and it presents a variety of ways that feminism deals with German films. Feminist film criticism, like feminism in general, is by no means monolithic; a number of theoretical approaches have been developed and applied in examining issues of gender. Some of the essays in these two volumes analyze cinematic technique, production, distribution, and reception; some debate the politics of representation – of women, of female sexuality, and of history in general. There are psychoanalytically based

1. Patrice Petro, *Joyless Streets: Women and Melodramatic Representation in Weimar Germany* (Princeton: Princeton Univ. Press, 1989). As we go to press, we are also happy to see another such publication: *Women and the New German Cinema* by Julia Knight (London: Verso, 1992).

investigations of visual pleasure in the cinema, there are socio-historical studies, and essays which draw on both approaches (as well as others). German films from a number of periods in the long history of German film production are discussed: from *The Doll* (1919) to the 1980s, from films made in the Weimar Republic and the Third Reich to films of both post-war German states. Films by both female and male directors are examined.

There is admittedly a strong emphasis here on films by women and on the representation of women in films by directors of either sex. If we are examining the ideological construction of gender in film and society, why the almost exclusive focus on the construction of the "feminine" gender? Our reasons are primarily pragmatic: once again, work by feminist film-makers and feminist critics concerned with the cinematic representation of women has for too long been ignored, especially with regard to German cinema. In addition, it is precisely such feminist work that initiated the broader project of investigating the dynamics of gender in the culture at large. "Men's studies," for instance, is obviously modeled after women's studies, and the more serious (and honest) adherents of such studies acknowledge the debt to feminism. The construction of masculinity is certainly related to the construction of femininity; indeed, they support the same dominant ideology. We welcome more work unmasking the social and psychic construction of the myths of masculinity. Nonetheless, as oppressive as such myths may often be – to men as well as women – one should not forget the obvious asymmetry in power relations between the two genders. Patriarchal societies do place burdens on men, too (especially men whose class, ethnicity, or sexual orientation is devalued by those societies), but it is clear that the burdens placed on women are almost always greater (by definition: in patriarchal societies, women are valued less than men).

Monique Wittig has asserted that only the female gender is "marked," that the male gender is conflated with the universal in patriarchal discourse, and the female is limited therefore to a particular "sex" (and thus with sexuality in general). It is thus only logical that a critical investigation of the female "gender" in particular would expose the contradictions of the ideological system called "gender."[2] There is, however, much theoretical

2. See for example Judith Butler's discussion of Wittig in *Gender Trouble: Feminism and the Subversion of Identity* (New York: Routledge, 1990), 18–21, etc.

debate around the category "gender." Constance Penley, in an introduction to her book of essays on "film, feminism, and psychoanalysis," maintains that the term "sexual difference" is preferable. She feels that "gender" can be "put on a level with other differences" – that is, with *social* differences – and the advantage to the category "sexual difference" is that it cannot.[3] As much as we acknowledge our debt (and that of many essays in these two volumes) to the psychoanalytical school of feminist film criticism to which Penley belongs, the idea that the psychic construction of sexual difference can be so neatly separated from the social strikes us as somewhat at odds with the feminist dictum that "the personal is the political." Any strict dichotomy between the psychic and the social, the "subjective" and the political, is contrary to that proposition. Teresa de Lauretis has called this the "fundamental proposition of feminism," and she asserts that it "urges the displacement of all such oppositional terms, the crossing and re-charting of the space between them. No other course seems open if we are to reconceptualize the relations that bind the social to the subjective." [4]

Judith Butler finds that "gender" cannot be "conceived merely as the cultural inscription of meaning on a pregiven sex (a juridical conception); gender must also designate the very apparatus of production whereby the sexes themselves are established."[5] Thus "gender" cannot be placed on either side of a "social/psychic" dichotomy, but rather is part of the process that produces that very dichotomy, as well as a whole system of dichotomies, including "male/female." Butler's radical questioning of gender and "sex" represents an important theoretical project: the deconstruction of any "prediscursive" essence attached to these terms. Her antiessentialist project also includes questioning the idea that "women" are the "subject of feminism."[6] Our focus, however, remains on "women" and "feminism," not out of any sympathy with essentialism, but rather on pragmatic – and political – grounds. We are concerned with the *social* reality (realities) of women (and not any monolithic female identity or prediscursive essence).

3. Constance Penley, *The Future of an Illusion: Film, Feminism, and Psychoanalysis* (Minneapolis: Univ. of Minnesota Press, 1989), xix.

4. Teresa de Lauretis, *Alice Doesn't: Feminism, Semiotics, Cinema* (Bloomington: Indiana Univ. Press, 1984), 56.

5. Butler, *Gender Trouble*, 7.

6. Butler, *Gender Trouble*, 1–7.

It was out of concern with the social experience(s) of women that feminism began – specifically, out of a concern with the oppression of women. This is by no means the only form of oppression, but nonetheless it is a real one, and one that still persists, in spite of any gains that have been made. Feminism's theoretical investigation of the cultural parameters and ideological foundations of women's experience(s) should never lose sight of real political struggles and real suffering. By "real" we do not mean anything "prediscursive" (although it may well include the "extra-discursive"). Systems of discourse require analysis (especially in terms of their relation to power), and the psychoanalytical insight into the split subject has been invaluable theoretically. Nonetheless there is a reality to social oppression that should not be effaced. Only a Faurisson could be interested in denying the reality of the crimes committed against the Jews, gypsies, and homosexuals in Nazi concentration camps. Similarly, we would assert that the suffering of Central Americans at the hands of death squads armed by the U.S. (especially during the 1980s) was real. The suffering of women is real – the suffering, for example, caused by pervasive sexual violence against women in many cultures (including the so-called "developed" countries) over many centuries. Our point is not that these examples of social oppression are the "same," but rather that, in spite of our skepticism about "positivism," there is a "positivity" to certain social and political realities, certain material conditions, that we feel it is irresponsible to discount. A connection to the political struggle of women has always characterized feminism. De Lauretis sees the productive tension between the "critical negativity" of feminist theory and the "affirmative positivity" of feminist politics as fundamental to the feminist project.[7] We agree: *both* are necessary.

History and the German Context

Our emphasis here on the political, the social, and the material is indicative of our training in certain German intellectual traditions that have influenced both German filmmaking and German feminism. Above all we are referring to the Marxist tradition and its "historical materialism." As in the United States, the

7. Teresa de Lauretis, *Technologies of Gender: Essays on Theory, Film, and Fiction* (Bloomington: Indiana Univ. Press, 1987), 26.

"second wave" of feminism began in the Federal Republic of Germany (West Germany) when women activists in the late 1960s distanced themselves from the male-dominated New Left. They rejected the rigid Marxism characteristic of many male activists in the student movement, for whom the "woman's question" was only a "secondary contradiction."[8] Nonetheless, a strong concern with historical analysis and material conditions remained important for many West German feminists – and feminist filmmakers – in a way less evident in the U.S., for instance, which has an intellectual tradition in which Marxism has been much more marginal.

Historical materialism has influenced our thinking about these two volumes to some degree, but we would not assert that it is equally relevant to all of the articles we have collected here. In any event, beyond the influence of the Marxist tradition in Germany, there are other, more obvious reasons why a concern with history would be so important for German intellectuals and filmmakers, female and male: above all, it has to do with the German experience under National Socialism. Intellectuals, writers, and filmmakers old enough to remember those years, or the immediate postwar chaos and instability left in the wake of fascism and the war, have often felt it their duty to come to terms with that historical legacy. The fascist impact on filmmaking specifically cannot compare to its larger crimes – above all genocide – but it was a negative one nonetheless. Many of the best directors fled Germany in the 1930s (Lang, Sirk, Wilder, Siodmak, et al.), and they left behind a mostly mediocre and politically compromised group of film directors who would dominate the film industry in West Germany into the 1960s. There are thus a number of reasons why any study of German cinema must emphasize history. It is our hope that this emphasis is obvious in both of our volumes – not just in Volume II, which deals specifically with the relation between German social history, German film history, and the depiction of German history on film, but in Volume I as well, which is concerned with a broad range of films made in the era of the "New German Cinema," that is, from the 1960s into the 1980s. Just as gender dynamics are a major focus of our "history" volume, so the vol-

8. See for example Renny Harrigan, "The German Women's Movement and Ours," *Jump Cut* 27 (1982): 42–43; and Edith Hoshino Altbach, Jeanette Clausen, Dagmar Schultz, and Naomi Stephan, eds., *German Feminism: Readings in Politics and Literature* (Albany, N.Y.: SUNY Press, 1984).

ume on gender and representation in the New German Cinema cannot ignore history.

Nonetheless, our stress here on history is not intended to imply support for the monolithic, totalizing model of history proclaimed by nineteenth-century positivism. That model claims "scientific objectivity" for its assertion of a single "History" – thus relegating so many other histories to silence. Following Walter Benjamin, we see this type of traditional historicism as being concerned with the history told of, by, and for the "victors," the conquerors: history from the perspective of the colonizers, not the colonized, of the owners, not the workers – and of patriarchal authority, not those who are most typically silenced by that type of authority: women. The historical approaches we favor are informed by a concern with those who have been the "losers" for most of Western history; they also openly acknowledge their own political agendas in the present. Habermas called this Benjaminian attitude to history "posthistoricism."[9] Today it might be more fashionably labeled a "new historicism," but perhaps a better label would be "feminist" historicism, for, as Judith Newton argues, much of what is "new" about new historicism was already pioneered by feminists in the 1970s trying to unmask the "objectivity" of traditional historicism.[10]

Because of the number of essays we want to publish, we have divided them into two volumes. The first volume is titled "Gender and Representation in New German Cinema," and by "New German Cinema" we mean the period from the 1960s into the 1980s. This era of German filmmaking is the one for which we provide by far the most thorough coverage, in large part because of our interest in the extraordinary number of women filmmakers who were able to start making films in the Federal Republic of Germany (West Germany) and West Berlin during those years; many of these directors made films that are informed by feminist perspectives. We also include in Volume I some coverage of films and filmmaking during the same era in the former German Democratic Republic (East Germany) and

9. Jürgen Habermas, "Modernity: An Incomplete Project," in *The Anti-Aesthetic: Essays on Postmodern Culture,* ed. Hal Foster (Port Townsend, WA: Bay, 1983), 5–6.

10. Judith Newton, "History as Usual? Feminism and the 'New Historicism,'" in *The New Historicism,* ed. H. Aram Veeser (New York: Routledge, 1989), 152–54.

Austria. Volume II is titled "German Film History/German History on Film," and it deals both with important films from earlier periods of German film history – the Weimar Republic, the "Third Reich," the Federal Republic in the 1950s – and with representations of German history in films of the New German Cinema. During the late 1970s and the early 1980s such films – made by both women and men – were produced in great number; they were primarily marked by a concern with confronting the direct and indirect legacies of the Third Reich, the most significant historical experience in twentieth-century German history. The centrality of that experience also bears on films made during the Third Reich (obviously), and on those made in its immediate aftermath, in the late 1940s and 1950s. It is significant for films made earlier as well, since films of the Weimar Republic obviously exist in some relation to the social and political conflicts of that era – including its gender dynamics – which led to the Nazi takeover in 1933.

What can the study of German film history from feminist perspectives bring to film studies? And the study of feminist and other forms of independent filmmaking in Germany? Among other things: an understanding of the potential (and limits) of filmmaking as an oppositional practice; the relation of specific aesthetic and commercial practices in filmmaking to the exclusion of women (on the screen, in the cinema, and/or behind the camera); the sociological, ideological, and linguistic constructions of genre and narrative, of social structures and history, of self and self-image. These are some of the issues that have been raised by women filmmakers in the German-speaking countries and addressed by feminist critics examining German film history as a whole. It is our hope that this volume can contribute to the same kind of feminist intervention in film studies and cultural studies in the United States.

Introduction

"New German Cinema," 1962–?

In the early 1960s, the film industry in the Federal Republic of Germany (West Germany) was in a period of intense financial and artistic crisis. Although competition from Hollywood films (and the control exerted by American interests over film distribution in West Germany) had made things difficult for the West German film industry over the entire postwar period, it was the growing popularity of television in the late 1950s that nearly destroyed the domestic industry. Besides its financial difficulties, the industry was plagued by artistic mediocrity to the extent that at the 1961 Berlin Film Festival no German film was considered worthy of the Federal Film Prize, the award that was supposed to be given to the best West German production.

At the same time, a number of independent young filmmakers were winning international recognition for their short films. The legendary moment usually considered the birth of what we now call the "New German Cinema" was the signing of the famous "Oberhausen Manifesto" in 1962 by a number of these young filmmakers. Actually, political lobbying led by cosigner Alexander Kluge was more important than the largely symbolic manifesto, since the lobbying actually led to funding for young filmmakers by 1965. What Kluge and the others wanted was a new model of government support for film production: the government, rather than supporting the commercial film industry (as had been done in Germany to varying degrees since the First World War), should instead provide funds for independent film production. The new model was meant to subsidize independent, "artistic" (rather than commercial) filmmaking; it could be compared to state support for the opera and the theater (although the much more expensive medium of film production never would get anywhere near the kind of money those less expensive arts enjoyed). This new model for public subsidy was only fitfully tried during the 1960s; broad financial support from a number of government agencies (especially the public television networks) did not materialize until the period between 1969 and 1982, when the Social Democrats were in power in West Germany.[1]

During these years the West German state seemed to exercise a certain degree of "open-mindedness" (or was it repressive tolerance?) vis-à-vis political critique within films. Commercial interests continued to receive a considerable share of subsidy support, and tolerance of political criticism served the government's desired image as a democratic state.[2] That tolerance had definite limits, as demonstrated in the controversies during the 1970s about terrorists, "sympathizers," the *Berufsverbot*, etc.. Nonetheless, a vibrant national cinema developed in these years, a "New German Cinema" that was critical both politically and in terms of its attitude toward cinematic conventions.

It probably is not surprising that at first it was primarily independent male filmmakers who benefited from the subsidy system. Women filmmakers struggled throughout the course of the 1970s to gain the same kind of access to funding. The women's movement in West Germany and Berlin was certainly an important influence on these women; many were active in that movement, and indeed filmmaker Helke Sander was one of its founders in 1968. In 1972 Sander and another filmmaker, Claudia von Alemann, convened the first international Women's Film Festival in West Berlin; in 1974 Sander founded the journal *Frauen und Film*, a journal that is today the oldest feminist journal on film anywhere. By the late 1970s a number of women had managed to get their film projects funded and to produce films which gained critical recognition: Sander, Mar-

---

1. See Thomas Elsaesser, *New German Cinema: A History* (New Brunswick, NJ: Rutgers Univ. Press, 1989), 24, 317–19. Among the many other good books in English on the New German Cinema are: Anton Kaes, *From Hitler to Heimat* (Cambridge: Harvard Univ. Press, 1989); Eric Rentschler, ed.,*Visions and Voices: West German Filmmakers on Film* (New York: Holmes and Meier, 1988), and Rentschler,*West German Film in the Course of Time* (Bedford Hills, NY: Redgrave, 1984); Klaus Phillips, ed., *New German Filmmakers: From Oberhausen Through the 1970s* (New York: Ungar, 1984); Hans Günther Pflaum and Hans Helmut Prinzler, *Cinema in the Federal Republic of Germany* (Bonn: Internationes, 1983); and John Sandford, *The New German Cinema* (New York: De Capo, 1980).

2. See Sheila Johnson, "A Star is Born: Fassbinder and the New German Cinema," *New German Critique* 24–25 (Fall/Winter 1981–82): 57–72.

garethe von Trotta, Ulrike Ottinger, Helma Sanders-Brahms, and Jutta Brückner are perhaps the most prominent names. They and others allied in order to lobby collectively so that women would not remain so underrepresented among the independent filmmakers favored by the subsidy system. The demands of the Organization of Women Working in Film in 1979 for 50 percent of all decision-making authority on film-funding boards and 50 percent of all production and distribution resources set a forceful agenda, and West German women did indeed become the most active national group of women filmmakers.[3] By 1989 West Germany had, as Thomas Elsaesser wrote, "proportionally more women filmmakers than any other national cinema."[4]

During the 1980s, however, things changed somewhat both for women filmmakers and for the New German Cinema in general. In 1982, the death of Fassbinder (of all the men in the New German Cinema probably the most interesting to feminists, although by no means unproblematic) was a great blow to the New German Cinema, if only because among its most prominent names, he had been the most productive and the most committed to remaining in Germany. But much more serious was another event of 1982: the coming to power of a government coalition led by the Christian Democrats. After that political change in West Germany, subsidies once again tended to go to filmmaking of a more commercial sort. This has made things more difficult for independent filmmakers, especially the many feminist filmmakers who had become prominent by the end of the 1970s. Nonetheless, they have continued to make films – indeed, at least five films by German women directors were shown at the 1992 Berlin Film Festival.

The West German example remains something of an inspiration to independent women filmmakers in other nations, and that is why this volume places so much emphasis on it. But there has also been filmmaking by women and films depicting gender

3. For more background on the history of feminist film culture in West Germany, see the articles by Miriam Hansen and Ramona Curry on *Frauen und Film* in volume 2 of this collection (*Gender and German Cinema*). Also, see for example Renate Fischetti, *Das neue Kino: Filme von Frauen. Acht Porträts von deutschen Regisseurinnen* (Dülmen-Hiddingsel: tende, 1992; Renate Möhrmann, *Die Frau mit der Kamera: Filmemacherinnen in der Bundesrepublik Deutschland. Situationen, Perspektiven: Zehn exemplarische Lebensläufe* (Munich: Hanser, 1980); and *Jump Cut*'s issues on West German women filmmakers, nos. 27 (1982) and 29 (1984).

4. Elsaesser, *New German Cinema*, 185.

conflicts in other German-speaking countries. In this volume, we devote one article (only one, unfortunately) to films made in the former German Democratic Republic (East Germany); we also provide discussion of the work of Austria's most influential feminist filmmaker, Valie Export, a woman whose films are all the more impressive when one takes into account the generally much less favorable conditions for independent filmmaking that have existed in Austria.

Beyond our interest in highlighting the achievements of women filmmakers, we have organized this volume to include articles that examine the function of gender both psychologically and politically, within the text of a film or in terms of a film's address to gendered spectators. The analysis of gender goes much further than taking note of the gender of a film director. The articles here do not uniformly condemn the depiction of gender in films by men, nor are they uniformly laudatory of its depiction in films by women. Feminism and a concern with the deconstruction of patriarchal conceptions of gender do in general mark the films of the women more than the men, but some male directors are clearly subversive of conventional understandings of gender – Fassbinder and Lothar Lambert especially. And an examination of the representation of gender in the New German Cinema demands a look at some of the most well known male directors of that cinema – among whom we have selected Fassbinder, Wim Wenders, and Alexander Kluge. Furthermore, just as the narrative and cinematic strategies of those three directors are clearly distinct, so too is it impossible to speak of any monolithic style among the women directors – from the more narrative cinema of von Trotta to the more experimental (yet nonetheless distinct) styles of Sander, Ottinger, or Export, there is a wide range of representational (and non-representational) strategies evident in the films discussed here.

"Narrative" vs. "Experimental" Cinemas?

One cannot discuss the representation of gender in a film without considering the question of cinematic representation in general. The films discussed in this volume certainly span a spectrum that runs from an orientation toward narrative cinema to more experimental attitudes toward conventional narrative forms. Thus we have divided the volume into two parts, one devoted primarily to more narrative films, the other to more experimental films. This is not meant to indicate our support for any "binary opposition" between narrative and experimental films. Feminism in our opinion works to subvert such oppositions, and in any case cannot be reduced to purely formal considerations. The division we have made here is not only for the most part a pragmatic one, but at times a bit arbitrary. We would also like to emphasize that the "experimental" films here are characterized not so much by a rejection of narrative as a playful appropriation of narrative to experimental (and feminist) ends, just as the "narrative films" here are not merely conventional in their use of narrative. None of them are products of the commercial industry; all are examples of independent cinema to one degree or another. They too represent experiments with narrative cinema, albeit more "accessible" ones. The success of a particular cinematic strategy obviously depends on an interaction of factors much more complex than the formal distinction at issue here. And one of the most typical characteristics of German feminist filmmaking has been precisely its experimentation with a number of forms that employ both narrative and techniques of distantiation to varying degrees.

Wim Wenders cannot really be considered a feminist filmmaker or an anti-narrative filmmaker, but his narratives are not conventional, either. Indeed, one characteristic of many of his films, especially in the 1970s, was his ambivalence about telling stories – and until *Wings of Desire* (1987), anyway, there was a definite aversion to love stories with apparently happy endings. As Kathe Geist demonstrates in her examination of the roles played by mothers and children in his films, Wenders's rejection of conventional romance does not lead to an especially sensitive depiction of those who are not adult males.

Compared to Wenders, Fassbinder was more oriented toward narrative – indeed, toward melodrama – and was at the same time more Brechtian; he was also much more interested in foregrounding female characters. In his 1972 film *The Bitter Tears of Petra von Kant*, there are only female characters, and Jan Mouton discusses his use of a silent female character in that film as the starting point for an exploration of the theoretical implications of women's silence in the cinema. Anna K. Kuhn also chooses a Fassbinder film for formal analysis, describing the distantiation devices, or "modes of alienation," in Fassbinder's

1974 adaptation of Theodor Fontane's novel *Effi Briest*. According to Kuhn, these devices enable the film to present a clear critique of patriarchal relations. Whereas Wenders tends to avoid or idealize gender conflicts, Fassbinder confronted the most troubling aspects of sexual relationships and sexual identity with an almost masochistic obsession. This is probably why Fassbinder is more interesting to feminists than the other famous male directors of the New German Cinema. Nowhere is the confrontation with sexual and gender identity more disturbing – and more radical – than in *In a Year of 13 Moons* (1978), as Sandra Frieden demonstrates in her article.

That such concerns have preoccupied women filmmakers should come as no surprise, and those who are more oriented toward making relatively straightforward narratives have often chosen to center their stories around relationships between women – friends, sisters, mothers and daughters, etc. Roswitha Mueller uses one of the first West German films made by a woman – Ula Stöckl's *The Cat Has 9 Lives* (1968) – and Margarethe von Trotta's *Sisters* (1979) to demonstrate dominant patterns of female identity and female interaction at two crucial points in the recent history of feminism and the women's movement. Von Trotta is one of the most well-known of German women directors, and Renate Möhrmann discusses her first solo project as a director, *The Second Awakening of Christa Klages* (1977), a film in which relationships between women prove especially subversive of the status quo. The film was also a popular success, and Möhrmann examines its ability to address a wide audience. Klaus Phillips writes about *Erika's Passions*, a 1976 film by Stöckl that, like her 1968 film and the two von Trotta films mentioned above, foregrounds female bonding. Relationships between women are also important in Stöckl's more surrealistic narrative, *Reason Asleep* (1984), which is, as Sheila Johnson asserts, a feminist appropriation of a patriarchal myth. Following the Johnson piece, we reprint an interview with Stöckl done by Marc Silberman just as she was making *Reason Asleep*.

Long before Doris Dörrie's hit comedy *Men* (1986), Heidi Genée made a comedy that was also popular, but centered on a female character and was openly feminist: *1 + 1 = 3* (1979). Gabriele Weinberger demonstrates that the film's feminist project is evident at levels other than mere plot; examining the film's use of language, she shows how the protagonist moves from silence into speech. In attempting to go beyond the West German boundaries of New German Cinema to cover other German-language filmmaking of relevance to the project of this volume, we include an essay by Gisela Bahr dealing with gender dynamics in a number of films made (by directors of both genders) during the 1970s and 1980s in the former East German state.

In the second section of our volume, we begin our look at more experimental filmmaking with essays discussing two films by Helke Sander. The founder of *Frauen und Film* in 1974 and one of those who initiated the "second wave" of German feminism in 1968, Sander was also a member of the very first class to study at the German Film and Television Academy in West Berlin, which opened in 1966. B. Ruby Rich compares Sander's first feature film, *The All-Around Reduced Personality – REDUPERS* in 1977, one of the first films of many by West German women to gain critical acclaim in the latter half of that decade, with Alexander Kluge's *Part Time Work of a Domestic Slave* (1974). Kluge and Sander are often compared, as both are among the more experimental West German filmmakers, and both have been described as belonging to the Brecht-Godardian modernist school. Rich however demonstrates the difference between Kluge's style and what she calls the "feminist modernism" of Sander. We also reprint here a short interview with Helke Sander done by Marc Silberman in which Sander discusses her early career and *REDUPERS*.

Ruth Perlmutter discusses two films released in 1984, Sander's *The Trouble with Love* and Ulrike Ottinger's *The Image of Dorian Gray in the Yellow Press*. Ottinger is a director whose films are usually connected to different traditions of experimental filmmaking (surrealism and/or camp). Sabine Hake focuses on Ottinger's *Madame X – An Absolute Ruler* (1977), her first full-length feature, stressing its camp sensibility and its use of masquerade. Miriam Hansen locates Ottinger's most famous film, *Ticket of No Return* (1979), within the contexts of West German feminism and of the debate on visual pleasure waged in Anglo-American feminist film theory. We complement the discussions of Ottinger by reprinting an interview with her by Marc Silberman.

As opposed to Ottinger, the team of Danielle Huillet and Jean-Marie Straub is usually connected to the Brechtian project.

Sometimes they are accused of a rather ascetic modernism, but Barton Byg argues that in their 1984 film *Class Relations*, the conventional – Oedipal – narrative is indeed problematized, but without destroying pleasure. Lothar Lambert is an underground filmmaker who would never be accused of asceticism, modernist or otherwise. Jeff Peck provides an introduction to the films of Lambert, which focus on people on the margins, socially and sexually, and employ a low-budget, graphic realism mixed with both melodrama and humor.

Valie Export is an experimental feminist director who has been making films since the 1970s; her work has achieved international recognition, and it deserves to be compared to that of other feminist directors discussed in this volume (and in the second volume of *Gender and German Cinema* as well). Because she is Austrian, she has too often been neglected, a situation we would like to help remedy. Margret Eifler provides a thorough analysis of the various discursive elements at work in Export's first feature, *Invisible Adversaries* (1977). Ramona Curry discusses a short experimental film by Export, *Syntagma* (1983), a playful critique of the cinematic representation of the female body. Finally, in a 1987 interview with Margret Eifler and Sandra Frieden, Export comments on her work as a filmmaker, describing her experimentation with cinematic signification in connection with her own commitment to feminism and political art.

It is this commitment that guides her "interventions" in film practice, and the same commitment has guided our efforts in editing both volumes of *Gender and German Cinema*. We hope that this intervention of ours will have an impact on the writing and teaching of German film history, as well as help to underscore the importance of feminist film praxis and theory within cultural studies.

Part I

Narrative Cinema

I

Mothers and Children in the Films of Wim Wenders

k a t h e   g e i s t

*K*athe Geist examines Wenders's characteristic depictions of mothers
and children in a number of films he made in the early and mid-
1970s as well as in one of his films from the early 1980s, Paris, Texas
(1984). Geist asserts that these depictions have much more to do with
what she calls the "fantasist" strain in his films, as opposed to the
"realist" strain. Noting his apparent difficulty in focusing on women
characters in these films and his tendency to idealize children, she
argues that his use of these characters has more to do with male fan-
tasies and projections – or at any rate with Wenders's fantasies and
projections – than with real women and children.
—THE EDITORS

With the exception of *The Scarlet Letter* (*Der scharlachrote Buchstabe,* 1973), Wim Wenders's films are all about men, and the
typical Wenders hero is alone – usually by choice – alienated,
adrift in society or making a living on its fringes, unable to communicate easily or relate well with people. For him human relationships are nonexistent or tenuous at best. Heterosexual relationships are fleeting, inconclusive or unsatisfactory,[1] a fact
which bothers Wenders's audience and about which he is often
asked. In 1976 he explained his pessimism toward male-female
bonding this way:

> I know maybe a dozen men quite well, friends or people I see
> often. Of these twelve, not one knows how he should live with his

---

1. This article discusses films made before Wenders's *Wings of Desire (Der Him-
mel über Berlin,* 1987*)*, the story of an angel who gives up immortality for love of a
woman. This film is somewhat of a departure from the patterns described in this
article, patterns which Wenders established in his first fifteen years of feature
filmmaking and to which the generalizations in this article apply.

wife, that is knew, because in the meantime he's given up. . . . The possible exceptions . . . were simply those who repressed the most.[2]

Three years later he told Robin Wood, "I still haven't seen any film that gave me a decent, utopian notion about it [male-female relationships]." Wood replied, "I'm not asking for a utopian notion." Wenders answered, "That's what I wanted anyway."[3]

Relations between these men and their parents are likewise tenuous. In *Alice in the Cities* (*Alice in den Städten*, 1974), Philip plans to take the child Alice to his parents' house after he runs out of money, but when the detective informs them that Alice's mother has been located, Philip forgets about his parents, whom he hasn't seen in several years, and accompanies Alice to Munich. In *Wrong Move* (*Falsche Bewegung*, 1975), Wilhelm Meister leaves his mother to go on his travels and remarks to himself, "Later, somewhere else . . . I would be able to remember her better." In *Kings of the Road* (*Im Lauf der Zeit*, 1976), Robert visits his father, whom he has not seen in eight years, but their encounter is brief and difficult.

Sometimes two men develop a relationship that lasts the length of the film, as in *Kings of the Road* and *The American Friend* (*Der amerikanische Freund*, 1977); but in both cases the friendship dissolves shortly before the film ends. The only relationship between one of Wenders's men and another person that is still intact by the end of the film is that between Philip and nine-year-old Alice in *Alice in the Cities*. This exception points to the only consistently viable relationship in Wenders's films, that between young children and adults, usually their mothers.

Though peripheral to the main action of the film in all but *Scarlet Letter*, the mother-child relationship is also important in *Alice in the Cities, American Friend*, and *Paris, Texas* (1984). In examining the role of mothers and children, separately and together, one must bear in mind that Wenders's films run conjointly on two tracks, the realist and what I will call the fantasist.

2. "Ich könnte zum Beispiel behaupten, daß ich ein Dutzend Männer ganz gut kenne; Freunde oder Leute, mit denen ich oft zusammen bin. Ich könnte behaupten, daß von diesen zwölf kein einziger . . . weiß, wie er mit seiner Frau leben soll, beziehungsweise das gewußt hat, weil er es inzwischen aufgegeben hat . . . Die Ausnahmen . . . waren nur diejenigen, die am heftigsten verdrängt haben." F.H., "Die Männer dieser Generation [The Men of This Generation]," *Filmreport* 5–6 (1976).
3. Edward Lachman, Peter Lehman, Robin Wood, "Wim Wenders: An Interview," *Wide Angle* 2 (1976): 178.

The pacing, the ordinary yet quietly desperate lives of his heroes and heroines, their language, and the attention to detail, all of which Wenders sees as making each film a kind of document, contribute to a realist facade which cloaks the fantasist nature of many elements in the films. For example, Wenders describes the scene in *Kings* in which Robert wakes up one night to find another young man mourning over his wife's suicide as like a dream:

> From the moment that Robert goes into this space [in the back of the truck] . . . in which the neon sight "Apollo," a juke box . . . and five projectors stand, that has nothing more to do with the fact that two men are spending the night in a basalt mine somewhere. Robert enters a space which is no longer the space of the truck; actually he enters his own dream.[4]

The "dream" is not separate from the rest of the narrative, however, for the young man is still there in the morning, Bruno meets him, and the suicide's wrecked car is towed away. Yet for Wenders it operates on a separate, "fantasist" level in the film. Mothers and children partake of this same fantasist level, and the tensions which arise between realist and fantasist readings of his text are never more evident than when one looks closely at the portrayals of mothers and children, which culminate in *Paris, Texas.*

To understand what mothers and children mean for Wenders and how they function on these multi-levels, one begins by examining their positioning in his narratives. Obviously the mother-child relationship is central to *Scarlet Letter*, adapted from Hawthorne's novel, because the child is the reason for Hester's public censure. Wenders wanted to make the film "precisely because of the idea of the mother and the child," but he felt he failed with the character of Hester, who turned out to be "the only lead character in any of my films for whom I did not . . . have any feelings."[5] Glamorous Senta Berger, who played Hester, had been forced on Wenders because of her star power and was unsuited to the role. Whether the miscasting was entire-

4. "Von dem Augenblick an, in dem Robert hinten in diesen Raum reingeht . . . in dem die Leuchtschrift 'Apollo' steht, eine Musikbox steht . . . und wo fünf Projektoren stehen; da hat das eigentlich nichts mehr damit zu tun, daß zwei Männer in einem Basaltwerk irgendwo übernachten. Robert betritt da einen Raum, der nicht mehr der Raum 'Lkw' ist, eigentlich tritt er da in seinen eigenen Traum von dieser Nacht ein." F.H., "Männer."

5. Jan Dawson, *Wim Wenders* (New York: Zoetrope, 1976), 4.

ly at fault for Wenders' lack of interest in Hester, or whether he
was too little interested in women generally to develop a major
female character, is hard to say, since he never tried again. Wenders's interest in the child Pearl, however, was very keen, and he
cast the young actress Yella Rottländer as the eponymous lead in
his next film, *Alice in the Cities.*

Alice is also a mother-child story, but Wenders took care to
write out the mother early in the film. Alice's mother Lisa (Lisa
Kreuzer) has come to the U.S. with her boyfriend, but unable to
speak English, helpless and alienated in the strange environment, she is determined to go back. Through the intermediary
of a pilots' strike, she meets another German trying to return
home, the journalist Philip (Rüdiger Vogler), who is suffering
from writer's block, and entrusts him with Alice. Fearing her
boyfriend might do something desperate if she leaves him too
abruptly, Lisa writes a note to Philip asking him to take Alice
back to Europe ahead of her to mandate her own return. Philip
complies, but when Lisa fails to meet him in Amsterdam as
arranged, he and Alice set out on a search for the next best person, Alice's grandmother. Unable to find her, the two are about
to abandon the search when a police detective informs them
that the mother and grandmother have been found. Philip and
Alice set out by train to meet them, and the film ends with a
happy reunion implied but not shown. The mother-child motif
is stressed, however, and shown to be salutary when, toward the
end of the film, Philip aims his Polaroid at a mother and child
on the Rhine ferry, his change of subject matter indicating that
his alienation has subsided. (His subjects previously have been
empty spaces and machines.)

The American Friend contains a mother-child relationship
which, like that in *Alice,* is central to the film's plot but peripheral to its action. Mother and child are central in that the terminally ill Jonathan (Bruno Ganz) agrees to become a paid killer
in order to leave money for his wife (Lisa Kreuzer) and son, who
are present throughout the film and to whom he expresses
great tenderness. Once initiated into the underworld, however,
Jonathan's friendship with the sleazy Ripley (Dennis Hopper)
and his fascination with male violence become the center of the
film, and mother and child are consigned to the fringes.
Although Jonathan intends to return to his son at the end of the
film, one understands that he is too sullied, too morally com-

promised, actually to achieve this. One accepts his death near the scene of his last crime as both logical in terms of the plot (he is terminally ill) and necessary in terms of the film's moral structure. With him when he dies, his wife can only look on helplessly. In Lisa Kreuzer's words, she is "a woman without a story."[6]

Wenders's most memorable mother-child story is *Paris, Texas*, whose script he wrote with American playwright Sam Shepard. Wenders describes the genesis of the story:

> Little by little we had the beginning of a story: a man who's lost, a little like Ulysses among the dead, who returns with one single idea, that of a woman. . . . The first person he meets is his brother and for a long time the film concerns just the two brothers. The search for the woman is limited to a desire. . . . One fine day there was a child, a boy. Sam always thought it was my idea. . . . Little by little it became the story of a family.[7]

The structure of the film reflects this genesis exactly. It begins with the father Travis (Harry Dean Stanton) alone on the Texas desert. He collapses, and his brother Walt (Dean Stockwell), a billboard designer, is summoned from Los Angeles. While the two travel back to L.A., Walt explains that he and his French wife Anne have been caring for Travis's son Hunter (Hunter Carson) since Travis's marriage to Jane (Nastassja Kinski) broke up four years before. Hunter is eight and doesn't know his father any longer. In an attempt to reacquaint them, Walt shows a home movie of a vacation five years earlier in which Travis and Jane play with the then three-year-old Hunter. Slowly Hunter warms up to his father, and when Travis, on a hint from Anne regarding Jane's whereabouts, sets out to find her, Hunter insists on going with him. Without saying good-bye to his foster family, he joins Travis in the search for Jane, telephoning Walt and Anne only at Travis's insistence and hanging up when they become upset.

6. Filmverlag der Autoren, "Der amerikanische Freund [The American Friend]," promotion brochure.
7. "Peu à peu, on avait le début d'une histoire: un homme perdu, un peu comme Ulysse chez les mort, et qui revient avec une seul idée, celle d'une femme... Le premier qu'il rencontre, c'est son frère, et pendant longtemps le film entier, c'était les deux frères. La recherche de cette femme se limitait au désir... Un beau jour, il y eut l'enfant, un garçon. Sam croyait toujours que c'était mon idée... De plus en plus, c'est devenu une histoire de famille." Michel Ciment and Hubert Niogret, "Entretien avec Wim Wenders [Interview with Wim Wenders]," *Positif* (September 1984): 10.

In Houston, Travis finds Jane working in a peep show, a sex club in which women in little cubicles talk to and act out fantasies for men who are separated from them by a pane of glass through which they can see the women, but not touch or be seen by them. At first Travis does not identify himself to Jane; he can, in fact, hardly speak at all. When he finds his voice, he asks her viciously if she goes home with her customers. Ashamed at his outburst he leaves and returns the next day. In a long monologue he identifies himself and recalls their married life and the spiritual/moral sickness that drove them apart. She was much younger than he, a teenager, and he became insanely jealous, fantasizing that when he was away at work, she was seeing other men. He brutalized her until she set fire to his bed one night and ran away. Awakening in time to save himself, he escaped the burning trailer and walked straight out into the desert, never looking back. Jane responds with a monologue in which she explains that after Hunter was born, she became restless and unhappy (a situation which inflamed Travis's jealousy even more). After leaving Travis, she found she could not care for Hunter and gave him to Walt and Anne, though she lived daily with the pain of being separated from him. (Every month she wires Anne a small amount of money for him.) Travis tells her that he has brought Hunter back to her, but that he cannot stay, for he can never wipe out the hurt his past behavior caused – and perhaps he is afraid he might repeat it.

Wenders explains Travis's decision this way: "In the end Travis realizes he's caused too much pain with his violence and there's no way to say it didn't happen. It happened, he realizes, and he's missed his chance because of it."[8] Travis leaves Hunter in a hotel room with a tape-recorded message explaining why he must leave. Jane goes to the hotel, and mother and son are reunited in a long embrace. The film's last shot is Travis looking up at the hotel room, then getting into his truck and driving away.

Thus the film apparently ends happily for Hunter and Jane but sadly for Travis, whose sins, like Jonathan's in *American Friend*, bar him from the family circle. Nevertheless Travis is heroic: he has reunited mother and son while denying himself the company of the only two people who love him, who could have made a home for him. In the face of such "nobility" added

8. Katherine Dieckmann, "Wim Wenders: an Interview," *Film Quarterly* 38, no. 2 (Winter 1984–85): 4.

to the tenderness of pure mother-love, one tends to forget that Jane's profession is hardly a suitable backdrop against which to bring up a child, that she presumably pursues this career because she has no other skills, that in whatever job she might take, she will be lucky to keep Hunter clothed and fed and will never be able to keep him in the style to which he has become accustomed. A steady paycheck would probably mean more to Hunter and Jane than Travis's noble self-denial.

The realist aspects of the film are further strained by Hunter's preternatural independence. No eight-year-old would voluntarily leave a loving and secure home to find a mother he cannot even remember, nor would he simply turn his back on people who had loved him and disciplined him – for what to his memory is his entire life – without a second thought.

While the situation Wenders presents in *Paris, Texas* is common enough – a broken home, an indigent mother and child, parental abduction – society does not usually view it in such positive terms. Such a discrepancy suggests that Wenders does not look at mothers and children in strictly realist terms, but that they have a specific, highly codified significance for him and therefore within his films.

In a telex message from the location shooting for *Scarlet Letter,* he wrote that the children in the film seemed like they were from "a science fiction film."[9] By this he meant that they seemed to come from another world and redeemed to some extent the misery he was experiencing while directing *Scarlet Letter* (the subject of the rest of the telex). "Children," he said later, "represent a sort of ideal view."[10] On the one hand children like Pearl in *Scarlet Letter,* Alice in *Alice in the Cities,* and Hunter in *Paris, Texas* represent an ideal view of personhood. They are whole, not yet forced into roles, uninhibitedly themselves. They are open to new experiences, unafraid, and wise. Neither Alice nor Hunter shrinks from accompanying virtual strangers on long journeys, and both insist on adding dimensions to the journey that the adults do not think of. Alice shows Philip around the city of Amsterdam while they wait, in vain, for her mother to arrive, and Hunter suggests buying dimestore walkie-talkies for the journey

9. Telex to PIFDA [Produktion im Filmverlag der Autoren], 17 November 1972 (Munich: Filmverlag archives).
10. Alain Masson and Hubert Niogret, "Entretien avec Wim Wenders [Interview with Wim Wenders]," *Positif* (October 1977): 24.

to Texas with Travis. Both come to the rescue of the adults. Hunter is the first to spot Jane when she drives into the bank where Travis expects to find her and wakens his sleeping father by means of the walkie-talkie. When Philip finds himself penniless and stranded in Cologne, Alice produces a one-hundred dollar bill from the pouch she carries around her neck and pays for his train ticket to Munich. These actions correspond to their saving of the adult men psychically, for both bring the emotionally damaged, alienated men, who have lost their ability to communicate, back to meaningful interaction with society.

Wenders thus idealizes the wholeness of the child's personality and, beyond that, attributes to children an innocence of vision which he compares to that of the ideal filmmaker. The latter will film what is right in front of him and in doing so will show people things they have never seen before because they have never looked. Wenders quotes Siegfried Kracauer, "The potential and rationale of film art lie in everything looking the way it is."[11] He uses children as examples of this fresh, innocent vision, this "ideal view."[12] The little boy at the end of *Kings of the Road* is writing down everything he sees. "As simple as that?" Robert asks after the boy describes his assignment. "As simple as that," the boy replies. In *Scarlet Letter* Pearl first sees the ship that will take her and her mother from the repressive colony just as Hunter in *Paris, Texas* is the first to see Jane. In *Alice in the Cities,* we *hear* the adults complain about the oppressiveness of New York City, but when we *see* Alice's view through the binoculars atop the Empire State Building, the city is transformed. Her gaze pans the tops of the skyscrapers, rests on one of the most beautiful, then follows the flight of a sea gull. In *American Friend,* the child is overtly associated with early (innocent) cinema: he plays with a zoetrope, then with a huge model of a Maltese cross; a moving light picture of a train called "The General" glows beside his bed. Early cinema, says Wenders, was a time when filmmakers "just photographed and were amazed at what they'd captured"[13] – the ideal view.

11. Dawson, *Wenders,* 23.

12. Masson and Niogret, "Entretien," 24. In a recent interview Wenders again lauded the child's view, calling it one of "wonderment" [verwunderten Blick]. André Müller, "Das Kino könnte der Engel sein," *Der Spiegel* (19 October 1987): 230.

13. ". . . die nur aufgenommen haben und sich gewundert haben, was dann auf dem Material drauf [sic] war." Heiko R. Blum, "Gespräch mit Wim Wenders [Interview with Wim Wenders]," *Filmkritik* (February 1972): 71.

In his portraits of children Wenders captures brilliantly the nuances of child behavior, which lend them a deceptive credibility; but they are not "real" children, described by someone who regularly takes care of children. Their needs in terms of security, stability, and ego are minimal, and they articulate these needs in a consistently charming rather than obnoxious way. They embody qualities of childhood instead of childhood itself, and these qualities – innocence, fresh vision, and spontaneity – are what the adult men need for their own redemption. (To understand the difference one need only compare Wenders's children to Lasse Hallström's in *My Life As a Dog*, which delights in children but centers on the child's need for security, reassurance, and love. Wenders's children need these things far less than the adults around them.)

The mothers in Wenders's films, for example, are far more needy than the children in terms of love, security, and sense of self, and the men in the films are inevitably unable to meet these needs. Although faithful in articulating the plight of these women, which includes the inadequacy of the men around them, Wenders ultimately shows little interest in them. He admits he lost interest in Hester; he wrote Lisa out of *Alice*; and he marginalized Marianne. In their place he has substituted the "missing mother," for whom his men yearn and search. When Alice demands a story from Philip, he tells her about a boy who spontaneously undertakes a journey and travels until he finally reaches the sea, at which point he remembers his mother. Alice falls asleep, and Philip never finishes the story, but the image of the wanderer who at some point changes course and tries to get back to his mother or a child's mother runs through Wenders's films. Burned out from his travels across America, Philip returns to Germany with Alice and searches for her mother. In *Kings of the Road*, Bruno and Robert briefly abandon their route along the East German border and drive to the Rhine to visit the house where Bruno grew up with only his mother. Finding only the ruined house, he weeps. In *Paris, Texas,* Travis returns to Houston with Hunter to search for the boy's mother.

For the adult male, the search for the mother is an elusive one. Although the restoration of Alice to her mother and a possible union between her and Philip is implied in *Alice in the Cities*, we never see the reunion. Bruno doesn't find his mother in *Kings,* and previously we have learned that Robert's mother is dead and that his father's mother died at his birth. In *Paris, Texas,* Travis finds Jane, but cannot stay with her.

The search for the mother corresponds to various structures in Wenders's films. In *Alice* it correlates with the hero's, and by extension Wenders's, search for a national identity in a Germany lost beneath the ruins of Nazism and the superstructure of American imperialism. Philip travels throughout America, feels lost and overwhelmed, then returns to Germany and rediscovers the part of it, the Ruhr, in which he (and Wenders) grew up via the search for Alice's mother/grandmother. Likewise the trip to the Rhine in *Kings* – ostensibly to visit Bruno's mother – allows the men to travel the breadth of West Germany and Wenders to work once again in the region where he grew up. (His family lived in Koblenz for a time and his grandmother in Boppard) After they return from the Rhine, Bruno tells Robert, "I'm glad we drove to the Rhine. For the first time, I see myself as someone who's put some time behind him, and that time is my story."

In *Kings* the missing mother also suggests a lack of nurture. Sufficient mothering in the past, the film implies, might have helped the men to get along better with women in the present. Robert accuses his father of dominating his wife (Robert's mother), which, we are led to suspect, may be the reason Robert could not make his own marriage work. As if by way of explanation, Robert's father tells him for the first time that he himself never had a mother. Bruno lives alone and is unable to relate to people, especially women. His one encounter with a woman that we see is awkward, chaste, and unfulfilling for him and the woman. Part of Bruno's thawing-out process is his trip home, a step which indicates his desire to return to a source of nurture, which in turn might help him overcome his difficulties with human society.

The inability to live with women is seen as a major stumbling block to the men's full integration into society and as a symptom of their regression. "If it [living with women] is impossible, you've got to make it possible," Robert tells Bruno. In *Alice,* too, Philip's alienation and writer's block are associated with his inability to get along with women, for when he complains about them to his girlfriend Angela, she suggests he has had these problems for a long time and throws him out. Evidently they had made him an insensitive companion. Thus the search for the mother is a search for reconciliation with one's self and with society.

Likewise in *Paris, Texas* the search for the mother is a search for reconciliation complicated by the fact that the mother is actually found. As the only "missing mother" who ever materializes, Jane must play a double role. On the one hand she is as needful as any other Wenders heroine and describes herself as such far more articulately (thanks to Sam Shepard): she is a lonely woman, abandoned by her husband and bereft of her child, guilt-ridden by her failure as a mother, and uncertain of her own identity. In fact her job allows her to change identities depending on the fantasies of the men who come to the peep show. On the other hand she is the *object* of Travis's fantasy and an image in his mind. Wenders admits that *Paris, Texas* is about "a man insisting on a certain image of a woman."[14] At first we see Jane *only* as an image within the film: her face on a strip of photomat pictures and the shots of her in the home movie. As seen by Travis in the peep show she is, in Wenders's words, "on the screen, or behind it, and is really the object of his imagination."[15]

As such she is not the needful person of her own self-description but the idealized "missing mother." She is a priestess, a mother-confessor who, separated from Travis by a pane of glass, hears his confession from the curtained booth of the peep show. His sin is jealousy, one of the seven deadly sins, a transgression of such magnitude that he cannot regain the paradise that Jane represents; in self-imposed penance he leaves the child, the innocent, who is still free to enter paradise. Reunited at the end Hunter and Jane become the "Mother and Child," an icon which for millennia has stood for redemption and the promise of salvation, Wenders's "utopian notion."[16]

The parallel between Hunter/Jane and Christ/Mary is pushed even further when one notes that Wenders sees Hunter as something like a substitute husband/lover for Jane. "At the end of my next to last film *Paris, Texas* a . . . little man takes his mother in his arms. The father leaves the stage free for this other love."[17] In keeping with the preternatural maturity of

14. Dieckmann, "Wim Wenders," 5.
15. Ibid., 5.
16. Lachman, Lehman, Wood, "Wim Wenders," 178.
17. "Am Schluss meines vorletzten Films, 'Paris, Texas', umarmt ein noch sehr kleiner Mann seine Mutter. Der Vater gibt die Bühne frei für diese andere Liebe." Müller, "Das Kino," 230. Cf. Helen Knode, "At long last, love: Wim Wenders," *East Village Eye* (November 1984): "I felt it was time to find another hero and, in the end, it's Hunter. . . . Everything I want to do for the next film is really based on the last film with Hunter and Jane, when he walks to her and takes her in his arms"(17).

Wenders's children, the son's love is seen as substituting for rather than merely complementing the father's. In Roman Catholic theology Christ is married to His Church, and Mary represents that Church.[18] Thus incest is implied in both mother/son relationships, a kind of theoretical incest, since both relationships are primarily symbolic.

In Wenders's films mothers and children belong more to the fantasist than the realist level, for both are extensions of the male protagonist's ego. The nuances of child behavior are real but the children are not. They are distillations, spiritual essences, that guide the men toward reconciliation and/or redemption. There is psychological realism in Wenders's portrait of the needful woman, but the filmmaker loses interest in her and his men do not get along with her. More often than not she is transformed into the "missing mother," who promises reconciliation and redemption without ever forcing the hero to confront his nemesis: the needs of women. There is a circular logic here, which Wenders recognizes when he admits, "Of course, Travis doesn't really have a future."[19]

18. The equation of Mary and the Church along with Christ's espousal to the Church was first formulated by St. Ambrose in the 4th Century and restated as recently as 1965 in Vatican II. The Coronation of the Virgin (by Christ) was frequently depicted in the Middle Ages and likewise gives the impression that, as Queen of Heaven, Mary is her son's consort.

19. Knode, "At long last, love"(16).

2

Women's Silent Voices

jan mouton

Jan Mouton's essay alludes to an obvious consequence of the use of sound in the cinema: the absence as well as the presence of sound becomes significant. Silence can indeed be more powerful than sound, and with this in mind, Mouton discusses the mute female character Marlene in Fassbinder's The Bitter Tears of Petra von Kant (1972). Noting that much feminist film criticism has dealt with the use of female speech in the cinema, but little work has been done on the topic of mute

Irm Hermand as Marlene in Rainer Werner Fassbinder's The Bitter Tears of Petra von Kant (1972).
(Photo courtesy of New Yorker Films)

female characters, she provides some historical background on the mute role in theatrical melodrama, and she then introduces concepts from Christian Metz and Jacques Lacan in her analysis of the power of the absence of speech. Discussing the role of Marlene in Fassbinder's film, she compares that role with another famous mute female role, Elisabeth in Ingmar Bergman's Persona (1966); she also cites similar examples of silence in films by women directors like Chantal Akerman, Marguerite Duras, Helma Sanders-Brahms, and Margarethe von Trotta.
— THE EDITORS

The girl wept and said, "Is there no way of saving my brothers?"
"No," said the old woman. "In all the world there's only one way

and it's so hard that you can't hope to succeed, for you would
have to keep silent for seven years, without speaking and without
laughing, and if you said a single word or if a single hour were
wanting from the seven years, all your trouble would be in vain,
and that one word would kill your brothers." Then the girl said in
her heart: "I know for sure that I'll save my brothers." She picked
out a tall tree and climbed up in it, and there she sat spinning,
and she neither spoke nor laughed.[1]

This tale of the Twelve Brothers from the Grimm's collection
is one of many that tell of the power of a woman's silence, a
power that has long been recognized not only in folklore and
other literary forms, but also as religious practice and political
expression. When we think of a woman's silence in the movies,
however, we do not associate it with her own power, but rather
with that of the patriarchal system which has silenced her, marginalized her, and turned her into a passive object of the male
gaze.

In her book *From Reverence to Rape*, Molly Haskell has pointed
out how Hollywood's various passive or silent women differ
from the active, autonomous heroines of some movies of the
1930s and 1940s. Regarding this latter group (which includes
heroines played by such actresses as Katherine Hepburn and
Rosalind Russell), she says:

> The more a heroine could talk, the more autonomous and idio-
> syncratic she became, and the more she seemed to define herself
> by her own lights. Conversation was an index not only of intelli-
> gence, but of confidence, of self-possession. The silent woman was
> more often a projection of the director's fantasies, an object
> manipulated into a desired setting, whereas the talking woman
> might take off on her own.[2]

As much as we might enjoy these roles of verbal wit – and,
indeed, agree with the general thrust of Haskell's argument –
we are nevertheless mistaken in assuming that fast-talking
(screen) women are the only ones who can hold their own in a
man's (screen) world. This article examines the phenomenon
of the mute female role and suggests some ways to understand
the innate power residing in these silent voices.

What are the origins of the role of the mute? Strange as it

1. Jacob and Wilhelm Grimm, "The Twelve Brothers," *Grimm's Tales for Young
and Old*, trans. Ralph Manheim (New York: Doubleday, 1983), 37.
2. Molly Haskell, *From Reverence to Rape* (New York: Penguin, 1974), 139.

might seem, these roles actually have their beginnings in the melodrama – that genre we associate with telling all. Clearly the melodrama is concerned with full expressivity, with characters who give voice to the meaning of their relationships and to their place in the world. But along with this tendency to tell all, the melodrama also always exhibits a fundamentally bipolar structure (the virtuous heroine against the evil villain, truth against falsity, the good hero against the wicked world). Within this schema, then, it is not surprising to find a mute hero or heroine playing a role complementary to that of the character who does tell all. The frequency with which mute roles occur in the melodrama has been noted by Peter Brooks:

> The different kinds of drama have their corresponding sense deprivations: for tragedy, blindness, since tragedy is about insight and illumination; for comedy, deafness, since comedy is concerned with problems in communication, misunderstandings and their consequences; and for melodrama, muteness, since melodrama is about expression.[3]

A further explanation for these mute roles lies in the simple fact that melodrama evolved out of the pantomime and tended to retain certain elements from that tradition, including an emphasis on gesture and body language and a corresponding de-emphasis of the spoken word. From among the traditional melodramas featuring such mute roles, we might consider an audience favorite, *The Dog of Montargis* (*Le Chien de Montargis*) by Pixerecourt (1773–1844). This play in fact boasts two mute heroes: the falsely accused Eloi and his faithful dog, whose mute gestures incriminate the real villain and thus work to save the innocent man. Since mute roles were extremely demanding, they invariably starred the most gifted actors, who used all their dramatic powers to convey meaning. Audiences always responded to these roles enthusiastically – possibly in recognition of their own inability to manipulate language – possibly too, in recognition of the innate inadequacy of language to express all we would wish it to. Stage melodramas established a popular tradition out of which many newer forms developed. Among these was Hollywood's so-called "woman's film," a regular item in studio production during the 1930s and 1940s, aimed at a female audience and located in a world of women's concerns. This

3. Peter Brooks, *The Melodramatic Imagination* (New Haven: Yale Univ. Press, 1976), 57.

genre has received considerable attention of late from feminist
film critics including Mary Ann Doane, Judith Mayne, Ann
Kaplan, Linda Williams, and Tania Modleski. Doane is the only
one who specifically considers the mute role, however, and she
does this as a part of her discussion of female protagonists who
are either ill or psychotic, and whose subjectivity is thus controlled and dominated by the knowledge of their male doctors.[4]

According to Doane these films, though they were made
specifically for the woman spectator, do not offer her viewing
pleasure; rather they invite her to participate in what is essentially a masochistic fantasy. Since the female spectator is called
upon to identify with a female figure who is powerless, victim-
ized, ill, and/or wounded, she cannot derive pleasure from this
experience, but only a greater sense of worthlessness. This
stands in contrast to the viewing experiences of the male spectator who, seeing in the male movie hero his more perfect mirror
self, derives pleasure through imaginary identification.[5]

Doane's reading works especially well when applied to a
movie like *Possessed*, where the mute woman – the Joan Crawford character – who alone knows her story, is incapable of
telling it until the male doctor, powerful possessor of the knowledge which will release her from her silence, makes the decision
to give her back her language. The film's structure clearly operates to contain the woman, to withhold power from her – even
over her own story – by keeping her discourse within the control of the male. But even in films where the woman character is
independent and exercises power on her own, as in the *film noir*
genre of the period, she can in effect be silenced if, through
voice-over narration, the male character controls the female discourse. This is the case, to cite two familiar examples, when
Waldo Lydecker narrates Laura's story in the film of that name,
or when the Orson Welles character speaks for Elsa in *The Lady
from Shanghai*. In *Mildred Pierce*, a *film noir*/woman's film in one,

4. Mary Ann Doane, "The 'Woman's Film': Possession and Address," in *Re-
Vision: Essays in Feminist Film Criticism*, ed. Mary Ann Doane, Patricia Mellencamp, and Linda Williams (Los Angeles: American Film Institute, 1984), 74.

5. Since Laura Mulvey's analysis in "Visual Pleasure and Narrative Cinema,"
Screen 16, no. 3 (Autumn 1975): 6–18, most classical Hollywood films have been
seen as texts of male address. The female spectator when confronted with these
films (in contrast to the women's films discussed above) has basically two modes
of entry – this according to Doane in "The Woman's Film": Possession and
Address" – "a narcissistic identification with the female figure as spectacle, and a
'transvestite' identification with the active male hero in his mastery"(79).

the Joan Crawford character remains a partial presence, a female subject denied wholeness by the patriarchal structuring which validates the detective's discourse and prevents her from telling her story from her point of view. In all these examples we see how Hollywood has contrived to render the woman silent by controlling her voice, even in films made specifically for women, even in films where the woman is ostensibly strong and active.

We are, however, dealing with a very different kind of silence when we consider the mute roles in Ingmar Bergman's *Persona* (1966) and Rainer Werner Fassbinder's *The Bitter Tears of Petra von Kant* (*Die bitteren Tränen der Petra von Kant*, 1972). These mute women, Liv Ullman's Elisabeth and Irm Hermann's Marlene, respectively, are voluntarily mute; they control their own voicelessness, and their silence has an eloquence which far exceeds the spoken words of the other characters in these films. This is true, too, of the muted women's roles which occur with surprising frequency in the films of contemporary European women directors including Marguerite Duras, Chantal Akerman, Helma Sanders-Brahms, Marleen Gorris, and Margarethe von Trotta.

My discussion of this phenomenon of a voluntary, powerful, female silence will be informed by some of the ideas Christian Metz develops in his influential article "The Imaginary Signifier," which appeared in *Screen* in 1975. Here Metz points to the link between the two perceptual passions – the desire to see (i.e., the scopic drive) and the desire to hear (or, the invocatory drive) – and to their obvious connection with the cinema. In the Lacanian system both these perceptual passions are defined as sexual drives and as such "challenge any straightforward concept of satisfaction."[6] Unlike the instincts, such as hunger for example, which can be satisfied by food, what characterizes the drives is not what they achieve, but their process. In this process, which is a kind of appeal, or a searching out (Lacan's terms), there always remains a degree of impossibility, something other than the satisfaction which is called for. This "something other" Lacan calls desire, and Metz follows his line of thinking by pointing out that desire is largely self-sustaining and independent of the pleasure obtained:

6. Jacques Lacan, *Feminine Sexuality*, ed. Juliet Mitchell and Jacqueline Rose (New York: Norton, 1982), 34.

In the end desire has no object, at any rate no real object; through real objects which are all substitutes it pursues an imaginary object (a "lost object") which is its truest object, an object that has always been lost and is always desired as such.[7]

Actually the perceiving drive has an even stronger relationship with the absence of an object than do other sexual drives, since the concrete distances of the look and of listening demand separation rather than fusion. Thus while it is true of all desire that it depends on the infinite pursuit of its absent object, perceptive desire (i.e., scopic and invocatory) is the only desire whose principle of distance symbolically and spatially evokes this fundamental separation.[8] It is, as Jane Weinstock says, "the drive that thrives on distance."[9]

Metz goes on to show that the cinema, existing as it does in a so-called "primordial elsewhere," is thus infinitely desirable. What defines the cinema is not only the visual and audible *distance* kept (the first figure of the lack), but also the outright *absence* of the object seen and heard:[10] no one is there when I, the subject, look and listen; I was not there when the object appeared and spoke. Metz concludes this section of his discussion by pointing out:

There is something to see, called the film, but something in whose definition there is a great deal of "flight": not precisely something that hides, rather something that *lets* itself be seen without *presenting* itself to be seen.[11]

What I would like to consider now are some of the audible possibilities suggested by Metz's notion of "flight." In the visual realm, as he says, the character does not hide; in the audible, however, he or she can decide to maintain silence, and the effect of this, as we will see, may be to quicken the viewer/listener's imagination in its pursuit of the desired, lacking object.

In making a connection between these ideas from Christian Metz and the mystery of the voluntarily silent Elisabeth Vogler in Bergman's *Persona*, we begin to understand why her lack of speech

7. Christain Metz, "The Imaginary Signifier," *Screen* 16, no. 2 (Summer, 1975): 60.

8. Metz, "Imaginary Signifier," 61.

9. Jane Weinstock, "Sexual Difference and the Moving Image," in *Difference: On Representation and Sexuality* (New York: New Museum of Contemporary Art, 1984), 41.

10. Metz, "Imaginary Signifier," 62.

11. Ibid., 63.

so fires the viewer's imagination. Though we see her infinitely communicative eyes, hands, and face, our desire to hear – to hear her story – to hear her tell her story – is never satisfied. This imaginary object has taken flight, and its absence is what keeps our desire alive. In an interesting reverse utterance, the doctor (in this case a woman psychiatrist) tells Elisabeth's story to her:

> You can keep quiet. Then at least you're not lying. You can cut yourself off, close yourself in. Then you don't have to play a part, put on a face, make false gestures. Or so you think.[12]

We receive these words from the doctor, but our desire continues to pursue the "lost object." Bibi Andersson's nurse provides another perspective:

> It's not easy to live with someone who won't talk, I promise you. It spoils everything. . . . I hear my own voice . . . and I think, "Don't I sound false." All these words I'm using. . . . But you've made things simple for yourself, you just don't say anything.[13]

We respond to these words as well; yet it is Elisabeth's silence that controls our desire.

This is true also of our viewing experience of Rainer Werner Fassbinder's *The Bitter Tears of Petra von Kant.* Here in a film which foregrounds excess – excess of emotion, excess of speech, excess of decor – the constant and pervasive background, or perhaps even the foundation itself, which structures the film and controls our response to it, is the mute role of Marlene, played by Irm Hermann with the same kind of intensity we saw Liv Ullman invest in her Elisabeth.[14] As in the traditional stage melodrama, so here in Fassbinder's particular filmic version of the genre,[15] the

12. Ingmar Bergman, *Persona* and *Shame*, trans. K. Bradfield (London: Calder and Boyars, 1972), 41.

13. Ibid., 73.

14. The privileged position of the Marlene character is indicated in the film's dedication ("dem, der hier Marlene wurde" [to the one who became Marlene here]), whatever meaning one takes from this rather cryptic phrase. For differing readings, see, for example, Wolfgang Limmer, *Rainer Werner Fassbinder: Filmemacher* (Reinbek bei Hamburg: Rowohlt, 1981), 80, and Harry Baer, *Schlafen kann ich, wenn ich tot bin* (Köln: Kiepenheuer & Witsch, 1982), 98.

15. Although Fassbinder's involvement with melodrama has been widely discussed, one succinct characterization by Timothy Corrigan is especially apt in the case of *The Bitter Tears of Petra von Kant*: "a film which appears late in Fassbinder's Hollywood phase and which makes use of what becomes one of the defining marks of his films during this period: Sirkian melodrama transformed into critical kitsch or camp, use of popular entertainment formulas but with a critical, self-conscious distance." *New German Film: The Displaced Image* (Austin: Univ. of Texas Press, 1983), 45.

compelling strength of the mute role resides in the withheld voice, the withheld story, the lost object. Though Marlene makes her presence felt – and intensely so through her powerful gazes, commanding postures, and communicative gestures – it is the voice which has taken flight that keeps our desire alive from the beginning of the film to its ending and beyond.[16]

Although Fassbinder himself withholds information from his viewer that Bergman provides regarding the nature of the muteness and its motivation, he does give us adequate evidence to conclude that Marlene's muteness is indeed volitional.[17]

Throughout the film we see too much of Petra (Margit Carstensen), constantly before us, too close and too overbearing. But what we hear pass from her lips is even more excessive: lying to her mother or to a professional contact over the phone, abusing her daughter, entertaining Sidonie, wooing Karin, and ordering, endlessly ordering Marlene. As viewers we must defend ourselves against Petra's verbal onslaught. At the same time we long to hear from Marlene, but this longing is never satisfied. It is her silence – as she gazes out of the darkness from behind her typewriter or stands watching beside one of the mannequins – which controls our desire and compels us to continue searching for the lost object. Fassbinder suggests something very similar himself when he says, "if the camera moves a great deal around something that's dead, it's shown to be dead. Then you can create a longing for something that's alive."[18]

Marlene exerts her control in the film through the force of her penetrating gaze – as when she hands Petra the ordered orange juice or listens to her lying stories. The audience always receives the direct impact of this gaze, since Michael Ballhaus's

16. This point is missed by Catherine Johnson in her attempt to apply Lacanian film theory to *The Bitter Tears of Petra von Kant* because she understands the nature of love to be fusion, and tries to read fusion into the Marlene/Petra relationship as well as into the Marlene/audience relationship. See "The Imaginary & *The Bitter Tears of Petra von Kant,*" *Wide Angle* 3 (1980): 20–24.

17. For example when we see Marlene pick up the phone, put the receiver to her ear, and appear as if to answer, only to have Petra snatch the phone from her at the moment speech would have begun; or when we hear the reformed, "post-Karin" Petra invite Marlene to "tell me about yourself," and we see the refusal in Marlene's eyes as she kisses her hand. Furthermore, one need only compare the viewer reaction invited by Marlene on the one hand with that of the mannequins or the doll on the other to appreciate the power of her volitional silence.

18. Christian Braad Thomsen, "Five Interviews with Fassbinder," in *Fassbinder,* ed. Tony Rayns (London: British Film Institute, 1980), 96.

camera is so positioned as to make Marlene's gazes at Petra audience-gazes as well. Fassbinder gives further control to Marlene's presence by placing her figure, always black-clad, in a framing position. This is particularly forceful in an early scene when we observe Petra and Sidonie in the background through a Venetian-blind grillwork; they wear neutral tones and are shot out of focus. The Marlene figure forms a heavy black three-quarter frame foreground as she stands silently with her arm outstretched, her head bowed, and her long fingers extended, resting against the window pane. While the position encircles and contains visually, because of Marlene's uncompromising muteness it simultaneously offers to the viewer's imagination possibilities for expanding and unfolding. This creates a dynamic tension which becomes a key structure in the film.

In another scene, faintly reminiscent of the figure-merging of the two women in *Persona*, we see Petra applying her makeup in the foreground in medium close-up while Marlene is sketching and using the same brushing and pencilling strokes at the easel in the background. Petra's change of position causes a body overlap, with Marlene's extended arms and hands visible and engaged in doubling – in effect, miming – gestures. Or, as Timothy Corrigan puts it, while Petra works on "the business of desire" she is superimposed on Marlene working on the "business of design."[19] During this sequence Petra is telling her story to Sidonie while Marlene gazes at her in disbelief; suddenly the camera begins to track forward to Marlene, holds on her face and its silent gaze in close-up, then suddenly zooms backward and racks her out of focus. Next it pans right and returns to its former focus on Petra, foreground, with Marlene again positioned and in clear focus in the background. Thus the viewer is constantly confronted with Marlene's framing, mirroring presence, which silently comments at the same time that it relentlessly withholds.

At the next stage in the film, marked by the arrival of Karin Thimm (Hanna Schygulla), Fassbinder gives Marlene an audible presence of sorts; now instead of sketching and silently gazing she begins to type – noisily and intrusively. In this we have another kind of withholding. Though we rarely see Marlene on screen in this sequence – one shot of her in profile at the typewriter dramatically sidelit in a very dark corner of the room – we

19. Corrigan, *Displaced Image*, 51.

have audible evidence of her presence in the form of an end-lessly clattering typewriter. This only heightens our sense of deprivation. A noisy typewriter is not a voice. And now we no longer have Marlene's eyes, hands, and posture to read.

Nor do the things said about Marlene by Petra and others help us in our pursuit of the lost object: the voice, her voice. The mysterious power of that missing voice continues to control the filmic and narrative scene and engage our imagination. It is with a mixture of anticipation and dread that we view the final sequence of the film: we do want Marlene to free herself from the exploitive, destructive Petra,[20] but as she walks out the door she is abandoning us, too, leaving us alone with our desire for-ever unfulfilled.

This eloquent power of the withheld voice, understood long ago by tellers of folktales and creators of melodramas, contin-ues to express itself today through the film medium. We might consider briefly a number of recent film heroines, who, though not totally mute as Elisabeth and Marlene, do choose to main-tain varying degrees of silence. Through this volitional act they link themselves to Bergman's and Fassbinder's heroines and to their fairy-tale sister whose brothers were saved by the mystical power of her silence. For the viewer of these silent women the process is again that described by Lacan: an appeal, a searching out, in which there always remains a degree of impossibility; there always remains desire. Almost all of Chantal Akerman's films deal in some way with the question of women's silence: in *Je, tu, il, elle* (1974) we experience the silent, empty time devoted to the reorganizing and regenerating of the protagonist's life; in *Jeanne Dielman, 23 Quai du Commerce – 1080 Bruxelles* (1975) the silent rhythm of the woman's daily routine of precise and detailed activities serving as a means for maintaining her sanity and selfhood; in *The Man with a Suitcase* (1984) the solitary pro-ductive silent space imaginatively guarded from encroachments and intrusions; and in *News from Home* (1976) the silent inner

20. Fassbinder did at one point (Thomsen, "Five Interviews," 84) claim that Marlene is not leaving in order to free herself, but rather will seek out another enslaving relationship. In evaluating this remark, however, we should keep two points in mind: Fassbinder said at the same time that he did not think Nora frees herself when she leaves Torvald in Ibsen's *A Doll's House*. Furthermore he has on several occasions made the point that a "pessimistic" ending – indeed, a "pessimistic" film – is intended to make the viewers think and feel and come up with alternate answers and solutions – for the film characters and for their own lives.

nurturing communion with an absent person, possible even in the presence of the chaos of external sights and sounds. In *Nathalie Granger* (1972) by Marguerite Duras we see the mutual understanding between two women which operates in a quiet realm beyond the fraudulence of patriarchal speech; and in Marleen Gorris's *A Question of Silence* (*De Stilte Rond Christine M.*, 1982) we witness the defensive, self-protective silence of a woman resisting questioning by a representative of the patriarchal legal system. Helma Sanders-Brahms, in *Germany, Pale Mother* (*Deutschland, bleiche Mutter*, 1979), presents us with another kind of self-protective silence that is her heroine's last-ditch retreat from the unbearable assaults and burdens of a too demanding world. And in Margarethe von Trotta's *Sisters or the Balance of Happiness* (*Schwestern oder Die Balance des Glücks*, 1979) we see a silently receptive sister who is able through that silence to maintain contact with the world of dream, fairy tale, music, nature, and memory, while in her *Sheer Madness* (*Heller Wahn*, 1982) the woman escapes into a realm of artistically creative silence as she searches for freedom from the constraints and demands of the patriarchal order.

In all these films women directors are seeking to explore the mystery of women's silence. As viewers we are engaged in the same endeavor. Together we recognize that silence is powerful and eloquent, but at the same time it eludes us and remains a mystery. Silence is "something other," there to remind us of the imaginary object which has taken flight.

Modes of Alienation in Fassbinder's
Effi Briest

a n n a   k .   k u h n

Anna Kuhn's discussion
focuses on Fassbinder's use
of various methods of "alienation" or "distantiation." Kuhn
translates Brecht's Verfremdung
with the English word "alienation"; "distantiation" and "defamiliarization" are two other
words that are often used to translate that concept. She examines
the various cinematic techniques to
create gaps or spaces that open the
story to a political critique – and
make clear the perspective from
which Fassbinder has constructed
his adaptation of Theodor Fontane's
novel Effi Briest. She demonstrates
that in his version of the story, Fassbinder attacks a patriarchal social
order in which oppression begins at its most basic, most "private" level –
in the institution of marriage.
—THE EDITORS

Hanna Schygulla as Effi, with Irm Hermand as the housekeeper,
who looks on. Rainer Werner Fassbinder's Effi Briest (1974).
(Photo courtesy of New Yorker Films)

Rainer Werner Fassbinder's *Effi Briest*, patently the most literary
of the New German Films, is literary in a uniquely self-conscious
way. Not only does the dialogue of Fassbinder's filmscript reli-
giously adhere to Fontane's novel – apart from insignificant stylistic changes, the film text corresponds verbatim to its literary
source – but Fassbinder also retains Fontane's third-person nar-

rator in a voice-over. The narration, spoken by Fassbinder, is augmented by frames of written tableaux taken directly from the novel and used as intertitles.

These inserted tableaux, a replication of silent film techniques, as well as the anachronistic use of black and white footage, must be seen as Fassbinder's attempt to recreate a period piece, to reproduce within his own cinematic medium the authenticity of Fontane's novel of mores in Wilhelminian society. Intertitles and voice-over narration together constitute the main vehicle of literariness in Fassbinder's film. Both serve to interrupt the spectacle, requiring the viewer constantly to switch from absorbing visual codes to aural codes, to reading and thinking discursively.

The title of the film already testifies to Fassbinder's indebtedness to his source: *Fontane Effi Briest*. To this title, however, he appends the subtitle: "Or many who have an idea of their possibilities and needs and nevertheless accept the prevailing order in the way they act and thereby strengthen and confirm it absolutely."[1]

The significance of Fassbinder's addition is striking, its ramifications far-reaching. While every cinematic adaptation of a literary text is already an interpretation, Fassbinder has gone one step further, from the outset, spelling out his reading of Fontane's novel. He does this explicitly and literally: the subtitle appears as intertitles over several frames after the title. Thus Fassbinder's claim to an objective rendition of Fontane (*Fontane Effi Briest*) stands in contrast to his sociopolitically engaged interpretation.

Fassbinder's subtitle, in its didactic formulation, is clearly more partisan than Fontane's narrator. It is precisely the juxtaposition of title and subtitle, the tension between source and interpretation, which determines the structure of Fassbinder's film. In examining how Fassbinder sets forth his interpretation of the novel through the film, I have chosen to focus on his use of stylization and narration. I show that Fassbinder's use of stylized images, the creation of disjunction between the visual and aural realms, estranges the audience as it elicits a critical view-

1. The German original reads: "oder/viele, die eine Ahnung haben/von ihren Möglichkeiten und/ihren Bedürf/nissen und trotz/dem das herr/schende System/in ihrem Kopf/akzeptieren/durch ihre Ta/ten und es so/mit festigen/und durchaus bestätigen."

ing of *Effi Briest*; and I examine Fassbinder's use of the narrator as his prime means of foregrounding the interpretative purpose of his film.

Stylization is of course hardly new to Fassbinder. Employed to varying degrees throughout his work, stylization is a favorite technique of the filmmaker's to inhibit viewer identification. The characters in *Effi Briest* are dispassionate creatures, devoid of spontaneity, their movements as static and ritualized as the society which has produced them. In *Effi Briest*, however, Fassbinder carries stylization to an extreme by freezing frames into *tableaux vivants*. Used to great advantage throughout the film, Fassbinder's *tableaux vivants* are particularly effective when they focus on Effi and Innstetten. To present the repressive dynamics of their relationship, Fassbinder has devised a recurring model: focusing on Effi, he has Innstetten enter the frame and then captures husband and wife in a frozen two-shot. The fact that the gray color tones become progressively darker in Innstetten's presence and that there is a corresponding shift in sound quality, with the tone becoming blurred or louder, testify to his oppressiveness for Effi.

Fassbinder's passion for enclosed spaces is used with optimal effect in *Effi Briest*. The characters are almost always framed within a shot by low ceilings, doors, windows, arches, curtains, or mirrors. The unrelenting use of confining framing shots, which can be seen as the visual correlative of Effi's social position, instills in the viewer a sense of claustrophobia. Notes Paul Thomas:

> Everything, people and objects, *looms,* ominously, the people oppress each other as their objects, settings and paraphernalia oppress them; but they watch each other all the time. The price of lack of liberty is the eternal vigilance of a .prim, repressed society, its code of loyalty, its frigidity, its poses.[2]

Effi Briest abounds in mirrors. Rarely do the characters address each other directly; instead, they speak either to their own reflection or to the mirror image of their dialogue partner. What on the surface appears to be mere narcissism becomes, in fact, the vehicle for expressing the isolation of the characters, their sense of alienation. It is as though these characters, staring blankly into their own reflection, were trying to wrest a sense of

2. Paul Thomas, "Fassbinder: The Poetry of the Inarticulate," *Film Quarterly* 30 (Winter 1976): 15.

self from the glass. Instead, the mirrors, which reflect not only the figures themselves, but also their surroundings, simply give back the vacuity of their world. These characters, in the rarefied perfection of their reflections, take their place among the other objects in their stifling, aestheticized world. This is especially true of Effi, who is virtually indistinguishable from the other *objets d'art* in her husband's house.[3] Thus the mirrors reflect the process of reification inherent in bourgeois marriage.

Narration in film is achieved through a variety of means, chief among them the semiotic sequence of images on the screen. In *Effi Briest,* Fassbinder, through the use of ellipsis, at times makes dramatic use of iconic narrative. More frequently, however, he reduces the narrative force of the images through his use of *tableaux vivants* and by giving greater weight to the voice-over narration and intertitles. It is my contention that the literariness of Fassbinder's technique in *Effi Briest,* together with his use of stylization, serve as alienation effects. The term "alienation" is used here in the Brechtian sense of *Verfremdungseffekt,*[4] that is, as distancing devices directed at the audience. Fassbinder's use of narration and stylization militate against identification with the characters and events on the screen. By calling attention to themselves, they remind viewers that they are watching a self-consciously artificial film. Both techniques are designed to jar us out of our passive stance, to awaken our rational faculties, and thereby to make us receptive to Fassbinder's engaged interpretation of Fontane's work.

In keeping with an authentic rendering of Fontane's text, Fassbinder retains the third-person narrator, who accompanies us from the opening description of Hohen-Cremmen to the closing one of Effi's grave. His role is not merely functional, that is, he is not simply called on to aid in those tasks generally considered difficult to realize in film, such as the articulation of abstractions or inner thoughts and emotions or the passage of time. By consciously resisting a cinematic rendering of even those scenes readily translatable into the purely visual medium

3. Fassbinder, in a significant change from the original text, omits all reference to the legacy of Captain Thomas, substituting for the ghost kitsch the bourgeois kitsch of baroquesque statuary and other ornate paraphernalia.

4. Fassbinder's use of Brechtian techniques goes back to his *antiteater* days. For a discussion of Brechtian devices in other films by Fassbinder, see my article "Rainer Werner Fassbinder: The Alienated Vision," in *New German Filmmakers: From Oberhausen Through the 1970s,* ed. Klaus Phillips (New York: Ungar, 1984), 76–123, especially 83–86 and 92–95.

(e.g., the description of Hohen-Cremmen and Effi's grave), Fassbinder underscores the literariness of his film. These descriptions serve as a sort of aural frame for the film and, as a complement to Fassbinder's much used visual framing devices, help create the aura of a hermetically self-enclosed world. Fassbinder, in granting his narrator a broad spectrum of narrative tasks, allows him to intrude continually on the consciousness of the viewer and thereby bestows on him the status of a persona in the film.

The narrator fulfills a dual function that corresponds to the double function of the film: Fontane-novel and Fassbinder-interpretation. In *Fontane Effi Briest*, Fassbinder has reduced the plot to skeletal form. Carrying Fontane's penchant for tableaux to an extreme,[5] the film presents us with a series of vignettes that are linked together and given coherence by the narrator. Of far greater import for Fassbinder's interpretation, however, is his manipulation of the narrator vis-à-vis the viewer for purposes of alienation.

The narrative framework of the film contains many levels of distantiation. These range from Fassbinder's playful teasing of Fontane cognoscenti[6] to the ironic underscoring of his own use of alienation effects. Fassbinder shows his highly developed sense of play by breaking off narration in mid-sentence and overlapping narration with the dialogue of an ensuing shot, so that the narrator's voice is drowned out or narration and dialogue run simultaneously, for example, in the scene between Effi and Innstetten at table or between Effi and Roswitha in the cemetery. The net results of such playfulness are, however, serious: viewers are induced to pay closer attention; they are prevented from participating in what Brecht called the "culinary" consumption of art.

By far the most effective use of the alienation effect within the filmic narration, however, is the disparity Fassbinder sets up

5. Recent Fontane scholarship has stressed the painterly component of Fontane's *oeuvre*. Cf. Peter-Klaus Schuster, *Theodor Fontane: Effi Briest–Ein Leben nach christlichen Bildern*, Studien zur deutschen Literatur, vol. 55 (Tübingen: Max Niemeyer, 1979); Richard Brinkmann, "Der angehaltene Moment. Requisiten–Genre–Tableau bei Fontane," *DVJS* 53 (1979): 429–62; Erdmann Waniek, "Beim zweiten Lesen: der Beginn von Fontanes *Effi Briest* als verdinglichtes *tableau vivant*," *German Quarterly* 55 (March 1982): 164–74.

6. Effi's devoted canine companion, her great solace in Kessin, does not appear in the film at all; yet Roswitha's allusion to Rollo in her letter to Innstetten assumes the viewer's familiarity with his function in the novel.

between the image on the screen and the spoken word of the narrator. The tension caused by this discrepancy between the aural and the visual realms disrupts the continuity of the already fragmented narrative still further. By disorienting his audience in this manner, Fassbinder effectively inhibits viewer-character identification and its resulting emotional catharsis; by accenting the artifice of the filmic medium, he appeals to his audience's critical faculties instead.

Significantly, the first aural-visual disparity occurs during the "engagement" scene. Here the narrator relates Frau von Briest's decision to break with convention, to capitalize on her daughter's ingenuousness, and rather than have Effi change into more "suitable" attire, have her daughter meet Innstetten dressed in her everyday clothes. Describing their gestures (Frau von Briest grasps both of Effi's hands in her own), he then recounts the conversation in which the mother informs her daughter of Innstetten's proposal and urges her to consider his offer seriously. There is, however, a disjunction between word and image; we perceive nothing of the gestures or interchange described. Instead, in the film's first *tableau vivant*, the camera closes in on the frozen figures of Effi and her mother standing on the stairs, with Effi's head on her mother's shoulder – a pose broken only by the entrance of Herr von Briest and Innstetten, at which point Effi rushes up to her fiancé and gazes into his eyes. Fassbinder thus makes viewers interpret what they know from the voice-over, but are not able to see, namely Frau von Briest's calculation regarding the encounter between Effi and Innstetten.

During Gieshübler's first visit to Effi, the narrator, after recounting the apothecary's emotions for Effi, also informs us: "Since his heart was strained to the bursting point, he stood up, looked for his hat, which, fortunately, he was able to find at once and, kissing Effi's hand, quickly withdrew, without having added a single word."[7] Instead of showing his departure, however, the camera focuses on the rather pathetic figure of Gieshübler, who remains immobile and whose nonaction belies the narrator's words.

7. The German original reads: "da . . . sein Herz es nicht mehr aushalten konnte, so stand er auf, suchte nach seinem Hut, den er auch glücklicherweise gleich fand, und zog sich, nach wiederholtem Handkuss, rasch zurück, ohne ein Wort gesagt zu haben." English renditions of Fontane's text are based on Douglas Parmee's translation of *Effi Briest* (Middlesex: Penguin, 1967).

An elaboration of this technique is found in Effi's long, soul-searching monologue during her second visit to Hohen-Cremmen in which, reviewing the events of the last few years, she speaks of "fear," "shame," and "the proper feeling."[8] Here Fassbinder has made two changes. First, he has given over Effi's interior monologue to the narrator, and second, he has moved Effi from the confines of the house to outdoors and changed the time from evening to day. These changes are significant in that Fassbinder ostensibly only introduces them to create disjunction between the aural and iconic realms once again. As the narrator speaks, we see Effi walking through a field in the rain with her parasol. The incongruity between word and image is underscored when the narrator, interrupting his narration of Effi's monologue, relates Effi's gestures: first, that she counts the strokes of the church clock, and second, that at the end of the monologue she puts her head in her arms and cries bitterly. Effi, however, does neither. Instead, she continues to stroll through the fields.

Confronted with the intricacies entailed in Fassbinder's execution of the aural-iconic juxtaposition in this scene, one asks oneself whether its sole function is to inhibit viewer identification. Since it would have been a simple matter to delete the narrated description of Effi's gestures, thereby lessening the tension between narration and image, the question arises whether Fassbinder is not calling the reliability of the narrator into question. Clearly, the cumulative effect of Fassbinder's use of word-image disparity, the viewers' inability to rely on conformity between what they are seeing and what they are hearing, is unsettling. Does Fassbinder retain a narrator only in turn to use him as a means of calling Fontane's narration into question? Or does he call for a reading against the grain?

Presumably it is our exposure to the filmmaker's techniques that prepares us to interpret Fassbinder's reading. In what is perhaps the most striking word-image discrepancy, the narrator describes the reunion between husband and wife after Effi's ghost scare in the house. We are told that Effi, looking very pale, enters the room on Johanna's arm and that, upon seeing Innstetten, rushes up to him and embraces and kisses him with tears streaming down her face. Yet, instead of showing us an anxious Effi seeking comfort, Fassbinder confronts us with that

8. German original: "Angst," "Scham," and "das richtige Gefühl."

sinister trio: Johanna, Frau Kruse, and the black hen – a major *source* of Effi's anxiety. The pan of the kitchen with its bizarre inhabitants[9] makes it clear that Effi will receive little solace in this house – an impression confirmed in the immediately following scene in which Innstetten rejects out of hand Effi's request to move. Thus, while the technique employed in this scene is similar to the earlier scenes, the interpretative burden, the challenge to active participation placed on the viewer, is far greater.

Fassbinder's challenge to the viewer is greater still in the scene at the train station. Innstetten's insensitivity constitutes the visual component of the scene in which Gieshübler's opinion of Tripelli,[10] related by the narrator, is juxtaposed with the image of the Innstettens at the station. Watching a train that will pass by Hohen-Cremmen move on, Innstetten asks Effi if she would like to be on it. As Innstetten continues to watch the passing train, a distraught Effi turns away, crying. Thus the camera and the viewer are privy to Effi's feelings of loneliness and homesickness, whereas Innstetten is oblivious to them. The sheer amount of disparate information contained in this scene places an enormous burden on viewers. Not only must they sift through and evaluate two discrete relationships (Gieshübler-Tripelli, Innstetten-Effi), but they must distinguish between appearance and reality within these relationships. In so doing it becomes clear that whereas Gieshübler's affection for his friend Mariette does not blind him to her social limitations, Effi is effectively invisible to Innstetten. His seemingly solicitous question stands in contrast to his insensitivity to her response. Struggling to absorb the various strata of information with which they are confronted, viewers are called upon actively to engage in the reading of the film.

9. Fassbinder here refers back to the previous kitchen shot, in which a lonely Effi, taking a break from her letter writing, enters, only to retreat in the face of the icily hostile (Mrs. Danvers-like) Johanna and the frightening Frau Kruse. The ominous pantomime of this scene is intensified by the long take of an axe on the wall above Johanna's head.

10. "Gieshübler was extremely fond of his gifted friend and valued her talents highly; but all his enthusiasm could not blind him to the fact that she had only been granted a modest share of social finesse. And it was on this sort of finesse that he prided himself personally." German original reads: "Gieshübler liebte seine Künstlerfreundin enthusiastisch und dachte hoch von ihren Talenten, aber all seine Begeisterung konnte ihn doch nicht blind gegen die Tatsache machen, daß ihr von gesellschaftlicher Feinheit nur ein bescheidenes Maß zuteil geworden war. Und diese Feinheit war gerade das, was er persönlich kultivierte."

The disparity between image and narration serves a different function in the sequence in which the socially ostracized Effi, returning home from a drawing lesson in a horse-drawn trolley, catches sight of her estranged daughter. We are never shown Effi's reaction to seeing Annie. Instead, Fassbinder interjects an amateurish sketch of the trolley and the street scene described by the narrator.[11] The following shots, again in tension with the narration, show Effi agitatedly walking up the stairs and through the empty courtyard into an official building.

Fassbinder's use of distantiation here transcends the mere word-image juxtaposition. What soon becomes apparent to Fontane readers is that Fassbinder has visually telescoped time by contrasting the narration of present events with the image of future actions. While the narrator relates Effi's immediate response to seeing Annie, the images record her reaction – they show her pilgrimage to the minister's wife, through whose intervention a meeting between mother and daughter is arranged. Thus the lack of synchronization between word and image not only activates the viewers' engagement by prompting them to synthesize divergent aural and visual information, it also lends a sense of determinism to the events depicted.

By extending these techniques, Fassbinder creates an aura of fatalism in the important dialogue between Innstetten and Wüllersdorf that seals Effi's fate. Fassbinder, by interspersing the dialogue with three shots of a speeding train and three of a horse and carriage – both modes of transportation which will be used by Wüllersdorf in presenting Innstetten's challenge to Crampas – establishes Innstetten's "decision" as a foregone conclusion. Directly upon Wüllersdorf's concluding words: "Our cult of honor is idolatry. But we must submit to it, as long as the idol stands,"[12] follows a closeup of the firing pistol which Innstetten uses to kill Crampas, symbol of the sacrifice to idolatry exhorted by an outdated code of honor.

The discussion of the statute of limitations, which ostensibly serves to air the options open to Innstetten upon his discovery of Crampas's letters, is shown by Fassbinder to be, in fact, the most striking example of the behavior of those alluded to in the

---

11. This sketch, presumably of the caliber of Effi's own artistic talents, is shown again just before Annie's visit.

12. German original: "Unser Ehrenkultus ist ein Götzendienst, aber wir müssen uns ihm unterwerfen, solange der Götze gilt."

subtitle. Innstetten indeed does have an idea of his possibilities and needs. He admits that despite everything, he still loves Effi and that the passage of time *has* made a difference, that he does not feel a personal need to kill his wife's lover. Nevertheless, he does accept the prevailing order – "that tyrannizing something which forms society"[13] – and, by challenging Crampas and sending Effi away, he does strengthen and confirm it absolutely. The visual compression of future action into the dialogue between Innstetten and Wüllersdorf, the closing in of the action on itself, evokes a sense of entrapment, relentlessness, and inevitability that is totally in keeping with that reaffirmation of the past, the outdated, undertaken on the verbal level.

As the analysis of Fassbinder's narrative technique in *Effi Briest* has shown, the filmmaker's use of the visual-aural disparity serves initially to estrange the viewer. Once having assured this estrangement, however, Fassbinder escalates his demands on viewers and ultimately leads them to his interpretation as formulated in the subtitle.

Whereas the narrator constitutes the aural component of the literary text, the intertitles constitute its immediate visual component. The fifteen projected inserts fall into two distinct categories, content-based and interpretative, which correspond to the two levels of the film (Fontane-novel and Fassbinder-interpretation).

On the *Fontane Effi Briest* level, the inserts crystallize pivotal moments of the plot. Through a tableau we learn of the Innstettens' twelve-hour separation, which precipitates feelings of loneliness and anxiety in Effi ("Then came the first separation for twelve hours").[14] The inserts of Tripelli's telegram ("Madame Baron von Innstetten, born Briest. Arrived safely. Prince K. at the station. More taken with me than ever. A thousand thanks for your kind welcome. Please extend my regards to the baron. Mariette Tripelli")[15] and the doctor's remarks at Annie's birth ("It's the anniversary of the battle of Königgratz today. A pity it's a girl. But the next one may be different , and the Prussians have lots of victories to celebrate.")[16] underscore the precarious

13. German original: "das tyrannisierende Gesellschafts Etwas."
14. German original: "Dann kam die erste Trennung auf zwölf Stunden."
15. French original: "Madame la Baronne d'Innstetten, née de Briest. Bien arriveé Prince K. à la gare. Plus épris de moi que jamais. Mille fois merci de notre bon accueil. Compliments empresses à Monsieur le Baron. Mariette Tripelli."
16. German original: "Wir haben heute den Tag von Königgratz; schade, daß es ein Mädchen ist. Aber das andere kann ja nachkommen, und die Preußen haben viele Siegestage."

social position of women. The situation with the ghost is alluded to in the intertitle: "It was utterly quiet in the house." Effi's adultery is referred to in two inserts attesting to her religious adherence to the "prescribed walks," her renunciation of them in Crampas's absence and their resumption on his return. ("Not a day passed without her taking the prescribed walks" and "While Crampas was in Stettin she had given up her walks to the beach and the plantation but now that he was back she started them again, undeterred by any unpleasant weather.")[17] After Innstetten is transferred to Berlin, we share Effi's hope for a new beginning, her resolve to put the past behind her ("A new era is beginning and I'm not scared anymore and I intend to be better than I have been up till now and try to please you more").[18]

After Effi has been cast out by Innstetten, we learn of her psychological state, her increasing melancholy, through an insert ("Until Christmas things went very well, but Christmas Eve passed very sadly and when the New Year came, Effi began to feel very melancholy").[19] And finally, after much loneliness and suffering, the telegram which constitutes a reprieve for Effi, her summons back to Hohen-Cremmen ("Come, Effi"), is inserted.

So too is the document which seals Innstetten's fate, his advancement to minister ("My dear Innstetten, I am glad to inform you that His Majesty has been pleased to sign your nomination").[20] It is only upon receiving this highest honor, in having attained his professional goal, that Innstetten recognizes the meaninglessness of his life. "I've made a mess of my life,"[21] he admits to Wüllersdorf. Thus the content-based inserts chart the main plot line of the novel of adultery, highlighting the cause, the progress, and the effects of Effi's infidelity.

17. German original: "Es verging kein Tag, wo sie nicht die vorgeschriebenen Spaziergänge gemacht hätte" and "Die Spaziergänge nach dem Strand und der Plantage, die sie, während Crampas in Stettin war, aufgegeben hatte, nahm sie nach seiner Rückkehr wieder auf und ließ sich auch durch ungünstige Witterung nicht davon abhalten."
18. German original: "Nun bricht eine andere Zeit an, und ich fürchte mich nicht mehr und will auch besser sein als früher und dir mehr zu Willen leben." This statement of course also reflects subservience and an unhealthy desire to please – a common theme of Fassbinder's.
19. German original: "Bis Weihnachten ging es vorzüglich, aber der Heiligabend verlief schon recht traurig, und als das neue Jahr herankam, begann Effi ganz schwermütig zu werden."
20. German original: "Mein lieber Innstetten! Ich freue mich Ihnen mitteilen zu können, daß Seine Majestät Ihre Ernennung zu unterzeichnen geruht hat."
21. German original: "Ich habe mein Leben verpfuscht."

The remaining inserts must be seen within the context of Fassbinder's interpretation. All are directly applicable either to Effi or Innstetten, who are for Fassbinder the microcosm of their society, and articulate insights which transcend the specificity of their situations and attain the stature of a generally accepted social truth. To this category belong:

"A story that ends in self-sacrifice is never bad."

"Of course a man in his position must be cold."

"What really prevents anyone from succeeding in life? Always too much emotion."

"Apart from the small fry, there must surely be some kind of elite."

"A sort of calculated means of inspiring fear."

"Guilt demands expiation: that makes sense. But a time limit is neither one thing nor the other, it's terrible."

"It's funny, but I can say 'almost' for lots of things in my life, really."[22]

The intertitle, "A sort of calculated means of inspiring fear," inserted twice, furnishes the key to Fassbinder's reading of *Effi Briest*. It initially appears after the Effi-Crampas dialogue at the beach concerning Innstetten's penchant for ghost stories; here it represents Effi's sudden insight into her husband's manipulation of her. It appears again after Effi's conversation with Innstetten during which he informs her of Crampas's unreliable nature, particularly regarding women, and cautions her that the best defense against such a character is a pure soul. When Effi attempts to change the subject by mentioning that she had believed Innstetten was merely joking about the entire matter, her husband responds: "I wouldn't say that, Effi. But be that as it may, one must behave in such a way that one doesn't

22. German original: "Eine Geschichte mit Entsagung ist nie schlimm." "Freilich, ein Mann in seiner Stellung muß kalt sein." "Woran scheitert man denn im Leben überhaupt? Doch nur an Wärme." "Es muß doch außer kleinen Leuten auch eine Elite geben." "Eine Art Angstapparat aus Kalkül." "Schuld verlangt Sühne, das hat einen Sinn. Aber Verjährung ist etwas Halbes, etwas Schreckliches." "Es ist komisch, aber ich kann eigentlich von vielem in meinem Leben sagen, beinahe." I am indebted to Helmut Schanze for this catalogue of intertitles. Helmut Schanze, "*Fontane Effi Briest*: Bemerkungen zu einem Drehbuch von Rainer Werner Fassbinder," in *Literatur in den Massenmedien–Demontage von Dichtung?*, ed. Friedrich Knilli, Knut Hickethier, Wolf Dieter Lützen (Munich and Vienna: Carl Hanser Verlag, 1976), 135.

need to be frightened of anything."[23] Directly upon Innstetten's sanctimonious phrase, Fassbinder again inserts the "calculated means of inspiring fear" intertitle, thereby underscoring the exemplary nature of the preceding scene. Thus we are made aware that we, along with Effi, have witnessed Innstetten in an act of emotional exploitation.

Fassbinder's preoccupation with the manifold social and interpersonal manifestations of manipulative behavior is well documented. Indeed, the theme of manipulation constitutes the unifying structure of his entire *oeuvre*.[24] From this perspective, his almost Expressionistic reduction of the Fontane novel to the figures of Effi and Innstetten becomes understandable. What better vehicle for portraying interpersonal manipulation could have presented itself than a traditional Wilhelminian marriage?[25]

The Effi-Innstetten relationship calls into question conventional marriage. The final two intertitles hold up other social conventions for scrutiny. By interjecting Innstetten's agonizing doubts about the validity of the theory of the statute of limitations immediately after Crampas's death, Fassbinder dramatically renders tenuous the entire Prussian code of honor. Similarly, Effi's poignant "It's funny, but I can say 'almost' for lots of things in my life, really" is meant to have the viewer question and ultimately reject a society which denies Effi more than this "almost."

Fassbinder's manipulation of the film's intertitles, by confronting viewers with what can easily be glossed over in the novel, is aimed at heightening their consciousness to elicit a more critical interpretation of *Effi Briest*. Thus without doing violence to the spirit of the literary text, Fassbinder's reading makes explicit the social criticism implicit in Fontane's novel.

23. German original: "Das will ich nicht sagen, Effi. Aber so oder so, man muss nur in Ordnung sein und sich nicht zu fürchten brauchen."

24. Thomas Elsaesser has stated it most succinctly. According to him, the "central experience – one might go so far as to call it the trauma that motivates his [Fassbinder's] productivity – is emotional exploitation. His films are fictionalized, dramatized, occasionally didactic versions of what it means to live within power structures and dependencies that are all but completely internalized, and as such apparently removed from any possibility of change or development." Thomas Elsaesser, "A Cinema of Vicious Circles," in *Fassbinder*, ed. Tony Rayns (London: British Film Institute, 1976), 25.

25. This particular interpersonal manipulation is, of course, only the working out of the greater underlying societal manipulation, which has dictated Effi's social aspirations and Innstetten's expectations.

The visual equivalent to the narrative alienation effects is Fassbinder's use of stylization. There is little of the child of nature in
Fassbinder's Effi; she is very much her mother's daughter, a
totally socialized being, susceptible to the ambitions of her class,
aware of the benefits of a good match. Fassbinder stresses this
aspect of Effi's character by including the conversation with her
mother regarding her social expectations and her rejection of
her cousin Dagobert. Significantly, as a visual corrective to this
conversation, Fassbinder interjects the silent scene with Dagobert in which Effi's attraction to her dashing young officer cousin
is made manifest. Thus the pantomime, as a means of direct
communication, calls the verbal level of communication into
question. This short pantomime is an eloquent indictment of
Effi's society, a society that encourages her to repress her natural inclinations and conform to expectations of family and class.
One wonders if Fassbinder considers Dagobert, who is clearly
more her peer, to be the "almost" of which Effi speaks.

In addition to the alienation effects produced by narration
and stylization, Fassbinder achieves another distancing device
through the use of white-outs. Vincent Canby has suggested that
the fades-to-white which separate individual scenes are reminiscent of the empty space at the end of the chapter of a book.[26]
Canby does well to point out the possible connection between
Fassbinder's white-outs and the literariness of his film. The fact,
however, that these white-outs are so brilliant and glaring as to
actually hurt the spectator's eyes indicates that they must be
regarded as another of Fassbinder's techniques for disrupting
the identification between the viewer and the characters and
events on the screen. This thesis is substantiated by Fassbinder:

> [*Effi*] works through two levels of alienation . . . [The white-outs]
> are one level, . . . like books which have white color and black
> print. According to Kracauer, when it gets black, the audience
> begins to fantasize, to dream, and I wanted the opposite effect
> through the white. I wanted to make them awake. It should not
> function like most films through the subconscious, but through
> the conscious. It's . . . the first time that I know of where the audi-
> ence is supposed to have its fantasy, like reading a novel – the first
> normal fiction film. . . . It's like a novel that one reads where you
> can have your own dreams and fantasies at the same time. When

26. Vincent Canby, "The Decline and Fall of Effi Briest," *New York Times*, 17
June 1977.

you read a book, a novel, you imagine your own characters. That's just what I wanted to do in this film. I didn't want to have predetermined characters made for the audience; rather the audience should continue the work.[27]

Fassbinder himself rejects the analogy between his distancing techniques and Brecht's *Verfremdungseffekte*, maintaining that in contrast to the playwright, who allows the audience to see emotions and then merely to reflect on them, never to feel them, he has gone further in letting the audience think *and* feel.[28] As with Brecht, however, there is a distinct disparity between Fassbinder's theory and praxis. Brecht's most successful plays, such as *Mutter Courage*, evoke an emotional response in the viewer/reader. So too, while Fassbinder might aspire to a balance between intellect and emotion, the scales are tipped in favor of the cerebral; the viewer's emotional response is circumscribed by the distancing devices he employs.

At the heart of Fassbinder's treatment of *Effi Briest* is the basic dialectic which informs his work: "I make films that have a bearing on the spectator's reality: this (in conjunction with the filmic reality) gives rise to a new reality in the spectator's head."[29] The relationship between Fassbinder's general philosophy of filmmaking and his treatment of *Effi Briest* is made explicit by the filmmaker himself:

> To show a narrative on film is like an author telling a story, but there's a difference. When one reads a book, one creates – as a reader – one's own images, but when a story is told on the screen in pictures, then it is concrete and really "complete." One is not creative as a member of a film audience, and it was this passivity that I tried to counter in *Effi Briest* . I would prefer people to "read" the film. It's a film which one cannot simply experience, and which doesn't attack the audience. . . . One has to read it. That's the most significant thing about the film.[30]

It is obvious that Fassbinder has a specific "reading" in mind, and that to elicit this reading he has introduced Brechtian distancing devices. If the chief function of these devices is to awaken the critical faculties of viewers, the question remains what

27. Quoted by Thomas, "Poetry of the Inarticulate," 14–15.
28. Quoted by Norbert Sparrow (interviewer), "'*I let the Audience Feel and Think*' – An Interview with Rainer Werner Fassbinder," *Cineaste* 8, 2 (1977): 20.
29. Ibid.
30. Christian Braad Thomsen, "Interview with Fassbinder (Berlin, 1974)," in *Fassbinder*, ed. Rayns, 46.

conclusions Fassbinder wishes them to reach. As with Brecht, the lack of identification is meant to deflect the viewer's focus of attention away from the outcome to the process of the action. We are not meant to identify with Effi's fate, but rather to judge it, to see the various junctures at which the seeming inevitability of events could have been circumvented. This is most obvious in the Wüllersdorf-Innstetten dialogue, where the events are presented as inevitable, but where the viewer is clearly meant to call this inevitability into question. We are meant to see Effi's fate as the direct outcome of the behavior of those who perpetuate the system even as they are aware of the strictures of the outmoded social system. Again and again Fassbinder, in pointing out the behavior of those who ultimately accept and thereby confirm the system, leads the viewer to his reading of *Effi Briest* .

In this context an explanation of Fassbinder's stance with respect to his narrator presents itself. Fassbinder has maintained that *Effi Briest* is about Fontane's attitude to society, which he describes as follows:

> He lives in a society whose faults he recognized and could describe precisely but all the same a society he needed, to which he really wanted to belong. He rejected everybody and found everything alien and yet fought all his life for recognition within that society.[31]

Despite his avowed affinity with Fontane's position,[32] the question arises whether Fassbinder has committed the biographical fallacy, whether he has equated the narrator of *Effi Briest* with the author Fontane. The calling into question of the narrator would then have to be seen as an indictment of Fontane for his acquiescence, for his failure to take the decisive step from the objective presentation of a questionable social order to an opposition to that order, for his failure to take the step from humanitarianism to engagement. The narrator-author would then be subsumed into the "many" of Fassbinder's subtitle against whom he directs his criticism. He too would be seen as one who, despite his idea of the possibilities and needs of his characters, nevertheless accepts the prevailing order and thereby strengthens and confirms it absolutely.

Reprinted from Seminar *21.4 (1985): 272–85.*

31. Ibid.
32. Ibid.

4

In the Margins of Identity: Fassbinder's *In a Year of 13 Moons*

sandra frieden

*exuality and gender
identity are at the
heart of Fassbinder's* In a
Year of 13 Moons
*(1978), and Sandra Frieden
demonstrates not only how,
within the film, the story
centering on the transsexual
protagonist Erwin/Elvira
plays havoc with traditional
gender roles (indeed, at the
very site of sexual difference:
the protagonist's body), but
also how this story disrupts
the conventional, gendered
patterns of spectator identification upon which narrative cinema is based. The film thereby
positions the spectator in a quite
different fashion, which Frieden*

Hacker (Karl Scheydt) forces Elvira (Volker Spengler) to look in
the mirror. Rainer Werner Fassbinder's *In a Year of 13 Moons*
(1978).
(Photo courtesy of New Yorker Films)

*asserts to be a new film-spectator relationship, "one which manifests
rather than represses the female as subject of desire."*
— THE EDITORS

The first frames of Fassbinder's *In a Year of 13 Moons* (*In einem
Jahr mit 13 Monden*, 1978) are dark and elusive: footsteps are
audible, but their source is not lit. A title discloses a place and
time: Frankfurt am Main, July 24, 1978. Light appears, first at
the edge of the frame, then forming a wedge in the center, but
never completely illuminating the faces whose silhouettes the

viewer discerns in the shadows. Strains of a Mahler symphony accompany a deep-focus shot of a tree-lined lane along the river. Two men meet. A rolling title explains:

> Every seventh year is a year of the moon. Certain people, whose existence is influenced mainly by their emotions, suffer from intense depressions in these moon years. . . . And when a moon year is also a year with thirteen new moons, it often results in inevitable personal catastrophes. (Fassbinder 1982)[1]

The titles then list all such years in this century, among them, 1978. On screen, money changes hands. The barely lit figures exchange an embrace behind the film's opening titles. A sudden close-up reveals luminous white silk underwear and a hand groping – awkwardly, confused – first from the front, then from the back. The camera retreats to show the two men: one pulls away and shouts at the other in Czech, "Are you a woman?" He calls to his friends – "He says he's a woman!" More figures appear and, to the side of the continuing titles, they strip and beat the hapless object of the confusion, who is left to crawl off into the darkness.

   This opening sequence introduces the last few days in the life of Elvira Weishaupt and establishes the tone and themes of the entire film. Darkness dominates Elvira's world, with strange sources of light intruding on the edges of the frame, but rarely illuminating the subject. Sounds and words lead – and more often, mislead – us; characters and events are shunted to the side rather than shown center-screen. Fate, money, sex, and brutality cohabit in the sphere of desire, and the expression of desire is permitted only within certain rules of gender identity. Indeed, here is the crux of the problem: Elvira's gender identity remains unclear, and this lack of clarity has consequences for how we view the film. A main character of indeterminate gender identity makes the process of identification highly problematic, since the conventions of cinematic spectatorship rely significantly on gendered viewer identification with a gendered protagonist.[2] And if

1. Rainer Werner Fassbinder (1946–1982) directed 44 films in 17 years.
2. For recent discussions of the complexities of viewer identification as related to gender and referred to in this essay, see Teresa de Lauretis, *Alice Doesn't: Feminism, Semiotics, Cinema* (Bloomington: Indiana Univ. Press, 1984); Kaja Silverman, *The Subject of Semiotics* (New York: Oxford Univ. Press, 1983); J. Dudley Andrew, *Concepts in Film Theory* (New York: Oxford Univ. Press, 1984); and Bill Nichols, Introduction to Laura Mulvey, "Visual Pleasure and Narrative Cinema" in *Movies and Methods Volume II*, ed. Bill Nichols (Berkeley: Univ. of California Press, 1985).

the usual process of viewer identification does not "work," then how will the film "work"?

Who – or more to the point, what – is this character? Each expository scene turns on the complexities of sexual relations and Elvira's gender identity but works to confuse the question rather than resolve it. Volker Spengler portrays the character Elvira Weishaupt, an actor whose hulking mass of body is insistently male, while voice, posture, gestures, and behavior attest to the distinguishing socialization of females in Western culture. In the sequence following the opening titles, Elvira quarrels with her lover Christoph, who, upon finding her in men's clothing and battered by her attackers, beats her even more, berates her for her ugliness and stupidity, and tells her that she is not, after all, a "real woman" (although Elvira certainly accepts this attack with all the masochism and self-recriminations of a properly socialized female). Next, Elvira tells her prostitute-friend Zora about her own young marriage to her childhood sweetheart Irene, about the fathering of a daughter, Marie Ann, and about Irene's loyalty, not divorcing her, "even after the trip to Casablanca." Then, we meet Irene, hysterical over a newspaper interview in which Elvira has apparently "told all" about an earlier relationship to a now powerful man, Anton Saitz. Irene is convinced that Anton will seek revenge – if not against Elvira herself, then against their daughter Marie Ann. Irene cries and says, "Erwin, I'm afraid." Elvira/Erwin comforts her, and promises to visit Anton and ask his forgiveness.

We eventually do learn more about Elvira/Erwin, but only after the fundamental issue of gender confusion has thoroughly undermined the viewing situation. We are told that she was indeed once a man, Erwin Weishaupt. After his marriage to Irene, Erwin fell in love with Anton and told him of his feelings. Anton replied, "That's nice. Too bad you're not a girl." With no further urging, Erwin went to Casablanca for a sex-change operation. Ridiculed and rebuffed by Anton on her return, Elvira was left to recover from a suicide attempt and to restructure a life for herself.

The apparent motivation of the remaining plot – fear of Anton's reprisal and Elvira's quest for forgiveness – turns out to be as irrelevant as a Hitchcock MacGuffin.[3] Anton Saitz couldn't

3. Hitchcock explains this purposely irrelevant plot-furthering device as the "gimmick" which motivates the characters, but is really of no other importance. "The name comes from an anecdote about two men in a train. One man says,

care less about Elvira; in fact, neither could anyone else in her life, and Elvira's quest loses all motivational significance. While friends and family are fond of her, they are not there when she needs them. Her wanderings lead to bizarre encounters on corners, in hallways, on rooftops with deafened, dying, suicidal individuals; and these episodes are accepted as mundane in a world where the cripple is the norm. Each scene of Elvira's life turns on the axis of gender identity and thus on her transgression of a dividing line basic to society. We are all too familiar with the economy of Elvira's world: sex is a commodity, purchased with money or servitude. But the commodity must be identifiable and desirable, and Elvira is neither. No longer a male, she can no longer act as a desiring subject; not accepted as a female – and though she is an object of derision – she cannot serve as object of sexual desire. As non-subject and non-object, Elvira is trapped in a social and sexual purgatory, and her frustrated needs provide her ongoing punishment. Relegated always to the edge of the frame, half-lit by hellish reds, oppressed by an excess of language that never elucidates but only heightens the awareness of despair, sure of herself only as spectacle, bitterly isolated and lonely, desired by no one and unable to say what she desires, her uncertain identity and blurring of roles pushing her to the margins of her world – Elvira kills herself.

* * *

The question of gender identity, sustained for the first thirty minutes of the film, works to discomfort the viewer. Just as the film characters seesaw in their reactions to now-Erwin, now-Elvira, so does the viewer: the need to know how to relate to this character builds, along with the awareness of our dependence on gender identity within social and cinematic relations, reflected in every scene of the film. By the time we learn how Erwin came to be Elvira, our attention has been so acutely focused on the ambiguity of this character's sexual identity that we are unable to dispel the discomfort.

'What's that package up there in the baggage rack?' And the other answers, 'Oh, that's a MacGuffin.' The first one asks, 'What's a MacGuffin?' 'Well,' the other man says, 'it's an apparatus for trapping lions in the Scottish Highlands.' The first man says, 'But there are no lions in the Scottish Highlands,' and the other one answers, 'Well then, that's no MacGuffin!'" Francois Truffaut, *Hitchcock* (London: Granada, 1978), 158.

Such uneasiness is intended to disrupt the viewer's expected interaction with the film – an intent based on an understanding of the psychological structuring of the viewing situation. In psychological terms, films work on us by invoking drives and fulfilling needs. As film theorists have observed (see note 2), narcissism leads us to identify with these larger-than-life figures upon the screen; voyeurism elicits our pleasure in doing so; and the need for stasis, equilibrium, and security propels us through a narrative structure in order to resolve ambiguities and confirm our place in the world. Along with class and race, gender is a powerful organizing principle of socialization which significantly determines our responses to these drives and our interactions as social beings and as cinematic spectators.

The patriarchally prescribed "look" of the camera has determined the gender-specific conventions of cinematic spectatorship: decisions to aim the camera in one direction as opposed to another, to foreground one subject as opposed to another, or to linger on one image as opposed to another reflect the perspective of the decision makers. And in the case of classic (Hollywood) cinema as the measure of our cinematic conditioning, the decision makers have been overwhelmingly male. The significance (or insignificance) thus invested in an image transfers to the spectator, an implanting of vision which at least corroborates and confirms – if not produces – existing social conditions and the male experience of the world. The female image on screen, powerless recipient of this look, provides the site of visual pleasure and offers the spectator an object of control. Thus, sexual politics is carried through the processes of spectatorship in a series of steps which seem to grant controlling power to the viewer, but, as Judith Mayne has pointed out, actually lock the viewer into the dominant way of seeing.[4]

This functioning of sexual identity in co-determining social interactions and subjectivity is conventionally repressed in cinema and in the process of spectatorship. The male viewer is provided a familiar perspective and finds heroic reflections of himself, or even antiheroic reflections of himself, at the center of attention and tailored to his view of the world. The female viewer is addressed as though she were male, is asked to identify not only with the male hero and male point of view, but also with

4. Judith Mayne, "Fassbinder and Spectatorship," *New German Critique* 12 (Fall 1977): 74.

the objectified female. This objectified female, the cinematic heroine (or un-heroine), is never the active center of attention. Her role in the narrative is predetermined by the structure of narrative itself: the movement of a (male) subject toward possession of a (female) object. The female image serves as the focus of the male gaze, as the reward at the end of the male quest, and as a behavioral model for the female viewer. Desire and pleasure within the film and within the viewing situation are thus male-defined, a situation leading Teresa de Lauretis to ask: what are the determinants of female desire as motivation, and where is a locus for the female viewer as subject?[5] De Lauretis suggests a different positionality within the film-spectator relationship – one which manifests rather than represses the female as subject of desire.

Such a "positionality," I maintain, is expressed in *13 Moons*. Whereas sexual difference – the gender-base of identity and identification – is conventionally repressed by both film and viewer, hidden within the processes of filmmaking and filmviewing, Fassbinder breaks this implicit contract by foregrounding gender issues and intervening in the familiar patterns of narrative/cinematic identification and visual pleasure. Just as the opening sequence establishes gender as a basis for relations, the ensuing scenes specifically thematize some issue of gender as the basis for identity, but always through the troubling persona of Erwin/Elvira. This character's strangeness defamiliarizes stereotypical gender-related behavior characteristics: Elvira's cowering, pleading self-abnegation and acceptance of abuse; the female body in service to the male, either through money or through availability; the female as property, bound through fear, custom, and law to the male. Elvira's stroll through a slaughterhouse and identification with the "sacrificial animal led to the altar" is a grotesque representation of the distortions perpetrated in the name of gender, distortions made all the more evident in that they are acted out by a character whose crossing over the gender line reveals both the rhetorical and the politico-economical power of gender socialization. Lest the viewer believe that such depictions are idiosyncratic to this one character, we are shown the "larger picture" in Elvira's world, a window to the society beyond the walls which encircle her: a "random sampling" of programs on Elvira's television set alter-

5. de Lauretis, *Alice Doesn't*, 141ff.

nate between a program on a dictatorship in Chile and a movie about a couple who mirror the power relationships we have seen elsewhere in *13 Moons* – global displays of totalitarianism in politics and in personal affairs.

At the center of every scene is not Elvira, but Elvira's displacement from a central role as active subject; on the edge of almost every frame, she remains on the edge of male-as-subject, female-as-object narrative gender models. Measured against the trajectory of traditional narrative, where the male-as-subject progresses toward the female-as-object, Elvira does not fulfill narrative/ideological expectations of "progress." On the contrary, Elvira *goes nowhere*. Immobilized within the mise-en-scène, she occupies an ideological no-man's land where there are (as yet) no words to articulate her desire except as an expression of despair ("What I fear the most is if one day I'm able to put my feelings into words, because when I do. . . ." – this, the writing of a lunatic soul mate discovered by Elvira and read silently). Elvira's "maleness" is a constant presence through her physique and, eventually, through her history (the insistent awareness of her "wound"), but her "femaleness" dominates her behavior. She attempts to return to a (male) position of initiation and articulation, but she can no longer occupy that privileged position. For the viewer, Elvira's predicament as once-male but now-female discloses the loss of privilege – a loss just as true for all the female characters in the film, but only made noticeable through Elvira's ambiguous identity. Desire in Elvira's world is initiated and fulfilled by men; *her* initiation of desire is a break with social norms. Her attempts at articulation are disembodied, captured on tape and played back when she is dead, her voice detached from her person and exploited. Conventional spectator relations are thus skewed and foregrounded in the viewer's unaccustomed access to female desire.

As viewers, we have all learned the pleasures of cinematic voyeurism; here "the look" yields only displeasure. Where the eye of the camera normally obliges the viewer to control and consume the beautiful object presented on screen, Elvira's ambiguous presence removes the site of pleasure, from within the film and within the process of spectatorship. As she is all too painfully aware, no one desires Elvira, and she acknowledges herself as spectacle. Her point of view is privileged, and we watch her, watching others watch her – in their discomfort, hers, and ours. To be sure, there are female characters who might normally serve as repositories of "the look" and therefore of pleasure, but the conventional way of seeing them is not presented to us. The men in the film who "look at" the women would normally serve as models for the viewers, directing our gaze both visually and ideologically to consume the female image, but the men are themselves objects of Elvira's gaze. Unaccustomed to such a reversal and unable to adopt (through identification) Elvira's point of view, we cannot participate in any pleasure in looking at the other women: the men's consumption of the image signals rejection for Elvira, both as consumer and image.

Sexual difference is thus exposed and foregrounded, not only among the characters and relationships within the film, but within the processes of spectatorship as well. The subjective view thrust upon the viewer is the uncomfortable ambiguity of Elvira, whose undeniable and constant presence as both male and female breaks with societal and cinematic rules of identification, leaving the viewer in a spectator's purgatory parallel to Elvira's. The level of visual displeasure sustains the discomfort, the unfamiliarity of the perspective: no comfortable comic interludes, no titillation, no promise of reversal offers relief from this point of view. The viewer scrambling for some familiar ground may turn to the melodramatic traits of the narrative, but Fassbinder's semblance of melodrama serves (as it so often does in his films[6]) as the mockery of the expected form: enigma, suffering, compromise – traditional driving forces of melodramatic narrative – set up an anticipation of resolution which never comes about. Indeed, the most traditional aspect of the narrative is the elimination of the female who dares to initiate desire. Narrative functions are broken down through resistance to identification, to visual pleasure, and to closure; and through these resistances, the exposure of sexual difference becomes the work of the film, opening up, as a possibility, the generally taboo territory of identification with female desire. Such a female positionality, in de Lauretis's terms, offers no solution, but only a possibility, a dislocated perspective from which to view the world – our world.

6. For discussions of Fassbinder's use of melodrama, see Mayne, "Fassbinder and Spectatorship," and Tony Pipolo, "Bewitched by the Holy Whore," *October* 21 (Summer 1982).

5

Images in Balance

r o s w i t h a   m u e l l e r

In this essay, Roswitha Mueller compares Ula Stöckl's first feature,
The Cat Has Nine Lives *(made in 1968, when a feature film by
a woman was a rare thing indeed in West Germany), with Margarethe
von Trotta's* Sisters, Or the Balance of Happiness *(1979). Each of
the two films depicts a problematic relationship between two women,
and Mueller analyzes each film as a documentation – and critique – of
dominant patterns of female identity and female interaction at two crucial points in the recent history of women's consciousness: in the late
1960s, just as women were starting to question a male-dominated sexual revolution (and male-dominated political movements), and in the
late 1970s, when a re-established feminism had consolidated itself –
but seemed on the mass level only able to influence the emergence of a
female careerism, as opposed to inspiring a more radical social solidarity. Beyond the critique of certain patterns of female interaction in the
films, Mueller finds suggestions of a more utopian model of female
identity, one that encompasses both autonomy and a capacity for
fusion.*
—THE EDITORS

Unlike American feminism, the organized German women's
movement of the seventies largely grew out of the political student movement of the sixties. Helke Sander's film *The Subjective
Factor* (*Der Subjektive Faktor*) documents this transition. It shows
the increasing discontent among women with the roles assigned
to them by men and their gradual breaking away from orthodox
positions. These positions held that the conflict arising from
gender difference was a secondary contradiction subsumed
under the primary contradiction. The latter, the contradiction
between the forces and relations of production, received all the
political attention, while it was believed that subsidiary conflicts
would fall into place once this primary issue was resolved. As a

result, subjective, interpersonal relations were not considered political and were relegated to the private sphere. In the seventies, women's insistence on the personal as political deepened the rift between the feminist movement and male radical politics, even though much of German feminism continued to be influenced by the precepts of the Left.

As could be expected, it was not until the later seventies that women became a tangible force in New German Cinema, at a time when the major male "authors" – Kluge, Herzog, Fassbinder, Wenders, and Schlöndorff – were already well established. A notable exception to this is Ula Stöckl, whose first feature *The Cat Has Nine Lives* (*Neun Leben hat die Katze*) is all the more remarkable in that it broaches specifically feminist questions at the height of the student movement in 1968, long before the women seceded from it. At the same time, however, the year 1968 is deeply engraved in the film's text. Stöckl, a student of Alexander Kluge and Edgar Reitz at the Institute for Filmmaking in the Ulm School of Design, was the Institute's first graduate of its five-year program. Kluge's style has definitely left its imprint on Stöckl's films – especially on this first feature film – even though closer comparison breaks down along the lines of point of view structure. Like Kluge, Stöckl works with an episodic structure in the Brechtian tradition, loosely stringing relatively self-contained scenes together, instead of developing a tight and cohesive/coercive plot. *The Cat Has Nine Lives* revolves around the friendship of two women: Katharina, a journalist residing in Munich, and Ann, a French woman, who arrives in town from Paris to visit Katharina. Grouped around this central pair are the chance meetings and encounters with other people, male and female, who are for the most part friends, lovers, and business relations of Katharina.

In Kluge's films with female protagonists (of which there are many), the randomness of this type of structure is usually firmly bound by factual information, quotations, subjective observations, and semi-omniscient insights into the various characters' psyches, provided by a male voice-over that represents the point of view of the filmmaker himself. As has been pointed out, this point of view is not always supportive of, or even fair to, the female protagonist.[1] Stöckl's film, in contrast, resorts to a differ-

1. B. Ruby Rich, "She Says, He Says: The Power of the Narrator in Modernist Film Politics," *Discourse* 6 (1984): 31–46 (reprinted in this volume).

ent device in order to provide a measure of coherence to the individual episodes. Short fantasy sequences are interpolated at certain intervals between the present events surrounding Ann's visit in Munich. It is difficult to determine the enunciator of these sequences. There is an instant temptation to see them as expressions of Ann's point of view. Some of the sequences delve into preconscious and unconscious states of mind that pertain both to Katharina and Ann. The fact, however, that Ann is more frequently represented both in the fantasy sequences and as the source of them defines her as the protagonist of the imaginary and sets her in opposition to Katharina, who rarely appears in this connection.

This opposition is elaborated in the rest of the film, in those sequences that show Katharina and Ann in their daily interactions. In this register of everyday reality, Katharina stands out as the more forceful character. Her career-oriented competence and her acquiescence in a marginal love affair with a married man mark her – in the language of the sixties and its Marcusian overtones – as representative of the "reality principle," whereas Ann, basking in polymorphous perversity, stands for the "pleasure principle."[2] What is interesting about Stöckl's treatment of this well-known sixties theme is that it shows what euphoria of sexual liberation meant concretely for women and shows this from their point of view.

Later in the seventies, other women filmmakers in the Federal Republic took up this theme with slightly different connotations, more attuned to questions growing directly out of the women's movement of that time. The most remarkable of these films is Margarethe von Trotta's *Sisters, or the Balance of Happiness* (*Schwestern oder die Balance des Glücks*). Made in 1979, the film investigates the love and dependency relationship between two sisters within the framework of their respective choices of roles available to women. As in Stöckl's film, the two positions are dichotomized with great clarity. Maria, the older sister, is a model of competence in the professional world, like Katharina, whereas the younger sister Anna shares with the character of Ann in Stöckl's film a greater investment in emotions, feelings, and concern about love and friendship. In short, Ann and Anna have chosen to remain closer to the traditional female domain

2. Marc Silberman, "Ula Stöckl: How Women See Themselves," in *New German Filmmakers,* ed. Klaus Phillips (New York: Ungar, 1984), 324.

and role pattern than either Maria or Katharina. On one level, the polarization within the two couples Katharina/Ann and Maria/Anna reproduces the distribution of roles in convention-al married couples, as the sister's mother makes clear when she points out that Maria, her older daughter, is taking after the father, while Anna is more like herself.

What invites comparison of the two films is not only their sim-ilar subject matter, but more importantly, the differences in the treatment of that same subject. Not the least of these differ-ences is attributable to the time lapse (more than a decade) between the making of the two films. To begin with, the posi-tions taken by Katharina and Ann in *The Cat Has Nine Lives* are not nearly so clear-cut as those of the sisters in von Trotta's film. While Maria is unconflicted in her professionalism, earning enough money as an executive secretary to be able to support her younger sister's medical studies, Katharina's work situation is fraught with dissatisfaction. Neither is Anna's melancholic despair over her dependent love for her sister and her inability to establish any relationships of her own with the outside world comparable to Ann's free spirit. Ann whimsically oscillates between self-assured aggressiveness and frustrating affairs casu-ally started. One reason for this divergence in characterization – complexity to the point of confusion in Stöckl's case versus clar-ity to the point of stereotyping in von Trotta's case – may be found in the conditions of production of the two films. *The Cat Has Nine Lives* was made with money from the *Kuratorium junger deutscher Film*, a funding agency that was established in support of the *Autorenfilm* in the Federal Republic in the sixties. This agency gave first-time projects by young "authors" a good chance of being subsidized, regardless of the commercial value of the end product. As funding policies changed in the seven-ties, filmmakers also began to take commercial standards into account to accommodate not an ideal but the actual audience. Margarethe von Trotta's films all reflect these changes, which is not to say that they are straightforward commercial films; rather, as with films by many New German Cinema "authors" – Fassbinder being a case in point – they are a compromise between the alternative and often idiosyncratic *Autorenfilm* and the success formulas of commercial cinema.

But aside from these questions of style, the two films approach the career-versus-private sphere dichotomy from opposing points of view. Both films are critical of the position favored by the cultural and intellectual attitudes of the respective decades of the films' making. Ann, whose position in Stöckl's film comes closest to a personification of the sixties discourse on cultural and political resistance, is portrayed as far from reaping the fruits of the promised land of dropouts. On the other hand, Maria's total and powerful investment in careerism, a position which reflects one of the major thrusts of the feminist movement in the seventies, is under serious scrutiny in von Trotta's film. In a way then, both films are posing the question that Helke Sander once substituted for the topic of feminist aesthetics, namely, "What do women want?" or more directly, "How do women want to live their lives?" This question touches on the larger discussion of roles, utopian or given, that women have initiated precisely to gain greater insight into that problematic.

Silvia Bovenschen has pointed out that "the idea of femininity is not exhausted by the actual social forms of female existence, but gains substance from the reality of image creations (*Imaginationen*)."[3] Bovenschen argues that these imagined constructs of femininity are not necessarily informed by the actual existence of women, but are set independently alongside of them. Interactions between the two registers take place in two ways: either women imitate or emulate the idealized notions of themselves, or else the phantasmal spills over into their lives, which is what gives these image creations the status of reality. Thus Bovenschen explains that the woman as witch was first created in the minds of men, but real women were burned at the stake. Historically, therefore, women had very little to do with the definition of themselves, finding expression instead in formulations alien to their experience. Strictly speaking, Bovenschen observes, the term "role" is not applicable to these different images of women, since the term implies an underlying, inherent property, the postulation of which would be tantamount to the hypothesis of an essential feminine. Bovenschen rejects this hypothesis, not on philosophical grounds but for reasons of impracticality. Such a construct would be so abstract as to elude representation. The only possibility for a genealogy of femininity, then, is to be sought on the level of image pro-

---

3. Silvia Bovenschen, *Die imaginierte Weiblichkeit* (Frankfurt/M.: Suhrkamp Verlag, 1979), 40. Translated by Roswitha Mueller.

duction, taking into account the interaction between phantasmal imaging and everyday forms of existence. The two films
under discussion contribute to this genealogy in that they map
two decades of real and imagined types of women.

A new element enters into this equation in *The Cat Has Nine
Lives* through the character of Ann, who follows the film's voice-
over proposition that "never have women had so many opportunities to make something of their lives. But now they must simply realize that they are capable of wanting." Ann, as befits her
role as the sixties flower child, is closely aligned with the realm
of fantasy and thus is able to break through the male hegemony
over representations of femininity by inventing woman in her
own image. Oddly enough, her invention is inspired by mythology's number one man-eater, the sorceress Circe, who turns
men into swine. The Circe (Kirke) of Ann's phantasmal imaging, however, is far from the vision of threatened male sexuality
with which we are familiar; rather, she is the woman Ann would
like to be. As such she takes on dimensions of superwoman. For
example, Ann describes her to Katharina in this way: "She does
what she likes. She can even blow up the Eiffel Tower. She is a
real woman." In fact, Ann is not dissimilar to Kirke. When asked
by one of her male acquaintances about her occupation, she
echoes her own description of Kirke: "I can do something different every day." But instantly she follows this pronouncement
with the "politically correct" explanation that she opposes
careerism because she is unwilling to "play the game." A latter
day Nadja of sorts, she contents herself with spontaneous
chance encounters with a series of men. Yet none of these
liaisons affords her any measure of contentment, and she seems
ready – like her fabled Kirke – to turn the whole lot of them into
swine.

It becomes clear that Ann is as much imaged as she is imaging: that is, her projections of Kirke are in large part the male
ideal of the sexually accessible woman of the sixties that Ann is
unconsciously or consciously filling, at the same time as she
fiercely defends her freedom. In her dealings with her friend
Sash, for example, she rejects any demands for constancy or
even consistency, thrusting him into Katharina's arms to rid
herself of his unwanted advances. She breaks down in frustrated
crying, however, when Katharina takes up the challenge and
spends the night with him. Her narcissistic universe is shattered

again and again in this manner; even Manfred, another admirer who thinks Ann a charming creature, is simply "too tired" to do justice to her needs.

Kirke, on the other hand, is free of such frustrations. Kirke, one might say, is an image of an image. She is carefree and plea-sure seeking, but she is more than that. She is also Ann's fantasy of power, the necessary power needed in order to safeguard this carefree position against the possibilities of frustration it so eas-ily holds for women. The power Kirke has is described on two levels – one realistic, one imaginary – which correspond to the ambiguous status of Kirke in the film: it is hard to tell whether Kirke is an actual character or solely exists in Ann's mind. The power she holds, accordingly, is on the one hand the power that can be gained by an ordinary character: "She is travelling. She has lots of money." On the other hand, she is also endowed with the power of the mythological figure, transmitted through Ann's imagination, as when she is seen turning a group of leer-ing men into giant hogs.

The equivocation around Kirke's existential status is an inter-esting commentary on Stöckl's part on the fluidity between image creation and social positionality. Yet, no great store of emancipatory hope is set by these flights of female fantasy, at least not from Ann's somewhat pessimistic view: "Few people can do more than they've learned. We can only imagine what has already existed." Is the failure of Ann's imagining – the fact that it does not connect with her own life – to be sought in its inauthenticity, in its recourse to already existing images of women?

Ann's quandary is that the power she dreams of, money and travel, she rejects in reality, by rejecting the obvious avenue of gaining it through a career. The odium of careerism that Ann scrupulously avoids attaches to some degree to Katharina. Although Katharina is a free-lance journalist working for a press which has clearly alternative guidelines for publication, her ambitions and her preoccupation with her work seem to be of a personal order. At one point she applies for a job as executive secretary just to see whether she could get the job and at what salary. The gratification she derives from her success in that field is more than mere vanity; it seems to be the basis of her self-esteem. In comparison to Ann's lighthearted indepen-dence, Katharina's more harried demeanor is at first view less engaging. Neither does her private life recommend her choices. Resigned to the awkwardness and lack of security that her relationship with Stefan, a married man, holds in store for her, she is unwilling to discuss the problem with Ann, insisting that neither divorce nor marriage is a solution to her situation. Gradually, however, Katharina is seen in a different light. Her sincere dedication to her job, and, more specifically, to the subject of her journalistic investigation, the singer-star Gabriele, contrasts positively with Ann's all too frequent states of frustration. The first time this contrast is presented is shortly after Ann's arrival at Katharina's flat. Katharina is absorbed in her work, poring over some papers, books, and her typewriter, while Ann occupies the adjacent room reading. But soon she loses interest and proceeds to burn holes into her stockings with her cigarette and sets a book of matches afire. Stöckl likewise pokes holes into the fabric of image creation. Ann, the ideal of femininity in the sixties, for all her charm and principled resistance to "the system," is also the other side of the ideal: a bored and frustrated child. It is precisely the conjunction of the ideal and the real woman in her that produces the ambivalence in her character. Katharina is, of course, no less ambivalent. Much more repressed than Ann and victim of an unrelenting superego, she compromises too much with the way things are to be admitted into the gallery of the countercultural idols. Yet from her dedication to her career emerge the contours of the freedom and independence that Ann is only dreaming about.

The other women in *The Cat Has Nine Lives,* Gabriele the star and Magdalene, the deceived wife of Stefan, are merely supplementary images, too undeveloped to be considered on an equal footing with the characters of Ann and Katharina. Magdalene's unsuspecting marital bliss and Gabriele's self-complacency, surrounded as she is by photos of herself, are little more that clichés even when they are transformed in Ann's fantasy into a jealous wife shooting her husband, or, in Gabriele's case, into the phantasmagoric object of all men's desire (Stefan standing in for all men in Ann's imagination). In a sense Gabriele and Magdalene are counterparts like Ann and Katharina, but they are too scantily drawn to merit lengthier analysis. In fact, their inclusion in the film is part of Stöckl's kaleidoscopic style, which, in an attempt to capture the complexity of these issues, broadens the field of investigation by piling episode upon episode – and these episodes are not necessarily related in space and time. The effect is often stimulation, especially in the fantasy sequences where the montage is well structured. At other times, the profusion of characters, situations, and various levels of reality results in mere suggestiveness, if not vagueness. Stöckl's first feature film nevertheless anticipated the great wave of women filmmakers in the Federal Republic by many years, broaching a number of issues that would continue to be discussed in the following decade.

Margarethe von Trotta's 1979 film *Sisters, or the Balance of Happiness* represents one such continuity. Like Ann and Katharina, the sisters Maria and Anna are polarized around notions of career versus private sphere. Yet, the accent is quite different. Maria, the successful business woman, has not questioned in her mind that her independence, her know-how in the world, and her monthly check are a big step forward in the life of a woman. Nor does the audience question this. Maria's competence is indeed impressive. Not only does she work eight hours a day, she also takes on extra typing for her boss in her leisure time. She not only supports her younger sister's education but also selflessly and generously takes on household chores when Anna is studying for exams. Unlike Katharina, who is professional with a bad conscience, Maria's ambition is seemingly undivided. The image Maria lives up to is one which men created for themselves and not for women. It also represents the *sine qua non* in the drive for equality of the feminist movement in the seventies. The difficulties that women encountered and still come up against in procuring such positions are captured in the ironic constellation of Maria's independence from men in her private life (as is evident in her reluctance about and final rejection of the advances of Maurice, the boss's son), while in the context of her work, she is entirely subordinated to the wishes and commands – however considerate and politely phrased – of her boss. Maria would have liked to go to the university herself, but was prevented from doing so when her father died. She compensates for the frustration inherent in her position by transferring her own ambitions onto Anna and urging her to finish her medical studies.

But Anna, like Ann, has no ambitions of her own; instead she has many scruples – not about careers in general, but about her own field. She talks to Maria about her inability to be neutral and scientific when it comes to subjects like genetic manipulation, and an entry in her diary reads: "to manipulate genes but not to be able to deal with love." Unlike Ann, Anna is not at all righteous about her position; on the contrary, she suffers from her inability to conform to her sister's demand to succeed with her studies. Her values are antithetical to Maria's way of life. Introspection, emotions, her love for her sister – desperate because so dependent – these are her primary concerns; they loom so large in her life that all her efforts at worldly competence are foiled again and again.

Thus, the classic male/female division of roles between the sisters is inevitable. Anna is not only unable to assume what used to be the male position as her sister had done, she is radically identified with the female image of yesteryear. To the audience von Trotta addressed in 1979, this image of a woman was no more appealing than Katharina was to Stöckl's audience in 1968. The tables are turned. What in Ann was expressed as the powerful euphoria of an expansive world view, appears in Anna as introverted and self-doubting weakness. And conversely, the halting uncertainty of Katharina's careerism emerges now in the form of Maria's matter-of-fact ambition.

Sisters is symmetrically and precisely structured around the two poles von Trotta has established. Each one of the sisters occupies her own physically and psychically distanced sphere. As a signal of her interiority, Anna is mostly associated with the house, their common apartment. There the ambience is characterized by melancholic retrospection both through the music she listens to – mostly sacred Renaissance and Baroque – and the richly glowing Rembrandtesque coloring of the furnishings. Here, Anna is seen doing the work of memory and dreams. She keeps a diary in which she records her thoughts and perceptions as well as the development of her tragic relationship with her sister. One of the first forebodings of the full extent of this tragedy is expressed in her diary entry: "The dream I have of life robs me of life." Anna is also the source of the flashbacks; that is, the sequence of Anna and Maria as children is mostly connected to the character of Anna. At one point this burdensome work of memory is shown to interfere with her activity in the outside world. In the scene where Anna is involved with her laboratory research, the objective conditions seem to allow for her smooth integration into the circle of colleagues surrounding her. But Anna appears to be dazed. The reason for her state of mind is revealed in the inserted flashback, which shows Anna and Maria as little girls putting on lipstick and gazing delightedly into the mirror at their perfect image of narcissistic union. Anna is unable to break through this magic circle, even though she tries. Once, she manges to smile at a fellow student at the cafeteria, but hastily flees when he takes this as an invitation to sit with her.

The sphere Maria occupies contrasts sharply with Anna's. Unlike her sister's flowing hair and dresses, Maria's well-tailored suits and severely combed-back hair are designed to complement the sober and cool simplicity of her office. There she reigns with efficiency, neatness, and a no-nonsense attitude which earns her the epitaph "angel" from her boss. This iron self-control gives her a measure of strength that can easily translate into power, especially over weaker characters like her sister Anna.

A subtle dynamic of dependency and control has developed between Anna and Maria. The perimeter of this power dynamic extends from the sisterly union of Anna and Maria reading fairytales, shown at the beginning of the film, to the brief insert of two old spinsterly sisters whose life together has gone awry. The opening shot is a slow tracking movement into the interior of a forest. It accompanies the fairytale text read – as we find out in the following shot – by the young Maria to her sister. Anna is cuddling up to her older sister's shoulder at the severity of the tale's injunction: "if we rest now, the wild animals will attack us in our sleep, and we will never get home." In this scene Maria's protective strength coupled with the potential of danger from without perfectly describes the sisters' predicament. Von Trotta's recurrent use of the opening shot as a structuring device, not just at the beginning and end of the film, but at crucial points of encounter between the sisters, emphasizes the importance of this scene. Their life together seems to be a continual struggle not to let protective strength turn into manipulative power, or affectionate feeling into total dependence.

The insertion of the old sister-couple points to the possibility of failure of this effort. In the case of this couple, the efficient rule of the older sister has reduced the younger one to fearful insecurity. Anna, who witnesses their interaction, is profoundly affected by it. At this point, she fully understands the stakes involved in her precarious juggling act with Maria. She realizes that much of Maria's altruistic support is also a means of keeping her powerless and dependent, and she accuses her of being "clever and heartless." Anna's decision to commit suicide, precipitated by her sister's affair with Maurice, is not just an act of jealous weakness, but the realization that, in order to survive, she would have to become more like Maria herself. Since she has nothing but contempt for this position, she prefers to die "in opposition" to her sister. "I don't ever want to become like her," reads her diary announcing her final act of defiant refusal.

Anna's story reads like the case history of a melancholic suicide. In all its symptoms, it corroborates Freud's classification of melancholia as a narcissistic disorder. A full elaboration of this observation exceeds the scope of this study. But a few remarks in conclusion in terms of different theories of narcissism are appropriate, not only because Ann in Stöckl's film is also conceived of as a narcissistic character, but more importantly, because in the genealogy of images of women, the "narcissistic woman" occupies such an imposing place. At least since Freud, there have been two interpretations of this image of woman. In one view narcissism is the result of greater self-sufficiency in women. According to the other it is caused by a greater narcissistic wound, that is, penis envy. Some psychoanalysts have seen the relatedness of these diverse views in the very nature of narcissism. Lou Andreas-Salomé, whose thoughts on narcissism apparently had some influence on Freud's article "On Narcissism: An Introduction" (1914), sees narcissism as the impossible desire for a total state of fusion, at the same time as it seeks individuality.

More recent psychoanalysts have placed the origin of this double determination in the prenatal stage of human development, when this condition of total autonomy and absolute fusion is indeed a given: "This borrowed economy (of the fetus) is completely unilateral, that is, not only is everything given to the fetus, but nothing is taken in return."[4] Based on similar psychoanalytic premises, the social and cultural theories in the sixties (notably those of Herbert Marcuse and other members of the Frankfurt School) saw in narcissism the possibility of another mode of sublimation altogether. Instead of repressing the libido, it would be extended and "the erotic body would come to make the whole world in its image."[5]

4. Bela Grunberger, *Narcissim: Psychoanalytic Essays*, trans. Joyce S. Diamanti (New York: International Univ. Press, 1979), 19.
5. C. Fred Alford, "Nature and Narcissim," *New German Critique* 36 (1985): 179.

It is easy to see how in Stöckl's film the character of Ann practices just such an extension of the libido. However, the limits of libidinal satisfaction – invested with such utopian hope by the theoreticians of the sixties – are also apparent. Ann's frustrations are depicted as oral regressions both with respect to the superficiality of her relationships and the most graphic level of voraciousness: she is constantly consuming bonbons, lollipops, and even flowers. Her dissociation from mature object mastery demanded by her ideological stance and abetted by her gender is shown to be the root cause of her frustrations, even though she fashions herself a badge of honor from the fact that she has no occupation.

Is Maria the answer then? Could it be that in assuming the traditional male model of fusion at home and autonomy or at least individuality outside, the impossible prerequisites of a narcissistic wholeness might at last be achieved? The price for this is paid, as the film shows, by the dependent partner, whether this be a younger sister or a wife. Anna's refusal to adapt to a world that is itself poor in narcissistic gratifications is an important, if negative, contribution to the imaging of women in terms of the lives women do *not* want to live. In *Sisters*, von Trotta is giving an explicit answer to these questions. After her sister's death, Maria gradually begins to change. Unable to deal with this loss in all its consequences, she replaces Anna with a younger colleague from the office, Miriam, by inviting her to move into her apartment. But Maria's attempt to reestablish the same relationship she had with Anna fails miserably in Miriam's case. After this second bitter loss, Maria is brought to face the fact that she will have to incorporate Anna's qualities into her own person in order to achieve the balance of happiness. At the office she literally and figuratively takes down her hair, while in her free time she now takes on the work of memory, diary writing, and dream recording. In this suggestion of a balance, von Trotta is projecting an ideal image, a woman with the capacity for fusion and the capacity for independence and autonomy that deserves to replace the old determinations of the narcissistic woman.

6

The Second Awakening of Christa Klages

renate möhrmann

Renate Möhrmann writes about Margarethe von Trotta's appropriation and reworking of the action film in The Second Awakening of Christa Klages (1978). The film deals with a female bank robber and makes direct allusions to the theme of political terrorism, but it is most subversive – and utopian – in its depiction of female bonding (which is indeed the source of the "second awakening" of the film's title). Möhrmann analyzes these various levels of the film's appeal in order to account for the film's reception (it was amazingly successful with the general public and the West German critics, two groups who generally do not agree on much). Her "reception analysis" evaluates the film positively for its ability to work on so many levels: precisely through this ambiguity, and its reliance on visual images of everyday reality rather than on a more didactic approach (which would stress a clearer political position), the film exposes a much wider audience to its underlying feminist politics than would otherwise be possible.
—THE EDITORS

Tina Engel as Christa in Margarethe von Trotta's The Second Awakening of Christa Klages (1977).
(Photo courtesy of Bioskop Film)

Premiere: February 24, 1978, International Forum of the Young German Film, *Berlinale* (Berlin Film Festival)

> Director: Margarethe von Trotta, Script: Margarethe von Trotta, Luisa Francia, Camera: Franz Rath, Music: Klaus Doldinger, Editor: Annette Dorn, Production: Bioskop Film/WDR (West German Radio), Cast: Tina Engel (Christa Klages), Silvia Reize (Ingrid), Katharina Thalbach (Lena), Marius Müller-Westernhagen (Werner), Peter Schneider (Hans)

Margarethe von Trotta's debut film, *The Second Awakening of Christa Klages,* enjoyed instant success. At the premiere on 24 February 1978, during the International Forum of Young German Film at the Berlin Film Festival, critics celebrated this film as *the* discovery of the festival and expressed unanimous praise. The official recognition entailed the *Bundesfilmpreis* (National German Film Award), the *Filmband in Silber* (Film Ribbon in Silver) accompanied by a bonus payment of 300,000 DM, an achievement surpassing all expectations. No one had ever expected that a woman who thus far had been known only as an actress, or as "Mrs. Schlöndorff," would present a film of this caliber.

However, not only the critics valued the film. After the Berlin Film Festival, *The Second Awakening of Christa Klages* appeared in public theaters, and the general audience, too, expressed utmost enthusiasm for the film. Such agreement between the public and the critics is unusual in the West German film scene. Whatever pleases the majority is normally branded as "mass entertainment" and arouses the suspicions of the critic. Rave reviews, on the other hand, appear equally suspicious to the general public and by no means result in box office hits. Hence the dilemma of the "New German Cinema": as subsidized cinema, it does not depend on public approval, but this freedom also has its disadvantages. It is very important to note that the West German film market is up to 80 percent determined by American productions and that the New German Cinema, from an economic perspective, plays only a marginal role. Against such a backdrop, the widespread popularity of *The Second Awakening* is that much more noticeable.

In the following discussion I shall investigate the success of this film and, at the same time, present a reception analysis from an aesthetic point of view. With this in mind, the definition of the term "debut film" must first be modified, since it often connotes amateurism. Von Trotta's first box office success as a "solo" director can in no way be seen as the kind of first accomplishment typified by Jutta Brückner's *Do Right and Fear Nobody* (1975) or Ulrike Ottinger's *Madame X* (1977). Labeling von Trotta's film a "first," nevertheless, illuminates significantly the prevailing working conditions of women filmmakers, who had been totally excluded from any discussion in film journals whatsoever. The press, for instance, simply discarded Ula Stöckl's first film *The Cat Has Nine Lives* (1968) as a "lady's film"; filmmaker Danièle Huillet was tagged an appendage of Jean Marie Straub; and the emergence of feminist short films and documentaries of the early 1970s was totally ignored. At any rate, in 1973 not one single prominent film critic attended the First International Women's Film Seminar in Berlin. No one in the Federal Republic besides the filmmakers themselves seemed interested in films by women. Thus, no one took note that as far back as 1970 Margarethe von Trotta had exchanged her place as an actress in front of the camera for a place behind the camera as codirector with Volker Schlöndorff. Her accomplishments ranged from directorial assistant in *The Morals of Ruth Halbfass* (1971), to writing 50 percent of the script for *The Sudden Wealth of the Poor People of Kombach* (1970) and *A Free Woman* (1972), to codirecting *The Lost Honor of Katharina Blum* (1975) with Schlöndorff. Only now, upon scrutiny of all of von Trotta's film accomplishments, is it possible to recognize her indelible marks in *Katharina Blum*.

Even the composition of her staff for *Christa Klages* was extremely professional. Unlike Helke Sander, whose film *The All-Around Reduced Personality* also premiered at the Berlin Film Festival in 1978, and who experimented with a production staff made up largely of women who had little professional experience, von Trotta used professionals instead. Her cinematographer was none other than Franz Rath, whose camera skills had been continually present since the very beginning of the New German Cinema – one need only recall his camera work in *Young Törleß* (1966). Von Trotta was of course well aware of Rath's skills from her collaboration with Schlöndorff. Equally renowned were her actors – no "buddies" lending a helping hand at the end of a shooting session. Tina Engel (Christa) and Katharina Thalbach (Lena), her main characters, are two of the best known actresses in the Federal Republic of Germany. The fact to be kept in mind is that unlike the majority of films made in the 1970s by women filmmakers, *The Second Awakening of*

Christa Klages is notably characterized by utmost professionalism – a fact playing no small role in the film's overwhelming success.

There are, however, other criteria still more responsible for the film's success. With this film, von Trotta offers the viewer a multitude of varying approaches and possible interpretations – a rare experience in the films of the late 1970s. That is to say, the film's levels of appeal are extremely diverse, and it possesses a remarkably high potential for ambiguity, a fact which also explains the diverse kinds of reception the film evokes, for it must be noted that the film *is* enjoyed for a variety of reasons. Helke Sander, for instance, praises the film's feminist qualities (*Jahrbuch Film* 78/79, p.71ff.); Brigitte Jeremias, on the contrary, favors the film for its non-feminist stance (*Frankfurter Allgemeine Zeitung,* 27 Feb. 1978).

Even the film's promotional announcement toys with viewer expectations. The audience, on the one hand, is led to expect a kind of female gangster film, since it promises the story of Christa Klages, who robs a bank with two of her accomplices, in order to put her alternative day care center on its feet again; on the other hand, the film is presented as a documentary of an actual event. A model for the main character can, indeed, be seen in the Munich "banklady" Margit Czenki, whom von Trotta personally knows. This connection with reality automatically presents the crime-by-a-woman theme and, at the same time, establishes a (perhaps) vague reference to terrorism: in terrorist groups, the participation of women was remarkably high. However, since the motif of a politically motivated crime appears in the guise of the soul-searching story of a woman's quest for identity, the titillation of the terrorist theme is immediately neutralized. The noble bank robber, in the end, regrets her action. And, thus, the realization in the "second awakening" of Christa Klages rests in the fact that her solo criminal pursuits provide no solution and that no ends – however noble – ever justify the means. This purging perspective is already briefly suggested at the beginning of the film. The first shot shows Christa squatting alone on the floor in an apartment which has been emptied out. Her voice can be heard: "Not until I created my own prison did I actually comprehend what had happened to me." The protagonist finds herself, quite obviously, in a state of isolation that she has inflicted upon herself like a penance.

A feminist interpretation is also offered by the film. In spite of

gangster-film elements such as action and suspense, the ultimate question posed is that of female identity and its right to
self-actualization. This was a relatively new issue in film, since
despite ten years of the women's movement, films by women
with a feminist touch were relatively rare in the Federal Republic. Another significant factor for the reception of the film was
the fact that feminist concerns generally reached public consciousness not through film, but rather by means of manifestos,
women's magazines, and yearbooks, or through militant actions
such as the fight for the amendment of the abortion law (1972).
Thus, the majority of the public, who at any rate felt no special
sympathies for the new women's movement, was under the
impression that feminism was necessarily proclamatory, rigor-
ous and, for that matter, not especially entertaining.

Since *The Second Awakening* was primarily promoted as a story
of a female bank robber ("they skipped town with the money in
the beige bag . . ."), it was possible to attract sections of the public who otherwise would not have gone to see a film with a feminist label. Those interested in a feminist film came to see it anyway. In this respect, von Trotta managed to appeal not only to
the interest of an audience whose taste is geared primarily
toward mainstream cinema, but also to the concerns of groups
with feminist goals. The film allowed both interpretations and
offered the possibility of identification for both groups. Thus
the bank holdup and the hostage sequence, as well as the
escape sequence immediately following, are depicted in a style
entirely true to the dramaturgical principles of suspense in
action cinema. However, the filmmaker gives such sequences a
different accent by shifting the emphasis within shots. The cus-
tomary American shot, with the revolver as the main focus, does
not dominate here, but rather the close-up concentrating on
the face, and specifically the face of a woman. Christa and her
hostage, Lena, look directly at each other. The attention of the
viewer at this point is shifted almost imperceptibly from the
expected tension of the holdup to the tense relationship
between the two women.

The film creates, thereby, a second field of tension, a feminist
one which continues to undermine the traditional pattern of
action. The long shot where Christa is holding her hostage and
threatens her with a pistol thus loses its dimension of terror and
almost suggests a love scene. The physical subjugation is con-

veyed by a sudden embrace. Lena, the bourgeois bank clerk, will never forget this break-in, which intrudes into her protected and regulated life. Her "second awakening" is thus introduced. The effort to interpret and comprehend her experiences visually is perceptibly etched into her face. She will refuse to testify for however long it takes her to learn the motives of the accused woman. And so, she commences a personal investigation and pursuit. The experienced enthusiast of detective stories will mainly notice Lena's strategies of pursuit and be thrilled by the tension between the hunter and the hunted. But von Trotta simultaneously portrays Lena's search to be a breaking-out of her accustomed limitations, a first look at unfamiliar ways of life. This bank clerk feels subconsciously that Christa Klages has seen and directly experienced a great deal more than she ever has. And during her lonely evenings in her small modern apartment, crowded with furniture, as she listens to operas by the glow of an artificial light, Lena puts her own photograph side-by-side with Christa's newspaper picture, thus visually "sitting down" next to her neighbor, the strange bank robber. At this point it becomes clear how much Lena's perspective has already changed.

A further theme of the film is thus touched upon: the gradual discovery of one's "own gaze" – one's own point of view. Helke Sander has said that women nowadays find themselves in a Kaspar-Hauser situation. They first must learn to see with their own eyes, and no longer through perceptual patterns created by men. Yet, while Sander renders such processes from an extradiegetic position and employs intricate narrative shifts with complex symbolic references, von Trotta – at least in *The Second Awakening* – does develop these learning processes in a seemingly incidental fashion, out of ordinary, everyday situations in familiar narrative patterns. The development of her protagonists' ability to see is accomplished through personal observation. In that respect, the director has considerably facilitated the viewers' approach to the film.

The third woman to complete the circle, Christa Klages's former schoolfriend Ingrid (Silvia Reize), has managed, in the meantime, to join the home-owning class as the wife of an army officer. Ingrid also experiences a remarkable emancipation process – again triggered by Christa. While fleeing from the police, Christa and her accomplice Werner seek refuge at

Ingrid's. Von Trotta again creates a double drama by offering different interpretive possibilities – the familiar detective story and a feminist story – yet always refusing didactic maneuvers of any kind. Von Trotta does not explain; rather, she simply transforms oppression into a picture. "A calculated mechanism of fear," the quote from Theodore Fontane's *Effi Briest* that has ever since signified female domesticity, finds with von Trotta its most vivid metaphoric depiction. Even though there is no Chinese ghost haunting the scene, something similarly threatening is in the air nevertheless. The dead eyes of "birds of the night" (bats) watch even during the absence of the landlord over his entrusted "property." Ingrid, a childless housewife who sees her husband only on weekends, is not even allowed to do as she pleases "inside" her mortgaged home. Even this traditional woman's domain is closed off to her – or, perhaps more precisely, obscured by bats. Bats in all forms and shapes occupy walls and ceilings. No place is spared, not even the toilet, as indeed Werner, the fleeing bank robber, discovers with horror. The viewer learns that the army officer is a passionate bat hunter who has made his home the altar for his trophies. There is absolutely no room for a woman's fantasies in this place. This masculine killer sport has left its traces even in the most private of spheres.

Thus, Ingrid's repressed fantasies soon turn toward Christa. They quickly become friends again. This marks the beginning of a thematic concentration that will play a predominant role in all of von Trotta's future films – friendships between women and also sisters. While the majority of women filmmakers of the 1970s portray women struggling alone, women in broken relationships with men, or women as victims of society or family, von Trotta is actually less interested in such stories of failures than in the experiences women have befriending other women. In pursuing this interest von Trotta does not believe in excluding the male, but rather finds a pictorial language which communicates the intensity of relationships between women and which directs the viewers' attention unobtrusively toward the female characters.

These female friendships bring to light a quality rarely encountered in the New German Cinema, and that is a little trust in the hope for something better, the faith that utopias can yet be transformed into realities and that humans do not have to be each other's worst enemies – wolves to each other. Von

Trotta never presents this principle of hope, however, as a doctrine, but always quite accidentally in the most diverse everyday situations and in simple human encounters. It belongs to the repertoire of the von Trotta dramaturgy. The scene in which the old man from Riga offers the emotionally exhausted Christa Klages a bowl of soup and encouraging words has no real function in the actual plot development. If, however, von Trotta enlarges and develops this scene anyway, then it is only because she needs such images as signs of her utopia. The uncertain content of these utopias allows the viewer to participate actively in the search for their meanings – hence the differing political evaluations the film has evoked, most pointedly demonstrated in the appraisal of the bank robbery. The political Left, for instance, praises in general the treatment of contemporary history, especially the theme dealing with politically motivated criminality and the sympathetic portrayal of the woman offender. Christa is unquestioningly the character from whom the strongest appeal to identification emanates. The politically conservative interpretation, on the contrary, values the recanting of the "political" crime, that is to say, her psychological return to her "private" self.

Quite interesting in this connection are the diverse interpretations of a key quotation cited in almost all reviews. The quote in question refers to Christa's confession to her girlfriend that she would never have committed the robbery had she really loved her boyfriend – a decisive remark, indeed, especially if taken seriously, for then it confirms the ancient bias which says that only unfulfilled, unloved women, "old maids" and "shrews," strive to be in the limelight and make a spectacle of themselves. This particular viewpoint nurtures the bias of conservative viewers who see in it not only a confirmation of their reservations toward feminist rebellion but, at the same time, a justification of their sympathies toward the woman bank robber. Christa just never found the right guy – as simple as that – bank robbery caused by lover's ennui.

The political Left could not tolerate such an interpretation. Even though they could not erase Christa's confession, they relativize it by simply blaming the director for it, dismissing the mistake as a "superficial, thus, unnecessary psychological analysis." (Wolfgang Limmer: *Der Spiegel,* Oct. 19 1978).

I would like to suggest a different interpretation for this statement. Undoubtedly, the discrepancy between Christa's state-ment and her actual behavior cannot be argued: she does, in fact, act in a contradictory fashion. One must, however, take note of the proportions of this contradiction. From the begin-ning till the end of the film Christa proves to be a woman of action. We see her perpetually in action, but rarely get to watch her reflect upon her actions. "I never thought a lot about myself," she admits in her self-inflicted isolation. The only tex-tual evidence in the film where she comments upon her actions can be found in her justification of the bank robbery. This, for one, signifies that words and actions do not carry the same weight. The viewer learns about Christa's character primarily through her actions. Through such a visualization of this char-acter, von Trotta subtly suggests Christa's "true" nature, which captivates all the people she runs across, implying that even the other characters within the story see Christa from this perspec-tive. That is to say, Christa's predominant behavior is not mere-ly constructed quantitatively, but is also rooted in qualitative and explicitly narrative structures. Her declaration that the bank robbery serves as a compensation for unfulfilled love could then just be the director's faux pas – and thus the only "mistake" in this otherwise tightly constructed film?

I think not. If Christa's actions and her assertions are differ-ent – labeled subversive on the one hand and affirmative on the other – this is an incongruity which can be substantiated. Such divergences appear repeatedly in the repertory of female char-acters, and not only in works by women. These deviations are evidence of the fact that the woman's emancipation process itself does not run "simultaneously" at all levels, and obviously can hardly be imagined as such. At the same time, we need to remember that even the New German Cinema did not create new women in accordance with feminist theory who could serve as models for successful emancipation.

Christa's lack of contemplative vision is closely connected to the fact that reflection is not one of her strengths. She is actual-ly stepping into foreign territory, so to speak, when she com-ments on her own actions. Without thinking, Christa uses exist-ing patterns of explanations, and thereby falls without realizing it into the trap of patriarchal discourse. That von Trotta does not iron out such contradictions in her subsequent films, but leaves them rather as they are, speaks much more for her being aware of them and intentionally using emancipatory incongruities such as these. Depending on one's own perception of emancipation, the viewer will find a meaning and fill the gaps, thus resolving any existing contradictions.

The film, however, offers yet additional interpretations, especially to the literary viewer. Some sequences allude very noticeably to Brecht, a phenomenon which incidentally is also apparent in numerous other films made by women. To mention only one: Helma Sanders-Brahms' *Germany, Pale Mother* (1980) alludes to Brecht with its very title. This, in fact, is somewhat surprising, since feminist writers usually denigrate and denounce Brecht unequivocally for being a "pasha" by virtually ascribing to Wilhelminian double standards when dealing with the topic of sexuality; thus women would not want to build upon such a writer. Women filmmakers obviously perceive Brecht differently, in a perhaps more relaxed way, molding him to their own needs just as Brecht freely adapted the classics to his needs. Filmmakers are not particularly concerned with "faithful reproduction" – such a practice would merely preserve cultural history as seen through men's eyes.

Along these lines, von Trotta uses Brecht's *Mother Courage and Her Children*, since she is interested in the correlation between anarchy and obedience in the *Second Awakening*. In order for Christa's actions not to appear purely criminal and even to transcend the context of a feminist interpretation, von Trotta places her protagonist into a traditional, literary framework of political "heroines," lending Christa Klages characteristics of the mute Kattrin. Thus, Christa's questioning the act of praying inspires Hans, the small-town pastor, to a sermon about the antithesis between the prayer of words and that of deeds, as does Brecht in the Kattrin episode. Von Trotta purposely suggests Brechtian connotations by focusing for a long time on Christa's stunned face in close-up, precisely at the moment when Hans demands understanding for Kattrin's not praying, and asks that her drumming be understood as a prayer or call for action instead. Interpretations of this kind find sympathetic ears, especially in those critics who trace the critical impetus of the New German Cinema back to Brecht and believe his theory of the epic narrative to be significant for today's films. In addition, such analogies have helped win over those political groups who had brushed aside obstacles to feminist emancipation as mere "sec-

ondary" contradictions. On the other hand, von Trotta's allusions to Brecht have also provoked opposition. The Catholic
Church has contended that a bank robbery, after all, could
never denote a plea or a prayer for action, and that an analogy
to that end would be far too simplistic.

Another fact has contributed decisively to the widespread and
enduring success of *The Second Awakening*. In the segmented,
overly specialized "culture-hierarchy" of West Germany, in the
aesthetic "caste-society" of our time, where the artist communicates only with the initiated few, von Trotta presents a film
which is popular in the best sense, as well as having great entertainment value. And in the Federal Republic, where the category "entertainment" suffers such a poor reputation, this constitutes no small victory .

I have had the opportunity to show and discuss *The Second
Awakening of Christa Klages* at numerous institutions in the Federal Republic, as well as abroad, a circumstance which has
allowed me to experience personally the extremely varied
receptions this film has received.

Translated by Lisa Cornick

7

Erika's Passions: Anatomy of a Female Partner Relationship

k l a u s   p h i l l i p s

K *laus Phillips's essay on Ula Stöckl's film* Erika's Passions *(1976) argues that although the two female protagonists are depicted in the film without men around, their attitudes toward each other are determined to a large extent by patterns of behavior learned in dealing with men, in order to gain male approval. These patterns must be overcome before they will be able to come to terms with each other – they must, as Phillips asserts, free themselves from the "male gaze" before they will be able to see each other. He interprets the film as a series of situations which force the two women to drop old patterns and defenses, so that each woman can face and accept her old friend – and herself.*
—The Editors

The characters in *Erika's Passions* (*Erikas Leidenschaften*) spend the final quarter of the film in the one room in Erika's apartment that is reserved for performing certain private rituals such as the cleansing of the body, the application or removal of makeup, the inspection of one's physical appearance in the mirror, and the elimination of bodily waste. Inadvertently locked into the windowless bathroom in the middle of the night with no prospect of release before morning at the earliest, Franziska and Erika transform the room into a candle-lit sanctuary, thereby establishing an interactively ritualistic contextuality that forces them to confront the resurfacing and gradually dissolving misconceptions of themselves and each other in order to explore the reasons for their failed relationship.

This analytical objective is characteristic of Stöckl's work. Marc Silberman has ably summarized the filmmaker's principal thematic concerns:

Ula Stöckl's films revolve thematically around the problems of affective relationships: marriage (what mechanisms of oppression it develops, how it fails as soon as the woman claims her autonomy), role-playing among women, the opportunity for women to engage in unconventional behavior, the impossibility or inability on the part of adults to express adequately their needs, and, finally, the search for forms of communication other than verbal. That is not to imply that Stöckl's films are only about women. Although men appear almost exclusively as peripheral, stereotyped figures, the lives of the women revolve around men implicitly and explicitly. Stöckl shows women who are breaking out of conventional relationships but who cannot find an alternative, women who refuse to be treated as objects of male prerogatives but who nonetheless conceive of their own emancipation in patriarchal terms.[1]

Shot in 16mm and black and white, and cofinanced with the ZDF (Zweites Deutsches Fernsehen – Network Two of West German Television), where it was first telecast on Thursday, 18 November 1976 at 10:15 p.m. in the series "Das kleine Fernsehspiel" ("Short Television Play"), *Erika's Passions* is the more accessible and intimate of the only two films by Stöckl in distribution in the United States.[2] Stöckl's two-character script reunites Erika and Franziska after a four-year separation in Erika's (formerly Franziska's) apartment, which they had shared for six years; in the course of one long evening their facades crumble – the facades that had prevented the two women from accepting themselves and each other for what they are. Eschewing the use of flashbacks, Stöckl uses calculated editing, medium shots, alternating high- and low-angle shots and a progressively larger number of close-up and slow zoom shots to reinforce the women's subjective view of each other.

    1. Marc Silberman, "Ula Stöckl: How Women See Themselves," in *New German Filmmakers From Oberhausen Through the 1970s,* ed. Klaus Phillips (New York: Ungar, 1984), 322.
    2. 16mm prints of both films are available from West Glen Films, 1430 Broadway, New York, NY 10001.
    The Cat Has Nine Lives (*Neun Leben hat die Katze,* 1968), 90 minutes; produced by Ula Stöckl and Thomas Mauch; written by Ula Stöckl; camera (Techniscope and color): Dietrich Lohmann; actors: Heidi Stroh, Liane Hielscher, Kristine de Loup, Elke Kummer. (Techniscope process requires a special anamorphic lens to "unsqueeze" image during projection!).
    Erika's Passions (*Erikas Leidenschaften,* 1976), 64 minutes; produced by Ula Stöckl for ZDF; written by Ula Stöckl; camera: Thomas Mauch and Nicole Gasquet; actors: Karin Baal and Vera Tschechowa.

We first meet Franziska, who is identified by a superimposed title, immediately following the sparse opening credits, as she prepares to enter the apartment building. Her inner turmoil is disguised by her seemingly self-assured behavior – she approaches the building with quick, determined steps and almost defiantly spits out a piece of chewing gum – until a voice-over verbalization of her thoughts reveals fears of finding that the apartment door may be opened by her ex-husband, that the divorce never happened, that she and Erika never lived there together. Once inside the apartment, having discovered that Erika is not yet home from work, Franziska rearranges the placement of a rocking chair and a potted plant, opens Erika's birthday champagne, uses some of Erika's perfume, and puts on one of Erika's tops. Articulated in a continual voice-over monologue, Franziska's thoughts vacillate between rationalizing her own past actions and blaming Erika for not making a greater effort to understand her (Franziska's) motives: "She did her thing so well that I wished she'd do it better still. I don't know why she never understood that." ("Sie machte ihre Sache so gut, dass ich mir wünschte, sie würde sie noch besser machen. Ich weiss nicht, warum sie das nie verstanden hat.") After scribbling a quick note to Erika, she leaves.

A superimposed title also identifies Erika for the viewer, or, rather, in keeping with Stöckl's training as a student of Alexander Kluge and Edgar Reitz at the Institut für Filmgestaltung in Ulm, it underscores the consciously episodic nature of the character expositions and indeed the entire film. We first encounter Erika as the reflection of her face is framed by the oval mirror in the apartment hallway when she enters the apartment some time later that afternoon and discovers Franziska's note. She promptly tries to telephone Franziska but is unable to reach her. When she realizes the plant has been moved from its usual spot, she smiles spontaneously, and we begin to sense that she has genuinely missed Franziska's presence. That sense of emptiness and unfulfillment in Erika's present condition is heightened when she prepares a quick dinner for herself and then eats it in front of the television. As she fixes a second portion for herself, the ringing of the doorbell startles her and she spills cooking oil on the kitchen floor. She is on her knees, trying to clean up the greasy mess, when Franziska enters the apartment. Erika rises to approach the other woman, but Franziska rejects her embrace, turns away, and, instead of offering a greeting, remarks: "God, you're filthy!" ("Mein Gott, bist du dreckig!").

The seven or eight minutes that comprise the film's opening sequence, reconstructed in relative detail above, serve as a prologue to the women's intense confrontation about their unwillingness or inability to perceive and accept each other (and, importantly, themselves) in a partnership in terms of their own individuality as women. We note that Franziska, immediately upon entering the apartment, indeed by the very act of letting herself in without Erika's knowledge, exhibits a domineering behavior pattern which violates Erika's individuality, a pattern which, it may be argued, derives from the traditional primacy of the male. Attitude, behavior, even appearance – she wears slacks, in sharp contrast to Erika's "feminine" business outfit – clearly reflect stereotypical masculine aspects. This is not to suggest that Stöckl actually had a heterosexual partnership constellation in mind, nor, for that matter, a lesbian one, although the undercurrent of the women's dialogue seems to hint at a potential for the latter. The ensuing discussions are a sort of autopsy on the women's failed relationship, punctuated by instances of resurgent power plays; in essence, these discussions are conducted against the backdrop of a male force which is unseen but felt.

Erika and Franziska had met as secretaries in the same firm ten years earlier because of the men in their respective lives: when Franziska found Erika in a restroom crying over an unhappy affair with a man, Franziska invited her to celebrate her own divorce and, subsequently, to move in with her. Erika, practical and also a romantic, ever ready to make sacrifices, provided monetary support for both women; Franziska, always rallying around some political cause and caught up in whatever issues were of interest to her at any given moment, but never able to make a meaningful commitment to any one activity, exploited Erika financially and emotionally. Their relationship, its format predetermined by each woman's conditioning in patriarchal society, became sadomasochistic. Erika, we (and they) discover, resented Franziska because she felt used by her, and she envied her boundless enthusiasm and eloquence. Franziska resented Erika for allowing herself to be exploited by her and admired her for being able to fall in love over and over, even though none of her affairs ever ended happily.

During the reexamination of the reasons for the failure of their relationship the women gradually comprehend that their relationship could not succeed because each had been seeing the other with a male gaze, i.e., from the only perspective patriarchal tradition had taught them. Erika at one point wants to know from Franziska, "Why did you always turn me into a guy?" ("Warum hast du immer einen Kerl aus mir gemacht?"), and Franziska later compares her to a hare caught in a car's headlights, attaining substance only through external illumination, i.e., in a man's eyes. Removed from his gaze, she does not exist. Erika's passions, her endless, unhappy love affairs, thus are conscious encounters with the "headlights," willful projections of her yearning onto her partners in the hope of attaining and maintaining form and meaning, at least for a while. In the brightness of the male view, she readily metamorphoses from companion to mistress to jilted lover, and, in identification with the male role model around whom her life revolves, in turn learns to modify his image at will, unaware that the resulting fantasy construct bears no resemblance to reality. Fundamentally, then, the two women's partner relationship could not succeed because, blinded similarly by the controlling male gaze, neither woman has been able to see and accept the other for what she is.

In this film, which relies so heavily on dialogue instead of visual images to carry out its analytical objective, it is no accident that Franziska is the more verbally accomplished of the two women. It is her greater force of words which, in combination with the other "male" traits referred to earlier, has enabled her substantially to govern their relationship. We recall that from the very start of the film Franziska's aggression contrasts with Erika's television-watching passivity. If, as Laura Mulvey (1975) has proposed, the dominant male look at the woman leaves no room for the woman's own pleasure in seeing, does it not follow, then, that dominant male language leaves no room for woman's speech? Theoreticians would be quick to point out that the bulk of mainstream cinema associates unreliable, thwarted, or acquiescent speech with the female subject, that "it is in large part through her prattle, her bitchiness, her sweet murmurings, her maternal admonitions and her verbal cunning that we know her. But her linguistic status is analogous to that of a recorded tape, which endlessly plays back what was spo-

ken in some anterior moment, and from a radically external
vantage."[3] Stöckl subtly introduces the notion of thwarted
female speech when Erika switches on her television to what
appears to be an action movie; we can barely discern a female
voice, "he bought me, and tonight he'll sell me to Garth" ("er
hat mich gekauft und heute nacht verkauft er mich an Garth"),
angrily countered by a male voice, "oh, shut your trap!" ("ach,
halt's Maul, du!"). Since she is thus prevented from having any
active role in discourse, the female subject has to find alternative, perhaps nonverbal forms of communication not defined
and delimited by the male voice.

In several of Stöckl's films, most notably *The Cat Has Nine
Lives* (*Neun Leben hat die Katze*) and the more recent *Reason
Asleep* (*Schlaf der Vernunft*), alienation from the male voice is
effected through women speaking (or claiming as their mother
tongue) a language other than German, here French and Italian, respectively. Stöckl, who had left Germany at the age of
twenty to attend language schools in Paris and London, has
expressed her belief that these languages do not feature the
degree of overt sexism inherent in German and, moreover, that
French and Italian men tend to show a greater sensitivity for
women's concerns than do their German counterparts, who
proclaim to be the most enlightened but in reality are chauvin-
ists.[4] Consequently, when Erika tells her friend of her impending transfer to manage her firm's branch in Milan and of her
facility with the Italian language, her announcement in effect
becomes a rejection of the male voice, which Franziska acknowledges by immediately challenging Erika's familiarity with the
foreign language.

Another alternative form of communication may be subsumed under the category of body language. During the first
part of the evening Erika and Franzisksa react to each other
rather than interact, they intrude on and interfere with each
other's space: at one point a mechanical device, a defective lock
on the bathroom door, creates a temporary break in their show-
down posturing. When they are trapped in the bathroom

3. Kaja Silverman, "Dis-Embodying the Female Voice," in *Re-Vision. Essays in
Feminist Film Criticism,* ed. Mary Ann Doane et al. (Frederick, MD: University
Publications of America, 1984): 131-32.
4. Renate Möhrmann, *Die Frau mit der Kamera. Filmemacherinnen in der Bun-
desrepublik Deutschland: Situation, Perspektiven. 10 exemplarische Lebensläufe*
(Munich: Hanser, 1980), 59-60.

together later in the evening, the spatial confinement unlocks their bodies from their artificial oppositional configuration. External appearance and spatial proximity of their bodies begin to reflect their spiritual state.

Perhaps the most constructive alternative forms of communication for Erika and Franziska – providing at the same time a powerful release for their emotions – are the shedding of tears and the sharing of spontaneous laughter. Each of the women sheds tears once in the course of their confrontation. Significantly, Franziska, the exploiter, is the one to cry first, when she realizes how much Erika had learned to hate her during their six years together. After studying her mascara-smeared face, the soggy mask of a sad-eyed clown, in the mirror, she ceases her earlier masculine role-playing.

Erika and Franziska break into spontaneous laughter on four occasions. The first time, when Franziska melodramatically drops her jacket in the middle of Erika's living room and justifies her action by saying, "a jacket in the middle of the room *can* be a work of art" ("eine Jacke mitten im Zimmer *kann* ein Kunstwerk sein"), the laughter acknowledges recognition of Franziska's characteristically male verbal rationalization; the sudden ignition of cooking oil inadvertently left on the hot burner in the kitchen parallels their spontaneity. They laugh again when Erika confesses that her current married lover, Georg,[5] no longer lives with his wife but another girlfriend; here the laughter underscores the ludicrous dimension of the affair. The third instance occurs when Franziska, all along the dominant figure in the relationship, asks Erika for help, and Erika admonishes her to be serious just once; their laughter suggests the beginnings of a role reversal and gradual realignment of their behavior patterns; percolating coffee which suddenly spills over the counter top functions as a parallel, similar to the burning oil before. The fourth and by far most sustained eruption of shared laughter happens when they conclude that the best way to get out of their hopeless situation (i.e., the locked bathroom) is to let the bathtub overflow in the hope of attracting someone's attention downstairs. Like the exploding and overflowing liquids, tears and laughter become images of liberation. The shared laughter, Stöckl's recurring motif for the

---

5. We catch a brief glimpse of Georg's picture: it is the American actor Donald Sutherland.

"moment that prefigures the elusive utopia of free, uninhibited relationships,"[6] reflects not only their optimism about a release from the bathroom, but also about their future.

Ula Stöckl's professional future did not look encouraging in the late 1970s and early 1980s. Her identification with television features made it all but impossible for her to reenter the commercial film market. Her belatedly attained reputation as one of the first feminist filmmakers in the Federal Republic failed to impress the (mostly male) members of the film funding agencies. In 1981 Stöckl wrote:

> For me it remains important to keep working toward my own radicalization. Only when I muster all my strength and reach the state of wanting that necessitates artistic expression can I imagine artistic results. A poetic dimension has to develop in order to provoke the imagination potential of viewer as well as creator.[7]

Like all of Stöckl's films, *Erika's Passions* provokes with its systematic examination of how women relate to each other, how they perceive each other and themselves. Because it treats these concerns as its central topic, not as byproducts, and thereby seeks to subvert the established patriarchal film code, the film occupies a particularly important place in Stöckl's oeuvre and in the development of women's films.

Reprinted from Schatzkammer *14.2 (Fall 1988): 104–110.*

---

6. Silberman, "Ula Stöckl," 332.
7. Letter to Klaus Phillips, 16 June 1981.

8

Modern Medea

s h e i l a   j o h n s o n

U la Stöckl's modern adaptation of the Medea legend, Reason Asleep (1984), focuses mostly on female relationships. The pro- tagonist's relationships with women close to her (besides her mother) are depicted negatively: in the final dream sequence, Dea's daughters and her female rival are dead, and here the rationale for the deaths does not appear to be mere vengeance against the husband, as in the traditional story of Medea. In Stöckl's film Dea is less troubled by her husband's betrayal than by the behavior of her daughters and her partner, who betray Dea's project of medical research in the service of women. What is utopian here is the film itself, a feminist appropriation of a patriarchal myth, as Sheila Johnson stresses in her essay. The film also presents itself as a model for working through archetypal rage (one age-old func- tion of myth) with fantasy and dream-work, but without the need for the actual bloodshed demanded by the traditional, misogynistic tale. —THE EDITORS

Ula Stöckl's 1984 film, *Reason Asleep* (*Schlaf der Vernunft*), rein- terprets the Medea myth from a feminist perspective. With her adaptation of myth as feminist political statement as well as her approach to form/content unity as aesthetic expression, Stöckl opens two important areas for detailed critical analysis of her film. Furthermore, she works from an explicit theory regarding her choice of myth generally and of the Medea myth in particu- lar. Examination of these clearly relevant factors constitutes my own point of departure. Moving from patriarchal myth inter- pretation to recent women's appropriations of mythic figures, I shall present Stöckl's own theoretical ideas relative to the use of myth and then analyze her thesis regarding her modern Medea. In conclusion, I shall look at the form and techniques of Stöckl's film, demonstrating how they work with its content.

It should be noted that classical myth interpretation has

been, until recently, a male province.[1] In standard German reference works, "myth" (*Mythos*) is defined by its function as an explanation of the world (*Weltdeutung*) or, more explicitly, as a means through which "the world is interpreted and explained in symbolic/poetic form." The male adapters of Greek and Roman mythology into German culture retained the patriarchal principles that were the dominant feature of not only the originating social systems for these myths, but also of their own particular European socio-religious concepts. Women, however, have begun to appropriate the mythical foundations of humankind by recognizing the role of humanity's other half. Such creative work has largely provided a shift of perspective; we have begun to hear female voices expressing women's own visions, experiences, and values. Within the context of feminist transformations of myths,[2] Ula Stöckl has provided a significant building block with her adaptation of the Medea myth. She has given us a truly modern Medea.

According to James Monaco, the filmmaker is confronted with three questions: first, what should be filmed? second, how

1. Neither Claude Lévi-Strauss with his anthropological/structural theory nor Roland Barthes with his linguistic myth theory offers relevant models for this article, although the absence of women's voices in their theories should be registered.

2. Within recent decades a number of creative women seem to have posed a common question: Whose myths are they anyway? For instance, we have the French theorist, Hélène Cixous, with her contra-Freud essay "Laugh of Medusa" (1976) on the subversive power of humor. B. Ruby Rich, with reference to Yvonne Rainer's films, speaks of "women as victim and the burden of patriarchal mythology." B. Ruby Rich, "In the Name of Feminist Film Criticism," in *Movies and Methods*, ed. Bill Nichols (Berkeley: Univ. of California Press, 1985), 347. Patricia Monaghan remarks in the introduction of her book *The Book of Goddesses and Heroines* (New York: Dutton, 1984), "stories are always told from the viewpoint of the god, even when the major character is clearly a goddess" (xiv); she proceeds to present the other side. Among prominent twentieth-century women writing in German who have given powerful reinterpretations of myths are Ingeborg Bachmann, Irmtraud Morgner, and Christa Wolf. Bachmann, through her Undine, rejects a world structured by and for men ("Undine geht," in *Das dreissigste Jahr*, München: R. Piper, 1961, pp. 231-244). Morgner counters the standard Hesiodic interpretation of Pandora as a "deceivingly beautiful bearer of misfortune" (*Amanda* 96) by building on the interpretation by Herder and Goethe, in which Pandora is the symbol of hope preserved; this positive interpretation informs the ideological core of Morgner's commanding antiwar novel, *Amanda* (1983). Irmtraud Morgner, *Amanda. Ein Hexenroman* (Darmstadt und Neuwied: Luchterhand, 1983). Wolf, too, breathed new life and power into the Cassandra myth in her novel, *Cassandra* (trans. Jan van Heurck; New York: Farrar, Straus and Giroux, 1984), narrated from the perspective of the title character.

should it be shot? and third, how should the shots be presented?[3] I shall address these questions sequentially, looking first at
"what" Stöckl decided to film. In a word she chose to film a
myth.

As the title of her first film, *Antigone* (1964), suggests, Stöckl
has been drawn to explore the possibilities of "myth in contemporary film"[4] for at least two decades. In a theoretical discussion
of *Reason Asleep* at the University of Texas in 1984, she established her position regarding the timelessness of myth, stating
that, while the mythic framework allows you to "tell your own
story," the core remains the unembellished, archetypal story
built around human tragedy.[5] Stöckl explained that in myths,
"each character has his or her very special, very own, very justifiable reasons for being and/or acting a certain way. Yet by
going deeper and deeper into the story, you will find out that
there is one eternal subject of all myths."[6] That subject is
tragedy; and the basis of tragedy is that "because we are
humans, . . . we have to die."[7]

Although this generalization might well be qualified by various exceptions, Stöckl is on solid ground when she points to an
aspect of tragedy which relates specifically to her film, *Reason
Asleep* :

> Tragedy arises always when [a] character tries to make time stand
> still, wants to make things eternal, [whereas] they have to go on. .
> . . Human beings . . . are like children – conservative in an
> absolutely absurd way: they always want to keep forever what they
> once had fallen in love with, whatever it was they once possessed:
> another human being, a theory, wealth, religion, whatever they
> [are determined] to keep. . . . Tragedy always comes when those
> people – the owners of love, wealth, theory, religion – are forced
> to find out that, without warning, they are on the way to losing
> everything they had been sure they possessed.[8]

Loss and experiencing the death of what one believes are essential parts of one's existence are central to many myths, and it is
crises of loss which are the basis of Medea's tragedy.

3. James Monaco, *How to Read a Film* (New York: Oxford, 1981), 132.
4. Ula Stöckl, "The Medea Myth in Contemporary Cinema," *Film Criticism* 10,
no. 1 (Fall 1985): 47.
5. Ibid.
6. Ibid., 49.
7. Ibid.
8. Ibid., 49–50.

The mythic Medea was a woman of great intelligence and
power; with her magical arts and wise advice, she enabled Jason
to take the Golden Fleece from the King of Colchis, her father –
predictably enough, Medea's skills, efforts, and sacrifices
earned her the designation witch.[9] Medea helped Jason escape,
bore him children, eventually married him, and was finally
rejected by him in favor of a younger woman, the daughter of
the King of Corinth, whereupon Medea killed the children and
flew away. Stöckl has some interesting comments on how she
lent a contemporary perspective to this traditional Medea
myth:[10]

> To make it a real "today" story, do you have to find the synonyms
> of profession, aims, social degree, and so on of your characters?
>
> For instance: a synonym for kingdom today could be a modern
> trust. A capitalistically run trust. With more than one director.
> The shareholders are the kings and gods of today.
>
> In the old Greek myth, magic is a very important fact. Today's
> magic can be scientific research: inventions like the birth-control
> pills (and [do not forget] their side effects).[11]

For Stöckl and her film, "Medea is the myth about the woman
who . . . killed her two children when her husband married
another woman."[12] Actually, a further important facet of the
Medea myth is that Jason deserts her, the mother of his children, for a younger bride whose father, the King of Corinth,
offers him an avenue to even greater power. Stöckl integrates

9. Edith Hamilton in the introduction to her popular *Mythology* (Boston: Little, Brown and Co., 1942) remarks that in Greek mythology "[t]here are no men
and only two women with dreadful, supernatural powers. . . . Circe and Medea
are the only witches and they are young and of surpassing beauty – delightful,
not horrible" (17–18).
10. Stöckl had to contend with pejorative versions of Medea in the writings of
Apolonius of Rhodes, Pindar, Euripides, Seneca, and Ovid. We see that there is
much meat for juicy interpretation. Apolonius and Euripides characterize
Medea as "child murderess"; Seneca calls her a horror of a witch. Austro-Ger-
man variations are commensurately negative. Elisabeth Frenzel refers to
Medea's acts as "Verbrechen" [crimes], Lessing makes her into the "lasterhafte"
[vice ridden] Marwood [1756]; Klinger's Medea is a sinning "Machtweib"
[power hungry bitch] [1786]; Grillparzer designates her "barbarian" [1821];
and the expressionist Hans Henny Jahn renders Medea as an aging "Negerin"
(Negress) [1920]. [Taken from Frenzel's *Stoffe der Weltliteratur: ein Lexikon dichtungsgeschichtlicher Langschnitte*, 2nd edition, Stuttgart: Kröner, 1963, "Medea,"
pp. 420–423.]
11. Stöckl, "Medea Myth," 48–49.
12. Ibid., 48.

this motif of the younger woman/rival with a powerful father into her film as well.

In finding a new perspective for the myth, Stöckl has turned around not only the negative image of Medea as witch, making her a sympathetic healer; she also has her actively countering modern "magic" used by men to control women's bodies and, at the same time, to make a sales profit. In *Reason Asleep* Stöckl calls her heroine Dea and presents her as an engaged and successful women's doctor, who, among other things, has been researching the negative effects of birth control pills for some ten years. The Jason figure, her husband Reinhard, is no longer the adventurous hero but rather a morally weak pawn of the capitalist system. His adventures are confined to secretly cohabiting with Johanna, the daughter of a "chemical king," Erdmann, the man for whom Reinhard works – and against whom Dea's research is directed. In a twist which puts female solidarity into question, Johanna is also Dea's medical partner. Dea and Reinhard's two children are young women who live with Dea but resemble their father in their lack of character and principles. At the outset of the film, Dea is still under the illusion that the love between herself and Reinhard is a given, nourished mainly by what she terms the imaginative unconventionality of their relationship; they have separate quarters and communicate through visits and phone calls.

The motivating factor of Stöckl's film plot is that Dr. Dea must pay the price for her own tragic flaw, which is falsely assuming that her own absolute love gives her the right to take those she loves for granted. Stöckl focuses on two days in Dea's life. On the first day the heroine loses most of what she believed she possessed absolutely: ten years of her medical research data are stolen; she is disabused of the last illusion that she and her two grown daughters share any sense of values (the older daughter, for example, takes the pill and also poses for pill ads); Dea's trust in her female medical partner is destroyed by Johanna's confession of the affair with Reinhard; Dea's husband then tells her he has long ceased to love her because she is too critical of his materialism; and finally, Dea's own fiscal security is threatened by a trumped-up charge of tax evasion.

How does Stöckl parallel these events in Dea's life with those of the mythic model? Medea became infamous for killing the children she had had with Jason and destroying her rival,

Jason's bride, with a magic corrosive robe. Stöckl, too, shows her Dea reacting to her losses by striking out at those she had loved. However, Stöckl's version of Medea's story differs from the traditional version in two significant aspects. The first difference is informed by her woman's perspective: she ties Dea's losses to social structures in which male domination and materialism still prevail. The patriarchal structure is exemplified by the relationship of Dea's husband to his submissive lover, Johanna, Dea's partner. The aspect of materialism is represented by her daughters, who lack ethical values, and by her nemesis, Erdmann, the drug magnate who is out to destroy her research. Dea's strong reaction becomes a feminist political statement, which illustrates Stöckl's own conviction that self-assertion on the part of a woman, in whatever form, constitutes a political statement. She is on record as maintaining: "Politics begins for me with the binary relationship (*Zweierbeziehung*) and can extend to world war. The concept of the political encompasses everything that concerns suppression mechanisms emerging during socialization. The claim 'a woman has no soul,' is to me a political one."[13] Stöckl's position on the value and necessity of women's political statements is clear.

The second significant difference of Stöckl's myth reinterpretation lies in the way she lets Dea avenge her losses. She approaches the problem of Dea's murders theoretically: "[Ancient] tragedy . . . starts with murder and blood. Because that is the only known way of defending [what] you value."[14] Then she goes on to define her own position:

> And here I start with my own new myth, or maybe my own new theory, my own new "possibility," by saying [that] the old ways of defining what you have, may have changed in [actual] practice, but not in the visceral necessity of being thought [through]. . . . If someone hits us, we must in some way hit back to restore our self-respect. But how? In [ancient] times the conflict could be resolved by eventually killing those who once were your most beloved . . . but, through betrayal, had become [the very ones] who had taken away your self-respect.[15]

Through the medium of cinema Stöckl lets Dea work through her visceral need for hitting back and thereby opens the way for

13. H-B. Moeller, "West German Women's Cinema: The Case of Margarethe von Trotta," *Film Criticism* 9, no. 2 (Winter 1984–85): 53.
14. Stöckl, "Medea Myth," 50.
15. Ibid.

her to regain her self-respect. Therefore, the answer to the question – how is Dea to regain her self-respect – is at the same time an answer to Monaco's second question: how should the film be shot?

It is a tribute to Stöckl's writing skill that she is able to make the disintegration and resolution of Dea's life unfold convincingly in a modern setting within the confines of one whole day and a few minutes of a second one, thus largely preserving the classic unities of time and action. Furthermore, Stöckl succeeds in keeping the viewer interested with skillful shots, although the space in which the film plays is limited largely to one place, Dea's apartment. As befits a tragedy taken at its turning point, the film is tense from the first scene to its resolution. This tension leads up to Dea's killing not only her children and rival, as in the mythic model,but also, in a logical extension of the myth, she kills her husband, too.

By realizing the link between myth and cinema, Stöckl allows Dea to draw on the cathartic potential of living out a mythic situation of vengeance and yet being able to go on in the modern world and "grow new things." Stöckl says:

> In mythology I see a great chance to show how the images of things and events are about all times and about all theories and are always alike.
>
> [Since] all those [mythological] images are images of separating, of death, of something coming to an end, . . . I decided that death in cinema is as real as your thoughts, and as unreal as cinema. Cinema is just the image of a certain kind of death imagined. And if you dare [to imagine], for example, an end of [a] relationship with a beloved person or a beloved idea, . . . just give it the image you choose. . . .
>
> The effect is amazing. By killing through images you manage to be born out of your [own] fantasy, you manage to separate definitely from what had already separated from you long ago.
>
> You just murdered an idea.
>
> You do not go to jail.
>
> Neither do your characters in your film.
>
> Nobody has to be sentenced afterwards or to be sent to a mental hospital.
>
> You just created new space for new possibilities.
>
> Myth always is the story of a bitter ending.
>
> Let it be a myth.[16]

16. Ibid., 50–51.

In her film, Stöckl realizes the aspects of her theory, pertinent to vengeance and regaining self-respect, by letting Dea's vengeance be played out in dream sequences – a device especially well suited to the film medium.[17] Dea has three dreams. Because the first dream is the opening scene and the last dream is the penultimate, they provide a slightly off-center frame for the film. In her first dream Dea anticipates her tragic loss and vengeance by pushing a seemingly devoted man, with whom she is swinging and cuddling, out of the swing they share. Unfortunately for the man – later we find out he is Dea's husband Reinhard – his trajectory sends him through an upper story window. Before the third dream she imagines that she slits his throat. In the third dream Dea kills both her daughters and finally Johanna, her partner/rival. I shall look at these sequences more closely later, but, first, I should like to complete my examination of Stöckl's ideas on combining myth and film, because in her version, unlike that of the mythic model, Dea's story does not end on a note of vengeance. In explaining her feminist negation of the Medea myth, which we have known only through male perspectives, Stöckl poses the question: "How could your self-respect be restored by killing someone you had loved before?" She provides her own answer: "Because killing is the most definite way to separate. . . . And how is one to separate at all? We never had a chance to learn how to separate properly. . . . There must be room to grow new things. Therefore you have to accept that the old stories are over."[18] Dea's acceptance of her separation is the new moral Stöckl lends the Medea myth.

The short final sequence, the beginning of the second day, shows Dea, a woman whose smiling face and relaxed body tell us that, having taken her vengeance through images, she has achieved separation and is prepared to pursue her own values alone, "to grow new things."

Beyond the cathartic potential of mythic tragedy, Stöckl found other characteristics of mythology fruitful for her theoretical purposes, particularly, the theme of the foreigner. In order to underline this theme, Stöckl adds a new character to the Medea myth, Dea's omnipresent *Moirae* - or *Parcae* -like[19]

---

17. Stöckl took her title from the Goya capriccio, "The Sleep of Reason which Gives Birth to Monsters."

18. Stöckl, "Medea Myth," 50–51.

19. Moirae (Greek) and Parcae (Roman) are names for the Fates or birth-goddesses. "Homer speaks of one Moira only, . . . who represents the moral

mother who sustains Dea throughout. Like the mythical Medea in exile, Dea is foreign, an Italian living in Germany; her house-keeper/mother speaks only Italian in the film. Stöckl deliber-ately alienates us from the mother by providing no subtitles of what she says. Dea's mother is the epitome of the defiantly for-eign outsider. This unbending Italian woman is a figure, whose presence alone conveys the concept of the tenaciously enduring female, long reduced to serving but innately unbreakable. Her obvious foreignness, reflected in Dea, whose German is strongly accented (the Italian actress, Ida di Benedetto, learned her role phonetically), illustrates how the strong-willed woman – here both mother and daughter – remains a misfit in a still patri-archically structured society.[20] By purging her rage in her dreams, by taking vengeance in the fullest measure, Dea is able to continue with her own productive existence as individual and modern woman. The content of the film thus shows a woman experiencing the necessity of and finding the way of separation – and that was the major task Stöckl set out to accomplish.

But how does she use the film medium to accomplish it? How do Stöckl's form and techniques work with and complement the content of *Reason Asleep*? How does she present the shots?

The visual impact of Stöckl's film lies in large part in her smooth integration of dream sequences, stylized confronta-tions, and surreal images with everyday reality (scenes in the doctor's office, the daughters giggling at the dinnertable, the tax auditors at work on Dea's books). She effects her transitions with rapid sequential editing and montage juxtapositions that produce a flowing together of "real" action and imagination. The background music, alternately ominous and pulsatingly repetitious, bridges her shifts from largely grim reality to the sequences which, though unreal, form a logical coming-to-terms-with this reality.

---

force by which the universe is governed. . . The Moirae are represented by the poets as [aged] stern, inexorable female divinities. . . . Painters and sculptors . . . . depicted them as beautiful maidens of a grave but kindly aspect." E. M. Berens, *The Myths and Legends of Ancient Greece and Rome: Being a Popular Account of Greek and Roman Mythology* (London: Blackie and Son, 1880), 1140. Dea's mother's relentlessly stern inexorability is ameliorated by her unbreakable bond, her innate kindness, to her daughter.

20. In a discussion of her film at the University of Texas – Austin (February 1986), Stöckl remarked: "It is important to show that she doesn't make much effort to be someone who adapts well."

In addition to making her heroine's story and reactions to its treacherous twists the center of interest, Stöckl has made it Dea's film through filming techniques. Analysis of three diverse levels of the film illustrates how Stöckl uses the medium to tell her story with maximum visual effect: (1) how she establishes Dea's character and shows her transformation when Dea realizes that those she loves have betrayed her; (2) how she integrates visual (and auditory) devices: e.g., her use of the chorus as *vox populi* ; her use of backlighting and selective focus for emotional effect; as well as a building and mirrors as leitmotifs; (3) how she structures the dream sequences.

First I shall look at how Stöckl conveys Dea's character and development. These scenes are all within the realm of Dea's everyday reality. The opening scene is a dream to which I shall return. The following sequence, however, establishes the woman, Dea, as a person of determined action. We see her eyes, in a beam of light, open from her dream, looking troubled; Dea rises quickly from bed, lovely, in a delicate nightgown; the camera pans to her feet, clearly on their way somewhere definite. The camera then rises quickly and follows her rushing dynamically – from screen left to right – through her apartment, passing by a room with two young women sleeping, to and then through a door whose lock she examines. Having slowed down, she then looks cautiously around two adjoining rooms, with shots changing from long shots of Dea to subjective deep focus ones of the office space she is exploring. The camera follows Dea to a filing cabinet in the second room, where she opens the top drawer. It focuses on her efficient hands; in a quick motion she thumbs through the files. The camera pans to her upset face, then back to her hands which fan through the file folders a second time, select one randomly, pull it out, and confirm by shaking it, that it is empty; the camera remains on her hands, which immediately reach for a telephone and dial. A pan to her face shows it cold – Dea speaks the film's first words: "Police Department? Please come to Reichenbergerstrasse #4. There's been a break-in here at Dr. Jannsen's office." [21] Speech is with-

21. "Polizei? Bitte kommen Sie in die Reichenbergerstraße # 4. Bei mir ist ein Überfall passiert. Praxis Dr. Jannsen." Because of the succinctness of Dea's message to the police, one tends to overlook that it is more a deliberately expository speech than half of the telephone conversation with a police station that it purports to be. Actually much of the dialogue in the early scenes is markedly expository rather than normal speech.

held through the extended first and second sequences, and the result is that attention is focused on the active, expressive parts of Dea's body. Stöckl has used the synecdoches of hands and feet as well as those of troubled facial features to make her narrative points. We are presented with a strong woman in crisis from without.

Subsequent scenes in Dea's medical practice show her interacting with patients – we see her more or less objectively through medium shots; these scenes introduce the viewer to her as a professional woman of warmth, understanding, and above all, strong principles.

Stöckl firmly establishes Dea's principles, ones which she shares, by using a variety of devices for narrative and symbolic purposes. Inspired by the structure of classic drama based on Greek myths, Stöckl experimented with adapting and realizing the device of the chorus in the medium of film. One form she chose was the conversations among women in Dea's waiting room. We hear and sometimes see – in pan shots – the patients discussing problems relevant to rights and responsibilities of, for instance, motherhood. Although those closest to Dea trample over her values, the *vox populi* reinforces them. The various voices act as indirect commentary on the main action. Several television clips serve a similar purpose – we both see and hear them as background to scenes in Dea's apartment, where her daughters keep the TV on constantly; the younger one does little else but sit passively in front of it, alternately awake and asleep. Stöckl selected the program clips deliberately, lowering the volume whenever it would interfere with dialogue, but making it audible in instances where the program text reinforces the ideas about women's ideas and problems with which Dea – as well as Stöckl herself – is concerned.[22]

Further filmic devices Stöckl uses are backlighting and sharp focusing. Through these she eloquently conveys Dea's affective transformations. Dea, as well as her mother, is often shown in different degrees of backlighting. The contrasts range from modified shadowing, where facial features are visible in varying degrees, often with highlighting and sharp focus on eyes and mouth, to pitch black silhouette; the deeper Dea's despair and

---

22. In a discussion (University of Texas–Austin, February 1986) about this aspect of her film Stöckl remarked: "In my movie, I tried to make the television talk about the same problems people really have."

anger grow, the darker the shadows on her face and form. In full shots, backlighting calls attention to the language of her emotionally charged body. Furthermore, backlighting adds to a prevailing sinister atmosphere which is always underscored by disquieting expressionistic music. The mother, an icon of defiance, as well as Dea's alter ego and support system, is one of the chief vehicles of this dark mood. Three times, at crucial junctures in the plot, she is shot in silhouette from a low angle, playing heavy chords at a piano (her arthritic movements have little to do with the music we hear, although both sound and image convey threat). Stöckl uses strong black and white contrasts in the manner of expressionistic directors. But it should be mentioned that her choice of the very able actress, di Benedetto, exemplifies her nod to realistic direction as well.

Most of *Reason Asleep* consists of indoor shots, usually in Dea's apartment and adjoining medical offices, but window shots are also used repeatedly (often out of and sometimes into Dea's windows), presenting more or less free space according to the stage of the plot development; for instance, when Dea is content we are shown birds flying in playful patterns. Shots looking out of Reinhard's apartment are more obvious, even rather heavy-handed filmic devices. His view, like his life, is dominated by the towering "Mondial" building, the drug company owned by his boss. This building also reappears, tilted threateningly, as a leitmotif signifying oppressive commerciality in the background of the soft-porn birth control magazine ads Dea's daughter poses for, and again in a collage scene in Dea's third dream. The imposing Mondial building, the ruthless drug magnate/boss, his health imperiling products, and his selfish values all represent the social corruption against which Dea is fighting; they are the forces which destroy the structures of her life and compel her to find new strength within herself. Such is the fate of the tragic heroine. Dea's dealing with her own fallibility provides the complicating factor of the film. A parallel exists between the complex shots in her apartment, which reflect the complexity of her problems and development, and the obviously symbolic shots elsewhere, which bespeak the shallowness of the other characters.

Another device Stöckl employs in presenting the motif of Dea's development is the mirror. Beginning in the middle of the film, mirrors appear three times, each time on a different level of reality. Actually, they come into play each time Dea has been confronted with a new facet to her tragedy. We see the first mirror in a dream Dea has after her partner Johanna, the "drug king's" daughter, has told Dea that she and Reinhard live together. Without seeing Dea fall asleep, we are set into the dream sequence; clearly she has begun dreaming about the worst things that could possibly happen to her. Ending the dream on a positive note, the same mirror then shows Dea with her mother standing by. The second mirror exists on the level of film reality. It is a full-length, free-standing mirror in Dea's appartment, which we are shown after Reinhard has told Dea he no longer loves her. We see Dea in long-shots from behind, standing in front of the mirror, isolated and frozen in shock. Interrupting this shot, three abrupt cuts are made to the dark figures of a man and woman prone and struggling; the woman slits the man's throat, and then we see that the figures are Dea and Reinhard. These are images of what is going on in Dea's mind. Only she can see her mirror image, and the viewer senses she is trying to convince herself she still exists apart from the violent things she is imagining. The final shot of this second mirror sequence is a cut to blackness relieved only by a lamp on each side of the frame. The camera pulls back slowly, revealing that the blackness was actually Dea, still paralyzed by her traumatic vision. A pan to a silhouette of the mother shows her looking at herself in a hand mirror, a repetition of Dea's self-confirming gesture. This third mirror, like the second one, is important as a symbol of truth and affirmation rather than for the actual image it reflects. The slow panning of the camera from Dea to her mother and the strong contrasts in lighting of this scene situate it somewhere between dream and reality; Dea's trauma is becoming *Traum* (dream). The mirror shots symbolize Dea's attempts to objectify the emotions she is experiencing and thereby subject them to "reason."

Reason Asleep, the title of Stöckl's film, prepares the viewer for the extensive use of dream sequences, and, indeed, Dea's three extended dreams comprise about half of the film. Each of the dreams is defined primarily by content, showing events which would or could only take place on the level of thought or imagination. Additionally, the quick cuts, shifts of focus, disorienting angles and settings, produce an atmosphere appropriate to psychic turmoil. Only through dreams can Dea depict the full extent of her despair and anger.

The first dream, backed by atonal but pleasant music, is the swing sequence which constitutes the opening scene – a scene that anticipates the end of Dea's happy but illusionary existence. A couple is swinging in a room toward a window; the initial shot is from the woman's side. Both are smiling, kissing. The camera shifts to his side; swinging, smiling, and kissing continue; her arm is around his shoulders, her hand on the rope swing is next to the camera. Twice the swinging camera focuses on the scene visible outside the window: the tops of buildings across the way. The couple swings a last time toward the window; the woman's encircling arm is shown moving forward, then it is empty. A quick medium-shot focuses on the woman's face and shows her torso pulling back from the window; she looks toward the ground outside, appalled; quick zoom to flecks on the concrete. Then church bells, and a cut to Dea waking, alone. This will be the story of a woman out of whose life a man disappears in a wrenching way, and yet she lives to go on.

The second dream begins after Johanna confesses to Dea that she loves Reinhard. This dream is more archetypal in nature than the first and third dreams. It consists of a series of disjunctive images and thereby emerges as the most visually varied but logically weakest dream. In the initial shot, we are shown Dea trapped and drowning in a bubble filled with liquid. Then two short sequences occur in which male figures appear who have no other connection with the film. In the first Stöckl cuts to a long shot of two unidentifiable, naked men struggling in a space through which run numerous pipes. Is Stöckl playing here on the struggle between Jason and Medea's father for the Golden Fleece, which is part of the original myth? Another long shot introduces the subsequent mysterious sequence. Dea, in silhouette, approaches a bed in which an unrecognizable man is lying; she calls him "Father," and climbs in beside him, like a child seeking comfort. This is the only instance in which Dea's father is mentioned in *Reason Asleep*; otherwise, the role of the mythological Colchian king has been totally eclipsed by Stöckl's substitution of the supportive mother figure. The camera next shows Dea lying asleep alone on her own bed, and we hear Reinhard's voice comforting her, but we do not see him. This second dream ends with Dea still struggling to get out of the bubble, a mocking metaphor for the secure life she believed was hers, until she had to face the fact that her illusions had dissolved about her and were threatening to destroy her. This dream precedes the "real" confrontation between Reinhard and Dea.

The final dream is prepared for when Dea withdraws from Reinhard by means of the three flashes of the struggling woman and man which she imagines. After he and Johanna leave Dea's apartment, Dea's break with her past reality is resumed and carried into the symbolic scene where Dea's mother is shown looking into the hand mirror. The door bell seems to break the spell and the tax auditors are back. Immediately they accuse Dea of a serious count of tax evasion. Her reaction: she breaks into uncontrolled laughter, and the tax men, as well as her otherwise stern faced mother, join her. The effect is one of relief and is at the same time grotesque. Dea must play out all of her horror stories ad absurdum. This laugh sequence of the third dream has its parallel in an earlier "real" scene where Dea's daughters and a girlfriend are shown giggling senselessly and uncontrollably around the dinner table. Reality has passed into surreality through a manipulation of content rather than visual effects.

At this point Dea's face, in a medium shot, slowly becomes solemn, and again a mechanical sound provides the cue for transition. The dream continues as the camera follows Dea and her mother down a long hall searching for the origin of the clicking sounds. With the two women we enter a photography studio (actually a room in Dea's apartment), where Dea's older daughter is posing for Mondial birth control ads. This scene presents the most technically complex shots of the film. A tilted image of the Mondial building is projected onto Venetian blinds in the background; after a series of cuts from mother to daughter and mocking comments on the daughter's part, an image of the chemical boss is superimposed onto the building. There is an exchange of sensual looks between him and the daughter; Dea is shown slowly raising her arms to throw an object; in a slow motion sequence, she shatters the huge plate of glass behind her daughter; the resulting rain of glass kills the daughter and destroys the Mondial/boss images. All the while the photographer is quietly going about his business in the background. Suddenly the younger daughter approaches the inexplicably orderly piles of glass around her sister (who is slumped over the bicycle she was posing on, dead); she smiles weakly at her mother and eats a handful of the glass. The second daughter is being eliminated. Dea is then separated into two images: one comforting her dying daughter, the other proceeding through a path of house plants to her partner, Johanna, whom she also finishes off in an unclear but horrifying maneuver, almost in parody of a gynecological operation, after which she withdraws her bloody hand from between Johanna's legs. Thus, in this third dream and the scenes of Dea's imagined struggle with Reinhard, which are its prelude, Stöckl has let her Dea kill the images of all those who have made her suffer because they have betrayed and abandoned her.

The final episode of the third dream begins with an overhead shot of a totally barren, hilly landscape looking like black dunes. The dark surface is broken only by particles in the dirt that reflect light like sand in the moonlight. The camera pulls back slowly, pausing on a stylized scene far below. At Dea's and her mother's feet, the daughters and Dea's rival are lying in a carefully choreographed frozen dance of death, each with the toes of one foot raised to touch the opposite knee, their hands joined to form a circle completed by the two women still alive. Reinhard appears smiling, and Dea says: "I'm giving them back" (*Ich gebe sie zurück*). He leaves and there is a closeup of Dea's foot burying her rival in the loamy black surface. For the first time, the background music is a song, "Mignon's Song" (*Mignonlied*), a poem by Goethe set to music by Hugo Wolf. [23]

The song continues into the final cut, the next morning, the day when Dea "wakes up." We see Dea in her nightgown and robe lying in a large, round lounge chair slowly turning herself on the swivel base. Her mother enters her bedroom and speaks to her in reassuring tones. Dea repeats her words of comfort in German. The music asks: "Where to? Where to?" (*Wohin, wohin?*). Dea smiles; she knows the answer. The last shot is out her brightly lit windows to a flock of birds circling in free formations above the buildings opposite. Having taken her revenge to the fullest through dream images, Dea has emerged separate and free, her basic values intact.

Whereas Stöckl's *Reason Asleep* rejects the values of patriar-

23. Goethe's "Mignonlied" (*Kennst du das Land?*) is named after a young androgynous character from Italy in his *Wilhelm Meister's Apprenticeship* (*Wilhelm Meisters Lehrjahre*, 1796).

chal society, she has not discarded, but rather taken as a point
of departure, the artistic lessons of male Medea interpretations. Like Euripides, Seneca, Grillparzer, Anouilh, and so
many more, she depicts her central character at a time of crisis.
Stöckl, however, has focused on Dea's own perceptions and
given her a socially valid alternative; no longer must she mount
a fiery wagon and fly away. She still has her work as a scientific
guardian of women's health. The "where to?" question posed
by the closing song has its answer in the cryptic, stylized final
dialogue between Dea and her mother. Dea echoes and thereby confirms the sovereign assurance her mother speaks to her:
"One has to act on one's own" (*Man muß es selbst machen*). Left
alone, she says: "You have everything within yourself" (*alles ist
in dir*), and stretches like a cat at home. Mignon's need to run
away to Italy, the country of her birth, is not Dea's. Stöckl's
integration of classical song text and music with her own conclusion, giving both positive resolutions, offers an ending in
which aesthetic and inner harmony have been achieved.

With her Dea, Ula Stöckl has created an effective film icon,
in the sense of presenting the viewer with a sign in which the
signifier, Dea, is at one with the signified, i.e., the strong
woman able to rise above her personal defeats. At the same
time Stöckl has given us an iconoclast, a modern Medea who
breaks through the traditional negative interpretation in which
she is portrayed as a destructive witch, a trap in which the patriarchal structure has so long kept strong women in check. In
Reason Asleep Ula Stöckl has realized not only her own theory
regarding the link between myth and cinema, she has also
made a very personal statement about the fate of strong
women, i.e. that such a woman must ultimately be a woman
alone, or at best one who can live only in the company of other
such women, hence the added mother figure.[24]

In her creation of a modern Medea, Stöckl's choice of cast,
her skilled use of black and white film, lighting, camera angle,
and editing in themselves make *Reason Asleep* a film worth viewing. If she also opens the viewer's mind to a new consideration
of the questions raised about women in today's Western society

24. Further aspects to explore might be: (a) the deeper significance of the
mother figure, (b) the fact that Italian women were chosen as the central characters, coupled with the implications of the final song which portrays Italy as the
ideal home, and (c) the symbolism of the burial scene in the black dunes.

– or inspires her or him to pose new questions regarding the values dealt with – then this film will have accomplished even more. In any case, *Reason Asleep* stands as an estimable advance in the growing tradition of German-speaking women reinterpreting myth.

9

Interview with Ula Stöckl: Do Away With Taboos

marc silberman

We reprint here Marc Silberman's interview with filmmaker Ula Stöckl. It was conducted before Stöckl was able to get funding for her film Reason Asleep (1984), the film discussed by Sheila Johnson in the previous article; she does, however, comment here on The Cat Has Nine Lives (1968) and Erika's Passions (1976), discussed in articles above by Roswitha Mueller and Klaus Phillips, respectively.
—THE EDITORS

I have had luck financing a film a year since 1968. Two of my early films were made with my teacher and friend, Edgar Reitz. After that I was able to get money from the TV networks, which supported an artistic climate here. In 1973 I received money from another network (WDR), but for the first time I was confronted with censorship. I was too modest then and too dumb to recognize it. The producer – a man I respected and considered my friend – asked me to reduce my budget by 90 percent. He said that was all he could give me, and I thought it was purely a matter of economics, not censorship. After I had rewritten the script to satisfy him, I suddenly had doubts about it and changed it – not to be more expensive but more radical. Production was stopped until I rewrote the script according to instructions.

I was one of the first women filmmakers in West Germany before the women's movement, and as far as the men were concerned, I was "just" a woman. I never conceived of my films as "women's films" or about "women's themes" but as stories about partners, either explicitly as in *A Quite Perfect Couple* or implicitly as in *Erika's Passions*. I have made no films about women alone, even if men are absent.

Perhaps you could call *The Cat Has Nine Lives* the first women's film in West Germany. I was interested more in women because I knew more about them. Moreover, I relegated men to the dream images they have of themselves as absent. We see no men in the film, just women who live only for their relations with men. Today, more than ten years later, I think the struggle has shifted to another arena: can people live together permanently at all?

Every person experiences this struggle, even men. My work "with" women also concerns the men with whom they live. For who could imagine women without their men? The women's movement is not just the province of women. At a time when women are completely without rights, we need the movement as an absolute necessity. Can men learn from us and begin to see their own misery at the same time that we women attempt to make films about emerging from our misery? If so, then the women's movement will have seen its time.

In *The Cat Has Nine Lives* I chose the characters as types: the not-yet-married professional woman, the recent divorcee confused about her future, the career woman, the deceived wife, and the ultimate dream woman – a legendary Circe. In this film the women seem to be sleeping because each thinks only of herself and that she has an advantage over the other. Each one thinks she has a recipe for happiness, or that being unhappy is her own fault because she's too dumb to be happy. In other words, these women cannot see their anxieties as having something to do with the society in which they live. They exhibit a lack of knowledge about how one could behave differently. In my films now, the characters perceive each other more clearly and recognize their shared misery as something they don't have to be ashamed of – as in *Erika's Passions*.

I haven't made a film since 1977. I worked for four years on a script which was rejected in blatant censorship by funding sources everywhere. Apparently my personal radicalism must have shocked producers who consider themselves "feminist." What I perceive as radical is to do away with taboos, to write down my dreams and images.

My script *Killertango* deals with three women – a grandmother, her daughter, and her granddaughter – and the pressure passed on from one generation to the next to fulfill contradictory demands. Dramaturgically I made the mother die, so as to free the daughter. It had to happen in a way that would teach the daughter something. That is, the mother died accidentally, when she sucked her lover's penis and he held her so tightly that she suffocated. For me this symbolized the daily suffocation millions of women experience as the result of male demands. Apparently this image was so violent that everyone rejected it out of hand. I am unwilling to drop it. Every artist reaches a point where she either accepts the conditions for continuing her work, conditions which make her lose track of the broader picture, or she refuses to compromise. (Translator's note: *Killertango* was never funded and Stöckl has given up on the project.)

I have never been active in the women's movement and have been criticized frequently for that. Yet the women's movement developed parallel to me. I was already making films when it began to organize and formulate goals. I considered radical separatism absurd. Moreover, the leaders of the organized women's movement in West Germany completely ignored my work. Indeed the fact that I had already achieved what they were still struggling for was counted against me. For them I was a "man's woman." In any case, I need a certain amount of independence and my commitment is more meaningful through my film work.

I have often been asked why I don't make films about women *workers*. The answer is directly related to my feelings about the left. In West Germany it was purely a student movement. Although I studied at the Film Institute for five years, I was never really a student and saw the left as elitist. Our aims were the same, but they were so involved in their word games and their struggles with one another were uninteresting. In the women's movement, too, women can never come together around common goals. However, I do confront the ideas of both groups as the very basis of my work.

In the film scene documentary realism continues to rule and imagination is unwanted because no one pays for it. The films we see are the ones "allowed." To make those, you don't need imagination. Backers are so confused about their ability to judge that they have lost all their courage. Behind every film lies the commercial question: "How much will it earn?" Ten years ago we experienced a paradise in filmmaking, but now we face an enormous bureaucracy. It is not that we are explicitly persecuted as radicals, but you don't live without fear in a country which keeps everything on file.

Reprinted from Jump Cut *29 (1984): 55.*

1 0

Language in Heidi Genée's Film
1 + 1 = 3

g a b r i e l e   w e i n b e r g e r

G *abriele Weinberger makes use of theoretical work by Laura Mulvey*
and Kaja Silverman in her analysis of language in Genée's film,
thus connecting her discussion to the feminist search for a non-phallo-
centric language. She investigates certain aspects of spoken language
in the film, demonstrating, for example, how Genée's female protago-
nist moves from silence to a kind of autonomous speech in the course of
the film.
—THE EDITORS

Laura Mulvey's observation of woman as object rather than as
subject of the gaze ("Woman as Image—Man as the Bearer of
the Look") in the traditional male-oriented Hollywood film is by
now axiomatic.[1] In the phallocentric discourse, man is in a privileged position while woman is defined through lack/absence.
In the dominant Hollywood cinema it is the male as subject who
has the greater power of language as well: "Within dominant
narrative cinema the male subject enjoys not only specular but
linguistic authority."[2] This in no way means, however, that
women are speechless in these films; on the contrary:

> The female subject . . . is associated with unreliable, thwarted, or
> acquiescent speech. She talks a great deal . . . it is in large part
> through her prattle, her bitchiness, her sweet murmurings, her
> maternal admonitions and her verbal cunning that we know her.
> But her linguistic status is analogous to that of a recorded tape,

1. Laura Mulvey, "Visual Pleasure and Narrative Cinema," *Screen* 16, no. 3
(Autumn 1975): 6–18.
2. Kaja Silverman. "Dis-Embodying the Female Voice," in *Re-Vision. Essays in
Feminist Film Criticism,* ed. Mary Ann Doane et al. (Frederick, MD: University
Publications of America, 1984), 131.

which endlessly plays back what was spoken in some anterior moment, and from a radically external vantage.[3]

Such language has been written for women by men; now feminist (script-) writers and filmmakers are no longer accepting it as their language. The empowering of women as active subjects requires the search for a nonphallocentric language as adequate expression of feminist consciousness. My intention is to investigate certain aspects of the language in Heidi Genée's film *1+1=3*.

The search for a different language is found in literature as well as in film.[4] While in literature such attempts must remain within the printed medium, in film one can present a commentary on language in a more complex fashion than with speech alone. Heidi Genée's critique of language in *1+1=3* encompasses formal and thematic aspects of verbal and visual representation: a) speech and nonlinguistic use of sounds and/or their absence; b) the relation between the image and voice; and c) the thematization of (women's) language and norms. In my analysis I shall use some of the film's most important elements from the above-named three areas, in order to demonstrate which status speech has in the composition of this film, to give a detailed analysis of the thematic and formal representation of language in this film, and to exemplify some approaches suggested by feminist film criticism.

The film starts with the protagonist Katarina, a young actress, discovering that she is pregnant. Bernhard, her boyfriend and father of the baby, at first reluctantly and then insistently proposes marriage. Katarina refuses: she wants to have the baby and keep up both her work and her independence. During a vacation, she meets Jürgen, who apparently is attracted to her only because of her impending motherhood. While in the beginning Katarina is in no way a maternal woman (countering the biologistic view of women as born mothers), she fights the traps of a seemingly modern, but still patriarchal society which pretends to offer her all she needs as a mother, while still

3. Ibid., 131–32.
4. The most prominent early example in German women's literature was Verena Stefan's novel *Häutungen*. A number of women directors in Germany could be named here. Most prominent politically is Helke Sander, the director of *The All-Around Reduced Personality - REDUPERS* and the founding editor of the journal *Frauen und Film*. Laura Mulvey's *The Riddle of the Sphinx* was also very influential for the German directors.

attempting to dictate her behavior. Katarina successfully finds
her own way and develops into a well-rounded, independent,
and happy person.

Aside from Katarina and her relationships with Bernhard and
Jürgen, the following groups and characters are involved: her
sister Anna and Anna's family; her theatrical agent Mrs. Berger;
the gynecologist; Vera (mother of the child Florian, whom Katarina babysits); and Vera's women's group.

The beginning of the film is programmatic in many ways, with
the first frame visually very limited. The viewer, however,
observes language acquisition, the fluctuation between silence
and attempts at speech in the appropriation of language, which
is the theme of this film. After some babbling, the voice of the
little "man" culminates in the sharp demand "Limo!" (lemon-
ade) through which he asserts himself. Katarina, the protagonist, does not interact linguistically but only mechanically. It is
significant that all through the first scene, she has no language,
until she finally murmurs to herself, "I could have had a heart
attack," and makes the vain promise, "your mom will be here
real soon." This, like her first remark, is directed more toward
herself than toward the child, since she knows very well that his
mother will not come for him for another five hours.

These first images establish the relationship between Katarina
and Florian, and they visually represent some of the psychological mechanisms of domination between women and baby boys
(which have been shown to differ from the interaction between
mothers and baby girls.)[5] This scene which precedes the credits
ironically represents the Lacanian transition from the pre-oedipal stage to the entrance into the realm of language and the
woman's definition through lack. It thus comments on the theoretical frame of the Lacanian psychology, which was the predominant theory that feminist film criticism was struggling with
at the time this film was made.

Katarina's relationship with Florian will later be characterized
as one that changes through different modes of speech. It is
important in this first scene that Katarina is defined as a woman
who acts, but does not have the power of language. When one
compares this scene with the final scene of the film, one finds
that Katarina, freed from both men, can speak freely and unpre-

5. See, for example, Elena Gianini Belotti, *Dalla Parte delle Bambine* [*What Are
Little Girls Made Of?*] (Milano: Gianciacomo Feltrinelli Editore, 1973).

tentiously with her two nieces. Jürgen and Bernhard are literally pushed out of the picture by the two girls. Both men in that
scene have no voice; all they can do is leave greetings and flowers. As Katarina becomes free linguistically she also commands
more space: in the initial scene she acts furtively in the dark,
narrow rooms – the camera is very close to and at eye level with
the child. This angle supports the impression of limitation and
is a visual representation of Florian's domination over Katarina
in this situation. At the end of the film, Katarina has not only
grown linguistically (e.g., as in the conversation with the girls
and the liberating "I think it's coming") and changed physically,
but she is also liberated in terms of the wide space that she occupies: the bank of the river and the large foyer that connects interior and exterior through glass doors.[6]

The relationships of the characters with each other are
defined through their respective communicative behavior. I
shall first discuss the relationship between Bernhard and Katarina as the most important one. Bernhard either talks to her in a
reproachful, admonishing manner or makes remarks that question her license to act the way she does, e.g., "Do you know that
we are supposed to be there at 12:00 noon?" or "Can you tell me
how you can possibly say something like that in the middle of
the night?" Through remarks of this kind, he criticizes both
Katarina's actions and way of expressing herself, questioning
her language and marking it as unacceptable. Especially revealing is the incident after her theater performance, when he
attacks her declamation of roles as fake because of its use of
unnatural and superimposed language. Katarina's profession as
an actress is a thematic representation of the existential problem of women in this society: like an actor in a theater troupe,
the women fill the position that has been assigned to them and
try – convincingly – to recite their texts, which male authors and
representatives of the patriarchal system have "put in their
mouths" and demanded from them. Women's personal manner
of expression is suppressed in favor of the one demanded by the
role. Bernhard, through his avoidance of the problem – his

6. See also Judith Mayne on the historical limitation of women to the home –
the "private sphere" as the adequate realm for women's activities, opposed by
the "public sphere" as the men's realm in traditional discourse in literature and
film – and the relevance of this limitation to the feminist discourse. "Female
Narration, Women's Cinema: Helke Sander's *The All-Around Reduced Personality -
REDUPERS*," *New German Critique* 24–25 (Fall/Winter 1981–82): 160.

attempt to hide it from Katarina – expresses at the same time a criticism of this lack of one's own language as well as his own helplessness in view of it: he cannot react to Katarina and deal with *her*. Instead, Bernhard becomes immersed in memories of his own experience as a school child: once, around the age of puberty, a female role in a Schiller play was imposed on him during a dramatic reading in class, and he felt deeply insecure in the situation. This traumatic experience, which until that time had not reached Bernhard's consciousness, resurfaces through the forced confrontation with Katarina's work. In order to overcome his pain and reassert control over Katarina, Bernhard uses a forced "macho" tone of voice and yells at her.

Whereas in this scene the acting profession is emblematic for women's alienation in the men's world, later, in the fight scene, Bernhard *explicitly* discusses male and female norms of linguistic behavior. Furious that Katarina only reacts either with gestures and a silent, but defiantly self-confident look or a matter-of-fact correction, he asks her: "Why are you putting on such a masculine act?" Bernhard is the one who, when desperate, retreats to wordy argumentation. The more he loses control, the more he seeks to regain it through language. Typically, he ends conversations with Katarina with the statement, "I will call you." Thus, he not only tries to have the last word, but he also manipulates Katarina into a position where it is in his power as to how and when he will approach her again. He often uses this kind of "remote control" through language: once when she stands at the window and only listens to the answering machine, and again in his New Year's Eve call in Tunisia. Katarina on the other hand cannot use the phone to her advantage as a tool to gain power over people: she either only listens, unable to say anything herself (e.g., in the phone conversation in Vera's apartment,) or the connection breaks (e.g., in Tunisia). Katarina, however, does not allow herself to be manipulated by Bernhard's attempts to gain control; her actions are not influenced by them.

Kaja Silverman's comment about women's speech in dominant cinema points towards the significance of Katarina's silent centrality in the image: "To permit the female subject to be seen without being heard would activate the hermeneutic and cultural codes which define woman as a 'dark continent,' inaccessible to definitive male interpretation."[7] Katarina becomes both a threat to the male partner and out of his reach. At the same time, her silence defines her in a new way: it becomes part of her way of expressing herself, which, far from being passive, defies the myth of the necessity to demonstrate power through language. The fact that Katarina does not play out the confrontation on a linguistic level is an objective deficiency which she does not allow to work against her, but in fact one which she transforms into strength.

During their farewell dinner, Bernhard tyrannically monopolizes the conversation, interrupts and ignores her until she gives up all conversational initiatives of her own, obediently submitting to his thinking aloud about his professional life. Katarina only draws the conclusions for herself and – in this instance as well as in the discussion among women at Vera's – this drives her to a linguistic capitulation. At the same time, however, it opens up avenues for her own initiation.

This evaluation of her interaction with Bernhard has to be qualified by a look at her behavior in other situations. The experienced mothers/feminists of Vera's women's group demonstrate their negative power over Katarina through language. During what amounts to a critical cross-examination, the overpowering strength of the talking women is accentuated through close-ups. These close-ups appear more overwhelmingly chaotic as they are shot with a hand-held camera, slightly out of focus. Each frame shows a number of talking women from a slightly low angle, as if they had crowded into the picture and in that way take away its controlled, framed character. While Katarina initially defends herself, she finally only shakes her head. The ensuing talk between the two friends, in which Vera gives Katarina short, direct answers without trying to influence her, serves as a positive counter-example.

The meeting of the women, like the scenes at the agent's and at the doctor's, shows forms of oppression through patronizing. The agent Mrs. Berger speaks in a "masculine manner" and her assumed superiority also becomes evident in the image: Katarina is shown from a high camera angle, placed in a chair, between two filmposters (the male discourse), while the camera angle on Mrs. Berger is low, and she is allowed to move around freely in front of the windows. Berger is a woman who competes with men on their own turf, and for that sake she gives up her own identity.

The scene at the gynecologist's is characterized by the doctor's speaking. The camera remains on his face even during Katarina's short questions and answers. In this scene, for the first time Katarina's body is dissociated from her speech; her body is deprived of a visual presence. First we only see her upper body mediated through the mirror, and later the spectator sees her hands grabbing the information brochures. While at first we still hear Katarina, but see the doctor, we finally see only her fragmented body, which has lost its language. While she actively collects the necessary information herself, the doctor already turns to the next patient. Katarina's character as object in the eyes of the doctor (as well as in the eyes of the agent) is visually represented through her fragmentation into body parts and the dissociation of her voice from her body. Kaja Silverman has pointed out the great importance of the body-voice unity of women in film.[8] In this film, the unity is absent in order to point out its problematic character, but it is not replaced with an off-camera voice of female authority.

Apart from the central figure, Katarina, through whom as protagonist the conflict is represented, the problem of women's language is thematized so as to include her sister Anna and her two nieces. In the beginning, Anna is part of a typical, "intact" modern family. Robert tries to press himself and his wife into the frame of his advertisement pictures. Each of his utterances expresses the norm that he establishes for his wife. Robert represents the patriarchal system and the purest form of the type of language it prescribes for humiliating women into servility. Anna looks down guiltily and keeps silent, looking like a dog afraid of punishment. Anna's liberation is represented through her moving out and attempting to express her needs toward her sister and her children. Again a metaphor is used: she learns a foreign language (French, in the language laboratory). Significantly, once she has freed herself and learned to express herself, it is she who helps a man learn to express himself in a different language.

Anna's youngest daughter Susi has been trained by her father only to react to his commands with looks and gestures. She represents the "ideal woman" who follows orders without claiming a right to language. Whereas she acknowledges the father as patriarch, she fights the female authority demonstrated by her

8. Ibid.

mother and sister, knowing that in the final analysis, this authority does not count and can easily be annulled. However, it is she
who has a high sensitivity to language and is shocked by her
father talking about "doing away with the baby" (*Baby weg-
machen*). She experiences the split between the male and female
world as an existential threat to herself. In psychoanalytic terms,
the alienation from patriarchal identification takes place, and
she seeks refuge in her mother's arms, attempting a reunification. Whereas at first her older sister tyrannizes her in the commanding tone her father uses, later their initially hierarchical
relationship becomes one of two equal partners who share the
same language.

Anna's older daughter, Barbara, understands that men are in
a position of power, and that this power is based on male language. She has learned to secure her position in the hierarchy
as the older sister – even against her mother – through her use
of her father's harsh, commanding tone. She feels that she can
confront even him with logical argumentation. On the other
hand, she senses the defensive position into which Katarina is
being maneuvered by her father and fights it ("One doesn't
have to apologize for one's baby.").

The film problematizes the norm of female existence dictated
by men and male language in this area. A group of businessmen
at PENATEN searching for a pregnant model for an advertisement believes that only the women using pillows to simulate pregnancy looked like mothers, whereas Katarina was unacceptable
by their standards, since pregnancy in general "looks unaesthetic
from the sixth month on." Bernhard's discussion with the counselor from the child protection league is also a discourse on language. The counselor insists on the importance of language in
the dispute between two partners ("The way you said it, I would
have been offended too."). However, he himself is insecure in this
realm and carelessly uses "*Geburtsverhütung*" (avoidance of birth)
where he meant "*Empfängnisverhütung*" (contraception).

Lacking legal means to pressure Katarina, the lawyer colleague whom Bernhard consults enjoys the opportunity to use
big headlines in cheap tabloids against another woman who
dares to make claims on her own behalf. He is very much aware
of this type of press language being a means of patriarchal
power, and he regrets that Bernhard does not stoop to this use
of language against Katarina.

The most important principle in the formal representation of language is the reversal of situations and oppositions which occurs throughout the film. Bernhard's fighting for his position in the relationship with Katarina is contrasted with the dynamics between him and his father. Bernhard's father is the caricature of a "hen-pecked husband." His insecure language mode, which is more typical for women, and the way he acts exposes "women's language" as ridiculous. At the same time, it addresses the men's fear of what happens if they lose/give up their old positions of power. In the same way Jürgen becomes a "womanish" character: during the dinner scene in Tunisia and when he takes Katarina home to her hotel, the roles are divided according to the old stereotypes, only reversed. It is Katarina who asks him, "Why don't you come in for a drink," and takes him along, grabbing his hand. He is coy: "It is already quite late." (This scene reminds the viewer of the scene in bed in Helke Sander's *The All-Around Reduced Personality – REDUPERS*.) Jürgen restricts Katarina to being an instrument of his parenthood. He is not interested in Katarina as a person, but only as a mother to a child he could care for. Jürgen wants to take over the role of mothering – even mothering Katarina as he takes charge of her high vitamin diet and the exercise program. In their talk in the baby's room, Katarina expresses her sense of degradation and objectification.

In the composition of single frames, we find formal oppositions, such as the dissociation between body and language, or the spatial crowding of the frame through a number of people, among whom Katarina almost gets lost (e.g., in the women's group). Such shots alternate with almost empty frames dominated centrally by Katarina expressing her strength. This technique is often combined with high and low camera angles marking a person as weak or as dominating the situation. In Robert's family circle, for example, we see Katarina alone in the frame and from a low angle, when she says with great self-confidence, "I am going to have a baby." In the course of the ensuing patronizing discussion, she loses this strength in the visual representation, and in the end she wins it back as she stands up and retreats, saying "I wanted to tell you something wonderful. If I needed advice I would not have come to *you*." The camera angle is also the most important formal expression of her strength when Katarina removes Bernhard's belongings from her apartment: as she (silently!) gathers his things together, the camera looks up to her from a low angle, and then down on Bernhard's "little bundle" of possessions.

Ultimately, it is in the hotel in Tunisia that we see Katarina's consciousness as a woman and her position toward society's norms changing. Initially, she retreats from the dining room in mute panic, but then returns to confront the situation and assert herself: she says what she wants. Significantly, she is the only person in the dining room who tries to speak French; everyone around her continues to speak their old language (i.e., they do not change). She risks expressing herself in the foreign language that is new to her and thus transcends her old limits. This self-affirmation continues in the following scene in her room. She stops the Tunisian music and language that is blaring in her ears (the intrusion from the outside world, the Moslem culture with which she, especially as a Western woman, has so little in common). She replaces these sounds with the music box (music is to be found everywhere in the film where Katarina lives her true self – with or without conflict). She plays with her round pregnant belly, covering up her belly button with a shell, thus symbolically cutting the umbilical cord that connects her with society's norms. She can now accept her body aesthetically and emotionally and develops a new relationship to her self. In her development as a woman, this is the decisive moment of detachment from the old values that are determined by patriarchal society.

While more examples of the use of language in this film abound, it is already clear from the foregoing analysis that the problem of language both co-determines and reflects Katarina's identity as a person and as a woman. This film creates an awareness of the political significance of language within the patriarchal system of roles and relationships and demonstrates the necessity for new strategies by which women consider and express themselves.

I I

Film and Consciousness: The Depiction of Women in East German Movies

gisela bahr

ot wanting to limit our discussion of contemporary German films to those made by filmmakers in the Federal Republic of Germany (West Germany), we have included Gisela Bahr's article, which gives an overview of cinematic developments indicative of the evolution of consciousness about women's issues in the other German state, the former German Democratic Republic, or GDR. If only for the reason that German reunification has turned out to be so difficult, we feel that the different conditions that existed in the East still need to be studied – and therefore, although this article was written before 1989, its insights are important. Bahr examines four East German films produced in the late 1970s and early 1980s, focusing not only on the change in cinematic depictions of women, but also on audience response to these films, as well as noting the difference when, as is the case for one of the films, a woman directs the film. Bahr investigates these cinematic texts, as well as aspects of their production and reception, for evidence about changes in the perception of the situation of women within GDR society in the 1980s.
— THE EDITORS

A woman in the Western world, still struggling against various forms of discrimination, might look with envy at her counterpart in the German Democratic Republic, because, for reasons of economic necessity as well as political purpose, East German women were given equal rights through legislative action early on in the development of their country. For years the GDR authorities have assumed equality of the sexes to be an accomplished fact in all areas of society, but this might be too quick an assumption. Recently in the GDR the authorities have perceived that legal status alone may not be sufficient to assure equal rights for all.

Following an order of the Soviet Military Administration in 1946 that everyone, regardless of sex or age, be given equal pay for equal work,[1] women were granted equal rights and opportunities in the GDR constitution, the new Family Code, the Work Code, and other measures enacted over the years. Specific steps were taken in two areas: (1) to give women equal access to education and work; and (2) to create favorable conditions for women to combine work with motherhood. In the first area, these steps included school reform and introduction of annual quotas for the training and promotion of women (*Frauenförderungspläne*). In the second area, these measures included generously paid maternity leaves, reduced working hours, priority allotment of day care and kindergarten openings, and a monthly supplement for dependent children. These provisions clearly show the government's strong interest in promoting women's productivity both as workers and mothers. However, abortions and free dispensation of contraceptives are legal, too. This means that a woman's right to make her own decisions about children and career, without outside pressure or interference, is meant to be guaranteed in the GDR.

The positive results of these comprehensive measures are reflected in the statistics: women, who constitute 53 percent of the population, make up 50 percent of the labor force today. Of the women of working age (between fifteen and sixty), 87 percent are working. There can be no doubt that the GDR economy would not be so strong as it is today without so many women in the labor force, nor would the GDR's standard of living be so high. This active participation in the national economy has also had a tremendous impact on the women themselves – on their lifestyles, their aspirations, and, last but not least, on their self-confidence. As one of the earliest West German reports on "the other Germany" put it: "The women are the best feature of the GDR."[2]

However, problems remain. Women have not yet advanced to upper level positions in industry, government, or the party

1. Order no. 253, 17 August 1946. Wolfgang Plat, *Die Familie in der DDR* (Frankfurt/M: S. Fischer, 1972), 19.
2. "Die Frauen sind das Beste an der DDR." Eva Windmöller and Thomas Höpker, *Leben in der DDR* (Hamburg: Gruner und Jahr, n.d.) 192.

structure – at least not commensurate with their numbers. To some degree this may be due to remnants of discrimination. But there are also indications of a reverse development. Many women no longer want to get involved in leadership positions. They refuse responsibility at work and decline opportunities for additional training and promotion. Instead, many are having a second or third child to be able to stay home for a year or more. This trend is generally attributed to the "dual burden" of work and family care that most women in the GDR still have to carry with no more than token help from their husbands.[3] Another sign of women's frustration is the divorce rate, one of the highest in the world and still growing.[4] These problems show that the laws alone are not enough to eliminate or even alleviate the "dual burden." Apparently, the GDR authorities are now faced with a problem that we have known in this country for some time: legal provisions are important prerequisites for obtaining equal rights, but they are not sufficient by themselves to change old traditions and ingrained habits. Real equality can be achieved only if and when the consciousness of men and women is changed.

One way of assessing a process as subjective as the changing of consciousness is to study films made in the GDR. Because, as Siegfried Kracauer said long ago, "the films of a nation reflect its mentality in a more direct way than other artistic media."[5] As a mass medium, he continued, movies "appeal to the anonymous multitude. . . . Popular screen motifs can therefore be supposed to satisfy existing mass desires."[6] This capacity to reflect the attitudes and concerns of a wide audience makes film particularly useful for our study of public consciousness. During the last decade, GDR filmmakers were able to revive public interest in movies by adjusting their products to an audience of which 75 percent are people in their teens and twen-

3. Christiane Lemke, "Social Change and Women's Issues in the GDR: Problems of Leadership Positions," in *Studies in GDR Culture and Society* 2 (Washington, D.C.: Univ. Press of America, 1982), 252.

4. The number of divorces grew from 1.4 (per 1,000 population) in 1960 to 3.0 in 1982. Cf. the Federal Republic of Germany with a divorce rate of 0.9 in 1960 and 1.8 in 1982. Harry G. Shaffer, *Women in the Two Germanies* (New York: Pergamon, 1981), 149; *DDR Handbuch*, 2 vols. (Cologne: Wissenschaft und Politik, 1985), 1: 314.

5. Siegfried Kracauer, *From Caligari To Hitler* (Princeton: Princeton Univ. Press, 1974), 5.

6. Ibid.

ties.[7] Consequently, the new film topics are more contemporary and youth-related.

More importantly, heroes no longer have to be exemplary all the time. The "positive hero" essential in Socialist Realism has almost disappeared from GDR literature and film, for several reasons. After the 8th Party Congress, in 1971, declared the GDR a "developed socialist society," the depiction of conflicts as class struggle in literature and the arts was replaced by "non-antagonistic" conflicts. Moreover, in a programmatic speech Honecker emphasized that if writers and artists started from a firm position of socialism, there could be no taboos either with regard to content or to form.[8] This declaration had a liberalizing effect on all artistic production, including film. In 1978, Hans Dieter Mäde, General Director of Feature Film Production in the GDR, stated that the future of the medium film would depend on its ability to reflect artistically not only changes in society but also in people's consciousness and on doing it in such a way that new movies would initiate further changes.[9] Therefore, the new heroes do not have to be models any longer. They may have problems without finding an answer, be in search of themselves, or question society and its values.[10] "Characteristic of these films," said film expert Kurt Maetzig, "is their absolute honesty and search for the truth, particularly in those that are being discussed the liveliest."[11]

Many of these recent films have women as their heroines. Women – says H.R. Mihan – are more representative of the changes that have taken place in socialist society. Scriptwriters often prefer women as protagonists because they perceive them as more spontaneous, more honest, more sensitive, and more

7. Günter Netzeband, Interview with Hans Dieter Mäde, *Film und Fernsehen* 5 (1978): 2–8.

8. "Wenn man von festen Positionen des Sozialismus ausgeht, kann es meines Erachtens auf dem Gebiet von Kunst und Literatur keine Tabus geben. Das betrifft sowohl Fragen der inhaltlichen Gestaltung als auch die des Stils." Volker Gransow, *Kulturpolitik in der DDR* (Berlin: Volker Spiess, 1975), 104.

9. Netzeband, Interview, 5.

10. Ibid.; Hans-Rainer Mihan, "Sabine, Sunny, Nina und der Zuschauer. Gedanken zum Gegenwartsspielfilm der DEFA," *Film und Fernsehen* 8 (1982): 9–12; Rudolf Jürschik, "Erkundungen. Filmbilder – Heldentypus – Alltag," *Film und Fernsehen* 4 (1981): 12; R. Jürschik, "Streitbare Spielfilme – sozialistisches Lebensgefühl," pt. 1, *Film und Fernsehen* 9 (1979): Supplement; pt. 2, *Film und Fernsehen* 11 (1979): Supplement.

11. Joachim Maaß, "Frauenrollen in DEFA-Filmen," *Neue Berliner Illustrierte* 37 (1982): 7.

articulate than men.[12] Generally, this trend is seen as reflecting
real, tangible changes that affect women and their place in
GDR society.[13] Typical themes in these film stories about women
are personal relationships, the quality of life, and the women's
search for happiness. Judging by their popularity, observed one
critic, one could say that these films hit a nerve in their viewers.[14] This study will discuss four movies about women, dealing
with a variety of topics, such as marriage, career, partnership,
and friendship. Considering them in chronological sequence,
we might see some progress in the treatment of women's issues.

The first example, entitled *Till Death Do You Part* (1978),[15] is a
rather melodramatic story. Sonja, a young saleswoman, and
Jens, a construction worker, are getting married. They look like
the "ideal" couple: they have good jobs, are strong, healthy, fun-
loving, and very much in love. After the birth of their child,
however, things cease to run smoothly. Jens wants Sonja to quit
her job and be a full-time wife and mother, which she did not
expect at all. Since they do not know how to discuss their difference of opinion, they have sex and hope the problem will go
away. But it persists and escalates. While Jens is at work, Sonja
takes a course, earns a diploma, and goes back to work. When
Jens finds out about this turn of events, he rapes and beats her
violently. Later he discovers that Sonja has had an abortion, and
he almost kills her. Finally, one day, she passively watches him
accidentally drink from a soda bottle that she has been using to
hold cleaning fluid. He survives but is crippled for life. Ponder-
ing her shattered dreams, Sonja cries out in total bewilderment:
"How did it all happen? . . . I did everything as I was supposed
to, but it all went wrong."[16]

This film story seems to address directly the problem mentioned above: the discrepancy between the new opportunities
GDR women now have and the lack of awareness that prevents
men and women from making use of them. The young couple
begin their married life with the old-fashioned notion that love
is all they need for happiness. But Sonja also expects to follow

12. Mihan, "Sabine, Sunny, Nina," 12.
13. Jürschik, "Spielfilme," pt. 2: v.
14. Jürschik, "Erkundungen": 12.
15. *Bis daß der Tod euch scheidet.* Dir. Heiner Carow. With Katrin Saß and Martin Seifert. DEFA, 1978.
16. "Wie's gekommen ist, will ich wissen. . . . Alles habe ich nach Vorschrift
gemacht. Und doch ist alles danebengegangen."

the new lifestyle of GDR women, that is, to go to work, have a baby, place him/her in day care, and return to work. It never occurs to her that motherhood might infringe upon her independence, because not until the birth of their son does Jens begin to act like the traditional male, anxious to keep his wife under his control. Neither family nor school nor society had prepared Sonja for such a conflict, said film director Heiner Carow.[17] Being so totally unprepared and unaware of her problem, Sonja cannot even communicate to Jens what her own needs and expectations are. All she is able to do is defy him behind his back.

This plot looks like a "classic" case for a consciousness-raising session, and an extreme one to the Western observer. However, director Carow did not see it this way. "There is always an equal rights issue involved, especially in a crisis," he said, "but it is not essential to the story. In real life, we are beyond the equal rights problem."[18] What he is concerned with are problems of living together. In his conviction that equal rights issues are practically solved, Carow may be in agreement with the official position in his country, but he is not in tune with his audience, as we shall see. Moreover, in his film he clearly shows a bias toward the male hero. Jens's outdated attitude (which, incidentally, violates the GDR's Family Code) is excused in the film by references to his background: the son of a working mother, Jens was raised by his grandmother and felt very much deprived. Therefore, he wants his son to have a better childhood. And the film gives other extenuating circumstances for the man. Jens's failure to complete his training for advancement is attributed to his troubles at home. His subsequent drinking and increased violence toward his wife, then, are the result of his failure at work. After the accident, all of his acts of brutality are forgotten, but Sonja's failure to prevent the accident is not. The injured Jens gets all the sympathy, while Sonja is seen as the perpetrator of a shocking, incomprehensible act, rather than as the battered wife who could bear it no longer. In the film's very emotional conclusion, Sonja is blamed implicitly as if she, and only she, had been lacking in understanding and selflessness.

17. "*Bis daß der Tod euch scheidet.* Interview mit Heiner Carow," *Progress. Pressebulletin Kino der DDR* 5 (1979): 6–8.
18. "Natürlich steckt da immer, besonders in Krisen, viel Gleichberechtigungsproblematik drin, aber sie ist nicht der Kern. Wir sind da in der Realität schon einen Schritt weiter." Ibid.

The film attracted large audiences and was widely discussed, for example, at audience forums, which are routinely held in movie theaters. Women, generally, had more understanding for Jens, while men tended to be harshly critical of this character. Many women also expressed relief that the film allowed them to speak freely about a problem they knew only too well but had been afraid to mention. "The beatings are not even the worst," one said, "but the war of words is."[19] This leads to the conclusion that the issue is not at all resolved. Intentionally or not, it seems that with this film Carow has broached a formerly taboo topic: namely, equal rights in the home.

Two years later, the film *Solo Sunny* (1980),[20] had a reception just as lively, although more controversial. Movie theatres were sold out in record runs, and viewers' reactions appeared in newspapers for weeks. The heroine, Ingrid Sommer, alias Sunny, is a young pop singer and member of a band that brings a mixed bag of entertainment to small-town audiences. Her goal is to get solo parts, and to be recognized by the audience as an artist. Previously a factory worker, she has left her familiar environment for the uncertain world of popular entertainment. Now she is determined to succeed in her new career and be taken seriously. It should be possible, she feels, to have one's own personality without the need to be famous.

If this sounds like a far cry from the usual film fare in the GDR, it is – and it is not. Director Konrad Wolf and script writer Wolfgang Kohlhaase created a heroine who wants something that does not strike us in the West as unusual: to have (1) a career of her own choosing and (2) a personality that is truly hers. In the GDR, however, unconventional choices like these are seen as new demands on society, and doubtful ones. Therefore, Wolf and Kohlhaase had some explaining to do after the film was released: in a socialist society, they emphasized, these are legitimate aspirations and should be encouraged.[21] To make

19. "Das Schlagen ist gar nicht das Schlimmste, schlimmer ist, sich mit Worten zerstören." Dieter Wolf, "Die Kunst, miteinander zu reden. 'Bis daß der Tod euch scheidet' im Gespräch," *Film und Fernsehen* 11 (1979): 9,10; Interview with H. Carow, 7.
20. *Solo Sunny.* Dirs. Konrad Wolf and Wolfgang Kohlhaase. With Renate Krößner. DEFA, 1980.
21. "Gespräch zwischen Klaus Wischnewski, Konrad Wolf und Wolfgang Kohlhaase," *Film und Fernsehen* 1 (1980); excerpts reprinted in *Progress. Pressebulletin Kino der DDR* 1 (1980): 6–8. Also "Es ist etwas im Gange. Spiegel-Interview mit dem DDR-Filmregisseur Konrad Wolf," *Der Spiegel* 15 (1980).

their point, they chose for their heroine not a highly gifted singer whose talents would enhance the cultural scene, but a rather average one whose career was vital to no one but herself.

Sunny lives in Prenzlau Hills, a dilapidated neighborhood in Berlin, where she fits in like an exotic bird. On the surface, she is street-wise, self-assured, independent-minded, and very out-spoken. "I sleep with a man if I feel like it, and I call a fucker a fucker."[22] But deep down she is insecure, sensitive, and vulnerable. In the band she is treated as a sex object, and when she refuses to cooperate, she is promptly fired. But she also refuses a comfortable life with a man she does not love. When she is betrayed by the man she does love, she breaks up with him because "people like you," she tells him, "have a way of draining people like me dry."[23] Nobody is to take advantage of her. These setbacks in her professional and personal lives lead to a period of self-searching and depression and to a suicide attempt. In the end, however, she is ready to try again, more determined than ever.

Sunny's attempts to liberate herself from a confining and often hostile environment are conveyed in the film through a variety of images. There is a winding, narrow staircase to climb, with a neighbor blocking her way; there is the view into a dark, steep backyard with only a narrow strip of sky above and an airplane soaring high. There is also a shot of Sunny and her lover sitting by the window, taken from the outside and showing just this window frame filled with two heads in a large, dark wall, like a small island in the ocean. Sunny's loneliness as a performer and her difficulties in communicating with an audience are made clear when the camera takes her line of vision and, blinded by stage lights, she is singing against what looks like a huge, milky wall behind which the audience can be heard, but not seen. Finally, just before her suicide attempt, we see her in front of her three part mirror, looking at herself somewhat perplexed and helplessly – an impression that is intensified by its triple reflection in the mirror.

Unlike Carow, Wolf and Kohlhaase explicitly deal in their movie with women's problems in a male-dominated world, such as sexual harassment, discrimination at the work place, and

22. "Ich schlafe mit jemand, wenn es mir Spaß macht. Ich nenne einen Ekenpinkler einen Eckenpinkler."
23. "Leute wie du haben eine Art, Leute wie mich auszusaugen."

partnership problems in the personal sphere. In addition, they bring up an issue that is not confined to the equal rights area: the issue of personal fulfillment. This aspect of the film turned out to be the most controversial in the eyes of the audience. While Sonja and Jens have the kind of problem that most viewers can easily identify with, Sunny's story appears to be somewhat ahead of its audience. The film was highly praised by Western critics but received a mixed reaction in the GDR. Some critics wondered just how justifiable Sunny's aspirations were,[24] while some viewers found the heroine outright unreasonable, an outsider, and not at all typical of young women in their society.[25] In comparison to conventional Sonja, Sunny clearly represents a new breed of woman. Without any role model or other encouragement, she embarks on a career that used to be beyond the reach of a worker, and, unencumbered by traditions or accepted modes of behavior, she sets her own standards, terms, and values. She wants to be an equal partner in her profession and in her personal relationships as well, no more, no less. The periods of self-doubt and, particularly, the loneliness she experiences in the course of her struggle are quite realistic. Her kind of woman is a rarity still – on screen as well as in real life in the GDR, so that it is not surprising that audience reaction was divided. A character like Sunny, observed one critic, presupposes (in real life) emancipation and an uninhibited relationship to the other sex.[26] Such an observation clearly implies that this is not yet the case in her country. Director Wolf, however, emphasized that a socialist society must do more than just tolerate or accommodate the Sunnys, because in the long run society will have to depend on individuals of this kind.[27]

The third film, *Apprehension* (1981),[28] was released only one year later, but its theme is more advanced. It is the story of Inge Herold, a divorcee with a teenage son and a married man as her lover. She works as a psychologist in a Family Counseling Agency. One day, a medical checkup reveals the possibility of

24. Hans-Jörg Rother, "Kino neuer Ideen im Meinungsstreit. Gedanken zu DEFA-Filmen aus den Jahren 1979/80," *Prisma. Kino- und Fernseh-Almanach* 12 (1981): 9–26.

25. "*Solo Sunny:* Kritische Diskussion," *Film und Fernsehen* 6 (1980): 3–7.

26. Brigitte Thurm, "Rückhaltlos und verletzbar," *Film und Fernsehen* 2 (1980): 7.

27. Wischnewski, "Gespräch", *Progress*, 8.

28. *Die Beunruhigung.* Dir. Lothar Warneke. With Christine Schorn. DEFA, 1981.

breast cancer, and an operation is scheduled for the next morning. This, then, causes the apprehension. The film focuses on
that last day before the surgery to show how Inge faces – not so
much the possibility of dying, according to Lothar Warneke, the
director – but the disturbing question: has her life been a meaningful and worthwhile one, or has it been wasted?[29]

As Inge searches for an answer, it is clear that she does not
measure the quality of life in terms of career or family or
lifestyle but simply in terms of human relationships. It turns out
that most of her relationships are rather perfunctory ones.
True, with her son she is able to resolve a crisis that day and
restore real understanding. But her dealings with her mother
are conventional, and with her coworkers collegial but not
close. This is surprising because friendships at work are often
depicted in the GDR as strong, supportive ties. Both Sonja and
Sunny have them, yet Inge has only one close friend – in West
Berlin. In the course of the day, she visits two former classmates
and inquires about others in her class, because she wants to
know what they did with their lives. All in all, the results of this
day in search of herself are quite meager. Could this be all there
is to life? Seeing one old schoolmate again who seems quite at
peace with himself as he rears his daughter alone offers just a
hint of alternatives Inge has never explored. Finally, there is
only her lover left to comfort her before going to the hospital,
but he stays away. That long, lonely night when Inge is waiting
for him to come, until his presence does not matter any more, is
shown to be the turning point in her life.

Inge is portrayed as what many consider an emancipated
woman. Her divorce, she tells her mother, was the most sensible
decision in her life. She will never remarry, and she has assured
her lover that they are both free to come and go, with no obligations on either side. A comfortable, unrestrictive arrangement
– only, it is just an escape. If she does not commit herself, she
cannot get hurt again. Of course, this arrangement fails the crisis test because it is not a true partnership. It is only after the
operation that Inge finds a real partner in this former schoolmate of hers who helps her cope with the aftermath of breast
cancer by giving her undivided love and moral support.

Like the other two, this film received much attention and

29. Joachim Maaß, "Film *Die Beunruhigung*," *Neue Berliner Illustrierte* 7 (1982):
20.

acclaim. At the Second National Film Festival in the GDR, Christine Schorn, who played Inge, received a prize, as did director Warneke and scriptwriter Schubert.[30] Critical reaction of viewers focused on the threat of cancer that was judged to be not realistic enough. However, the cancer scare is not the issue, but rather the quality of life or the fear of wasting one's life, as Warneke has explained.[31] For him and scriptwriter Helga Schubert, a strong, meaningful woman-man relationship is central to the quality of life. This is exemplified by the structure of the film, which begins with Inge and a new partner, a year after the operation. Knowing the happy outcome, the viewer can concentrate on Inge's learning process and on the differences between the two men in her life. The film ends with the continuation of the opening scene, that is, with an emphasis on partnership. Inge and her new man support each other so completely that they can allow themselves to be both stronger and more vulnerable, and this seems to be the key concept. What Sonja cannot even express yet, and Sunny has been looking for in vain, Inge is able to achieve, but only after an adjustment of her values and attitudes. Particularly, she has had to correct her misguided idea of an emancipated woman. "As for the relationship between man and woman, we are just beginning our search for new forms," said director Warneke, "and I admit my helplessness."[32]

To emphasize the tentative, searching nature of their story, Warneke and Schubert created an experimental film (in black and white) using lay actors for many parts and, more importantly, asking their actors and actresses to improvise their lines, rather than play from a prepared script. They wanted their product to reflect real life more closely than a conventionally made film. By relying on the spontaneity of their acting staff, they avoided an overdramatization of the cancer scare in favor of Inge's probe into relationships. As in a real-life situation, Inge goes through a number of seemingly unrelated, everyday occurrences, like a flirtation in a coffeehouse and a visit with a large, happy family, which, however, become significant in rela-

30. *Prisma. Kino- und Fernseh-Almanach* 14 (1984): 25.
31. Lothar Warneke, Interview, *Progress. Pressebulletin Kino der DDR* 2 (1982): 8.
32. "Was die Beziehung von Mann und Frau betrifft, da befinden wir uns am Anfang der Suche nach neuen Formen, ich gestehe, daß ich auch hilflos bin." Ibid.

tion to her frame of mind and her search for new meaning in her life. By making the story line somewhat unstructured, i.e. by simply allowing the heroine to follow her impulses and chance encounters, as well as by creating the impression that time is suspended on that afternoon between her notification and the actual operation, the film focuses on the inner process Inge goes through. And by chosing an improvisational approach, letting their performers contribute their own ideas about the characters they play, Warneke and Schubert captured a kind of reality that makes their story particularly believable. Warneke, it seems, is acutely aware of the changes occurring around him which he can no longer control. "The more clearly we understand the humanity of our society," he said in a discussion with other film directors, "the more we also understand our own powerlessness."[33]

The last movie to be discussed here is *Pauline's Second Life* (1984),[34] a film made for GDR Television. It differs from the other three in that it is directed by a woman, Christa Mühl, who also wrote the script. She wrote it for two actresses and allowed them to contribute significantly to the development of the story line. This, then, is a film by women and – as we shall see – for women.

As a point of departure, Mühl chose divorce, a relevant topic in light of the GDR's high divorce rate, although she was neither concerned with statistics nor with divorce as a means of liberation. Rather, she said, conversations with divorcees led her to conclude that divorce often changes a woman's life more radically than a man's. While it seems easy for him to find a new mate and resume the life he is accustomed to, she often stays alone much longer. Mühl wanted to investigate how a woman copes with being on her own and with changing her lifestyle.[35] Her heroine, Pauline, is a woman of about fifty who, after thirty years of being a supportive wife and devoted mother, is being divorced by her professor husband for a younger woman. The divorce robs her of everything she has: her purpose in life, her sense of identity, and her financial security.

33. "In dem Maße, in dem wir immer klarere Vorstellungen von der Menschlichkeit unserer Gesellschaft gewinnen, wird uns auch unser eigenes Unvermögen klarer." Discussion between Kurt Maetzig, Konrad Wolf, Lothar Warneke, Ruth Herlinghaus, pt. 2. *Film und Fernsehen* 7 (1980): 6.
34. *Paulines zweites Leben.* Dir. Christa Mühl. With Annemone Haase and Walfriede Schmitt. DEFA, 1984.
35. Vera Böhm, Interview with Christa Mühl, *FF Dabei* (29 Oct. - 4 Nov. 1984): 44–45.

At a health resort where she is supposed to recover from this blow, Pauline shares her room with an energetic, resolute working woman by the name of Wally. Divorced by her husband many years ago because she cannot have children, Wally appears undefeated. She is successful at work as a team leader in a laundry, full of zest, optimism, and practical common sense. The unlikely friendship that these dissimilar women develop is the backbone of the film.

Used to following her husband's lead, Pauline now follows Wally's – she manages to get hired into Wally's team as a laundry worker. In due course, Wally's unconventional ways, unencumbered by traditional tastes and values, help Pauline shed the habits and traditions of a middle-class housewife – though not so easily. At first her inexperience and pedantic perfectionism cause problems with her coworkers because they hurt the team's productivity and earnings. While Wally stays out of the conflict, Pauline is on her own to resolve these problems. Slowly she learns the give and take of dealing with people, at work and elsewhere, gaining self-confidence and a greater awareness of her surroundings and of herself. Ironically, as Pauline begins her "second life," Wally's life falls apart when her partner of many years decides to go back to his wife, and she turns to Pauline for support. In the end, then, the strong, courageous, optimistic Wally proves to be more vulnerable and the soft, delicate Pauline more resilient than expected – a reversal that brings the two women closer together and makes them more compatible and more human.

The film was highly praised by most GDR critics. That it received four art prizes from the Federation of Trade Unions (for the director, the two leading actresses, and the camera operator) can be taken as an indirect, favorable audience response, since these prizes are determined by membership vote. Direct audience reactions were published in newspapers and magazines. Critics and viewers agreed on the realism of the story and its truthful, unadulterated portrayal of contemporary life and problems in their society.[36] Much of the praise centered on the realistic depiction of the workplace – with one viewer claiming that Wally's part represented "one of the most beautiful portraits of a worker in many years"[37] – and the fact that the

36. *FF Dabei* (3–9 Dec. 1984).
37. Helmut Drechsler (Leipzig), *Berliner Zeitung* (16 Nov. 1984).

heroine found her liberation through her work experience. In this respect the film is a loyal illustration of the socialist belief that working means emancipation for women and will solve all questions of identity, self-realization, and happiness.

But there is more to the film than that. It is the story of a consciousness-raising process – a term that is not exactly a household word in the GDR. Throughout her married life, Pauline had been a follower, accepting the traditional sex role in her marriage and subordinating herself to her self-assured, patriarchal husband. After the divorce, Wally becomes a role model for Pauline, introducing her to such new traits as assertiveness, spontaneity, and compassion, and liberating her from her self-pity and middle-class values.

At the laundry, the consciousness-raising process continues, not simply because of the new work experience and the need for Pauline to find her place on the team, but, more importantly, because all the team members are women. Hard working and efficient, with different temperaments and personalities, different problems and life experiences, these women contribute significantly to Pauline's "awakening," helping her to recognize who she really is and which options are available to improve her life. As one critic noted, there is no sentimentality among these women but a great deal of warmth, solidarity, caring for one another, and humanity; and they do their work with sensitivity, expertise, and cheerfulness. These are unusual words to describe a workplace, but apparently the critic (a woman) felt solidarity with the women workers and chose to identify particular qualities that we associate primarily with women.[38]

As in *Solo Sunny*, the capital city of Berlin again plays a significant role in this film. It provides not only the atmosphere, the tempo, and the sights for the story but, with Wally, also the prototype of the proverbial Berliner – in language, sense of humor, and vitality. In one scene, the two women are sitting on a bench in the middle of busy Alexander Square, "feasting" on barbecued chicken and champagne and acknowledging the attention they are getting from male passers-by with amused nonchalance. Mühl also employs symbolism to demonstrate Pauline's growth. After her divorce, Pauline is left with a turtle to take care of. As her struggles to find a new place in life and at work

38.   Gisela Hoyer, "Paulines Aufbruch zu sich selbst," *Der Morgen* 5 (Nov.1984).

unfold, her reactions can easily be identified with either with-drawing into, or coming out of her "shell." Not until the turtle dies of neglect does Pauline realize how self-centered she had been, and begins to face her problems in a more open way.

Pauline's "second life," then, is that of a hard-working, self-supporting woman who has freed herself from the restrictions of traditional role expectations for the risks, and adventures, of exploring herself, her potential, and her environment. But as part of this new life, she exchanged the company of a spouse and other family for the unaccustomed life of a single woman. Mühl points here to an acute problem: as women leave their tra-ditional roles behind and become self-reliant, independent, unique persons – as conditions in the GDR encourage them to do – they often leave men behind, too, because many men – and this is not confined to the GDR – are still quite comfortable in their dominating sex roles and see no need to liberate them-selves. Therefore, the new kind of woman has fewer prospects of finding a congenial man. Neither Pauline nor Wally will be so "lucky" as Inge Herold. In the conventional view, this must make them lonely and unfulfilled. As one critic observed, "their concrete prospects for happiness are slim."[39] However, Wally and Pauline achieve something not seen in the other films: the freedom to be themselves. How they are going to use this free-dom and reshape their lives is left open. Significantly, there is no suggestion that they might seek their fulfillment in the ser-vice of society. Instead the emphasis is on individual relation-ships and the private realm, and the film leads both women to the point where it is up to them to take charge and go in any direction they want.

The four movies discussed here were made within only six years of each other, but in theme and perspective they seem far apart. As we have seen, the directors' (and scriptwriters') own level of awareness regarding the place of women in their society differed considerably. We can assume that this made a differ-ence in their choice of topic and also in their perception of what their audience needed. In *Till Death Do You Part*, Heiner Carow refused to acknowledge women's rights as a problem that still needs to be addressed in the GDR, at least in regard to marital and other personal relationships. Audience reaction to

39. "Ihre konkreten Glücksaussichten sind gering." Ursula Materny, "Zwei 'Maßrollen,'" *Die Union* 9 (Nov. 1984).

his film, however, highlighted this need. In *Solo Sunny*, Wolf and
Kohlhaase suggested that women could go much further in
their demands and aspirations for a fulfilling life than they currently do. They used their film as a vehicle for encouragement
to the women in an environment that is still male-dominated in
certain areas. With *Apprehension* Warneke and Schubert invited
the audience to participate in their search for a new, more
promising, and truly equal partnership between women and
men. They did so by focusing on the learning process of the
heroine who at first is not aware of her own needs and does not
know what kind of male partner she really wants, until a crisis
shakes her out of some superficial assumptions. Finally, in
Pauline's Second Life, Christa Mühl presented us with the story of
two very different women who exemplify the joys as well as the
pains of being their own persons. This film, too, is encouraging
to women by providing role models and a number of learning
situations that are easy to identify with.

Do films like these, and their reception, offer clues to the
Western observer as to what the level of awareness in the GDR
might be with regard to women's issues? At least, I believe, they
give us some idea of the subjective side of the equal rights issue
in that country. And although criteria like viewers' reception
and directors' intentions can be elusive, they should not be
overlooked. We might even conclude that the women in the
Western world have little cause for envy since their GDR counterparts still face some of the same obstacles as they do, but
often don't quite know even today what is missing in their lives,
and why.

Presumably, movies like these will continue to receive wide
attention, due to their topics as well as their directors' promi-
nence.[40] Whether or not they will be effective in the long run
not only in reflecting changes in people's consciousness but
also in stimulating learning processes, so that women and men
in the GDR can form new relationships based on equality,
remains to be seen. It is worth watching.

40. Konrad Wolf, the most prominent of the four, died in 1982.

Part 2

Experimental and Underground Cinema

12

She Says, He Says: The Power of the Narrator in Modernist Film Politics

b . r u b y r i c h

Two members of the collective of women photographers carry their photo to the Berlin Wall. Helke Sander's The All-Around Reduced Personality – REDUPERS (1977).
(Photo courtesy of Helke Sander)

*I*n discussing the role of cinematic strategies for distantiation or defamiliarization in more experimental films, one must note that such strategies have origins that predate feminism's "second wave" (i.e., before the 1960s). Those origins can be found in the ideas of modernism and the avant-garde dating back to the first few decades of the twentieth century. In order to emphasize the issue of gender and the contributions of feminism to subsequent developments of the modernist ideas, we include B. Ruby Rich's influential article comparing *Alexander Kluge's* Part-Time Work of a Domestic Slave *(1974) and* Helke Sander's The All-Around Reduced Personality – REDUPERS *(1977). Both Kluge and Sander are among the more experimental West German filmmakers, and both of them can be specifically placed in a tradition which goes back to Brecht via Godard. Rich distinguishes, however, between Kluge's cinematic modernism and what she calls the "feminist modernism" of Sander, focusing on the use of voice-over narration in the two films.*
— THE EDITORS

> In the construction of their own new forms, women may well react
> against some elements in modernism and will almost certainly
> challenge some current definitions of what an artist does and
> what her relationship to her audience can be.
>
> ANN BARR SNITOW[1]

As the 1970s have shifted into the 1980s, certain parallel aesthetic and political trends have edged close enough to shed
light upon one another. In the area of film criticism and filmmaking, this closeness has proved particularly provocative in the
juncture of modernist and feminist film practice. In this article
I take up two films which together constitute a nearly axiomatic
case in point: Alexander Kluge's *Part-Time Work of a Domestic
Slave* (1973) and Helke Sander's *The All-Around Reduced Personality – REDUPERS* (1977). In their intense similarities and differences, these two films can illuminate for us both the nature of
feminist film practice and the implications of a modernist film
form. Most pertinent, in both cases, is the role played by the
narrator in relation to the central protagonist as well as to the
audience – a role which raises serious questions concerning the
actual politics of a modernist film practice.

Part-Time Work of a Domestic Slave examines the contradictions
attending the life of one Roswitha, a wife and mother of three
who gives up her work as a part-time abortionist and, together
with her friend Sylvia, instead undertakes a political investigation of her chemist husband's employer, the Beauchamp Factory, which covertly plans to move its operations out of the country and shut down its present plant. Such is the bare-boned narrative line.[2] Throughout, consistent with modernist film style,
Kluge interrupts, inflects, and retards the forward movement of
the story by the insertion of other types of materials into the
film. These include pictures taken from moralistic German children's books, excerpts from *Kuhle Wampe* and from the Soviet
realist film *Chapayev*, songs and rhymes that indirectly comment
upon Roswitha's situation at various points, intertitles that sup-

1. Ann Barr Snitow, "The Front Line: Notes on Sex in Novels by Women,
1969–1979," in *Women: Sex and Sexuality*, ed. Catherine R. Stimpson and Ethel
Spector Person (Chicago: Univ. of Chicago Press, 1980), 161.

2. Space here obviously does not permit a full discussion of the film. For that,
see: Jan Dawson, *Alexander Kluge and the Occasional Work of a Female Slave* (Perth:
Perth Film Festival Publication, 1975).

ply key information at other points, and, of course, the ubiquitous voice-over that directs our view of the images and transactions on the screen. The structure of the film is derived, not
from any narrative progression or character development, but
rather from the course which Kluge's narrator pursues in conjunction with the viewer. It is the voice-over, together with the
intertitles that constitute its point of view, that exercise organizational control over the film.

Two questions demand our attention: What is the function of
the narrator in the film? And, what is the effect of the narration
upon the viewer? While Roswitha is not a properly constituted
character in the realist sense of character unity and psychological motivation, she is nevertheless a compelling presence on
screen and the nominal focus of the film. Her persona as well as
her distillation of the film's narrative and political concerns do
lead to an audience engagement with this "Roswitha." In the
best modernist style, such an engagement is then distantiated
and fractured by Kluge's devices of narration, extrapolated references, etc. Thus cut off from the characters (who in fact
remain a mystery to the viewer, devoid of any visible subjectivity
and relieved of all psychology) and from the possibility of identification with these characters, the viewer must turn elsewhere.
It is commonly assumed that such a viewer, blocked from character identification, turns instead to the higher strata of non-
identificatory responses. With Kluge's help, I would disagree.
The narrator holds a position of omniscience as a *deus ex machina* privy to information unavailable to the film's characters and
inaccessible within the film text. In this guise of omniscience,
the narrator quickly becomes the favored replacement for the
viewer in search of identification. The narrator, in his display of
wit and wisdom, wins the respect of the viewer over the course
of the film. The viewer, in turn, repays this narrative generosity
with a downright chumminess, uniting in a spirit of smug superiority with the narrator over and against the character(s). In a
film such as *Part-Time Work*, in which the filmmaker and narrator are male and in which the protagonist is a woman, the sexual politics are sharply etched within the film's form. The narrator, "in league with" the author (Kluge) whose point of view he
comes to represent and whose words become inflected in the
intertitles, consistently undermines the film's female protagonist by a process in which the audience is actively complicitous.

A simple but clearcut example of this process can be found in Kluge's presentation of the Beauchamp Factory's impending move. The viewer learns this crucial fact via intertitle. Having discovered the fact with such ease, the viewer then has little respect for the characters' diligent uncovering of the same knowledge. The narrator's omniscience undercuts the protagonist's power. The effect is even more decisive later in the film, when Kluge frames Roswitha's investigative efforts with a damning title, "Under pressure from the work force and the public, the management decides – independently of Roswitha and Sylvia – to scrap the planned closure." In the context of the film, the title is received as an hilarious send-up, a final jab at the Sisyphean haplessness of Roswitha's mission. We are not told just what did motivate the management's decision, nor why the narrator is so sure that it was made "independently." The film has shown the nighttime raids conducted by the two women, the desperate trip to a newspaper editor for better coverage, the meetings with union representatives, and even Roswitha's solo journey to Portugal to verify the prospective site being readied there by Beauchamp. How can the narrator be so sure that all this work was not only ineffectual, but totally and utterly without effect? More important, how can the viewer accept this "fact" without question? It is a testimony to how thoroughly the viewer is under the sway of the narrator by this point in the film that, indeed, the assessment is accepted and the character thereby further disempowered. Severe judgments become the rule of thumb, couched in irony and ridicule, proffering jokes to be shared by narrator/author and viewer. A voice-over describes the women's activity in another scene: "Having found no better way of experiencing reality, Roswitha and Sylvia learn a song by Brecht by heart."

All the trouble is not located in the narrator's treatment of the characters, however. Once a reassessment of the role of the narrator (hitherto considered benign) has begun, the film's facade starts to reveal other fissures. A new layer of contradiction emerges.

"The more contradictory a situation, the more contrasts you need to describe it."[3] The words belong to Alexander Kluge and presumably refer to the sorts of contradictions between the interests of the family and those of society, between the private

3. Ibid., 40.

and the public spheres, between the individual and the historical process, between logic and chaos. There are other contradicitions, though, within his film's own parameters. They are contradictions that have been lodged there by the author to throw off the balance, not unlike the thumb applied to the scale by the corrupt merchant to cheat the customer. Two central tenets of Kluge's own political praxis provide the guideposts for our inquiry. (1) "It's the spectators who produce their films."[4] And, (2) "Materialist aesthetics (is) a way of organizing collective social experience."[5] Both statements demand a consideration of the social context (Kluge made his film in 1974) in order to assess what relation it might have to its subject and, furthermore, what social experience spectators could, indeed, find there.

Part-Time Work of a Domestic Slave was made at the height of the campaign to abolish Paragraph 218 and thereby make abortion legal in the Federal Republic.[6] In the Federal Republic, as in the U.S. or France or Great Britain, the pro-abortion campaign has served as an index to the force of the women's liberation movement during this period. Curiously for a film that states so adamantly its concern with public and private spheres, this paradigmatic struggle to claim the public right for a previously "private" act has been totally omitted. Indeed, the entire social and political context of the time within which Roswitha can be presumed to be working is omitted. The omission serves a very clear purpose for Kluge: once the evidence of the highly political nature of any abortion activity in the Federal Republic of 1974 has been precluded, then the coast is clear for the narrator's redefinition of Roswitha's abortion work as individualistic and apolitical. Instead, her work as an abortionist is defined by the narrator as one of the film's precious contradictions: "In order to afford more children her own, Roswitha runs an abortion practice." The memory must struggle to recall that this is not the tale of a backstreet abortionist fleecing customers in the 1950s, but rather a woman engaged in supplying crucial women's healthcare in the midst of a political crisis threatening both her livelihood and the lives of her patients (toward whom Kluge is pained to show her great, if "apolitical" concern.)

4. Ibid., 31.
5. Ibid.
6. See, for example: Monica Jacobs, "Civil Rights and Women's Rights in the Federal Republic of Germany Today," *New German Critique* 13 (Winter 1978) and other articles in the same issue for background information.

Omission is but one tactic employed by Kluge to combat the feminist position on abortion. Together with his sister Alexandra, who plays the part of Roswitha and who is credited with substantial input to the film (in particular its handling of abortion), Kluge chose to present a more direct attack on the pro-abortion campaign by including a graphic, emotionally jarring shot within an abortion sequence. At the time of the film's release, a counterattack was launched by the members of the *Frauen und Film* collective (including Helke Sander). In their published critiques of the film, they questioned its moral and political ambivalence toward the abortion issues and its sensationalistic handling of the mock-clinical surgical sequence that ended with the instruments being tossed into a slop bucket atop what seemed to be a fetus. Sander et al. censured the film as "a slap in the face" to the women's movement by Kluge.

"It's necessary to have in your nerves a sense of what constitutes a false choice."[7] The words, again, belong to Kluge; once again, they indicate a damning view of his own film. Kluge has constructed a false contradiction between abortion work (apolitical) and political work (workplace organizing). The spectator is led to accept the false choice posed to Roswitha of sleazy abortion profiteering versus the righteous work of combatting multinationals. Her abortion work, futhermore, is peculiarly privatized in contrast to the collective struggles that surrounded such work in the year of the film's making. When Roswitha is busted by the police (due to a vindictive tip by a rival abortionist), her case is no *cause célèbre*. Left with Kluge's depiction, we might well be in the 1950s. Further, the most basic politics of abortion are altered. The major villain is the rival *woman* abortionist who does sloppy work and informs on Roswitha; there is not a word about the medical profession that has been complicitous in the deaths of countless pregnant women for ideological reasons. The one male doctor is pictured as professional but callous, skilled but fed up with these messy women. It is the women abortionists upon whom Kluge focuses as self-motivated, medically incompetent, and vengeful – this at a time when a number of politically dedicated women are running abortion and health clinics coming under severe (and often physically violent) attacks from the right. Whence this portrayal? Whence Kluge's oft-expressed doubts about abortion rights when there is no such doubt about

7. Dawson, *A. Kluge and Occasional Work*, 42.

such "clear-cut" cases as yellow journalism or multinational cor-
porations that are depicted negatively in the film?

An analysis of the film's perspective can thus clarify the reactionary view of reproductive rights which Kluge has couched
with apparent objectivity and ironic neutrality. There is more at
stake here, however. How does the spectator come to accept
these views within the experience of the film's exhibition? How
is the spectator made into a passive consumer of authorial
authority, unquestioningly constituting the film's meaning
according to the false choices dictated by the narrator?

The clues are lodged in yet another set of fraudulent contradictions, which are basic to this film and much of Kluge's other
work and are imposed upon the audience by the narrator at the
very beginning. The very first spoken narration tells us that
"Roswitha feels an enormous power within her, and films have
taught her that this power really exists." The words are coupled
with an excerpt from *Chapayev* (Sergei and Georgy Vasiliev,
USSR, 1934), the film that marked the turn from montage to
socialist realism as the feature of Soviet cinema. The "power"
that "really exists" is one of the political abilities as defined in a
revolutionary battle situation circa 1917. In the film excerpt,
the emotional peasant leader Chapayev, who is obstinate and
prone to acting instinctively, is taught "rational" leadership by
his comrade Lenin. Roswitha's character in Kluge's film may be
seen as a dramatic literalizing of this peasant metaphor. Kluge
assigns her to an essentially preliterate, irrational locus, consigned by her sex and her role within the family to act out, without mediation, illogically, and – consistently – ineffectually. The
narrator leads the viewer in laughing at this buffoon and her
stupid ways. In one case, even a feminist analysis of the film fol-
lowed this lead in praising the "screwball" comedy effected by
Kluge.[8]

In interviews, Kluge himself has denied that the humor
ridicules or demeans the character, indeed denies that
Roswitha's actions are necessarily intended as comedic. Instead,
Kluge offers a different view of the female characters that popu-
late his films: he idealizes the irrationality he had imposed upon

8. The best example of this is the piece written by Karyn Kay, originally
appearing in *Film Quarterly* and available now as "Part-Time Work of a Domestic
Slave, or Putting the Screws to Screwball Comedy," in *Women and the Cinema*, ed.
Karyn Kay and Gerald Peary (New York: Dutton, 1978).

them, praises the "chaos" from which new choices can potentially be constituted, and blasts logic as a supreme value. The
seeming contradiction between Kluge's praise of irrationality
and his film's ridicule of Roswitha's same irrationality provides
the clue to the film's most basic problem. The female/male
chaos/rationality dichotomy is, after all, a familar schema. In a
discussion of Althusser and psychoanalytic theories, Elizabeth
Wilson characterizes the nature of the discourse in a manner fit-
ting Kluge as well. She cites it as:

> the language used in political debate since time immemorial,
> whereby anarchy on the one hand and law and order on the other
> are posed as antagonistic opposites in order to discredit anarchy,
> i.e., chaos. Feminists should know better than to be taken in by
> this kind of language which constantly seeks to mask the progres-
> sive or revolutionary aspects of rebellion; rebellion is always stig-
> matized as flouting law and order and producing chaos.[9]

With Kluge, we encounter a minor variation on the theme.
Rather than stigmatizing chaos, he heroizes the stigmata with all
the fervor of a Noble Savage devotee. Deprived of rationality,
derided for this lack within the film even as she is lauded for it
by the author outside of the film, the character of Roswitha
must struggle to consciousness like some sort of primordial slug
struggling to emerge from the muck into life.

Kluge's true attitude regarding rationality (which Jessica Benjamin has so convincingly characterized as the religion of the
Federal Republic's fatherless patriarchy) is revealed in his
choice of narrative voice.[10] Despite his fervent support of irrationality, Kluge carefully preserves his narrator and narrative
voice from any such taint. In discussing the function of the
voice-over commentary in Kluge's film, Miriam Hansen pointed
out that "its own status remains unquestioned."[11] Kluge's disembodied voice clearly assumes the position of authority and
shapes the film according to its maxims. Chummed and
charmed by narrative complicity, the viewer identifies with the
narrator whose role as Kluge's surrogate is, by now, clear. Mean-

9. Elizabeth Wilson, "Psychoanalysis: Psychic Law and Order," *Feminist Review*
8 (1981): 76.
10. Jessica Benjamin, "Authority and the Family Revisited: Or, A World Without Fathers?" *New German Critique* 13 (Winter 1978): 35–38.
11. Miriam Hansen, "Cooperative Auteur Cinema and Oppositional Public
Sphere," *New German Critique* 24–25 (Fall/Winter 1981–82): 55.

while, the distantiated clinical treatment of Roswitha blocks her own subjectivity from view, just as the modernist avoidance of any realistic character construction prevents the viewer from making any sense of her motivations, goals, needs, or even identity. A modernist victim, Roswitha can claim no subjectivity in exchange for the rationality she forsakes. Nor does Kluge ever permit his own subjectivity ever to be at issue. He conceals his own biases and agendas beneath a layer of pseudo-factual contradiction. Behind this cover of false choices, however, he can be found manipulating the viewer into his corner through the use of an authoritarian narrator completely equipped with voice, titles, supporting texts, and even appropriate snippets of relevant films.

The narrator takes on the guise of a meta-character, offered up unproblematically for audience identification, smoothing over the real contradictions of the film's form in order to displace attention upon false contradictions taken to represent impossible obstacles to political consciousness or action. Pretending to offer a sympathetic analysis, Kluge instead offers a frame-up. Caught in it are not only the female protagonists of his films, but the women in the audience as well.

The writer Christa Wolf has called for a prose capable of giving people "the courage of their own experiences."[12] From Kluge, that is impossible. From Helke Sander, whose film quotes the words of Christa Wolf, that is requisite.

Helke Sander's *The All-Around Reduced Personality – REDUPERS*, like Kluge's film, focuses on the issues surrounding a particular period of time in a woman's life. Like Roswitha, Edda Chiemnajewski is a mother (but not a wife). She is also an artist and journalistic photographer, seen during the time that her women's photography group has received a commission from the city of Berlin. The issues of representation and political meaning that mark the women's project are equally those which dominate Sander's film.

Unlike Kluge, Sander does not construct a character outside the realms of language and logic. On the contrary, the film opens with a demonstration of Edda's mastery of language, as she translates an English message to her postman. Later, Edda is

12. Christa Wolf, "The Reader and the Writer," in *The Reader and the Writer: Essays, Sketches, Memories*, trans. Joan Becker (New York: International Publishers, 1977), 193.

seen in a number of freelance situations. She photographs an old people's party at which – as is typical for someone in a free-lance position trying to invest her work with a feminist con-sciousness – she overinvests her time and emotions. She demon-strably cannot collect enough money to pay for the time spent in this place, nor can she sell the photos she takes other than the banal man-at-podium snaps she has been assigned. Her involvement produces a surplus for which there is no compen-sation. This imbalance, consisting of the constant inability to tally an emotional and artistic accrual against a photojournalis-tic ledger sheet, builds throughout the film. It marks as well her other columns of imbalance: her home life balanced against her public obligations, her assignments versus her own photo project, etc. These imbalances produce the contradictions that permeate the film and which, in turn, form the subject which the film seeks to investigate. Unlike the Kluge/Roswitha ver-sion, here the contradictions are manifested not by an omni-scient narrator's instructions to the audience but instead through the direct visualization of the material conditions of Edda's life on the screen. The film's leitmotif is its central con-tradiction: the all-consuming wall is dividing the city in half ide-ologically, it seems, whereas in reality it is walling in West Berlin.

Most critics and viewers agree that the Kluge and Sander films are both located within a particular area of contemporary film-making which could be termed, more or less, modernist. In such a recognized, if vaguely defined, area as contemporary modernist cinema, certain assumptions are operative. The tenets hold that a self-interruptive text provides the appropriate rupture with linear narrative or transparent narrativity; that an uninflected voice-over provides the distinction necessary to pre-vent an unmediated identification with a character that, after all, is not a "character" at all; that nonpsychological progres-sions, furthering formal requirements rather than plot con-cerns, shape the structure; that such a structure, meditative in tone, combining elements of realistic depiction with materials drawn from other films and sources of representation, ensures that the viewer will have to construct the film actively from its parts, thus in the process securing liberation from the trap of passive consumption; and that a mix of fiction and documen-tary modes will disrupt genre conventions, throw the elements of genre into dialectical opposition, and throw into doubt the notion of a fixed "truth" representable on screen, thereby securing the viewer's complete engagement in the labor of producing meaning. Assuming that these criteria are equally supported by the two films under consideration here, any differences become of paramount interest. Ann Snitow, in the article cited above, called for an investigation into "the problems and contradictions in the way modernism descended into the female line."[13] The comparison of Sander's film with the parallel Kluge work demonstrates forcefully the causes of such problems, given the nature of modernism, and casts doubt upon the radical political claims made for its form once viewed within a feminist context.

The narrative voiceover in *REDUPERS* is more discursive, self-interrupting, and nonhegemonic than the corresponding voice in the Kluge film. Unlike the male Klugian narrator, the female voice of Sander's film does not set out to control audience response or to undermine the protagonist with superior wit. There are marked shifts in the narrative locus from scene to scene, opening up the route of identification from an individual bonding to a collective process.

Frequently, the voiceover offers entry into the thoughts of the protagonist, though devoid of any attendant drama or motivational closure. As Edda photographs an anti-rape demonstration, the viewer is told that "she thinks that not enough of her socially significant photos are bought." At other times, the observations seem less those of an observer than the interior voice of a self-deprecating character: "At age thirty-four she decides to do something for her body." At certain points, the position of the narrative voice shifts from this sympathetic proximity to a more Klugian, detached, data-prone chronicler, as in one scene of a meeting of Edda's women photographers' project: "The group continued the futile discussion for some time." Shortly after, though, the narrator turns downright low-key, remarking only that "all kinds of people come to her" as a pair of art-world hustlers try to con her. Similarly, as her schedule careens out of control with overload, the narrator remarks "Monday – the Sunday paper – have to keep up to date."

Such jibes are not entirely out of line with those of the Klugian voice, yet the effect of the voiceover in the Sander film is utterly different, both in its effect upon the film text and upon

13. Snitow, "Sex in Novels by Women," 161.

the spectator. The most reductive explanation, and a persuasive one, focuses on the difference between Sander's utilization of a woman narrator to speak for and comment upon a woman character, whereas Kluge imposes a male voice upon a female subject. It is a fundamental and determining difference, but for formal reasons rather than simply those of gender identification. The difference arises from the disparate sources of the two styles, with Kluge proceeding from the political base of a post-Frankfurt-School modernist aesthetic and Sander proceeding from the feminist political base of writing and filmmaking made by women for an audience of women. At a few points they may coincide, as when Kluge's narrator quotes proverbs and moral tales with a panache of irony, while Sander matches the proverbs with a very different popular-culture source: the radio. Yet Sander's narrator goes on to quote from the writings of Christa Wolf. The difference in film quotations are even more revealing. Kluge picks *Chapayev* as one model, whereas Sander sandwiches three different films made by women onto the screen at once. The three films (by Valie Export, Yvonne Rainer, and Ursula Reuter-Christiansen) are layered atop a newspaper that fills that frame, which is itself overlayed by the words of a letter read on the soundtrack. Over the facts of women's lives asserted within the newspaper, Sander superimposes the private words of women's letters and the unprecedented film images of women's imagination and self-definition of daily life.

The major break with Kluge's narrative model might be pinpointed in Sander's rejection of hegemony and authority as narrative qualities. A clue can be found in one otherwise unexceptional scene: in the home darkroom where she prints her photographs, Edda is finishing up her latest order. A voiceover, assumed to be the narrator initially, turns out to belong instead to an off-screen character carrying on a conversation with Edda. The same confusion occurs again in a meeting of the women's group, at which a seemingly authoritative narrative pronouncement turns out to be spoken by another character. Such confusion would never transpire in a Kluge film, for there is no possibility of any such case of mistaken identity. Kluge's characters do not share in the narrative authority granted to his *deus ex machina*. There is no possibility of inclusion: his woman protagonist suffers the same exclusion from her own history within the film that women have suffered for years under patriarchal record-keeping. In Sander's films, the other characters do not just share in the narrative authority; rather the authoritarianism of narration is avoided in favor of a relationship that sounds at times more like conversation than any hierarchical ordering of narrative truth. In earlier writings, I have contended that such structuring and narrative voice in the feminist cinema can be termed a "cinema of correspondence" due both to its base in the historical unpublished writing of women and to the correspondences between women's lives and the shape of these works.[14]

As Christa Wolf's writing is quoted extensively in *REDUPERS*, it is particularly appropriate to refer to an assessment of Wolf in light of the feminist tradition in the United States. Myra Love assesses the narrative style of Wolf's work in terms that fit *REDUPERS* equally well:

> The prose writing of Christa Wolf . . . makes use of the self-inter-rupting and non-linear methods of communication which charac-terize conversation. . . . She demystifies authorship by removing it from its traditional position of depersonalized authority and returning it to its function as a means of social communication.[15]

The link between author and viewer is a solid one for Sander. It is a link that proffers an easy crossing to the narrator without any need for pulling rank. After all, *REDUPERS* was made in the spring of 1977 (not yet the fateful autumn of Kluge's next film contribution), as the state apparatus was coming down soundly on the heads of the women's movement in the Federal Republic. The comrades in arms invisible to Kluge's Roswitha – the femi-nist health workers – were being busted under the very same laws used against so-called terrorism.[16] Sander was a part of this situation and at one with this world, and it shows. Her narrator speaks *to* as well as *with* both character and viewer. The narrative voice may be fragmented in its identity, free to float from locus to locus, but it is absolutely unified in terms of its sympathies.

Given such a style and voice, *REDUPERS* is able to pose con-tradictions to us, not as a trump card of doom, but as an

14. See my own "The Crisis of Naming in Feminist Film Criticism," orginally published in *Jump Cut* 19 (1979): 9–12, and republished in different form as "In the Name of Feminist Film Criticism," in *Heresies* 9 (1980): 74–81.

15. Myra Love, "Christa Wolf and Feminism: Breaking the Patriarchal Con-nection," *New German Critique* 16 (Winter 1979): 34.

16. See the materials presented in *New German Critique* 13, as well as the sum-mary of the *Frauen und Film* critiques of Kluge quoted and summarized in Daw-son's *Alexander Kluge*.

inevitable foundation upon which lives and ideologies may be, however provisionally, constructed. In place of Kluge's false contradiction of privatized political fervor tilting against overwhelming state power, Sander provides a view of collective work in the very area of representation (a women's image-making project) within which the film being seen is itself inscribed.

The differences between the two films are extended and further accentuated when their treatments of the function of "seeing" are examined. In *Part-Time Work*, Roswitha's trust in her own act of seeing is a foolish and naive one that undermines her political work and diminishes her strength in the eyes of the viewer. This is a key scene. Wanting to prove that the Beauchamp factory is indeed being built in Portugal and thus expose their denial as a lie, Roswitha drives all the way there to find out for herself. Sure enough, she finds the site of the factory construction. She returns with the knowledge of the site, but she does not think to replicate the knowledge in the form of a photograph. She does not realize that her personal vision, externalized as a photo, would become evidence. The Klugian narrator therefore presents the viewer with this monumental miscalculation as a self-destructive act of political folly. When Helke Sander and the other editors of *Frauen und Film* (then newly formed) attacked the film, they particularly cited this stupidity which had been foisted upon the character. Kluge was prone to justify the choice *not* to make a photograph: in a peculiar fetishization of "lack of access" as a positive value, Kluge has chosen to frame the non-action as a touching testimony of the working-class faith in words. Thus, with an element of perversity, Kluge transformed exclusion from technology into an act of choice.

Given the chance four years later, Helke Sander redressed the balance. In *REDUPERS*, the women have an ease with the technology of representation and free access to the world of imagistic "truth," yet the true fundamental problems that had been masked by Kluge's tactic here persist. First, the women's ability to create photographs carries no assurance that the photographs will be granted legitimacy as any sort of evidence. When Edda visits an editor to encourage the publishing of a photo portfolio in his magazine, she is treated badly and turned away; when a newspaper publishes her photojournalistic photo, she is not credited and most likely not even paid. For Kluge's film to imply a change of fate based on the mere taking of a photograph in Portugal is for Kluge to indulge in uncharacteristic political naiveté. Further, for his film to equate the taking of a photograph with the political understanding of image-making is to reveal just how far from a feminist aesthetic we have wandered. To be able to make images, women must still overcome the obstacle of discovering how, truly, to see. In a paper presented at Graz, Austria, in 1977, Helke Sander wrote:

> Women today find themselves in a situation which is perhaps best comparable to that of Kaspar Hauser or the wild child. They must first learn to see with their own eyes and not through the mediation of others.[17]

Thus Sander draws the opposite lesson from the same comparison motivating Kluge. Whereas Kluge can celebrate woman's exclusion as a sign of purity, Sander is looking for the route out of the situation.

At one point in *REDUPERS*, the narrator comments that Edda is "obsessed with daily life as other women see it." The emphasis is upon the act of seeing, both as a metaphor for and an acting out of feminism. Sander is not content to describe woman as inscribed within patriarchy or as, in Kluge's idealist view, outside the gates of the city and the limits of logic. *REDUPERS* reveals its feminist assumptions within its language, images, and structure. The emphasis on vision is collectivized and thus granted the dimension of a political struggle. The inclusion of the three films by women, all concerned with the surreal banalities of everyday life, represents the shared concern of women artists in the 1970s "to see with their own eyes." By including these films in her own, Sander is claiming the political dimension of the filmmakers' work and supporting the claim made by Snitow on behalf of women novelists: that the making of "visionary recombinations" is one kind of political work.

Like all political work, this one carries its attendant risks. The risk, as might be guessed from the vaunting tone of Kluge's narrator, is a familiar one for feminists: ridicule. In one of the key moments in *REDUPERS*, the women's photography group is

17. Helke Sander, "Feminism and Film," trans. Ramona Curry, *Jump Cut* 27 (1982): 50. From a talk originally given at Graz, Austria, 1977, entitled "I like chaos, but I don't know whether chaos like me." See the entire Special Section in this issue of *Jump Cut*: "New German Women's Cinema," especially the contextualizing essays by Renny Harrigan and Marc Silberman, for a sense of German feminist film activity.

preparing a billboard-sized blow-up of one of Edda's photographs of the Berlin wall. They are seen mounting the giant photograph onto a frame to carry out into the streets of the city on a test expedition aimed at evaluating their plan to install a number of such billboards equipped with their photos. Unsure how successful the images will be on this scale, out in the unsheltered, ungallerylike jungle of representational overload, the women have agreed to try one outing as a test. The narrator intervenes with some added information for the viewer, to wit: "a male friend makes fun of them for carrying out their ideas." In other words, the women are ridiculed for literalizing instead of conceptualizing their process. The women's distrust of stopping at working the idea out on paper (of merely *imagining* the effect) is held by this unseen commentator to be a ludicrous deficiency, an inadequacy to be squelched with ridicule. The women's commitment to physical process is perceived by the male friend as a lack of abstract conceptual ability. Such a perspective hearkens back to the familiar Kluge narrator, casting a rather jaundiced light upon that narrator's smug ridicule of Roswitha's activities as irrational blunders meriting ridicule. Here, male ridicule is subject to bounds of containment: it is held to an off-screen account, mediated by a different narrative voice, meant as a necessary reminder of a major patriarchal weapon (ridicule) used against early feminist activity, against women's efforts to embody a new vision, and revived increasingly now as a tactic of the anti-feminist backlash.

Through her choices of which material to visualize on-screen, which to sequester off-screen, and which remarks to assign directly to the narrative voice, Sander continually demonstrates an effort to encourage women to see with their own eyes and speak in their own voice. The effort marks the two final points that require attention here: the significance of the term with which the female protagonist is named ("I" or "She") and the significance of the other voices which the narrator/author quotes to substantiate an identity. Judith Mayne, in her extensive analysis of *REDUPERS*, has concentrated on this issue of articulating an evasive self-definition.[18] Mayne situates Sander's

18. Judith Mayne, "Female Narration, Women's Cinema," *New German Critique* 24–25 (Fall/Winter 1981–82): 155–171. Mayne goes into far more detail on the film than I have been able to cover here, and is the best source for a coherent description of both its narrative and stylistic qualities. See especially her comparison of the film with its Godardian counterpart.

film within a feminist novelistic tradition and follows the film's lead back to the words of Christa Wolf, whose narrator/protagonist in *The Quest for Christa T.* is engaged in a search for:

> the secret of the third person, who is there without being tangible and who, when circumstances favor her, can bring down more reality upon herself than the first person: I.[19]

The difficulty of saying "I" has been a central subject for many contemporary feminist authors, most notably Monique Wittig. The extent of alienation, silence, and containment has been so vast that women, accustomed to speaking for so long in the voice of a male syntax, have had to undertake a political struggle to reclaim language. In the cinema, of course, this language encompasses the lexicon of images as well as words. The shadowy "I" has to be located, often hidden in the domain of the "she." The narrator in *REDUPERS* fulfills this very function of struggling to adapt/invent language. The lack of an hegemonic narrative voice, as pointed out earlier, reflects in all its shifts and contradictions this precise struggle to name the self by finding the voice of that intangible "third person." The shifts between an interior and exterior discourse, between an objective and subjective narration, are precisely the tactics of stalking the self. The narrator may be seen, then, as an active agent working in conjunction with the active viewer; the two become partners in the collective enterprise of fashioning a feminist voice.

Part of this enterprise is the enlistment of allies and sources. Within *REDUPERS*, the narrator refers to the words of Christa Wolf and the films of a trio of women filmmakers, while the characters themselves appeal to friends, old allies, and experts in their quest for reassurance. In the Kluge film, the lessons of *Chapayev* are paramount; Roswitha reads theoretical texts, takes tours of workers' housing, and learns the songs of Brecht; but she never finds the words of other women, nor does the Klugian narrator have any occasion to quote them. The Sander film can be inscribed within a context of feminist writing and filmmaking in part because this context is itself inscribed, by Sander, within the film. The anti-feminism of the Kluge film can be discerned, just as plainly, from its exclusions of similar material. Criticism is prone to the same examinations: a feminist critical

19. Christa Wolf, *The Quest for Christa T.* (trans. Christopher Middleton, New York: Delta, 1970), 170.

context depends upon the ongoing work of building ideas, quoting sources, extending arguments. If feminist critics sometimes falter on this point, it may be that we suffer from a problem that Myra Love, in her article on Wolf, pinpointed as a trouble spot for feminist novelists. Love hypothesized that the longtime silence of women in literature was due, not entirely to a lack of the means to use written language, but rather to "the lack of practice in occupying the position of authority which has traditionally characterized authorship."[20]

REDUPERS is a particularly significant film in that Sander takes as her subject the real labor of representation – photography, picture making – and positions that work ambiguously out in the world: as collective labor, as political process, as hard and contradictory and inevitable. The usual power relations which dominate the interaction between male narrator and female subject are not replicated, as they are so cleverly by Kluge. More important, neither are the power relations that have long characterized, covertly, the interaction between the male narrator and the female viewer . . . or female critic. A feminist modernism insists on holding the narrator to the same codes of anti-authoritarianism and nonhierarchical processes that have long characterized the women's movement. In place of the exempted and fetishized author, there is a demystified author intent at working together with the view to construct, not merely the film text, but a new vision, a different society, a feminist locus of production and reception. The least that we can do, as feminist critics, is to match this accomplishment with a worthy critical theory. It is an obligation reiterated with some urgency by Elizabeth Wilson in her divergence from current psychoanalytic feminism:

> The last thing feminists need is a theory that teaches them only to marvel anew at the constant recreation of the subjective reality of subordination and which reasserts male domination more securely than ever within theoretical discourse. . . . To change the conditions of work – in the work and in the home – might do more for our psyches as well as our pockets than an endless contemplation of how we came to be chained.[21]

The creation and explication of a feminist modernism is important to any further development of a feminist film aes-

20. Love, "Breaking the Patriarchal Connection," 41.
21. Wilson, "Psychic Law and Order," 76.

thetic or its theory. It may be that the two dominant modes of contemporary cinema which we discuss today – namely, capitalist escapism and patriarchal modernism – will continue to characterize film culture in our alienated society for some time to come. In the cinematic tradition of patriarchal modernism exemplified by Kluge's *Part-Time Work of a Domestic Slave,* irony and distanciation replace identification, the absent but controlling author stands in for the visible father, rationalism is simultaneously deployed and derided, and woman (when such a figure appears) is merely the figment of an idealist imagination. Sander's *The All-Around Reduced Personality – REDUPERS* presents an alternative to such a modernist hall of mirrors. In this example of modernist cinema as descended into the female line, the narrative is discursive rather than controlling, the narrator is female and benign, contradiction is an accepted assumption, daily life is a proper subject for visualization, the choice of subject can encompass the political in all its manifestations, humor does not mitigate against the characters, and an engagement with the viewer is an essential requirement. The narrator is not a figure set apart at the top of a hierarchical pyramid, analogous to the absent father-figure signing his name to the movie. Rather, the narrator in a work of feminist modernism problematizes the power relations within the viewing process, much as the earliest works of cinematic modernism first sought to problematize the power relations within the film text itself.

Only by undertaking a study of feminist modernism, in Sander and other filmmakers (especially those engaged in the "cinema of correspondence"), can we assess its true significance and begin to recognize the power of the narrator in a film politics that has gone unexamined too long.

* * *

Thanks are due here to Ramona Curry, who first prompted my thoughts on this subject by inviting me to give a lecture at the Chicago Goethe Institute as part of the Kluge retrospective she had programmed there in 1980. Readers should note that, due to my own lack of fluency in German, all seeming quotations are actually taken either from printed texts or from subtitles on the screen (a notoriously unreliable referent).

Reprinted from Discourse *6 (Fall 1983): 31–47.*

13

Interview with Helke Sander: Open Forms

marc   silberman

We reprint here Marc Silberman's interview with filmmaker Helke Sander, which first appeared in Jump Cut 29 (1984). Sander discusses the beginnings of her career and her film REDUPERS.
—THE EDITORS

I was always ahead of my time with my films. In 1969 a project of mine about the women's movement was a novelty, and no one was interested. What's more, the funding commissions told me since a known feminist couldn't possibly be objective, I couldn't do it. Then they were so disgusted with my film project about menstruation (to be called *Red Period*), they didn't even want to deal with the topic. It was meant to be neither an educational nor a documentary film, but a film about myths; for it, I was advised to try for ten minutes on the weekly TV health program! The projects I have devoted a lot of work to, the ones I really wanted to make, never succeeded.

I became politically active with the Springer film (*Crush the Power of the Manipulators*, 1967/8). I didn't want to adapt some crazy popular idea of art. We filmmakers had discussions then trying to figure out how to still make films, didactic ones that relied on a form that was understandable and accessible to the audience. Yet a completely false conception of filmmaking was developed in this school of Berlin Workers' films. My next film, *A Bonus for Irene*, in the tradition of the Berlin Workers' films, in some ways critiques the tradition. I strove to translate political content directly into film, and only slowly moved away from that position, recognizing that it came to no more than slogans.

I also faced a problem of isolation. If a film took up a political issue, television networks wouldn't make funding available, so we had to produce films for political meetings with little money or material. Many filmmakers felt obliged simply to document something when officially there was no information about it. And political groups were suspicious of "aesthetics." This reductionism was mutually conditioned.

In *REDUPERS* I took up once again something I had already done, but now with a different consciousness. In the sixties I'd been doing theatre and made some short films, but I was interrupted when the whole political movement began. *REDUPERS* reflects on what was left behind. I did not intend to *show* change but rather *how* minimal changes may come about, how things happen simultaneously. I tried to examine how we think and in what categories we articulate feelings, and what the consequences would be if we were to think like the women in the film. In other words, I ask the viewer to consider a given situation from an alternative perspective, namely a divided Berlin from a woman's perspective. It's a subversive procedure, perhaps even a form of utopia. The viewer must think out the consequences on her/his own.

I vehemently resist any attempt to ghettoize my films as "women's films." Men or women can interpret any situation. The way I see life necessarily has something to do with my experiences, and women's experiences are, of course, different from men's.

I have had some experience in trying to gain access to institutions. For example, in 1974, founding the film journal *frauen und film* represented our effort to articulate the problems that women have in this profession. We faced unbelievable criticism, a defamation of the whole attempt. Professional female film critics did not want to participate at first in something so controversial, something that might fail. Women filmmakers doing their own thing were not really looking for publicity. The journal strove to codify women filmmakers' problems in order to remedy them, and it has made a real contribution here. We reviewed the few films by women that existed at the time, which were too often rejected by festivals because we had no lobby and only men in the juries, who didn't understand what the women were doing in their films. In addition, as a result of the women's movement, public consciousness no longer brands everyone as crazy who points to sexism in the media.

I am especially concerned with developing new production methods. When we receive a contract and financial support (from a network, prize money, or producers), we have to show results very quickly – for example, a completed script. I would prefer to work more essayistically, filming very slowly, and then maybe finishing up quickly. I don't want a filming schedule which says you film the script in thirty consecutive days, engaging each actor weeks in advance. I want to write *while* filming and work together *with* the actors. I don't want to chase them through a scene, each one standing in the 'right' corner for the 'right' angle.

I imagine preconceived situations, with an idea about how they will look in the film; elements of tension and changes come when I see actual image. That is my point of reference, not some idea about an image: concrete images come into relation with other concrete images. I can imagine a rather open form somewhere between fiction and documentary – as in *REDUPERS* – where fictional people enter documentary films. I want to continue working in this direction, but find no money for such a form. We get money based on our scripts, which must be completely written to submit to the various funding commissions. That implies certain compromises if I do not want to accept the repressive nature of the script.

Reprinted from Jump Cut *29 (1984): 60.*

14

German Grotesque: Two Films by Sander and Ottinger

r u t h   p e r l m u t e r

Ruth Perlmutter discusses Helke Sander's The Trouble with Love *(1984)* and Ulrike Ottinger's The Mirror Image of Dorian Gray in the Yellow Press *(also 1984). Ulrike Ottinger is the daughter of painters and was herself trained as a painter, and the images created in her surrealistic films have often been called "painterly" (although her sensibility has also been described by Angela McRobbie as "lesbian/punk"). Helke Sander, as we have noted previously, can be seen to stand in another avant-garde tradition, the tradition of Brecht* The press ball in Ulrike Ottinger's The Mirror Image of Dorian Gray in the Yellow Press (1984). (Photo courtesy of Ulrike Ottinger)

and Godard. Perlmutter chooses a category intended to cover films by both of these very different directors, describing Ottinger's Dorian Gray *and Sander's* The Trouble with Love *as "baroque neo-grotesque."*
—THE EDITORS

I.

Working individually, and largely in control of their own work, Helke Sander and Ulrike Ottinger produce uncanonized films that are generally inaccessible to a mass audience. They seem to spurn as well the popular "auteur" role adopted by Herzog, and (although begrudgingly) by Fassbinder.[1] Although stylistically disparate, they are bold, aggressive, and have as their goal the invention of new visual and auditory models for politically subversive comedy. Their humor relies heavily on a dismantling of linear narrative, a strong dose of the grotesque, and a kind of sullen, abrasive black humor, unlike the more entertaining appeal of American black humor. From an American perspective, given only the few works we get to see – and these, certainly not on the commercial circuit – their recent films, *The Trouble With Love* (1984), and *The Mirror Image of Dorian Gray in the Yellow Press* (1984) appear to contribute to an emergent style in German filmmaking today. One could call it baroque neo-grotesque.[2]

In their tendency to wild hyperbole and farce, they bear a family resemblance to some of their artistic predecessors. The flamboyant delirium of Ottinger's work reflects the tableaux effects of Syberberg's avant-garde epics and Werner Schroeter's parodies of opera and film. Sander makes use of Kluge's compilation "strands," whereby an interspersion of highly stylized fictions and archival collage material explores the "power of emotions" (title of a Kluge film), that is, the problematic of a patriarchal society in its principal struggle between the needs of the individual or the family and the constraints of the political economy. Both filmmakers seem to be influenced by Fassbinder's brand of brooding, absurdist kitsch – garish, unsentimental, and often revelling in intentional bad taste.[3]

In terms of a correspondence with external realities, their texts tend to mirror pre-unification West German issues, such as a frenzied consumerist buildup, divisiveness caused by Berlin's separation and a continual obsession with the effects of Nazism and the war's useless destruction. As prominent women filmmakers in Germany, their feminist stance is markedly satirical, not only of male manipulation of media and personal relation-

1. Thomas Elsaesser, "Achternbusch and the German Avant-Garde," *Discourse* 6 (Fall 1983): 93.

2. This new mannerism has extended beyond German borders to disparate films like Beneix's *Moon in the Gutter*, the American musical *Pennies From Heaven*, and some recent work of the Coppola studio, like *One From the Heart* and *Hammet*.

3. This trend is mostly exemplified by Fassbinder's later period, especially *The Third Generation* and *Querelle*.

ships, but also of feminist naiveté. Rather than a positive clarion call for altered ways of seeing the objectified image of women based on the male gaze, these new films seem to ridicule men for their childishness, while they also satirize women who try to supplant men with the same sexist models.

II. The Trouble With Love

Although Helke Sander's feminism is immersed in contradiction and pessimism, it stems from questioning the false idealism of a smug, uncritical, middle-class passivity. *The Trouble With Love* continues the formal and political concerns of her first film, *The All-Around Reduced Personality*, 1977 (also called *REDUPERS*). Again, she creates separate discourse shifts and sound/image "strands" (melodrama, parody, documentary) that register different planes of reality. Her montage method provides a kind of eccentric ironic humor that tends to undermine the surface of seriousness. As in *REDUPERS*, despite the visual and verbal puns that poke wry fun at a particular emotional state, *The Trouble With Love* is tinged with despair about the inescapable link between sexism and social and political repression. Both films suggest that elemental tensions in political and personal life build walls that prevent full development of a whole personality, while the complexity of the political economy of Germany and Europe offers no easy solutions.

The title of Sander's new film implies that "the trouble with love" is that love or, at least, open relationships, are troublesome. (The title in German is even more emphatic: *The Beginning of All Terror is Love*.) In Sander's film as in those of her mentor, Alexander Kluge,[4] every personal tale refers not only to the larger political milieu of postwar Germany, but also to the ever-present awareness of the Nazi period and its legacy.[5] Thus, the triangular love relationship of two women who alternately share one man and suffer fits of jealousy because of this emotional

4. B. Ruby Rich, "She Says, He Says: The Power of the Narrator in Modernist Film Politics," *Discourse* 6 (Fall 1983) (reprinted in this volume). Rich suggests that Sander's strong feminist stance as exhibited in her particular voice-over style differentiates her work from Alexander Kluge's.

5. Lenssen, Fehervary, Mayne, "From Hitler to Hepburn: A Discussion of Women's Film Production and Reception," *New German Critique* 24-25 (Fall/Winter 1981-82): 172-185. Lenssen suggests that it is important for feminist filmmakers in Germany not to "ignore fascism and its historical context as a significant segment of recent German history" (173).

ping-pong game is presented as an extended metaphor of "troubled waters," with continual linkages made between the errors of the past, the male dominance struggle, and personal freedom. As in *REDUPERS*, Sander repeats the inescapable connection between sexism and social/political repression.

Her method is paratactic: a string of disjunctive sequences, repeated images, shifting female narrative voices, and points of view set up opposing metaphoric relationships. Contrary to the "under-narrative" practice of silent denial and rejection as a feminist stance, as in Akerman's *Jeanne Dielmann . . . and Handke's The Left-Handed Woman*,[6] the female narrative voices in Sander's film are overtly aggressive and hostile toward men, as well as self-mocking.[7]

Here is Freya, the protagonist (played by the filmmaker), phoning her lover Traugott and begging him to come to her. As she phones him, she watches him on a mini-TV on her lap as he is interviewed about his political beliefs. Meanwhile, the narrative voice-over evaluates the quality of their emotional relationship. She says, "In this relationship, it is now 1933," at which point there is a still photo of the burning Reichstag. On one hand, here is a woman whose life revolves around a man, and on the other hand, a political comparison is made in conjunction with her personal struggle. Thus, each sequence opens out to the next without definitive resolution or explanation, yet suggesting various stages of a disaffected love affair and with inserts that hint of connections between male domination, war, and fascism.

Image/sound correlatives for the degradation of Freya's relations with Traugott accumulate in the ensuing sequences. As Freya walks along the Hamburg harbor, the image disjuncts to a dark wood, and she bays to the moon like a love-struck wounded animal (a pose she affects throughout). She then sits on the harbor steps, accidentally putting her hand into a pile of feces, while a disjunctive cutaway to Traugott in his doctor's uniform shows him standing in a bathroom stall, with defecation pour-

6. See my article on under-narrative films and feminism: "Visible Narrative, Visible Woman: A Study of Under-narratives," *Millenium Film Journal* (Spring 1980).

7. Sander's own description of *REDUPERS* implies her general *comedic* intent, which, I believe, she exhibits in *The Trouble With Love* as well. She sees *REDUPERS* as a "rather comic contribution to the question of why women so seldom make much of their lives." John Sandford, *The New German Cinema* (New York: DeCapo, 1980), 142.

ing from a drain above him (Freya's wish fulfillment?). These signs of their degenerate relationship are reinforced by the irony of the mythical significance, especially in German culture, of their names: Freya, Wotan's wife, was Goddess of the hearth and of marital fidelity, and present-day Freya battles with her jealousies, fluctuating between love and despair, while exhibiting feminist anger and desire for vengeance. The name Traugott has a patriarchal ring. Meaning "Trust in God," it is attached to an unregenerate, self-involved egotist.

Metaphoric relationships constitute part of the paratactic method of *The Trouble With Love*. The film opens with a whole tongue being sliced, accompanied by images of a mother and child – one of many dialectical pairings – severing/male-female dissension vs. bonding/infantile state. The tongue and the mother/child dyad operate as feminist references both to castration and to the desire to invent a feminist "language." As if to reinforce female authority, the off-screen female narrator comments on the emotional desires and justifications for some of the images. At one point, along with a shot of Freya and Traugott together, the voice-over wryly states, "That's why she loves him." At another time, when Traugott is campaigning for the rights of prisoners, the voice-over states, "The screenwriter found a good man for Freya." As in *REDUPERS*, the images and the voice-over operate as separate independent strands: the protagonist as filmmaker, who presents her subjective feelings, the "I"; the public expression of all women, the "she"; and a "third person," the voice of the new feminist who is conscious of altering male-centered discourse and therefore has another (feminist) perspective on language, history and cinema.[8]

Sander uses repeated images to intensify her metaphoric connections. She continually cuts to the images of a tugboat – both a toy one on a stormy "sea" and a real one in Hamburg harbor – to symbolize the tempestuous relationship and its adolescent affinities. On one hand, the toy boat is associated with the growing realization that the shared male love object is infantile and must be abandoned. On the other, the actual boat is where the male lover operatically drags off Freya's rival. His sadistic indecisiveness about his commitment to each woman is ascribed to

8. Christa Wolf, a contemporary German woman novelist, raises these pronominal distinctions as an issue of female narration. See Judith Mayne, "Female Narration, Women's Cinema: Helke Sander's *The All-Round Reduced Personality/REDUPERS*," *New German Critique* 24–25 (Fall/Winter 1981–82).

his shady fascist lineage (his father was an SS officer), although he has compensated by becoming a doctor and by defending political prisoners. He is concerned about others on a public level but remains woefully adolescent in his personal relationships. The metaphor of childishness is humorously extended when Traugott contracts a children's disease and again there is a cutaway to the toy boat on stormy waters.

Uncertainty about the sexism women masochistically tolerate is also expressed through connections between images/sounds and metaphor. A woman knits in a maternity ward. Scenes of people knitting are repeated, and later, we see completed hand-knit socks in Freya's bedroom. Another time, Freya examines a honeypot sent by Traugott, and then is seen in a restaurant, desolately lapping up jam from a jampot, as if substituting with sweets for the lack of a love object. Still later, indicative of Traugott's accumulated conciliatory gestures, we see a lineup of preserves, ranged on shelves above Freya's head. Both sets of sequences are witty metaphors for the passage of time that also record the mercurial changes in the unrequited relationship. Since these images occur when Freya is in a sentimental self-pitying mood because of the breakup with Traugott, they suggest that traditional feminine preoccupations and sublimations are self-destructive.

Masochistic uncertainties over the sexism that women permit are also expressed through references to other films. Sander intercuts a scene from *The Lacemaker*, in which Isabel Huppert shyly explains to her lover that she has no friends and then contradictorily suggests that she had already been to Mykonos with someone else. Somewhat later, Freya and Traugott discuss *The Lacemaker*, which they agree demonstrates that people should never be excessively dependent on love. Underlying the choice of that particular film with its description of female dependency is a critique of Freya's tacit consent to self-denial in her obsessive *amour fou* with Traugott. Another time, a group of women stand in front of a poster of *Manhattan*, arguing about how the character Woody Allen played wanted to run over his wife and her girlfriend because they were lesbian lovers. A double irony in a film about sexism, these movie references to sexism in films by men exemplify the "passions" in and out of film that manipulate and seduce women. They also attempt a critique of real relations rather than those engendered by the constraints of commercial cinema. In "worrying" over cross-gender problems which are reflected in the oscillation between jealousy, passionate female-to-female affections, and a genuine distaste for adolescent male pride, the film grapples with problems of sexual difference, symbiotic bonding needs, and the underlying political basis of all relationships.

Somewhere toward the end, once Traugott has sailed away with the other woman, a more dispassionate Freya quotes a line from Adorno: "Take care lest your own powerlessness and the powers of others defeat you."[9] While the quote is a warning about the troubling nature of love, it also reflects on the equally troubling linkage between sexual politics and the public realm. As in *REDUPERS*, Sander presents the contradictions in feminist aspirations and obdurate social realities. The ironic theme of the film suggests that while feminism is an irreversible political force, its goals have not yet been tested in the arena of real personal relationships.

III.

Ulrike Ottinger's film, *The Mirror-Image of Dorian Gray in the Yellow Press*, parodies the misogynistic grounding of genre films. Instead of Fritz Lang's male conspirator, Dr. Mabuse, the film's villainess is Frau Dr. Mabuse, who rules over a video-dominated "metropolis." Lang's heavy melodrama is replaced by Ottinger's highly theatricalized allegory and radical comedy. Color and costume-coded props, practical jokes, and personified characters mock the superficiality of the clichés, sexism, and social conventions of traditional movies.

Originally a painter, Ottinger plays surrealistically with many levels of theatrical representation and film parody. In her use of campy flamboyant sets and costumes, she is distinctly heir to Werner Schroeter's wild and often outrageous parodic innovations.[10] All her own, however, is the startling way she allegorizes the female assertiveness of her protagonist. Played by Delphine Seyrig (favorite of the feminist avant garde, in Duras's *India Song* and Akerman's *Jeanne Dielman*), Frau Dr. Mabuse is the

9. After the Cannes screening in 1984, Sander herself acknowledged that this quote had come from a Kluge film. She neglected to mention which.
10. Roswitha Mueller, "Interview With Ulrike Ottinger," *Discourse* 4 (Winter 1981–82). Ottinger affirms her admiration of Schroeter, with whom she had worked.

head of a multinational press organization. Revamping the media's male sexist manipulations of gender, beauty, and sensationalist story telling, Frau Dr. Mabuse methodically conjures up a new Narcissus, Dorian Gray, to be the "willing victim" of her Machiavellian strategies.

The film opens with an exquisite visual tableau reminiscent of David Hockney's limpid canvases. In a high-vaulted, empty space that is festooned with a triangle of gaily colored flags, the playboy/girl, Dorian Gray (played by the model, Verushka) sits suspended on a pedestal pulling on giant oars. While the credits blink across in the style of teletype, the scene switches to a cavernous sewer along which move small neon-lit boats covered with green plastic, and three women, dressed like Futurist versions – in high heels and black leather – of the witches from Macbeth, troop after Frau Dr. Mabuse into her conference room. There, representatives of the world newspapers, Mr. Charles Chronicle, Mr. Standard Telegraph, Mr. Pogo-Pogo Express, give a financial report that explains their failure to control the events of the day. Frau Mabuse shows her displeasure by exploding their cigars. She then announces her plan, called "Operation Mirror," to take Dorian Gray, who is "handsome but boring," and mold him/her into the protagonist of a serial romance that will addict and expand readership.

Unlike his/her namesake in Oscar Wilde's novella, Ottinger's Dorian Gray is fashioned more for political than aesthetic purposes. S/he is designed to furnish the yellow press with fictitious scandals and catastrophes. As Mabuse claims: "We will build him up, seduce him, destroy him and thoroughly exploit in word and picture each and every phase in every conceivable way for our media." In order to stage newsworthy stories, Mabuse, like a latter-day Dante, leads Dorian through a nightmare world, into a series of self-reflexive situations, evocative of the "mirrorings" suggested by the title. A cross between a Lacanian mirror-stage spectator and a figure in a Las Menianas-like allegory of the strategies of viewing, s/he watches himself suffer in some eternal theatrical time warp.

Ottinger, like Sander, grounds her own unique grotesque vision in a framework of visual and verbal jokes. Although camera action is often the instrument of comedy (the camera pulls away from Frau Mabuse's "American" breakfast to reveal a tray full of vitamins and pills), the major sources of humor stem from:

1. An occult assortment of eccentrics with weird costumes and behavior in equally weird locations.

A crew of Diana Arbus-like freaks engage in covert pursuit to undermine Dorian in settings that are a cross between industrial sleaze and hi-tech elegance. Frau Mabuse conducts Dorian into an underworld of sewers, pipes, and boiler rooms, bizarre contrast with her own neo-1950s Futurist offices and his/her Aalto-inspired postmodern loft.

Frau Mabuse herself is decked out in a wide-brimmed black hat and stark Mephistophelian outfit that is a cross between a 1950s haute-couture suit and a highly styled tux. Out of her outsized white lapels emerges an antenna from which she receives news of Dorian's escapades from her crazy band of spies: a paper-bag lady; Alpine-hatted twins who look and act like Chico Marx; and a stout diva dressed in gold who puts makeup on in a phone booth and opens garage doors by singing high "c."

2. Skits that recall the mindless antics of the Marx Brothers' zany combination of verbal nonsense and sight gags.

A slapstick chase is parodied when the two Alpine-hatted spies pursue Dorian. Inquiring which way Dorian went, they stop to ask twin tots in a stroller who are dressed exactly as they are. One says "right," the other "left," and then their father claims they are saying their names, not giving directions. Meanwhile, behind them, drolly satirizing filmic self-consciousness, three men wave fly swatters because the sound of a buzzing fly is heard on the sound track.

3. Intentional parodies of movies, as in the Newspaper Ball, where women in gowns made of newspaper dance in a room with newspaper-lined wallpaper. Their movements to slow languorous music echo a similar scene in *Last Year at Marienbad*, in parodic homage to Delphine Seyrig, who played a very different role as an entrapped woman. A funeral cortege, with the hearse pulled by a camel ridden by a monkey and hung with whitened auto tires for wreaths, recalls Rene Clair's *Entracte*.

4. Sometimes, there are embedded political jokes. When Frau Mabuse tunes in to Hamburg to check the increase in circulation due to Dorian's escapades, the newspaper is being used to package fresh fish, while in East Berlin there are no visuals, only written information, mocking that somber society.

5. A biting satire about the stagey theatricality of cinema.

Dorian sees him/herself in an opera about the conquistadors

who have captured the Happy Islands for the Church. As the Spanish Infant King, s/he is having a hopeless love affair with an aboriginal princess, Attamana, who is also the woman s/he loves in "real" life. As with everything in the film, the costumes and events are askew or anachronistic – the prince's guards carry shields of gilded washboards, and one carries a cross made of bone and feathers. The opera is performed on a "real" beach and observed by Dorian and Frau Mabuse from a box seat carved into rock. At one point, the opera leaves its framed proscenium arch and moves onto a highway between the mountains where natives in modern dress ride in open cars. With Frau Dr. Mabuse as an emissary of the Pope, the opera represents a grand scene of embedded linkages between imperialism, Catholicism, contemporary third world politics, and the artifice of representation.

6. Surrealist delirium.

Mabuse conducts Dorian down a manhole into an infernal horror show – homosexual sailors in a knife-fight; Dorian's beloved in an S/M costume play; a Marat-like civil servant in a bathtub railing against someone who urinates in his tub; a wild transsexual striptease with a stout man in a corset doing the goosestep under a huge dollar sign; gilded Siamese twins dancing in a huge stone shell; a rabbi carving a pig's head that is then pulled by a little boy on a leash (a strangely idiosyncratic reference to the Holocaust – or is it Nazi guilt or a revived anti-Semitism?).

Somehow, we are supposed to believe that all these excesses have been watched around the world and Dorian has become notorious, a "monstrous" success as "Playboy of the Underworld." Thus, a media-created monster/androgyne becomes the "mirror and window" for news, slander, and staged extravaganzas.

The multiple endings are wild and ambiguous. Dorian is dead – within his/her nightmare – yet alive – within the opera and the film. The last shot shows him/her running across the mountain that had been part of the opera's "real" set.

In a blend of "estrangement" techniques, anti-illusionist clichés, and mannerist melodrama, Ottinger demystifies cinema and theater. Underlying the kinky fantasy are some radical feminist notions: principally, that women filmmakers must appropriate the male filmmaker's territorial imperative – the manipulation of gaze, fantasy, and pleasure – in order to challenge the traditional notions of heroism, to question authoritarian control of the media, and to refashion styles of storytelling. Although the works of both Ottinger and Sander share the stylistic departures of works by prior male filmmakers of their generation, they are also trying to develop a form of political feminist comedies composed of varying degrees of outrage and the grotesque, often its visual equivalent.

Reprinted (revised) from "German Grotesque: Two New Films by Sander and Ottinger," Film Criticism *9.2 (1984/1985): 67–73.*

To my knowledge, *Dorian Gray* is not available for distribution in the United States. *The Trouble With Love* is available from Provobis Film, Hamburg. *REDUPERS* is available for rental from West Glen Films, New York.

I wish to thank Miriam Hansen for her help and suggestions.

15

"And With Favorable Winds They Sailed Away": *Madame X* and Femininity

sabine hake

> *S* abine Hake sees Ulrike Ottinger's campy Madame X – An
> Absolute Ruler *(1977) as a very pleasurable deconstruction of*
> *narrative realism – and more specifically a deconstruction of the repre-*
> *sentation of femininity. The film, Hake asserts, does not represent a*
> *revolt against men and masculinity (men remain rather irrelevant in*
> *Ottinger's films), but rather a playful critique of mediated images of*
> *femininity. Not at all a social-realist attempt to present "positive*
> *images" of lesbians, the film, she maintains, is connected to what she*
> *terms a "homosexual sensibility" primarily through its use of masquer-*
> *ade. She sees* Madame X *as a subversively pleasurable evocation of*
> *"an atmosphere of female eroticism that extends beyond the lines of*
> *social roles and identities."*
> —THE EDITORS

To begin with names, Madame X is a woman's name that stands
in for the ideal of femininity and its deconstruction. *Madame X* is
also a film title that recurs throughout the history of cinema.
The mystery around *Madame X,* then, is about the problem of
representing femininity, with the chiasma X as the marker of her
universal exchangeability, yet also as witness to her threatening
absence. As part of this tradition of inventing Madame X, the
film's previous designs of 1920, 1929, 1937, and 1965 finally lead
to 1977, when, in the contribution of filmmaker Ulrike Ottinger,
woman becomes the product of her own imagination.[1] Turning

1. As a film title, *Madame X* has almost become the generic term for a group
of films that investigate the problem of femininity in the most varied narrative
frameworks. Examples include films directed by Frank Lloyd (1920), Lionel
Barrymore (1929), Sam Wood (1937) and David Lowell Rich (1965).

from the riddle of femininity to that of sexual difference and object choice, we now accompany Ottinger's title figure on her journeys aboard the "Orlando," the ship named after Virginia Woolf's novel *Orlando,* whose title figure changes his/her sex at the age of thirty.

Madame X – eine absolute Herrscherin (1977, *Madame X – An Absolute Ruler)* opens with a promise: "Madame X, a strict, unremitting beauty, the uncrowned and cruel ruler of the Chinese Sea, proposes a message to all women who are willing to exchange their comfortable and secure but almost unbearably monotonous everyday lives for a world full of dangers and insecurity, but also full of love and adventure."[2] With seven women leaving their dull lives behind, the pirate ship "Orlando" subsequently embarks on her illegitimate journey through the inner landscapes of power and desire. Aboard, the women instantly succumb to the tyrannical rule of Madame X, her power doubled in the ship's mysterious figurehead. While each participant obsessively continues to stage her contribution to femininity in increasingly detached rituals, traces of something new emerge, traces laid out by the rhythm of desire and seduction propelling and, simultaneously, disrupting the "Orlando"'s predatory mission. The narrative reaches its point of implosion with the rescue of a shipwrecked hermaphrodite, the absurd staging of a masculinity-femininity personality test, and the attack on a luxury yacht. After that, the schemes of desire and jealousy, power and revolt increasingly take their toll. Most of the women are killed at Madame X's request. Yet in the end, a new crew embarks in another port; the "Orlando" continues her adventurous quest – with the old crew of women in new costumes.

In light of its promise of worldly and sensual goods, *Madame X* is not, as has been claimed, about "the actions of a band of women who, bored with men and masculinity, escape to carry-

2. *Madame X – eine absolute Herrscherin.* Script, direction, cinematography and sound collages: Ulrike Ottinger. Costumes: Tabea Blumenschein. With Tabea Blumenschein (Madame X), Roswitha Janz (Noa-Noa), Monika von Cube (Karla Goldmund-Freud), Irena von Lichtenstein (Blowup), Yvonne Rainer (Josephine de Collage), Lutze (Betty Brillo), Mona (Omega Centauri), Orlando (Ulrike Ottinger), Claudia Skoda (Flora Tannenbaum) et al. Release: 1977, 141 min., Filmwelt München. No American distribution at this time. This quote (and all subsequent quotes) is from the book *Madame X – eine absolute Herrscherin. Drehbuch* (Berlin/ Basel: Stroemfeld/ Roter Stern, 1979): 2.

out piracy on the high seas."[3] Instead, it offers an escape from
the boredom inherent in these categories. The circumstances in
which the women receive their calling seal the structural
absence of men from the outset and prove that the women are,
in fact, bored with femininity. Their boredom is elaborated by
Ottinger in humorous vignettes that show each woman figure in
her own typical domestic or professional environment. The
Polynesian native Noa Noa, the European artist Josephine de
Collage, the German ranger's wife Flora Tannenbaum, the psychoanalyst Klara Freud-Goldmund, the American housewife
Betty Brillo, the model Blowup, the Australian bush-pilot
Omega Zentauri: each woman stands for one particular "success
story" of female identity formation, each also plays that choice to
its grotesque limits. The film's seven models of femininity – a
veritable freak show – are culled from the iconography of high
art, mass media, and advertisement, but not, as many feminist
critics have assumed, from social stereotypes or reality. First,
each figure is easily recognizable through her "uniform," such as

3.   Angela McRobbie, introd. to Erica Carter, "Interview with Ulrike
Ottinger," trans. Martin Chalmers, *Screen* 4 (Winter/Spring 1982): 34. For the
controversial reception of *Madame X*, see Cillie Rentmeister, "Frauen, Körper,
Kunst: Mikrophysik der patriarchalischen Macht," *Ästhetik und Kommunikation*
37 (1979): 61–68 and the insightful essay by Monika Treut, "Ein Nachtrag zu
Ulrike Ottinger's Film 'Madame X,'" *Frauen und Film* 28 (1981): 15–21. For
reviews, see Norbert Jochum, "Kino als Collage. Ein Portrait der Regisseurin
Ulrike Ottinger." *Die Zeit* 48 (23 Nov. 1979); Klaus Kemetmüller, "Triumph der
Phantasie und die traurige Wirklichkeit," *Neue Zeit* (8 Nov. 1977). For an assess-
ment of Ottinger's work, also see Renate Möhrmann, *Die Frau mit der Kamera.
Filmemacherinnen der Bundesrepublik Deutschland* (Munich: Hanser, 1980); Marc
Silberman, "Cine-Feminists in West Berlin," *Quarterly Review of Film Studies* 5, no.
2 (Spring 1981): 217–232; the interview by Gesine Strempel, "Nicht einfach nur
klauen mit einem Tonband und einem Fotoapparat. Gespräch mit der
Filmemacherin Ulrike Ottinger," *Courage* 3 (1979): 40–45; and Ottinger's own
programmatic statement in "Der Zwang zum Genrekino. Von der Gefährdung
des Autoren-Kinos," *Courage* 4 (1983): 18–21. For a discussion of the collaboration between Ottinger and Blumenschein, see Renate Wolf, "Tabea Blumenschein und Ulrike Ottinger," *Zeitmagazin* 14 (25 Mar. 1977) and Barbara
Schlungbaum and Claudia Hoff, "Eindruck – Ausdruck. Tabea talks." *Frauen
und Film* 26 (1980): 34–38. For discussion of other Ottinger films, see Miriam
Hansen, "Visual Pleasure, Fetishism, and the Problem of Feminine/Feminist
Discourse: Ulrike Ottinger's *Ticket of No Return*," *New German Critique* 31 (Winter
1984): 95–108 (also reprinted in this volume); Roswitha Mueller, "The Mirror
and the Vamp," *New German Critique* 34 (Winter 1985): 176–193; Karsten Witte,
"Dame and Dandy. Ulrike Ottinger's Films," in *Im Kino. Texte von Sehen & Hören*
(Frankfurt/Main: Fischer, 1985): 61–70; Renate Fischetti, "Écriture Féminine in
the New German Cinema: Ulrike Ottinger's *Portrait of a Woman Drinker*," *Women
in German Yearbook* 4 (1988): 47–67.

Betty Brillo's 1950s polka dot dress or Josephine de Collage alias
Yvonne Rainer's fashionable overall and roller-skates.[4] Second,
each figure is marked as the sounding-board for male voices of
authority, with quotes, puns, and innuendos at times accessible
only to the insider: examples include Flora Tannenbaum's
Goethe recitals, Noa Noa's affiliation with Gauguin and Melville,
etc. Hence the promise of a new femininity is bound up not with
the invention of new images, but with the textual strategies of
irony, exaggeration, and simulation through which Ottinger
appropriates the old images for her subversive purposes.

In the following discussion, I will focus on the representation
of female homosexuality in *Madame X*, traceable in the film's
distinct play with masquerade, the references to orientalism,
and the appropriation of psychoanalysis.[5] Rather than presenting "positive images of lesbians," to phrase it polemically,
Madame X invokes an atmosphere of female eroticism that
extends beyond the lines of social roles and gender identities.[6]
Madame X derives much sensual appeal from displaying its costumes, their texture and patterns, from the play with color, jew-
elry, flowers, feathers, makeup, accessories, and, finally, from
the camera's discrete investigation and celebration of that mate-
riality. This emphasis on costume is primarily the result of
Ottinger's collaboration with her companion Tabea Blumenschein, the star and costume-designer of most of her films. The
film does at times seem to collapse into a dubious fetishistic sce-

4. Other than the other actresses in *Madame X*, the American avant-garde
filmmaker Yvonne Rainer obviously plays herself. This is evidenced by her delivery of a statement on the state of art and the artist, written by Rainer herself.

5. The space available limits me to the discussion of one particular aspect of
Madame X, thereby doing injustice to the film's other qualities. *Madame X*
deserves a detailed analysis of its aesthetic strategies, particularly of the appropriation of the genre of the pirate film, the elaborate sound track, the relation
between film book and film, and, finally, its position between feminism, the traditional avant garde, and postmodernism. These aspects will be discussed at
length in a forthcoming longer essay, "Gold, Love, and Adventure: Postmodern
Piracy of *Madame X*," in *Discourse* 11, no. 1 (Fall/Winter 1988/1989), 88–110.

6. Following Freud I use the term "female homosexuality" rather than "lesbianism." As is evidenced by the feminist reception of *Madame X*, the relationship between emancipatory movements (like the feminist/lesbian movements)
and avant-garde practices can prove problematic. In the case of *Madame X*, specific preconceptions and expectations typical of an emancipatory notion of lesbianism caused some feminist critics to dismiss the film's sadomasochistic eroticism as antifeminist (see in particular Rentmeister). For that reason I prefer to
avoid affiliations – even at the price of certain blind spots – that suppress the
film's textual complexity instead of liberating it.

nario, but through a clear refusal of the voyeuristic perspective, Ottinger's painterly frame compositions create an all-pervasive atmosphere of desire instead – a desire that is not reduced to the interaction of individuals, but is located in the fissures and crevices in between. Hence, in *Madame X* the act of representation emerges as the erotic itself.

To that end, costumes are utilized here as the material of woman's masquerade – of pretending to be what she is not – and, in relation to the film's specularity, as one of the major sources of the film's erotic appeal. The ordinary functions of dress, namely of marking social status and sexual difference, are left behind for more disquieting ones, namely those linked to masquerade – until everything is exposed to the test of changing surfaces and identities. Stolen from the media's arsenal of second-rate identities, costume and role thus are disengaged from each other, and costume assumes a meaning of its own, namely that of playful choice. Following Oscar Wilde in his rejection of all hierarchies between inside/outside and surface/core, the women figures, just like the film's constantly moving site of action and signification itself, escape fixation altogether. Some consequences of that operation of simulation and play have been discussed by Mary Ann Doane in her insightful essay "Film and the Masquerade: Theorizing the Female Spectator."[7] She describes masquerade as the possibility for women spectators to produce a distance and, in that drifting apart of signified and signifier, to regain access to their own desire in looking.

Intimately connected to the film's erotic investment of costume are its references to orientalism.[8] Initially, Ottinger's own expressed interest in Chinese history led her to discover fascinating figures like the Chinese woman pirate Lai Cho San, who became one of the models for Madame X. Yet aside from such concrete sources of inspiration, orientalism in *Madame X* functions as an operating principle through which a particular erotic imagery is generated. As the fictionalization of a specific eroticism placed at the outskirts of Western culture, the oriental

7. Mary Ann Doane, "Film and the Masquerade: Theorizing the Female Spectator," *Screen* 23 (Sept./Oct. 1982): 74–87.

8. For a discussion of orientalism, see Edward Said, *Orientalism* (New York: Random House, 1979) and Malek Alloula, *The Oriental Harem*, trans. Myrna Godzich and Wlad Godzich, introd. Barbara Harlow (Minneapolis: Univ. of Minnesota Press, 1986).

scenario is alluded to in the film's intimate relations between desire and death, lust and decay, domination and submission, and, in particular, all those subtle hints of perversion – a rather "unfeminine" infliction, one might add – that have become the bone of contention in the film's critical reception. Through Ottinger's appropriation of the oriental scenario, these relations are activated in order to link the problem of femininity to colonialism, thereby establishing colonialism as the important other strategy of exclusion within the patriarchal discourse. As the forceful interpretive strategy of defining the Occident against the Orient, orientalism stands for one specific form of representing the Other; it likewise becomes the demonstration object through which Ottinger unmasks, almost by proxy, the violence behind the categories of gender. In a world of permanently slipping signifiers, sexual difference, as *Madame X* suggests, does not reside in a linear movement of affirmation, liberation, or identity, but in a spiral-like energy wavering between exclusion and inclusion, a choreography of permanent non-identity. It is there that patriarchy and its guises will get their second chance – as the source of women's laughter.

To further explore the significance of orientalism in *Madame X* and, even more importantly, to perceive it as part of the film's distinctly homosexual sensitivity (if one chooses to use that phrase), I would like to invoke a central scene within orientalism, a scene characterized by a similar excess of femininity and claustrophobic mise-en-scène: the harem. Yet whereas the odalisques are removed from the circle of exchange for the exclusive pleasure of one man, namely the Father of the primal horde, the women of the "Orlando" voluntarily agree to follow another Freudian archetype: the phallic mother.[9] Represented

9. A brief note on the psychoanalytic terminology used throughout this essay: the term "pre-Oedipal" refers to "the period of psychosexual development preceding the formation of the Oedipus complex; during this period attachment to the mother predominates in both sexes." (Laplanche/Pontalis, p. 328) The pre-Oedipal is characterized by the oral phase ("sexual pleasure . . . is bound predominantly to that excitation at the oral cavity and lips which accompanies feeding" [287]) and the anal phase ("characterized by an organization of the libido under the primacy of the anal erotogenic zone" [35]). Both lead to the phallic phase and the achievement of a heterosexuality under the sway of the castration complex. The latter can be defined as the "complex centering on the phantasy of castration which is produced in response to the child's puzzlement over the anatomical difference between the sexes (presence or absence of the penis): the child attributes this difference to the fact of the girl's penis having been cut off." (56) It is obvious that the castration complex is experienced very differ-

by the figure of Madame X, this revengeful return of the pre-Oedipal and the threatening specter of an older bisexuality are already perceivable in the film's anarchic sense of humor. In addition, the protagonists can only shed their dreadful past by entering a circle of death and desire reminiscent of the tyrannical absoluteness of the oral and anal stages. The symbolic significance of those scenes dedicated to and constructed around the problem of unconditional nurture/nourishment (devouring, poisoning, drowning, robbing) are ample proof of such an interpretation.

Female homosexuality as an object choice, finally, enters the film at three levels. An element of the narrative, it propels the chain of desire and seduction toward the ultimate solutions sought in murder and suicide; a chain, however, that is phantasmagorically saved from termination through the return of all protagonists and, metaphorically, the resurrection of homosexual desire. Homosexuality, as implied by the film's ending, defies mortality. Secondly, *Madame X* is characterized by a specific homosexual appreciation of the aesthetic, brilliantly analyzed by Susan Sontag in her essay "Notes on 'Camp.'" On the level of visual spectacle alone, the film's obligations to Camp are most obvious in the fetishization of clothes described above, the narcissistic indulgence in self-reflective gestures and glances, the stylized rituals of seduction, and the privileged position attributed to looking. Yet in order to maintain its rule of taste and style, Camp, according to Sontag, also requires detachment, the love of artifice and exaggeration, and the recipient's active participation in this celebration. Commenting on congruencies between Camp taste and homosexuality, she writes: "Homosexuals have pinned their integration into society on promoting the aesthetic sense. Camp is a solvent of morality. It neutralizes moral indignation, sponsors playfulness. . . . Obviously, its metaphor of life as theater is peculiarly suited as a justification and projection of a certain aspect of the situation of homosexuals."[10] Even when transforming the serious into the

---

ently by the little boy and the little girl; the image of the "phallic mother" ("woman endowed, in phatasy, with a phallus" [311]) is evidence of the persistent influence of the castration complex. All definitions are taken from Laplanche/Pontalis, *The Language of Psycho-Analysis*, trans. Donald Nicholson-Smith (New York and London: Norton, 1973).

10. Susan Sontag, "Notes on 'Camp,'" in *Against Interpretation* (New York: Farrar, Strauss and Giroux, 1967): 290.

frivolous, Camp is never cynical – precisely because it believes in the small fallacies rather than the existential problems of human existence. Its refusal of judgment is a form of love. The primacy of stylization, ironization, and other camp elements in *Madame X* and other Ottinger films thus can be interpreted as the attempt of introducing female homosexuality as an aesthetic and not only a sexual choice, a project perhaps only shared by filmmaker Werner Schroeter.

As the third contributing factor to the film's slipping representations of female homosexuality, psychoanalysis intersects the narrative and interpretive strategies in *Madame X* on all levels. The film almost shamelessly utilizes psychoanalytic concepts to construct its narratives and, in ironic anticipation of its reception, provides a self-analysis, yet only to escape the dogmatism of both the psychoanalytic and the feminist readings. Again, irony becomes the mode of transformation. Just as the film's generic elements represent a disrespectful imitation of the pirate film, and just as its protagonists are constructed from the vast archives of femininity, so does psychoanalysis provide the material with which to work through the problem of representation and interpretation. As a powerful metanarrative, psychoanalysis introduces the element of the dramatic. Yet precisely by providing an interpretive framework devoted to cause and effect, Ottinger deploys the mechanism to eventually collapse itself.

At first glance, the truth behind *Madame X* appears to be entirely tied up with psychoanalytic terms. Upon further inquiry, however, it becomes obvious that they only participate in creating a mere apparition of power, a mirage of patriarchy. This use/abuse of psychoanalysis is most poignantly captured in the film's representation of *Madame X* and her double, the ship's figurehead. Her body's statuesque posture, the angular movements and aggressive gestures, the angry stare, and all the ceremonial paraphernalia doubled in the figurehead contribute to the overall striking appearance of Madame X. In significant opposition to traditional images of femininity, the body of Madame X is modeled on the phallic imagery of patriarchy, thus representing the return to/of the overpowering phallic mother, the object of desire for both sexes. Yet, with her missing hand, she is also represented as flawed, thereby embodying the double image of the phallic and the castrated mother. In order to interpret her lack in relation to the film's representation of female homosexuality, the position of this castration within the narrative becomes crucial, particularly when taking into account Freud's claim that the denial of castration constitutes one of the sources of female homosexuality.

The film *Madame X* reverses this traditional narrative of castration by placing it after the homosexual choice of the object has already been made. As Hoisin explains to the astonished crew members, Madame X had once loved a woman, the woman in whose honor the ship was later named "Orlando." Reaching into the waters to fetch a beautiful flower for her mistress, Orlando (played by Ottinger herself) misrecognized what turned out to be a poisonous jellyfish and, consequently, was pulled into the depth. In the attempt to rescue her lover, Madame X lost her right hand, since then wearing a fitted leather stump with a sharp blade attached to it. Hence, the lack and its concealment can, in accordance with the psychoanalytic narrative, be interpreted as a symbol of the vagina dentata. Yet Ottinger's apparently playful retelling of women's castration receives an even stranger twist in light of the figurehead's function as signifier of phallic power and its absurdity. As an important prop within the film, the figurehead represents a stylized wooden replica of Madame X. Equipped with an uncanny secret mechanism that makes it speak, look, and kill, it guards Madame X's absolute power at all times. But as a double in the psychoanalytic scenario, the figurehead represents the absent phallus, but it does so with ironic implications: after all, its powers, as the film unequivocally concedes, rest exclusively in a few simple mechanical devices and two primitive light bulbs that create its effective piercing stare.

It was *Madame X*, her first long narrative film, that made Ottinger known to a larger public with its release in 1977. At the same time, the film's spectacular iconography and its complex references instantly placed it at the center of bitter debates about feminism and a new feminine/feminist aesthetic. Since then, with the rise of a ubiquitous postmodern appreciation of second-hand images, *Madame X* has acquired the dubious status of the cult film, thereby becoming the subject of an appreciation that does not necessarily reflect its actual qualities. For instance, when Angela McRobbie praises Ottinger's films as "landmarks in the development of an erotic women's cinema,"[11]

11. McRobbie, "Interview with Ulrike Ottinger," 34.

she tends to neglect their substantial contributions to the
debate around postmodernism and a feminist avant garde. In
my opinion, *Madame X* resists mainstream as well as subcultural
readings which eagerly strive for fixed meanings, and thereby
seems to have no stake in the glorification of male power games,
sadomasochistic thrills, or cheap media images. Through a
remarkable act of piracy, the film appropriates all symbolic values and then uses them for a critique without denying pleasure.
With the pirate ship "Orlando" as the vehicle on which femininity leaves for new horizons, *Madame X* can be read as an immoral
allegory about glorious departures. In that sense, the film offers
to its crew – those aboard and those in the cinemas – one possible escape from the deadly Scylla and Charybdis of a decrepit
patriarchy and a boring realism.

Reprinted from Discourse *11 (1988/89): 88–110.*

16

Visual Pleasure, Fetishism, and the Problem of Feminine/Feminist Discourse: Ulrike Ottinger's *Ticket of No Return*[1]

miriam hansen

In this 1984 article Miriam Hansen situates Ottinger's film in various contexts: the politics of West German filmmaking, the film's controversial reception by West German feminists, and the context of feminist film theory. Hansen discusses the apparent conflict between Ottinger's visually stunning film (which exhibits a style one might describe as surrealist-aestheticist) and what she calls "the feminist injunction against visual pleasure," an injunction associated with a 1975 essay that has had a formative influence on feminist film theory: Laura Mulvey's "Visual Pleasure and Narrative Cinema." Hansen contends that Ottinger mobilizes visual pleasure in such a way as to liberate it "from the gender hierarchies inscribed in classical narrative cinema."
—THE EDITORS

According to J. Hoberman, *Ticket of No Return* is "the funniest, most inventive, and totally befuddled attack on demon rum in the 50 years since D. W. Griffith's much misappreciated swan

1. *Bildnis einer Trinkerin* (*Picture of a Lady Drinker*); Berlin, 1979; 108 min; Center for Public Cinema. New York. The English title, *Ticket of No Return* (actually a translation of the French subtitle of the film) echoes the words of the officer at the beginning of *Morocco*, following Dietrich's first appearance when getting off the boat: "Oh we carry them every day. We call them 'suicide passengers' – one-way tickets. They never return." This essay is the slightly revised version of a talk sponsored by the Feminist Film Society, Yale University, November 1982.

song, *The Struggle.*"[2] Social realism, lighted by an experimental
and even humorous touch; avant-garde comedy, redeemed by
social consciousness, either way, and praise and irony notwith-
standing, a male film critic once again integrates a woman's
work into the "Great Tradition," not accidentally as represented
by a minor work of a major director. Angela McRobbie, on the
other hand, emphasizes precisely the film's distance from such
a tradition when she describes *Ticket of No Return* as "a celebration of lesbian punk anti-realism." Where traditional criticism
invokes an establishment precedent, the feminist critic focuses
on the possibility of an alternative tradition, a tradition that
aims to subvert the gender-specific hierarchies inscribed in
patriarchal cinema. Thus Ottinger's film, according to McRobbie, represent "landmarks in the development of women's erotic cinema."[3]

Not all feminist response to Ottinger's work shares such
enthusiasm. In her home country, in particular, Ottinger has
remained relatively marginal to the mainstream of feminist film
culture. Paradoxically the term "mainstream" here refers to a
phenomenon that is itself defined by an extremely marginal status as well as a scandalously short history. Barely a decade ago,
women working in German cinema appeared in the credits as
editors, scriptwriters, actresses, or subordinate partners of
teams, the best known outside Germany being Margarethe von
Trotta and Volker Schlöndorff. Ever since 1978, when the first
women's seminar was held in Berlin, the situation has begun to
change: today there are over twenty German women directing
their own films.

The marginality of women filmmakers is further compound-
ed by the peculiar history and economy of West German cinema. Like all independent filmmakers, women have had to struggle with the professional machinery of commercial cinema, i.e.,
with the hegemony of Hollywood and its Common Market sub-
sidiaries. Partly owing to the unique – though (now more than
ever) precarious – film subsidy system in the Federal Republic, a

2. *Village Voice*, 20 April 1982, 46. Surely, Hoberman forgets W. C. Fields's sub-
lime short, *The Fatal Glass of Beer?*

3. Angela McRobbie, Introduction to "Interview with Ulrike Ottinger," by
Erica Carter, trans. Martin Chalmers, *Screen Education* 41 (1982): 34. Also see
Roswitha Mueller's interview and filmography in *Discourse* 4 (1981/82): 108–126
and Marc Silberman's interview with Ottinger in *Jump Cut* 29 (1984): 56 (also
reprinted in this volume).

number of male directors have succeeded in challenging commercial control and establishing an audience for their films both at home and abroad. While "New German Cinema" in this country has become a brand name for the work of Fassbinder, Herzog, Wenders, and Schlöndorff, this lucrative label is rarely conferred upon films by Ula Stöckl, Helke Sander, Jutta Brückner, or Ottinger, films whose showings depend upon noncommercial outlets such as the German Embassy, the Goethe Institutes, women's film festivals, and academic conferences. Competing with both commercial cinema and the relatively established male avant garde, women found themselves facing enormous difficulties in financing their films and often incurred considerable personal debts. Only gradually did they manage to tap the same sources of funding that had supported their male colleagues, including co-productions sponsored by German television stations. While the latter form of subsidy guaranteed a moderate degree of access, it also proved problematic in its ideological restrictions concerning areas and issues crucial to feminist projects (e.g., family, sexuality).

The more consciously feminist women filmmakers did not see their goal as the addition of a few women to the pantheon of New German *auteurs*. Since the first wave of women's filmmaking had gained momentum with the new women's movement of the 1970s, its program developed in close interaction with this political impulse. Thus, the aim was to create a women's cinema as a public space where women's experience and interests could be articulated and organized, where specifically female modes of perception (problematic as this might be) could find an artistic and public expression. As a first step in this direction, feminists emphasized the need for an organizational substructure, a basis for exchange and cooperation among women working in film that would also link them to the budding oppositional public sphere of the women's movement. In 1974, a group of filmmakers and critics (mostly from Berlin) founded the journal *Frauen und Film* – to this day the oldest surviving feminist film journal in Europe – whose function ranges from that of a newsletter to that of a forum for feminist criticism and theory.[4] Other efforts toward a feminist film culture focused on distribution and exhibition outlets specializing in women's films. In

4. Cf. Hansen, "*Frauen und Film* and Feminist Film Culture in West Germany," *Heresies* 16 (1983): 30–31 (also reprinted in this volume).

1979, finally, the Association of Women Film Workers was formed; its program demands equal representation in production, training, funding committees, and public access.

The orientation toward an oppositional public sphere (*Gegenöffentlichkeit*) that seems typical of women's film practice during the 1970s is reflected in most of their works in terms of genre, mode of representation, and subject matter. It is not surprising that many women filmmakers work in documentary, attempting to make visible those aspects of women's lives that are traditionally relegated to the private sphere. Even a number of so-called fiction films integrate documentary footage or stage their narratives in documentary situations. Many of these films address themselves to politically relevant issues such as abortion, childcare, women in the work place, or the status of housewives, with the intention of raising consciousness regarding these issues. Generally, these films tend to emphasize the personal in the political, and, by the same token, bring out the political dimension in personal relationships, whether they cast mothers and daughters, sisters, husbands and wives, lovers, or communes. Significantly, most of these films contain references to Germany's catastrophic history and its equally repressed consequences for the present state of West German society.

To the degree that German women filmmakers understand their work as an intervention in the West German public sphere, they adhere to an overall realistic mode of representation. The search for a nonpatriarchal, feminist discourse may include the testing and appropriation of modernist devices – most remarkably achieved in the work of Helke Sander – or it may emphasize a strongly subjective, often autobiographical point of view, as do the films of Claudia von Alemann, Jutta Brückner, and Jeanine Meerapfel. The majority of women's films, however, avoid a radical break with narrative linearity and spatial continuity, the conventional props of realism. On the contrary, the articulation of a specifically feminist perspective in these films usually hinges upon diegetic reference to a recognizable everyday world as well as traditional strategies of identification.

Although she recently joined the Association of Women Film Workers, Ottinger does not consider herself part of the German women's cinema in the sense of a movement. Unlike most of her colleagues, Ottinger neither graduated from one of the film academies, nor did she get her training in a male director's team. Her first and foremost vocation was painting. During the 1960s, she lived in Paris, working as a freelance painter and photographer. In 1969, she returned to her hometown, Konstanz, where she founded a film club, a gallery, and small press. At that period, she also became involved in staging a series of happenings with Wolf Vostell (the person who appears at the artists' table in *Ticket of No Return* with a coat of bread loaves). In 1972, Ottinger moved to Berlin and started making films – together with Tabea Blumenschein, the costume designer and lead actress of both *Ticket of No Return* and *Madame X: An Absolute Ruler* (1977). In all of her films, including her latest, the five-act epic *Freak Orlando* (1981), Ottinger herself is behind the camera, controlling the visual composition of her films with rare intensity and precision.

In *Madame X*, Ottinger's first feature film, Blumenschein plays a lesbian pirate queen who attracts women from all corners of the world with the promise of "gold-love-adventure." Once on board the junk Orlando, however, the utopian quest turns into a regime of terror. In a parodistic display of masks, costumes, and murderous paraphernalia, *Madame X* moves through rituals of love, power, and death to a new beginning, as the cast is brought back to life and embarks on yet another experiment in freedom and desire. The film provoked predominantly hostile reactions in the feminist film community and did not even get reviewed in *Frauen und Film* until a recent shift in editorial policy.[5] Ottinger's highly stylized exploration of the erotic fringe, her foregrounding of sadomasochistic and fetishistic tendencies as culturally constructed (and constructing) signs, obviously presented a challenge to essentialist positions which would condemn such tendencies as "naturally" male.

If *Madame X* was ignored by *Frauen und Film*, Ottinger's second feature film, *Ticket of No Return*, was ruthlessly panned by the same journal.[6] The crucial function of costumes in this film was seen as yet another instance of Ottinger's penchant for fetishism and similar sexist heresies. Moreover, Ottinger was accused of indulging in a decadent aestheticism – instead of dealing with the problem of women's alcoholism in a properly

5. See the excellent essay by Monika Treut, "Ein Nachtrag zu Ulrike Ottingers Film *Madame X*," *Frauen und Film* 28 (1981): 15–21.
6. Claudia Lenssen, "Mit glasigem Blick"; Ilse Lenz, "Die öde Wildnis einer Schminkerin"; Karin Reschke, "Frau Ottingers (Kunst)gewerbe," *Frauen und Film* 22 (1979): 23–29.

critical, socially responsible, and realistic manner. The more serious objections to the film articulated the fear that any visual pleasure derived from representations of the female body is intrinsically voyeuristic and therefore something which caters to the male spectator. Such fear is certainly not unfounded, as Laura Mulvey has shown in her analysis of visual pleasure as the keystone to patriarchal narrative cinema.[7] What some of these critics rightly perceive is that *Ticket of No Return* is concerned with visual pleasure rather than with the "problem" of alcoholism; what they fail to see, however, is that Ottinger radically subverts the terms in which patriarchal cinema has monopolized visual pleasure on behalf of the male gaze.

The film opens on a frame of red. The surface begins to drape, becomes visible in its texture and lighting, and recedes at the margins to reveal itself as a costume. As its bearer walks away from the camera in a direction perpendicular to the base of the frame, the marble floor reflects the whole figure in perfect symmetry. In this opening shot, Ottinger demonstrates her basic visual codes: color, lighting, texture, costume, figure, reflection – the transformation of one kind of surface into another. The "character," a rich foreigner, is introduced then as the focal point of these codes, an artificial figure which is at no point to be confused with a real human being. The voice-over locates her origin in a mythological place, La Rotonda, presenting her through comparisons with mythological women – Beatrice, Aspasia, Mona Lisa, a pre-Raphaelite beauty. From the start, she appears as a work of art, a poem or a painting, an image that consummates centuries of women's idealization (and their concomitant oppression). In such highly allegorical terms "She" descends, in flared red coat and white high heels, upon the actual city of Berlin, following her impulse to live her destiny, her passion for drinking. Equipped with a sightseeing guide she found on the plane, she maps out her boozer's itinerary: a fantasy conceived in what the voice-over calls her "pessimistic-narcissistic cult of loneliness" will be put to the test of reality.

Reality, however, turns out to be a rather unrealistic setup. In the deserted, impeccably clean, and modernistic airport of Berlin-Tegel, an official voice requests "Reality, please" over the loudspeaker. Ordinary spaces are rendered strange by means of

7. Laura Mulvey, "Visual Pleasure and Narrative Cinema," *Screen* 16, no. 3 (Autumn 1975): 6–18.

static extreme angle shots in which the character moves from close-up to long-shot distances or the reverse; throughout the film, this technique of spatial defamiliarization – combined with highly selective or entirely suppressed diegetic sound – will serve to transform authentic locations into theatrical platforms for the contradictory gestures of female desire. The arrival of the strange lady seems to place a spell upon the workings of reality: accidents proliferate, suitcases and pushcarts tumble and eject their contents, objects rebel against their everyday function as if *her* refusal to function as a subject were encouraging them to do the same.

The arrival scene also introduces a set of characters who will be crossing the protagonist's path in a series of chance encounters throughout the narrative. Three houndstooth-checkered ladies, going by the names of "Social Question" (Magdalena Montezuma), "Common Sense" (Monika von Cube), and "Accurate Statistics" (Orpha Termin), appear on the scene like Fates, personifying the reality principle at its most petit bourgeois. Never tired of discussing the problem of women's alcoholism, their chatter will accompany or counterpoint the protagonist's behavior on the image track. Significantly, they never relate to the Lady Drinker other than as peeping toms; the only communication that takes place between them occurs in a section in which the drinker envisions herself in various professional roles – a kind of fantasy within a fantasy. Although these three ladies can be expected to turn up in the same spaces as the protagonist, they obviously exist on a different plane of reality. They are little more than well-choreographed mouthpieces of types of social discourse in the film's overall collage, adding one more level of meaning, which, nonetheless, remains fragmentary and unassimilated. Like other elements that Ottinger assembles in this manner – found objects, places, texts, and characters (mostly drunk) – the houndstooth-checkered sisters can hardly be integrated into the fictional homogeneity of a conventional realist narrative.

The most allegorical figure to materialize at the airport – right after the Lady's first drink – is the Dwarf (Paul Glauet), with whom she will be on excellent terms. Personifying her death wish (or the Nirvana principle), the Dwarf acts as a Master of Ceremonies, initiating sequences of fantasy or states of anxiety and self-hatred, thus punctuating the transition from objective to subjective moods of narrative. The section enacting the drinker's job fantasies, for instance, is bracketed by symmetrical sequences showing her in a park in successively closer (respectively longer) shots, each intercut with extreme close-ups of her eye. In the first of these sequences, the Dwarf enters frame left to deposit a photograph of himself at her feet; the second sequence, which closes the job fantasy section, has him enter frame right to remove the photograph again. Thus nested, even the most positive images she can conceive of herself – as underlined by her own eye's imaging capacity – are marked as deeply interwoven with the death wish as externalized in the image of the Dwarf.

The transition from a relatively objective mood to one in which the Drinker's emotional disposition takes over is further underscored by a deliberate muffling or even complete elimination of simple diegetic sound exquisitely engineered by Margit Eschenbach. The absence of any realistic background noises in the Drinker's perception emphasizes both the dominance of the interior space and the sense of social isolation that usually accompanies a loss of hearing. Its counterpoint, throughout the film, is the protagonist's abstention from speech, a rather pronounced form of silence. The few times we actually hear her voice, as in the pre-credits sequence, we do not get to see a speaking face. When she envisions herself in talking roles in the job fantasy section – first as acting Hamlet, later as an advertising consultant – the sound is dubbed over her mimicking, thus creating a ventriloquist effect that calls attention to the distance between speaker and discourse.

The only occasions on which the Drinker seems moved to suspend her social isolation are prompted by a fascination with another woman (or, almost, an "other" woman). The motif is introduced as she is leaving the airport and gets caught between two sets of automatic doors. In one of the few unambiguous shot/reverse-shots of the film, a cleaning lady appears on the other side of the glass door, matched to the Drinker's face as it is being blurred by the cleaning liquid on the glass pane. This encounter prefigures her relationship with the bag lady, played by Lutze, the only person with whom she engages in any kind of consistent interaction. Lutze, the sub-proletarian drinker, is probably the most traditionally realistic character in *Ticket of No Return*: she is at home in the bars, stations, and public places and maintains a modicum of contact with other people, including men. By contrast, the Lady Drinker appears all the more artificial and displaced. Even in this rudimentary relationship, she maintains her habitual silence – an indication not only of the effects of drinking but also of the underlying assumption that the bag lady is just another version of herself, of the same impulse which has become her identity.

The Drinker's desire obsessively revolves around her own image, an image which seems to be both cause and obstacle to her quest. When, during her visit to the Casino, a man attempts to hold her hand, she dispassionately withdraws it and reaches for the glass of wine – an obvious renunciation of heterosexual forms of desire. She seems to enjoy the company of women yet is hardly moved to any sexual activity. She likes to picture herself as a young man in black leather but performs ritual attacks against this image, stabbing a knife around his/her photograph on the wall. Desire in *Ticket of No Return* takes on a less personal, more interdiscursive, pervasive shape. It is most palpable in the constant interplay of costumes, gestures, lighting, and other aspects of mise-en-scène and finally blends into the visual pleasure evoked by Ottinger's cinematography. In centering the movements of desire around the protagonist's image, its power of fascination as well as inevitable lack, the actual body and the textual body more than ever seem to coalesce.

At this point, it is crucial to recall the function of visual pleasure in dominant patriarchal cinema. In Mulvey's oft cited analysis, visual pleasure revolves around the representation of the female body through a system of looks organized and legitimized by a narrative structure which puts the male subject (filmmaker/character/spectator) in control over the woman's image. And controlled it must be – in the interest of the circulation of male desire – because, according to Mulvey, the image of the woman's body not only offers pleasure but also poses a threat, through her lack of a penis, the threat of castration. One route by which patriarchal cinema deals with this threat is that of fetishization. In order to assure uninterrupted if not heightened visual pleasure, the woman's body is idealized into a phallic substitute – the classic instance is Sternberg's representation of Dietrich.[8]

8. Claire Johnston, "Women's Cinema as Counter-Cinema," in *Notes on Women's Cinema*, ed. Claire Johnston (London: SEFT, 1973), 26. Mulvey takes up on Johnston's point but considers a potentially subversive angle to Sternberg's particularly excessive fetishization of Dietrich's image in that he breaks "the powerful look of the male protagonist (characteristic of traditional narrative film) . . . in favor of the image in direct erotic rapport with the spectator." Mulvey, "Visual Pleasure," 14.

Costumes traditionally play an important part in the fetishistic containment of women on the screen. Moreover, along with make up, accessories, and other techniques of beautification, costumes have been a predominant focus of women's aesthetic impulse for centuries because women were barred from most other forms of expression. The aura of self-sufficiency Freud observes in female narcissism may be seen as the highly ambiguous result of this historical inversion of the aesthetic impulse. As a trace of woman's exclusion from social signifying systems, however, it collapses agent and object and thus overdetermines the female body as a site of representation. Hence, while still testifying to the deflected impulse, the aesthetic-erotic effect of self-sufficiency is ironically linked to the cultivation of appearance and reflection in another's gaze – mechanisms by which female narcissism conventionally plays into voyeuristic and fetishistic structures of spectatorship.

Tabea Blumenschein's exquisitely bizarre fashion show in *Ticket of No Return* engages both fetishism and cinematic voyeurism in a double move. By foregrounding the fetishistic character of her costumes, she parades them precisely for what they are: representations, signs, masks of femininity. This masquerade puts a distance between the woman as aesthetic agent and the woman's body in that it hyperbolizes the means of representation and thus allows her to assume some measure of control over them. The masquerade, according to Mary Ann Doane, acknowledges "that it is femininity itself which is constructed as a mask – as the decorative layer which conceals a non-identity."[9] Blumenschein's game becomes increasingly precarious to the degree that this critical distance diminishes, as in the course of the film her costumes become more and more scanty, brittle, metallic, and inflexible. Her last costume is made of a shiny silver material reminiscent of all the mirror surfaces in which all along she has attempted to drown out her image. Eliminating the difference between self-stylization and mirror image, she seems to precipitate her eventual collapse.[10] This col-

9. Mary Ann Doane, "Film and the Masquerade: Theorizing the Female Spectator," *Screen* 23, no. 3–4 (1982): 81–82.

10. This motif, in particular in the mise-en-scène of the Drinker's collapse on the staircase of Bahnhof Zoo, is strongly reminiscent of Fassbinder in *Fox and His Friends* (*Faustrecht der Freiheit*, 1974); variations on the same theme can be found throughout his oeuvre, most poignantly, however, in later works like *Veronika Voss* (*Die Sehnsucht der Veronika Voss*, 1982).

lapse, however, is not the last word; it eludes narrative closure. Having taken an aesthetics of narcissism to the point of no return, the film offers an alternative in its final shot. The high heels are marching again, this time shattering the mirrors that reproduce the deceptive geometry of cinematic space.

"Use your high heels to crush the mirrors" seems to be the line along which Ottinger's cinematography supports Blumenschein's masquerade. The whole film attempts nothing less than to disentangle visual pleasure from the voyeurism inherent in the codes of patriarchal cinema. As Ottinger perceives the source of visual pleasure in the aesthetic potential of female narcissism, she is equally aware of the dangers in this source. The contradictions in store for an aesthetic cult of narcissism are amply illustrated by the metaphor of alcoholism: the gesture of refusal encoded in the never-ending binge finally defeats itself since the very desire for fusion only produces isolation, just as the aesthetic distance maintained towards the physical self evaporates with the number of drinks.

Aware of these contradictions, the film not only reconfirms but also renegotiates visual pleasure – in a systematic effort to dissociate it from traditional forms of cinematic voyeurism. Ottinger consistently avoids the standard editing devices of illusionist/voyeuristic cinema, in particular eyeline matches and shot/reverse-shot. Whenever she does resort to such devices, as for example in the job fantasy section when the drinker plays a secretary, the reverse shot (showing Kurt Raab as her outraged boss) is taken from such an impossible angle that it prevents the sequence from adding up to a consistent space, thus mocking the very concept of diegesis. The same sequence includes a shot of the three Fates curiously pressing their noses against a window; yet their location in relation to the scene observed remains as unclear as the spatial position of the spectator.

Moreover, voyeurism becomes thematic as the stereotypical social response to the appearance of the Drinker – on the part of men as well as women, most obtrusively the three Fates and the ubiquitous media. Unlike the classical Hollywood film – which also tends to contain figurations of the look – *Ticket of No Return* refuses to give this voyeurism a narrative support system. The voyeurs in this film cannot conceal their activity in the course of narratively meaningful actions, nor are they fleshed out as characters who would offer instances of identification. By the same token the film refuses to naturalize voyeurism for its spectator. Rather, the spectator is alerted to her/his own position as a voyeur, for instance when the Drinker acts out a fantasy of herself as an advertising consultant, and when a reverse shot reveals the camera's position to have been adjacent to that of a curious crowd watching from the street. Caught in the act, the spectator is urged to abandon the privileged position of Invisible Guest and to enter into a relationship with the figures and events on the screen that is both more distanced and more direct.

Extricated from the voyeuristic context of traditional narrative, visual pleasure in *Ticket of No Return* is reconnected to its source, female narcissism. Given the problematic nature of that source, visual pleasure may not always be that pleasant or pleasing, a delight easily to be consumed. The contrast between the Drinker's increased alienation and the beauty of the images conveying this process is actually quite painful. Yet, Ottinger also gives us glimpses of mutual enjoyment of the aesthetic impulse, though they are moments at best – recall the joy that radiates from the drinkers (Lutze wearing her rich friend's clothes) when they join punk star Nina Hagen in a Berlin bar or when they immerse themselves in bubble bath and champagne).

This mutual pleasure, finally, is what the film tries to evoke in its interaction with the spectator. More than any film to have come out of Germany in recent years, *Ticket of No Return* indulges in a succession of visually stunning compositions, reflecting Ottinger's background as a painter. Her images are constructed in a most classical manner, strongly emphasizing geometrical perspective, balance, and symmetry. But – to return to the feminist injunction against visual pleasure – has not classical composition been the mainstay of patriarchal cinema, the most fetishistic form of representation, over and over asserting the centrality of the spectator's position, his possession of the image, and, thus, of the woman?

Geometrical perspective seems to be to Ottinger's cinematography what Blumenschein's costumes are to the drinker's masquerade. Ottinger foregrounds the fetishistic quality of her images to the point of parody. Where Sternberg emphasizes the pictorial surface, the two-dimensional quality of the screen rather than the illusion of three-dimensional depth, Ottinger omits no opportunity to demonstrate the illusionist quality of her compositions, having her character sweep through spaces in almost perpendicular directions. The three-dimensionality of these spaces is not given, in a realist sense: Ottinger inflates them before our eyes like a cluster of balloons. Whereas Sternberg, exercising control over the woman's image, still subjects his self-consciously fetishistic representations to the plausibility of narrative, Ottinger increases the distance between representation and narrative to the point where one subverts the other. The allusion to *Morocco* in the film's final shot is indicative of this revisionist strategy: while Dietrich presumably discards her high heels to follow the fatal scenario of desire, Blumenschein refunctionalizes the fetishistic emblems as a weapon against the very system of representation that governs the narrative of women's lives. By reversing the traditional subordination of looking, display, and fascination to the logic of narrative, Ottinger sets visual pleasure free from gender hierarchies inscribed in classical narrative cinema.

The emancipation of visual pleasure through a parodistic display of its fetishistic guises is not least a function of the overall organization of the film's narrative. Avoiding standard patterns of temporal progression and closure – along with devices of identification and motivation *Ticket of No Return* effectively challenges the traditional hierarchy of time over space as well as the transmutation of both into a fictive logic of narrative events.[11] The movement of the narrative is spatial rather than temporal. There is no development, no anticipation, no past, no attempt to spell out the chronological order and duration of the various parts of day or night (except for the causal connection between the Drinker's misdemeanor in Cafe Möhring and the arrival of the *Bild-Zeitung* carrying her story, which someone anonymously pushes through her door the next morning). The disintegration and eventual collapse of the protagonist appear as predictable fulfillment of a self-chosen destiny, although we are not entirely spared the pathetic connotations of the process. The Drinker's fate, however, seems secondary to her idiosyncratic sense of geography that structures the narrative as a sequence of spaces. As Blumenschein puts on one new costume after the other, Ottinger presents a series of Berlin locations – the airport at Tegel, the Casino, the glass tower in the botanical garden, the

11. Cf. Stephen Heath, "Narrative Space," in *Questions of Cinema* (Bloomington: Univ. of Indiana Press, 1981).

skating rink, the Wall, a lesbian leather disco, a Turkish bar in Kreuzberg, the whale-shaped pleasure boat called "Moby Dick" on the Wannsee, the waste land of the West Harbor, the passages and caverns of the Bahnhof Zoo. These locations are rendered strange by means of camera angles, lighting, sound, or absence of everyday traffic; they are transformed into stages for the protagonist's purposefully purposeless quest. Such places do not add up to a social topography – as they might for the bag lady – but represent allegorical stations in the protagonist's experiment of lived-out fantasy.

In its spatialization of narrative, *Ticket of No Return* recalls literary traditions of urban odysseys, in particular Breton's *Nadja* and Aragon's *Paysan de Paris*. Ottinger endows the deserted landscape of Berlin with an enchantment similar to the Surrealists' visions of Paris: spaces that have long lost their unique aura through social habit and economic rentability are recovered by the motions of desire, turning into a mythical arena for chance encounters where waking and dreaming states, reality and fantasy intersect. The difference between the media of film and literature, moreover, is counterbalanced by an elective affinity of style. As the surrealists' writing deliberately juxtaposes distinct levels of reality as well as heterogeneous materials (including drawings and photographs), Ottinger's visual/aural interweaving of discursive fragments echoes the principles of the surrealist collage.

Despite the obvious influence of surrealism on Ottinger's narrative style, the Lady Drinker – as the subject connecting the landmarks of desire – is not an idealized female figure like Breton's Nadja whose construction as a muse depends largely upon "feminine" qualities such as spontaneity and unpredictability. The Drinker already carries the historical traces of women's idealization on her own body, displaying them in both apparel and attitude. Thus she appears closer to the figure of the Dandy,[12] the creation of a literary sensibility distinctly less heterosexual than that of the surrealists, who were to claim it as part of their heritage. The Dandy's repetitive touring of urban spaces reflects the static spatial arrangement of a world that can no longer maintain the promises of progress and change, a social landscape that has reverted to the barbarism of mere nature. In

12. Karsten Witte suggests this connection in his review of the film, "Der Dandy als Dame," *Frankfurter Rundschau*, November 13, 1979.

this world, fashion symbolizes the eternal recurrence of same-
ness in the guise of the new – an emblem of modernity that
belies the linear narrative of bourgeois history.[13]

The Dandy's obsession with surfaces, poses and gestures is
synonymous with his rejection of the key values of bourgeois
ideology – rationality, morality, progress. No writer has stated
this rejection more elegantly than Oscar Wilde, and Ottinger
pays homage to Wilde throughout her work. *Ticket of No Return*
testifies to this influence from the allusion to *The Picture of Dorian Gray* in the film's German title to the satire on "liberal uplift"
as personified by the three Fates. Ottinger's self-conscious display of artifice and style, over and against the human interest
story, provocatively reasserts Wilde's relegation of ethics under
the aesthetic imperative. Upon returning to her room with the
bag lady, the Drinker meticulously peels an orange while Lutze
welcomes the prospect of getting her liquid diet supplemented
with vitamins; the drinker, however, throws the orange away and
muses over the peel, now shaped like a starfish. This gesture
encapsulates Ottinger's commitment to the aesthetic tradition,
with its emphasis on the risks of interpretation: "All art is at
once surface and symbol./Those who go beneath the surface
do so at their peril./It is the spectator, and not life, that art really mirrors./ . . . All art is quite useless."[14]

Aestheticism, finally, is the stylistic equivalent of the cult of
narcissism. The Drinker, like the Dandy, is at the same time
artist and artifice, using her body as the surface of her art. In its
neurotic fixation, narcissism yields an aesthetic potential, along
with the semblance of autonomy; traditionally, this has been
linked to the socialization of women and – by a similar though
mediated logic – to gay sensibility. The feminist recourse to the
tradition of aestheticism reactualizes the cross-dressing involved
in this predominantly male tradition. For the Dandy's emphasis
on appearance, fashion and decor both absorb and displace the
aesthetic impulse of female narcissism. What the male Dandy
cultivates in the manner of a sublimated transvestism serves the

13. Particularly relevant here are Benjamin's fragments on Baudelaire and
Paris, partly translated in *Charles Baudelaire: A Lyric Poet in the Era of High Capitalism*, trans. Harry Zohn (London: Verso, 1983) and in *Illuminations*, trans. Harry
Zohn (New York: Schocken, 1969 and 1978); cf. ibid. his "Theses on the Philosophy of History," pp. 253–264.
14. Wilde, "Preface," *The Picture of Dorian Gray* (1890). Ottinger's current project is entitled *Dorian Gray in the Mirror of the Yellow Press*.

Lady Dandy as material for her masquerade, doubly distancing the representation from its object. Ottinger merely reappropriates the aesthetics of narcissism for a feminist rather than a traditionally feminine discourse, reflecting the problematics of reappropriation through a many-layered, parodistic masquerade of her own trade.

Reprinted from New German Critique *31 (1984).*

17

Interview with Ulrike Ottinger: Surreal Images

marc silberman

We reprint here Marc Silberman's interview with filmmaker Ulrike Ottinger, which first appeared in 1984. In it she primarily discusses her film Ticket of No Return, which is called Portrait of a Woman Drinker here, the literal translation of the film's German title, Bildnis einer Trinkerin.
—THE EDITORS

I find myself rather isolated in the German film scene, particularly among my women colleagues, because my films come out of the tradition of fantasy and surrealist filmmaking. Besides that, my experience as an artist, especially in Paris during the sixties, is rather unusual for a filmmaker. My eyes have become extremely sensitized to visual images. My film *Portrait of a Woman Drinker*, for example, on one level offers a sight*seeing* tour through Berlin. I construct my films with images. I use a syntax of images, whereas most German women filmmakers seem conventionally tied to dialogue. I seek new images for the new content which is proposed by a woman's experience. This may be why spectators often complain about my films' length and dense imagery. They are not accustomed to an associative style, beyond psychological motivation.

I don't think it is adequate to show things "as they are" in a film. I don't think you can do that today. There was a counter-movement ten years ago against formalist films; even fiction films then presented things "as they were," certainly an unpretentious goal. In my film *Portrait of a Woman Drinker*, quasi-documentary scenes alternate with extremely stylized ones. I introduced this technique because I realized that Berlin filmmakers often made the quasi-documentary with tremendously precise film content, but formally lifeless. The public for these films has already developed a critical consciousness and watches a familiar reality on film – so familiar that the public doesn't see, or doesn't want to see, what goes on around them.

I work self-consciously with fragments of reality in a collage process. For example, in *Portrait of a Woman Drinker*, I have integrated many other noises – both artificial and real – into the original sound track to broaden associative possibilities. Earlier I never had the money to record on-the-spot sound; here I could afford a sound crew, but still used the old process. Basically, I attach little value to traditional narrative film. I work in a completely different way. In my films I introduce ironic "quotes" of films or images. In other words, I use traditional cinema's cliches for my own purposes.

I had so little money for *Madame X* that I was forced to work collectively from the start. I wrote the script and did the camera work. I had the notion of a pirate film: the ship as a metaphor for awakening, basically into the adventure of reality. Then I began to consider which women I could possibly work with, according to the roles. An artist on roller skates justifies her escape to Madame X because of her dissatisfaction with the academic culture industry; she speaks directly into a microphone. A beautiful prostitute with wonderfully developed body language had to find another way to articulate herself, and I just let her move. Nor does the third-world woman speak; she expresses herself by means of gestures and dance. Yvonne Rainer plays the artist (I had intended to play the role myself originally) and obviously could write her own text. I dissolved the shots of her into details – the roller skates, her hands, her mouth. Another woman spoke a curious mixture of several languages. With her, I'd write something and then ask her how she would say it. In this way, the film incorporates many expressions typical of the women.

Although the film focuses primarily on the moment of awakening, I try to make clear that the enthusiasm of waking up cannot last because reality itself offers a mixed bag of pleasant and unpleasant experiences. Nonetheless, desires for escape and change should remain. All the characters die. All their traditional, socialized patterns of behavior must die or at least be disrupted to create new possibilities. In addition, the film investigates role playing, the impossibility of rationally determined female or male role playing.

I consciously formulated the contradiction between Madame X as a master and her promise of freedom. Madame X does not represent a person at all but rather a kind of power machine. She moves mechanically, just like her image, the ship's figure-head. She represents me, power, and traditional hierarchial structures of behavior. I find it remarkable that awakening, which has become a mass gesture in the women's movement, runs its course within the same hierarchial, patriarchal patterns. I wanted to show this contradiction as our reality, one that stuns and disturbs, and to emphasize that we have to take seriously the residue of behavioral structures which have been chiselled into us for centuries.

Amazingly, I find that there is always a figurehead which the women's movement follows – and above all, within these tradi-tional patterns. I find the movement itself very important, but I still need to gently critique it. We have given too little thought to the power of traditional structures. Surely, they must be bro-ken down, but each of us falls back into the old patterns. There-fore, women in the film find a new identity that is only slightly different, not an ideal one. Yet changes only come step by step. I find it unrealistic to make a film in which women revolt and triumph gloriously.

Reprinted from Jump Cut *29 (1984): 56.*

18

Straub/Huillet, Feminist Film Theory, and *Class Relations*[1]

b a r t o n   b y g

B *arton Byg investigates a film by two directors who will never be part of the mainstream pantheon: Danièle Huillet and Jean-Marie Straub, long associated with the "Brechtian-Godardian" avant-garde project. In his essay on their 1984 film,* Class Relations *(an adaptation of Kafka's novel-fragment* Amerika*), Byg cites Teresa de Lauretis's belief in the possibility of problematizing conventional narrative without destroying visual pleasure, and his analysis attempts to demonstrate that this is indeed what Huillet and Straub achieve in* Class Relations: *surpassing the avant-garde minimalism with which they are usually associated, they have made a film which allows the spectators pleasure precisely in its subversion of the Oedipal narrative.*
—The Editors

One of the most important women working in the postwar European cinema remains almost totally ignored by film criticism: she is Danièle Huillet. One reason for this is as scandalous as it is simple: since Huillet and her collaborator Jean-Marie Straub have refused to stylize themselves in any particular way as "artist personalities," the sexist assumption of the 1950s that Straub is the principal *auteur* of the two has remained unquestioned. Yet in an interview in *Frauen und Film*, published in 1982, Huillet removed all doubt that the works of Straub/Huillet are truly collaborative, and always have been.

1. This paper is a revised and expanded version of a presentation in the Literature and Film session offered by the Division on Twentieth-Century German Literature at the 1986 MLA Convention. I am grateful to New Yorker films for providing a print of *Class Relations* for the purposes of this study. *Class Relations* (*Klassenverhältnisse*). Dir. Danièle Huillet and Jean-Marie Straub. Janus Film und Fernsehen, 1983. New Yorker Films, U.S. distributor.

It is difficult to approach the reasons for Huillet's lack of recognition. She has not sought to call attention to her work on the films and has not identified herself as a feminist. Instead, for years she has stayed in the background, especially since she suspects that interviews and discussions – in which Straub more readily engages – may do the films more harm than good.[2] Without presuming to impose consciousness-raising on Huillet, however, the Straub/Huillet division of labor and the perception of it certainly reflect sexism in the institutions of cinema. Critics even continue to assume falsely that Huillet and Straub are married, and frequently include Huillet only by way of the term "the Straubs."[3] Male critics have never felt it necessary to query Straub on this issue, and his greater visibility and volubility feed the assumption that he dominates in their teamwork. Furthermore, the single area where Huillet does leave decisions to Straub is the aspect of filmmaking that has been reified into the directorial "signature" – the set-up and framing of shots. The areas of more equal collaboration – e.g., script and mise-en-scène – and especially those areas where Huillet is more in charge – sound, editing, "scene design," and many producer's functions – all fit more readily the stereotype of women working behind the scenes.[4]

One could argue that Huillet's toleration of this situation is in itself a result of sexism. On the other hand, any familiarity with the aesthetic project of Straub/Huillet films immediately puts such hierarchical thinking itself into question. From the very beginning, a principal aspect of their aesthetic has been to subvert the primacy of the visual in cinema by having the text, sound, duration, and editing clash with, rather than support, the image. For this reason, a feminist reception of Straub/Huillet might begin by cooperating with Huillet's concern for the films first and the gendering of authorship afterwards. In her words, "what interests us are the products and not the names."[5]

Further study would then certainly be warranted on the gen-

2. Danièle Huillet, "Das Feuer im Innern des Berges," interview with Helge Heberle and Monika Funke Stern, *Frauen und Film* 32 (June 1982): 6.
3. The name Straub/Huillet, which applies only to both together, is both convenient and accurate as a shorthand term for two individuals working together with no concern for assigning credit. It does not erase the problematic fact that Jean-Marie Straub is still often regarded as the more significant, if not sole, *auteur.*
4. Huillet, "Feuer im Innern des Berges," 5–7.
5. Ibid., 5.

der (and political) issues raised by Straub/Huillet's work methods and their reception. This is not to say that Huillet has never stated a position on feminist issues. She did so in her 1982 interview, but always in the context of her work and the realities of history and everyday life. Even the radical cinema she and Straub have developed collaboratively she does not ascribe to their creative will alone: "Yes, but that came about also through our living" ("Ja, das kam aber auch durch unser Leben").[6]

When questioned about her position on gender oppression and the presence or absence of women in Straub/Huillet films, Huillet gave a three-part answer. First, she pointed out the presence of women in the documentary aspects of the films, seen going about the work of everyday life. And if women's work is less visible on the streets and in the factories, that is part of the documentation the films provide. But Huillet objected to modifying the historical texts used in the films to include women after the fact: "To place a woman into the middle of Brecht where he had none would be false, also for the woman."[7] Her second answer was to point out that the film *The Bridegroom, the Comedienne and the Pimp,* (*Der Bräutigam, die Komödiantin und der Zuhälter,* 1968) – although constructed from previously existing texts like all their films – very clearly shows the oppression of women.[8] This, too, arose from a documentary impulse: Huillet and Straub developed the idea for the film after walking by chance through the prostitutes' area of Munich, seen at the opening of the film. Third, Huillet stressed that she sees the liberation of women as more quickly attainable through general revolution – as in the resistance struggles of the third world.[9] And finally, consistent with the scrupulous respect for "reality" evidenced in Straub/Huillet films, Huillet categorically refuses to use film to fabricate a history for women using the methods of the "dream factory." "The dreams one has come only from reality and are only partly different from reality and are an attempt to escape from it," she says. "But always from reality and not from nothing."[10]

Furthermore, Huillet does not see her work as part of a countercinema that simply destroys the pleasures of the convention-

6. Ibid.
7. Ibid., 9.
8. Ibid., 10.
9. Ibid.
10. Ibid., 12.

al narrative by reversing the system: "But I don't believe that one can replace one oppression with another and I also don't believe that one can fight one system with another, because then a thing becomes simply too rigid."[11] To the suggestion that Straub/Huillet films, too, seem to be built on a strict system, based on renunciation, she replied: "I hope not *only* that. I hope that one can feel sensuality and pleasure [*Lust*] at the same time. Can sense the fragrance of things."[12]

What Huillet primarily distanced herself from in this interview is that aspect of feminist film that Gertrud Koch has traced from the *cinéma militant* through the theoretical emphasis on film language and identification.[13] Straub/Huillet films are instead more relevant to the reintroduction of Brecht and the Frankfurt School into the discussion of feminist theory, as proposed by Koch and Elin Diamond, for example. Diamond stresses the importance of Brechtian theory for feminism in theater because it allows space for "gestus" within the process of subverting the conventional means of representation. Koch's article on Critical Theory, on the other hand, suggests invoking phenomenology and existential psychoanalysis for film theory, examining the prelinguistic levels of the unconscious rather than the linguistic formations analyzed by Lacan. Koch's return to the fundamentals of perception and to the origins of film parallel Straub/Huillet's emphasis on a documentary attitude and a search for cinematic pleasure that is not predetermined by the culture industry and the "patriarchal orchestration of the look."[14] Thus Straub/Huillet move beyond the renunciation of pleasure of what de Lauretis calls the "Brechtian-Godardian" program of the materialist avant garde.[15]

This utopian force will now be examined on the basis of Straub/Huillet's film *Class Relations* (*Klassenverhältnisse*, 1983), based on the *Amerika*-novel by Franz Kafka. Here we will discover an example of the liberation from and through the cinema postulated by Walter Benjamin. Gertrud Koch poses this utopia as an alternative to the renunciation urged by Mulvey in the 1970s:

11. Ibid., 11.
12. Ibid., 12.
13. Gertrud Koch, "Exchanging the Gaze: Revisioning Feminist Film Theory," *New German Critique* 34 (Winter 1985): 140–141.
14. Koch, "Exchanging the Gaze," 142.
15. Teresa de Lauretis, *Alice Doesn't: Feminism, Semiotics, Cinema* (Bloomington: Indiana Univ. Press, 1984), 60.

If one follows Benjamin's utopia of the emancipated camera-"eye," however, its implications seem to run counter to the distancing effect desired by Mulvey: 'Thus, for contemporary life, the filmic representation of reality is incomparably more significant (than that of the painter), since it offers, precisely because of the thorough-going permeation of reality with mechanical equipment, an aspect of reality which is free of all equipment.'[16]

In regard to the novel *Amerika* and the film version *Class Relations*, we will explore Straub/Huillet's subversion of the Oedipal narrative, especially in spatial terms. This will allow us to address the fundamental dilemma shared by Kafka, Straub/Huillet and feminist (film) theory: how to envisage a realm of freedom for ourselves in this world when the language we have to describe it is one of the means of our enslavement.

Kafka sought to overcome this paradox in literature by challenging the mechanisms of narrative representation. As Klaus Ramm has demonstrated, Kafka reduced the presence of a narrator in his prose as much as possible, thus frustrating the reader's tendency to identify with either the narrator or the protagonist. A similar strategy is developed in feminist theory, which seeks to find a space in cinema that is not entirely dominated by the Oedipal narrative. Feminists have raised the possibility that every narrative is inherently a sadistic repetition of the Oedipus drama, the struggle of the son to become the father. In this drama, woman has no space of her own, but is seen only as an obstacle or as the currency of exchange.[17] The dilemma resides in the fact that in existing society such narratives are a source of pleasure and social cohesion as well as oppression. Therefore, the task is to employ narrative and undermine it at the same time.

An example of Kafka's subversion of narrative can be illustrated briefly by considering the plot of the short story *Das Urteil* ("The Judgment"). In this simple inversion of the Oedipus drama, Kafka constantly builds up in the reader an expectation of a narrative whole, a narrative trajectory. In the first few sentences, this trajectory is repeatedly traced from Georg Bendemann in his room, outside to the row of houses along the river, and then to the green hills beyond, and perhaps to the friend in Russia to whom Georg has just written. The plot of the story then proceeds to undermine the reader's expectations about all

16. Koch, "Exchanging the Gaze,"
17. Cf. de Lauretis, *Alice Doesn't*, 103–157.

these elements. Finally, rather than taking him to the distant
hills or to a reconciliation with his friend, Kafka cuts across
Georg's expected trajectory, having him drop himself *off* the
bridge instead of crossing it. Both the expected narrative movement and Georg's actual path have a fateful character. But by
placing two narrative wholes in opposition to each other, Kafka
has left for himself and the reader a structural gap promising
freedom from the narratives' closed Oedipal logic.

The challenge to closed narrative structure articulated by
feminist film theory echoes Kafka's narrative strategies. Much
avant-garde and feminist work has tried to frustrate the impulse
toward narrative wholeness in film, but often at the expense of
visual pleasure. This project was theorized most prominently by
Laura Mulvey in 1975 in her article "Visual Pleasure and Narrative Cinema." At its most extreme, this feminist theory calls for a
renunciation of all the "satisfaction, pleasure and privilege"
offered by the conventional cinema.

Partly on the basis of E. H. Gombrich's theories of perception, Teresa de Lauretis has recently argued that Mulvey's
"Brechtian-Godardian program" was unnecessarily brutal in its
denial of pleasure, and that it could not logically succeed without abolishing cinema entirely.[18] De Lauretis proposes an alternative analysis of conventional narrative, using Gombrich's theory of the "phantom percept."

The phantom percept is an illusion present in all sensory perception. It is fundamental to human survival, since it allows us
to reconcile the fragmentary data of our senses with the unified
whole we expect to perceive. Hence we tend to see a whole circle even if a segment of it is obscured from view. The success of
illusion in the visual arts rests on the exclusion of contradictory
percepts that would not fit into the expected pattern, "the social
contract by which external consistency is given up or traded
against the internal coherence of the illusion."[19]

De Lauretis believes that it must be possible to undermine
conventional narrative without destroying the basis of visual
pleasure. Therefore she asks the following:

> With regard to avant-garde practices which foreground frame,
> surface, montage, and other cinematic codes or materials, includ-
> ing sound, flicker, and special effects; could contradictory or

18. Ibid., 60.
19. Ibid., 62.

phantom percepts be produced not to negate illusion and destroy visual pleasure, but to problematize their terms in cinema?[20]

A problematization of narrative illusion and the pleasure it affords is found in Kafka's works as well as in the films of Danièle Huillet and Jean-Marie Straub. Let us now turn to Straub/Huillet's film *Class Relations*, based on Kafka's novel-fragment set in America. Through a visual problematization of Karl Rossmann's subjectivity, Straub/Huillet's film achieves many of the goals of feminist film practice without destroying visual pleasure.

The first reel of *Class Relations* corresponds to "Der Heizer" ("The Stoker"), the opening chapter of Kafka's novel. Kafka was less happy with "The Stoker" segment than with its companion piece, "The Judgment." He called it a "bald imitation of Dickens," perhaps because it at times seems to postulate a privileged narrator who reveals accurately Karl Rossmann's subjective percep-tions.[21] For instance, when he first enters the ship captain's office, the seat of power and justice, Karl looks out at the majestic spec-tacle of ships in New York harbor. The description concludes, "Yes, in this room one knew where one was."[22] Soon thereafter, as the stoker is clearly failing in his plea for justice, the view shifts to small motorboats darting about and "peculiar floating objects," and the description concludes, "A movement without end, a rest-lessness, carried over from the restless element onto helpless humanity and their works."[23] The subjective impressions are inconsistent but perfectly logical if we assume there is a superior narrator who is merely revealing Karl's state of mind.

Most film treatments of Kafka have seized precisely on this subjective identification and have tried to depict the images described. Straub/Huillet, on the other hand, use their film to explore the relations between the figure of Karl and the narra-tives within which he is placed. They do so solely on the basis of the pared-down utterances they have selected from the novel-fragment, in a manner of speech which Wolfram Schütte has called "an arena where struggles of power and class take place."[24] It is clear at the beginning of both the film and the story that

20. Ibid., 63.
21. Franz Kafka, *Tagebücher 1910–1923* (New York: Schocken, 1949), 535.
22. Franz Kafka, *Amerika* (Frankfurt: Fischer, 1973), 12. Translation by B. Byg.
23. Ibid., 16.
24. Wolfram Schütte, "Arbeit, Gerechtigkeit, Liebe," in *Frankfurter Rundschau*, February 24, 1984, p. 12.

Karl's position in matters of class and power is very important. This position is explored by Straub/Huillet through Kafka's use of language and his method of narration as well as through their own construction of the narrative space of cinema.[25]

As Karl Rossmann arrives by ship in New York, his narrative takes a sudden turn from his vision of the Goddess of Liberty back to the lower decks of the ship. He searches there for his lost umbrella (a connection to his family and the Old World) and finds a German-speaking ally and father figure in the person of the stoker. The conditions of this alliance are tenuous, however. Karl is drawn to the stoker only because they have suffered similar humiliations. But when the stoker says "there must have been a reason" for Karl's exile, Karl responds, "Now I could also become a stoker. To my parents it's quite indifferent now" (*Class Relations*, subtitles). He refuses to reveal to the stoker the true basis of his sympathy, that his parents have disowned him for getting a servant pregnant. At the same time his reference to the stoker's job betrays his presumption of superiority.

Their solidarity continues to rely on this lack of communication. Karl explains why he does not expect to study in America with a series of speculations, concluding with the assumption, "Besides, people here have a prejudice against foreigners, I believe." Not only is the word "here" ironic, since he hasn't "arrived" anywhere, but the stoker heightens the irony by responding, "Have you learned that, too, already? Well, then that's good. Then you're my man." In fact, Karl has not learned/experienced (the word is *erfahren*) anything new up to this point, and the stoker's ensuing complaints about his Rumanian supervisor on a German ship build up a nationalistic bond between them. Karl's invented solidarity betrays his presumption of superiority as he tells the stoker not to stand for such treatment and later impulsively speaks up for him in the captain's office. The speciousness of this solidarity is fully exposed in Karl's last theatrical attempt to impress the captain with its longevity: "To me you have always depicted it so clearly,"

25. "Narrative space" is a concept developed by Stephen Heath. It describes the way in which narrative cinema leads viewers to construct a unified sense of space out of the fragments offered by the shots of a film. Common devices employed are establishing shots, point-of-views-shots, reverse angle shots, and eye-line matches. For a fuller explanation, see Heath, "Narrative Space," in *Narrative, Apparatus, Ideology*, ed. Philip Rosen (New York: Columbia Univ. Press, 1986), pp. 379–420.

he admonishes the stoker. Karl has attempted to fabricate a long-standing bond out of a shared feeling of victimization. Yet it becomes clear through the narrative that their two stories have nothing in common, since their social circumstances remain different.

In addition to social roles, the power to narrate is another means by which characters' relative positions are revealed. By transferring this power from figure to figure, Kafka reveals class relations and subverts narrative identification at the same time. The entire work is Karl's story, after all, but by the end of the "Stoker" sequence he is the one character with no story to tell. Karl himself raises the issue of narration, since he believes the stoker's failure lies in his inability to use his own tale of victimization effectively to gain sympathy. Yet Karl's support of the stoker has nothing to do with the stoker's story, either, despite Karl's lie. Karl's own narrative is more pertinent. In Kafka's novel, Karl's narrative is summarized in a dependent clause within the opening sentence, but is narrated thoroughly only by the uncle, with Karl's comments revealed by internal monologue. In the film, both the initial summary and Karl's unspoken commentary are dropped. Only the uncle has the privilege of explaining Karl's journey and eliciting our sympathy for him. The uncle's narrative, one of the longest speeches of the film, takes away the central position from the stoker. It is delivered with polished theatricality by Mario Adorf, whose vocal style is one extreme of a broad spectrum of voices in the film. With this narrative, the uncle places Karl back into continuity with the past, in fact embedding Karl's exile into his own fantastic success story. Now that the relationship is clear, the uncle usurps Karl's right to speak by repeating his statements, almost mockingly. For example, "It did him no harm!" – referring to the ocean crossing below decks. The uncle also takes over the words that had propelled Karl in his actions – words such as "right" and "justice," which Karl has been repeating as in a school lesson but with the belief that they might have some power on their own. In the face of the uncle's impatience over the attention given the stoker, Karl insists, "But that isn't important in a matter of justice." The uncle then takes over the phrase "matter of justice," subordinates it to a "matter of discipline," and declares both subordinate to the judgment of the captain. The uncle finally uses his superior position and understanding to

steer the plot of the story itself: "I understand perfectly your way
of acting, but precisely that gives me the right to conduct you
hence most quickly."

To this assertion of power over him, Karl responds by turning
to the stoker's oppression, not his own. Using the intimate form
of address for the first time – as if talking to himself or to a family member – he asks the stoker why *he* doesn't resist. But since
the relationship Karl has hoped for has been destroyed,
Straub/Huillet cut the upper body of the stoker out of the
frame as Karl kneels and holds his hand, telling him he must
leave him on his own.

The final speech in this section of the film, closing the stoker
episode, again has the uncle as omniscient narrator: "You felt
abandoned, there you met the stoker, and now you are grateful
to him; that is very laudable. But don't push that too far, if only
out of love for me, and learn to comprehend your place." The
word "place" (*Stellung*) is the achieved end of the entire
sequence. Lost in the ship, sent to America, Karl had only an
assumed "place" in regard to the stoker. The slender legacy he
has brought from home, however, has expanded to the point
that it temporarily determines his identity and fate: it is a long
tracking shot from a very low angle, showing the facades of
Uncle Jacob's endless harbor warehouses. The father's power
and Karl's dependence and vulnerability are given material substance in composition, montage, and duration. Straub/Huillet
have no need to repeat Kafka's summation, "It was truly as if
there were no stoker anymore."[26]

If there is no hope of freedom in Karl's narrative, is there at
least hope for Karl? Or is there hope for the viewers of this film?
Their task is not an easy one. By eliminating many of the familiar
supports of film narrative, such as establishing shots and reverse
angle shots, Straub/Huillet make it much more difficult to construct a complete narrative space out of the fragments filmed.
Karl's inability to provide us with an intentional direction of the
narrative is also an inability to present an overview of its locations. We are left with the fragile unifying function of Karl's mere
presence, variously placed within the class relations of language
and – as we will now examine – space. It is in the spatial gaps of
this narrative construction that we will look for hope.

Karl's presence in the two locations of "The Stoker" segment

26. Kafka, *Amerika*, 30

is never comfortably established in terms of space. Most of the shots of him consist of only two quite two-dimensional compositions. In the stoker's cabin he is perched precariously on the edge of the bunk. We see none of his retreat below decks, only his knock at the stoker's cabin door. He does not move freely into the cabin but is conducted there. His confinement is emphasized when he rises to look for his suitcase and the stoker's arm enters the frame to push him back onto the bed. Similarly, in the captain's office we see Karl step forward out of the frame of the shot, in order to defend the stoker, but we have not yet seen the space into which the words are spoken. He steps into a void, a feeling instinctively shared by the audience since no "phantom percept" can be constructed.

The space of the captain's office – like that of most of the film – is never unified by conventional narrative use of the camera, which would establish an overview of the space and would unify it by movement from one shot to another or at least by solidly connected eye-line matches. Instead, the three positions occupied by the characters in the confrontation are carefully framed and prevented from overlapping. The stoker and later his foreman and others stand against the door or near it. The captain, the uncle, and the officers sit in easy chairs with windows behind them in a roomier shot of the interior. Karl stands alone along a paneled wall in the most two-dimensional composition, a medium close-up. The only movement between these fragments of narrative space is the invasion of Karl's space by the uncle as he takes over Karl's right to speak.

Any unity attributed to the space of this office must be constructed through an effort by the viewer. But this effort calls attention to the undefined space between the three basic compositions, just as the rigidity of the frame and the delivery of the text call attention to the constructed nature of the language we hear. Who could inhabit this abstract, undefined space?

One possible answer would be Karl, and in a conventional *Bildungsroman* this would be the audience's expectation. But despite the fact that the viewers must use Karl as a visual organizing principle, they are constantly reminded that other reference points often have greater influence on the connections between filmed spaces. By the end of the film, Karl loses all the external characteristics that make him a narrative hero. The family tie to his uncle is abruptly severed, he loses his only memento of his parents (their photograph), and finally he gives up his name for the label "Negro." But Straub/Huillet find the optimism in Kafka's novel in the separation between its protagonist and the external narrative devices that make him "Karl Rossmann." It is one of the major achievements of this film, I believe, that the performance of Christian Heinisch is visually and acoustically so doggedly consistent. His measured, articulate recitation of Kafka's text functions as a tonic chord among the voices in the film, which range from professional stage rhetoric to the straining memorized speech of non-German speakers and lay actors. As his links to the past are cut, Karl also maintains the determined yet well-meaning appearance he had at the beginning. As a photo caption in *Der Spiegel* put it, "Not a hair is disturbed."[27]

Throughout the film, Karl is carefully located in regard to the narratives of others, usually in an insecure position of his own. He speaks less and less until, in the final scene, he is completely silent. His narrative role diminishes – from protagonist to witness – but his importance to the film does not.

Straub/Huillet often show Karl alone on screen, watching and listening. Most often his gaze is directed inward, toward the center of a room or any space to which he is confined. For example, later in the film Karl hears Robinson's story on the balcony of Brunelda's apartment. Robinson and Delamarche are subservient to Brunelda, and they want to enslave Karl. As Robinson talks to Karl, the view from the balcony is never revealed. The space around the two is limited to a door, a low wall, and a drainpipe. Later, when Brunelda forces Karl to look out at a political parade through her opera glasses, Karl insists he does not see anything – and neither does the viewer. He sees enough already, Karl maintains. The effect of this is twofold. It implies that Karl's experiences do indeed contain sufficient political information to understand class relations. Furthermore, the frustration of the viewer's gaze exaggerates the illusion of confinement, yet calls attention to the film frame as one source of this illusion.

So far, this might seem to be an example of the Brechtian frustration of visual pleasure as urged by Laura Mulvey. But Kafka's aesthetic is not exhausted in revealing the unreliability

27. Helmuth Karesek, "Niemandsland Amerika," *Der Spiegel* 38 (27 Feb. 1984): 184. Translation by B. Byg.

or the fragmentary nature of his subjective narration. Similarly, since we are allowed to share Karl's position as witness, as listener, we are tempted to construct some future that would be implied by his experience, even if he does not. We know that he sees less than the camera can show, and this reminder disrupts conventional visual pleasure and provokes our escape from the narrative – to insist on seeing more, and differently.

It is in basing the pleasure of their narrative on the impulse to escape the structural confines of cinema that I see the connection between Straub/ Huillet and feminist theory. In this regard, I believe it would be a mistake to consider Straub/Huillet as predominantly "minimalist" or "structuralist" filmmakers, or to assume they have issued a "blanket condemnation of narrative and illusionism." It is important to distinguish the strategies of Straub/Huillet as described here from "the minimalist strategies of materialist avant-garde cinema," which de Lauretis criticizes for being "predicated on, even as they work against, the (transcendental) male subject."[28] Indeed, it is the desire for an alternative basis for the film practice and narrative structure that gives dramatic force to the composition of Straub/Huillet's work.

A decisive example of Straub/Huillet's separation of visual pleasure from (transcendental) male subjectivity occurs in the filming of the story told Karl by Therese, the hotel secretary. Karl and Therese stand at a white window, beyond which is supposedly snow. Therese looks out, while Karl looks somewhat more toward her and the camera. As Therese begins her story, the camera tracks in from the shot of them both to a close-up of Karl listening. As the story is completed, the process is reversed – the camera tracks out from Karl to the initial shot of both figures together.

This sequence sums up the narrative lines of the film and reveals the possibility of freedom beyond them. First, the story Therese tells is simple, linear, and hopeless, and it is given an unforgettable delivery by Libgart Schwarz, counterbalancing the bombastic rhetoric of Mario Adorf earlier in the film. After a night without shelter in winter, Therese's mother goes with her child to a building site where she is to obtain work. Immediately she climbs a scaffold and walks along it with miraculous agility to its end, where she topples over a pile of bricks and falls to her death. The physical separateness of Therese and Karl can

28. de Lauretis, *Alice Doesn't*, 68.

also be described in terms of straight lines, since they face at oblique angles across the axis of the camera. Yet two devices imply a connection. In the only such shot in the film, the tracking camera has indeed set up a coherent narrative space that they share on equal terms. The use of reverse cuts during the story, although implying separateness, are nonetheless an acknowledgement of communication and are all the more powerful due to their rarity in the work of Straub/Huillet. At the end of the sequence, the camera tracks out to rejoin Karl and Therese, again on equal terms in the composition.

The fact that their gazes cross the axis of the camera conveys both separateness and complementariness. There is no indication that Karl can do anything with this story except hear it. But there is one more element along the linear structure of this scene that gives it a hopeful balance. This is the empty window, which is at the center of the frame at both beginning and end, a counterpart to the camera and the screen themselves. The window lights Therese's face as she looks out, in a composition reminiscent of earlier films by Straub/Huillet. Far from frustrating visual pleasure, this shot uses the subjective point of view (so freely exploited in the empty promises of commercial cinema) to suggest unlimited possibility.

Whatever solidarity Karl and Therese achieve in this scene produces no concrete change in their fates as characters, but it is profoundly significant for the viewer. Nothing is visible in this white window, but as the mediating space between Therese speaking (remembering) and Karl listening (perhaps understanding), it stands as a potential realm where the justice Karl originally spoke of could truly be located. The Father and the Law, represented by Uncle Jacob and the Captain in the "Stoker" sequence, are nowhere to be seen. Recalling Benjamin's utopian vision, the realm of freedom is outside the space which the film can construct, but still a construction of the cinema.

The conclusion of the film resonates with this structure. In the last sequence, no more of Kafka's text is spoken at all. Karl and another elevator boy, Giacomo, are shown sitting next to each other on a train bound for Oklahoma. They exchange smiling glances, then a close-up shows Karl finally looking out the window. Then, with thoroughly conventional cinematic logic, we are allowed to see what Karl sees: the passing landscape of the Missouri River Valley.

This subversion of the Oedipal narrative allows us to consider an alternative to the linguistic model adopted by feminist film theory from Lacan. Koch proposed exactly this type of attention to the "mimetic" impact of objects and landscapes in film.[29] As Huillet said of their film *Too Early, Too Late* (*Zu früh, zu spät,* 1981), "But there are landscapes and they are treated exactly as if they were people."[30] I would argue that *Class Relations* achieves what Koch admires in the "aesthetically most advanced films" of the feminist avant garde: "[T]hey anticipate an expanded and radicalized notion of subjectivity . . . a type of subjectivity that transcends any abstract subject-object dichotomy."[31]

The final shot of the river and the initial few seconds' view of the Statue of Liberty are the only such "traveling" shots in the entire film and the only shots filmed in America. The motion of the arrival in New York Harbor is negated by Karl's return to the narrative of his past. A Kafkaesque suspicion would be that the cycle would repeat itself in the second instance, but Straub/ Huillet's construction of contradictory percepts reveals that neither metaphysical forces nor Karl's supposed "true nature" makes this unavoidable. In fact, an audience that refuses to let go of the memory of Therese at the window will finally see that, although the film does not present an image of freedom, it does point to a freedom beyond its own structure. I do not believe this process involves the sacrifice of visual pleasure. Instead, I believe Straub/Huillet allow their audiences a fundamental joy in constructing the phantom percept of this freedom. In doing so, they meet the challenge of feminist cinema de Lauretis described as follows:

> Not to deny all coherence to representation, or to prevent all possibility of identification and subject reflection, or again to void perception of all meaning formation; but to displace its orientation, to redirect "purposeful attending" toward another object of vision, and to construct other ways of seeing.[32]

29. Koch, "Exchanging the Gaze," 144–45, 148.
30. Huillet, "Feuer im Innern des Berges," 9.
31. Koch, "Exchanging the Gaze," 151.
32. de Lauretis, *Alice Doesn't*, 63.

19

The Films of Lothar Lambert

jeffrey m. peck

Jeffrey Peck provides us with an introduction to the films of under-ground director Lothar Lambert, whom he has also interviewed for this article. Lambert lives in what we used to call West Berlin. He is gay, but he is not interested in being identified as a "gay filmmaker"; rather, he wants to continue making films which subvert rigid social stereotypes about gender and sexual identity and encourage people to become more accepting of themselves and others. His films examine sex-uality quite graphically, focusing on people on the margins, both sexu-ally and socially – but not in a glamorous or trendy sense. Content to continue making "no-budget" underground films, he has no interest in becoming part of the film industry, but does not consider himself at all "avant-garde" or experimental, either. His films mix a sort of seamy verité and almost sentimental melodrama with a strong dose of self-irony.
—THE EDITORS

Lothar Lambert is unlike any other German director, at least those with whom one popularly identifies German cinema, such as Fassbinder, Herzog, von Trotta, or Wenders. Although one would be more inclined to include Lambert in a list of German filmmakers such as Ulrike Ottinger, Elfi Mikesch, Helke Sander, or Rosa von Praunheim, he still maintains a very personal style that has, in fact, become his trademark. While the creative wave of the more celebrated (although not necessarily more interest-ing) group of directors has subsided and the German New Wave has been eclipsed by Spanish or Soviet cinema, Lambert's low-budget productions keep coming, most often with the same troupe of actors. After completing his seventeenth film, Lam-bert's work might be seen as a cross between directors as diverse as Andy Warhol, Russ Meyer, and you, filming your own home movies. His films have, however, a very special Berlin touch, as one might gather merely from the ironic title of his film that refers to his beloved home, *Fucking City.*

Born in 1944 in Rudolstadt, Thüringen, raised in Berlin, the backdrop for almost all of his films, Lambert studied journalism (*Publizistik*) at the Freie Universität in Berlin before he joined the editorial staff of the Berlin newspaper *Der Abend.* He has worked for many years as a free-lance and television critic in Berlin while making his films.

While his films often have gay characters, his work cannot be identified with any one sexual orientation or subculture. He clearly identifies with outsiders, often those from the seamier side of life – pimps, prostitutes, drug addicts, transvestites – but he is even more preoccupied with less flamboyant outsiders, such as the Turkish guest workers (*Gastarbeiter*) in Berlin, and the rest of the utterly "normal" population who lead, at least in Lambert's eyes, rather banal and boring lives. But all of Lambert's characters, from whatever side of the tracks, are searching for fulfillment at the most fundamental of levels: they all seem to want just a little love, understanding, and happiness.

What saves Lambert's films from disintegrating into mere melodrama, however, is the irony and humor with which he treats these characters and situations, whether it be the meek bank employee who is liberated from his dreary existence by performing at night as a transvestite, as in *Drama in Blond,* or the lonely and frustrated pharmacist's assistant who tries to become a film star in New York, as in *Fräulein Berlin.* His "simple" stories, as he repeatedly calls them, reflect the simplicity of the people he wants to present. By exposing people's most basic emotions, often in the most intimate of situations, he uncovers that side of them that is the most vulnerable and at the same time the most human. Lambert's superrealistic technique, often rough and brutally direct, unmasks people at their most private moments. Such frank and explicit display has, in fact, provoked charges of obscenity or pornography. Although in this context we are not inclined to admit it, we cannot help identifying with these characters who are experimenting with something new or even dangerous. We cheer them on, at least secretly, since they are able to liberate themselves from middle-class and conventional social constraints in ways that we might not dare.

Sex and sexual identity figure prominently in all of Lambert's films, as does the city of Berlin. The city today is gray and dreary; a decadent veneer of its faded elegance may remain, but the glamour and glitter are dimmed and considerably drained. Yet a metropolis like Berlin creates spaces for meeting, opportunities for chance and exciting encounters between groups of people who might not "normally" come together: different nationalities – Germans, Turks, Pakistanis, Arabs, and Americans – and various sexual orientations – gay, straight, bisexual, asexual. The city and sex are not far removed from each other.

In one of Lambert's most popular films, *Tiergarten* (the first that he directs and does the camera work and cutting), West Berlin's most famous and popular park becomes the setting for such encounters and his usual commentary on life in the big city. Inhabited by freaks, "weird types," and social outcasts that the average park visitor may never notice, the daily sojourns of a frustrated well-to-do housewife cum poetess draws our attention to a subculture that is trying to make a place for itself in this seemingly idyllic and protected city environment of trees and lakes. Against this backdrop, the Tiergarten may be an escape for some, like this housewife, but her encounters with this underbelly of the world only show her how much they have in common. She seems to find temporary refuge in the park by masquerading in various wigs and costumes to join the parade of strange people. Yet Lambert only uses this character to draw the audience into the lives of the many unusual denizens of this demimonde: a drunken cabaret actress who tries to seduce Turks, a drug-addicted prostitute, unemployed guest workers, and even an old man who has lost his wife and just wants a little human warmth. A cross between low-budget (the film only cost 15,000 marks), human interest, social commentary, and documentary, the film touches the audience. We get to know this array of characters and care about their plight, because the urge for love, intimacy, and empathy transcend class, profession, race, or sexual orientation. These "flipped-out types" in the park may indeed suffer more without the comforts of a luxury apartment like our heroine has, but her tragic ending only emphasizes the hopelessness of human existence in general.

Life is survival. For Lambert's characters this task requires not only individual energy to shore up their fragmentary existence, but also solidarity among the disaffected. Meaning is not to be found without a struggle. Lambert's ironic treatment, however, saves the film from mere kitsch; the structure of the film – disconnected scenes, poor lighting, and a grittiness in his 16 mm production – reinforces the disjointed sense of life that he wants to expose. We leave the theater having been confronted with lives that we probably did not know before, but perhaps strengthened in our conviction to make life better, to fit the pieces together more coherently. This is not to say, however, that the films are moralistic and leave us with a message. They merely point to the sadness and hopelessness of many peoples' lives, and we are left to our own conclusions.

In one of Lambert's more recent films, *Drama in Blond,* the same kind of theme evolves toward a more optimistic conclusion. Lambert himself plays a shy bank employee who is dominated by his sister with whom he has an unusually "close" relationship. He is liberated, quite literally, from his dreary existence when he visits a local drag show in the company of a younger colleague who turns out to enjoy dressing in the clothes of the opposite sex. Lambert's character is simultaneously being coyly pursued, however, by the everpresent and overly helpful female neighbor. The woman finally begins to untangle his curious and frustrating ambivalence towards her when she hears loud music blasting from this otherwise tranquil apartment – and suddenly meets a female version of her neighbor! The bank employee does turn into a drag queen, or at least a parody of one. But more importantly, he frees himself from the oppressive constraints of a conventional world that will not give people like him the freedom to be their real selves. Lambert asks us here to question what constitutes such a self. The play on dressing up and transforming one's identity takes the cliché of fantasy being more than reality a step further. Here imagination takes people into new worlds that are frightening, extreme, decadent, even "perverse" and "deviant," whether transvestite or S&M porno star. Lambert obviously sees how our sexual urges and desires can take us further into ourselves and become a vehicle for expressing sincere human needs, warmth, and closeness. Sex is not to be feared, but to be entertaining and to be enjoyed, since it is a way of reaching out to other human beings. Without moral judgments, Lambert liberates sexual desire and pleasure from traditional sexual orientation and gendered roles by throwing all traditional categories up for grabs.

In another Lambert production, *Paso Doble,* the most well-funded at 200,000 marks, the title of "Double Steps" is taken quite literally. The plot revolves around a middle-class couple who wants to escape their boring family life in West Germany. After returning from Spain, the traditional vacation for this class of Germans, the marriage begins to fall apart after they both have extramarital sexual encounters: she with a Persian masseur and he with a Spanish hustler. Through these unusual experiences, husband and wife confront the boundaries of their traditional existence as man and woman, husband and wife, father and mother, and recognize that once they have freed themselves of these constraints, they can now get to know each other as people. The final scene of the film with husband and wife dressed in the other's clothes and dancing with each other in reversed gender roles reminds us that happiness is not based on adhering to the rules or codes of social norms but following one's feelings. Caught up in a crazy and often lonely world, only the individual can establish ethical categories that are based on very simple criteria – human kindness, warmth, openness, and generosity – that are nevertheless difficult to find.

In his own way, Lambert contributes to the breaking down of traditional gendered roles, fixed sexual preferences, and rigid categories that prevent rather than encourage free expression. Lambert gets down to the "nitty-gritty" of life in films – called "kleenex" or "throw away" – whose production values may seem to reinforce the transience or disposable quality of lives represented in these productions. But this is not the case: although nothing is quite sacred or hidden for Lambert, he respects human dignity even when he is revealing its basest elements.

In fact, all of Lambert's work seems to be a kind of "coming out" story. This exposure is not just meant sexually, but a metaphor for everyone who is "closeted" in life and just does not seem to fit. For Lambert, everyone, no matter how conventional they may appear, is yearning to be liberated from some constraint or conventional mores to which they have had to conform. Ultimately, the audiences who watch Lambert's films, whether outsiders or the middle class, recognize themselves in his work. While they might not fancy themselves one of the "stars" of his productions, they can imagine what it feels like to be in the predicament of his characters. Lambert captures through the simplest of technical and cinematographic means the complexity of human life, reduced however to its most fundamental instincts. Lambert's egalitarian ethic that strips away the facades of everyday life spares no one, neither those who are often excluded and disenfranchised, nor the self-righteous middle class that thinks it has all the answers. But by poking fun at both these groups, he manages to get us to notice sides of life that we may well have ignored or taken for granted, those that are often invisible and those that are much too dominant. Lambert's "slice of life" cuts very sharp, and we must commend him for making this possible.

The following interview took place in August 1987 in Berlin. It was conducted almost entirely in English at Lambert's request, and I have edited the transcript of the tape with Lambert's approval.

Q. I feel compelled to start out with the most obvious question for such a volume on gender perspectives. How would you characterize for your work the relationship between gender and sexual preference?

A. I think that the individual profile of a person is a combination of both the male and the female, so sexual preference doesn't really have much to do with sexual characteristics. The typical clichés – that *this* is typically male or *that* is typically female – have nothing to do with the individual or bodily constitution of a person. They are generalities which cannot be coordinated with the sexual wishes and expectations of an individual. This masculine and feminine behavior which one finds in society is mostly only learned (*antrainiert*) and socialized. It has little to do with how people really are when they are in their rooms in the dark where their neighbors can't see them, and they do as they wish.

Q. How would you define specific gender categories of masculinity and femininity?

A. We need to move away from the prejudices I just spoke about. One confronts of course complete confusion about what is masculine and what is feminine. One can say it is masculine to admit weakness, and that is really strength. Strength defined as holding oneself back and giving oneself up for someone else is categorized as typically feminine. One doesn't get very far by characterizing people with these categories. I think it would be better to focus on the human (*menschliche*) in people, what brings men and women together and not what divides them. In fact, I would say that if one wants to differentiate people, better categories would describe those who are mature or childish, self-reliant or dependent (*fremdbestimmt*), because it would include all kinds of gender differentiations.

Q. To take the question of the "mixing" of gender directly into your films, I wanted to ask you about your use of transvestites as characters. Is this a specific vehicle for you to deal with this issue?

A. First, I think it is simply fun for people to dress up (*verkleiden*) in costume; it brings out the comic and the ironic. These kinds of figures have always been popular in theater and in film. I enjoy especially playing with "Sein" (existence) and "Schein" (appearance), to show how so-called "machos" fall for another man when he is dressed up like a woman and consequently learn something about themselves.

Q. How would you respond to the charge by feminists that transvestites, as merely a parody of women, promote negative stereotypes of women?

A. Basically I am in favor of parody, not only about femininity, but also about so-called masculinity. Parody is an exaggeration of reality and can therefore make reality clearer through comedy and laughter; it can portray what one otherwise might only be able to represent through tragedy.

Q. Looking at the broader ramifications of what we have been talking about regarding gender, do you think that the presentation of characters that break down gender differences ultimately contributes to subverting the traditional family, which incidentally does not come out looking very good in your films?

A. I would not want to say that, except that it is clear that the traditional family has brought much unhappiness to many people who have been trapped by its strict rules and are afraid to get out. When I show family, I also parody the traditional family. I show how characters suffer in it and want to break out and find out who they are. This doesn't mean that I am against the family, but it must be flexible enough to accommodate the individual members' desire to be free (*locker*) and to take the roles which fit them. Children should be able to take more responsibility, for example, or parents to have the chance to feel freer with themselves and their children.

Q. How would you describe your films in general as they deal with the problems of sexual identity?

A. My films are personal and defined by my need to express myself through this medium which I have loved since childhood. It was then that I had my first practical experience when I did the sound for my family's 8mm films by adding music to them. You might say I am the grandfather of the music video. Even today you can see this montage style in my work when I put music and scenes together to create new content. To get back to your question. I have a position which can't be identified with either sex. As a man I can still feel what a woman needs and desires. I feel the oppression which societies use against people, men or women. I identify with the problems they have fulfilling their lives, especially regarding sexual concerns. I am not trying to make socially critical movies. I want to show reality as I see it, with irony. I leave it to the onlooker to interpret it as tragic or comic, just like life. I am interested in how you judge what you see. I am often amused by what critics see in my films since they interpret them so differently. Some reviewers will see the same film as a tragedy or as a comedy.

Q. Your style of filmmaking, which has been called low-budget, "no-budget," "kleenex," or throw-away filmmaking, is certainly different from commercial Hollywood films. How would you describe the differences?

A. I make my films by myself; in that way I differ from Hollywood. I do my own production, directing, camera, script, and editing (it is the cutting which I actually like best). I never say I will work from the beginning to the end of the month. My work is spontaneous; I get friends together and then we begin to film. The people I work with are not professional actors, but my friends. If they are interested they can work for me. Their talent is secondary to the consideration that we can all be together. Comparisons which have been made between me and Fassbinder, then, are not appropriate. I don't think that the people who work for me are indebted to me, especially since they don't get paid or get famous. I don't make films to get rich or famous.

Q. Are you surprised then with the notoriety you have received?

A. Since I am a film critic myself, I see many bad films and therefore understand why my films get recognition. If you bring personal things into films, people respond.

Q. Some critics have identified you as a gay film director. What do you understand by that, and would you compare yourself then to directors such as Rosa von Praunheim or Frank Ripploh?

A. I see myself as quite different from them. I happen to be gay, but am not just a gay film director. I often have gay characters in my films and of course they interest me because of my

personal life. But I hope that I integrate these characters naturally into my films just as I do heterosexual figures. I can make
fun of both. I have often been reproached by gay people that I
am promoting clichés or prejudices. I am merely representing
what I see around me in a homosexual world, and unfortunately the homosexual often acts according to his own parodies.
This can be funny, it can get on one's nerves, or one can also see
the tragedy behind it. But this is the complexity of reality and I
try to present it in my films.

Q. Does every one of yours films raise the issue of sexual identity?

A. In my life sex is very important. I see why sex becomes even
more important for those people who don't get enough. It is
really the motor of people's lives. It gives people power and is at
the root of human instincts. It is the motor of what one doesn't
see on the surface. I am only a little freer by talking about it in
my films. Some people miss this freedom in conventional films.
I do not want to exploit sex to make more money. My films are
both more honest and more radical.

*Q. Do you think your films are sexually shocking? To put it bluntly,
are they pornographic?*

A. I don't think they are pornographic, since I would see
pornography defining itself by trying to arouse sexual desire,
and my films do not do this. In fact they sometimes literally turn
people off. They kill desire because they often show sex without
a romantic or idealistic context.

*Q. Do you think there is a difference between sexual desire in men and
women, at least in the way you depict the sexes in your films?*

A. To say that they have the same sexual desire would be too
general. Each person is different. In general the differences are
not so great as feminists, homosexuals, and machos would like
to depict. Everyone needs to be loved. Everyone needs tenderness and suffers from loneliness. These basic needs become
problematic in our society. It may sound banal or mundane but
I am not afraid of banality in my films, because that is what most
people suffer from, not from the major problems of the world.

*Q. You are so concerned with the issue of outsiders, those who don't fit
into society, those with unconventional sexual desires, everyday people
who are lonely. Do you see a relationship between the outsider and the
problem of sexual identity?*

A. For the outsider who doesn't have responsibility to a family
or a profession, let's say, it is much easier to realize what s/he

really needs. People who are bound in conventional ways hardly find out who they really are, and they just act as they are expected. I am very much interested in the conflict that arises when these people's facades are exposed and they are brought into conflict about who they are.

Q. Do you have a specific public you are trying to reach, specifically male or female for example?

A. It depends on the film. When I made the film *Nightmare Woman* (*Die Alptraumfrau*), many women identified with it more easily because it centered on a female person, but on the other hand, when I was a kid, I always identified with the female stars and not with their male partners. It depends on the conflict. If you have someone who has a quarrel with his/her parents, then the viewer can identify with this problem whether s/he is a man or a woman because he or she sees common problems. It depends on the presentation of the film. If the viewer really feels for the actor, the sex is not important.

Q. How do your films connect the issue of sexual identity and the city of Berlin, which is the location of your films as well as your home?

A. It is always easier in a big city like Berlin to lead a double life and have a double morality. In a small town it is not possible to let anyone look behind your facade. In the big city there are so many ghettoes, and you can find people who have the same wishes and needs, and therefore find solidarity. This relieves much of the pressure.

Q. What are the types, the characters that fascinate you in a city like Berlin?

A. Oh, that is difficult to say, because somehow I am still a naive filmmaker, although I have learned many tricks about how to keep people interested in a story for one and a half hours. I am still naive enough to get interested in a person in real life, and like keeping a diary or a photo album, I want to remember them and put them in a film – especially if they are strong individuals and different. It is more interesting or fascinating to keep them. Looking behind the facade of a bourgeois person, one finds strong hidden talents which society never allows to come out. I find these types very exciting. People don't have to be exotic. I am not interested in fashion. I don't want to make a new wave film or punk film, because that would be too much on the surface. Although I feel I am banal, somehow I am more interested in the person who is behind the trends. If the person needs fashion to protect him/herself, that is interesting, but a punk scene alone, for example, is far removed from my way of making modern film.

Q. You often appear in your own films. Do you do this merely as a kind of trademark, or do you really think that you can better dramatize characters or issues which are important to you?

A. When I was young, I had the naive or childish wish like many children of my generation to be a film star. Today perhaps adolescents want to be rock stars. This was part of starting to film and act myself, since naturally no one else would put me in a film. This wish comes back from time to time, not too often, thank God. I have fun, making fun of myself. I like to laugh about other people as part of a feeling of solidarity, and I don't mind if they laugh at me. It's only fair that if I ask them to be naked psychologically in front of the camera, I should do the same. I believe if we are are colleagues, we should both be able to be friends on the same level.

Q. I think I'll have to take the cue from your reference to psychological nakedness and ask you about nudity in your films. In almost all of your films, people spend a lot of time taking their clothes off. Is this essential for the issues that concern you?

A. It is more interesting to see how people behave when it comes to love or sex, to see if they are tender or brutal. This fascinates me more than seeing how they eat their breakfast because these intimate moments reveal so much.

Q. Why do you think that sex is so telling about people's behavior?

A. Because most people do not have the chance to be free about sex, it is very interesting to see how they deal with sex, how they overcome their sexual conflicts. This tells a great deal about how they overcome problems in their daily life.

Q. Your responses really show how aware you are about the struggle between people's individual desires and social expectations. But do you think presenting these problems as you do will change those who come to see your films?

A. I can only tell you about the kinds of responses I get from those who come to talk to me after a film or write to me. Sometimes I have a discussion after a film, and if a girl comes with her boyfriend, she does not dare to say what she thinks of my film because it is too intimate. So, often the girl leaves her friend and comes to me privately and thanks me for what I have presented in the film. She found it important for her.

Q. What might she talk about?

A. For example, about the sexual dreams of women in *Nightmare Woman*. If it comes to a discussion, people remain silent because they are not used to speaking about the sexual desires in their dreams. They never tell them to their partners or even dare to confess them to themselves.

Q. Do you think, then, your films have a sort of liberating quality?

A. That would of course be the best possible effect. But people who are too repressed or inhibited often react aggressively. So sometimes after my harmless television pieces which deal with marriage, I get anonymous phone calls. Even this was too strong for the average television viewer. They called it dirty to look into a bedroom of a couple and see that there is anything but the harmony and love one would expect in kitsch novels.

Q. Since your films often provoke such extreme responses, do you have difficulty financing your films?

A. I finance my films by my journalistic work. Even with television, if they ask me to do something, I have to do what they call more harmless scenes. They overlook the fact that the theme is the same, but I make some compromises. For example, I don't continue the scene to the finish, or make an earlier cut, or I reduce the brutality and use more humor and irony. You can show the same theme from different sides. Because I have something to say to the normal television viewers who would never come into a movie theater to see one of my films, I have to try to make them understand too. I get a big audience, and it gives them the chance to look into the mirror at themselves. But even then the announcer once had to warn the audience about my film and say that it was not pornographic and had been given a good rating (*besonders wertvoll*). They themselves were not sure if it would shock the audience. It was an eight o'clock showing, and I heard that afterwards they had big fights among the producers (*Redakteuren*) in the TV station. Naturally they cut parts of it (*Paso Doble*).

Q. What kinds of theaters are your films shown in and what groups go to your films? Has the response been different in Germany and America for example?

A. My films are viewed mostly by young people in both countries in festivals and student film theaters. Normally my special Berlin sense of humor is better understood in Toronto or New York than in Munich or Hamburg. The openness of Berlin is closer to big cities outside of Germany, since West Germany is stiffer and behind the times.

Q. Would you consider yourself an underground director?

A. If underground means you have no money and are free to choose topics which might be taboo, in that respect I am underground. If it means you are really avant-garde and try new forms and styles of filming, then I am not. I cling to the same style of filming, and if you see my last film, it has the same style as my first film. This is why some critics say that if you've seen one of my films, you've seen them all. But no film directors can change so much that they can make totally different films. You have to recognize my style, because I am honest to myself. If you look at famous filmmakers like Fellini, you notice right away that it is a Fellini film, whether you like it or not.

Q. Would you compare yourself with any other directors, whether in Germany or America?

A. That is very hard. Do you mean, do I have models (*Vorbilder*) or see similarities in my work to other filmmakers? I think there are very few people who really have clung as long as I have to this simple way of filming. Many started as I did, sometimes often imitating my primitive style. But then they take the first chance to make a big movie, and then while making bigger movies they sometimes lose their personal touch. So I can identify with certain films of some directors, but not with their filmmaking in general, such as with Jim Jarmusch's *Permanent Vacation*, which impressed me (he's also in one of my films), or with different debut films of the *Nachwuchs* (newcomers to German film).

Q. How would you describe your personal style of filmmaking?

A. If I can talk about a personal style at all, then this style is very influenced by the technical means (*Mittel*) at my disposal. Formally, I stay close to the documentary, often adding music in order to move towards the melodramatic. The 16mm technique gives me a directness (*Grobheit*) of images which corresponds to the blatant statements I want to present. Therefore any larger format or more complicated technique like stereo sound or wide screen would be superfluous, even destructive to what I want to present.

Q. You've used the word simple or naive to describe your work. Do you mean this technically as well as thematically?

A. I think my films are easy to understand; the stories have no intellectual pretensions or puzzles to figure out. They have no complicated narrative with flashbacks, no costumes or expensive sets. They don't take place in the past. They just bring that which is closest to me into the picture.

Q. Have you been changed by your own films? Has your own sexual identity or freedom to express yourself changed?

A. I haven't been changed by my films; I have been consolidated. My psyche has been stabilized by my films.

Q. How would you see the role of film in general today in comparison, say, to literature or other media for self-expression?

A. Years ago when one had something to say about the world or oneself, one wrote a diary. Today the camera, film, or video camera replaces the diary as a medium of expression. Today young people, when they have something to say or are dissatisfied, take a camera rather than a pen in hand. Film is simply the medium of our time.

Q. Since you see film as being such an important medium for expression and, as you mentioned before, even having the power to provoke a reaction from the audience, whether positive or negative, do you think films – or at least your films – can have as liberating an effect as a movement?

A. I don't think films can have the same effect as a social movement. I never felt I wanted to join a homosexual political movement or organization. My films reflect this extreme privateness. I am my own interpreter somehow, since I am a professional film reviewer, and I would say that my films are extremely political at the same time.

Q. Do you think that dealing with the kind of gender issues or sexual topics you deal with is being political?

A. Yes. It becomes more political the more you confront a society which is oppressive, like Turkey. I deal in my films very often with the problems of the Turkish young people who are here. They don't know to which society they belong. This is a very interesting issue for me, which gets increasingly more acute.

Q. So you see yourself then as a politically engaged person because of the films you make?

A. Yes and no. I am engaged in that which is most urgent to me personally (*nah liegendst*). Politics means nothing more than the problems of living together in a city, like the original definition of *polis*. There is not much more than that.

Q. For the future, how would you wish the issue of gender or sexual identity to be resolved?

A. Societies will never be free of conflicts. If people would simply have more tolerance, then these conflicts would not lead so easily to war and other human catastrophes. Sexual tolerance can lead, I think, to more general tolerance and mutual respect – whether you are in a majority or minority, male or female.

* * *

Lothar Lambert's films have appeared in New York, San Franscisco, Chicago, Toronto, Montreal, Paris, Rotterdam, Florence, Goteborg, Australia, and of course throughout Germany, at museums, international film festivals, gay festivals, and retrospectives on German cinema.

1971 *Kurzschluß* (with Wolfram Zobus) (*Short Circuit*)

1972 *Ex und hopp* (with Wolfram Zobus)

1973 *Ein Schuß Sehnsucht – Sein Kampf* (with Wolfram Zobus) (*A Touch of Longing – His Fight*)

1974 *1 Berlin-Harlem* (with Wolfram Zobus)

1976 *Faux pas de deux*

1977 *Nachtvorstellungen* (*Late Shows*)

1978 *Now or Never*

1979 *Tiergarten*

1980 *Die Alptraumfrau* (*Nightmare Woman*)

1981 *Fucking City*

1983 *Paso Doble*

   Fräulein Berlin

1984 *Drama in Blonde*

   Der sexte Sinn (*The Sexth Sense*)

1986 *Die Liebeswüste* (*The Love Desert*)

   Gestatten, Bestatter! (*Heartbreaker and Undertaker*)

1987 *Verbieten, Verboten* (*Forbidden to Forbid*)

20

Valie Export's *Invisible Adversaries:* Film as Text

m a r g r e t   e i f l e r

argret Eifler's essay examines Invisible Adversaries *(1977) by the experimental filmmaker Valie Export. Describing Export's origins in the Austrian avant garde, Eifler then analyzes in detail the various discursive elements in her film. The various discourses she identifies do not blend together harmoniously into "story," but rather present different perspectives that make clear not only Export's feminist critique of conventional relationships, but her critique of conventional artistic depictions of reality. These different discursive levels in the film work to subvert the illusion of the real – so essential to conventional fiction – by pointing outside the fiction, exposing its limits and artificiality.*
—THE EDITORS

Valie Export,[1] an up to now underrepresented Austrian filmmaker, is slowly but surely gaining attention in the international arena of U.S. film criticism.[2] Since the cultural-political forces of

1. Born 1940, Linz, Austria. Resides in Vienna. Major film works in their original titles: *Unsichtbare Gegner* (1977), *Menschenfrauen* (1979), *Syntagma* (1981/83), *Die Praxis der Liebe* (1984). Her films are currently in distribution from: Foreign Images, 1213 Maple Avenue, Evanston, IL 60202, Telephone: (312) 869-0543; or on video from Facets Video, 1517 W. Fullerton Ave., Chicago, IL 60614; telephone: 1-800-331-6197.

2. *Invisible Adversaries* has been extensively discussed in the *Village Voice* and other New York, Chicago, and Toronto art scene journals; academically it has been treated by Roswitha Mueller, "The Uncanny in the Eyes of a Woman: Valie Export's *Invisible Adversaries*," *SubStance* 37 and 38 (1983). Other lengthy articles: Joanna Kiernan, "Films by Valie Export," *Millennium* 16, 17, 18 (Fall, Winter 1986–87) [special issue]; Ramona Curry, "The Female Image as Critique in the Films of Valie Export," in *Schatzkammer*, Vol. 14, No. 2 (Fall 1988) [also reprinted in this volume]; Margret Eifler, "Valie Export: Feministische Filmautorin," in *Österreich in Amerikanischer Sicht* (New York: Austrian Institute, 1990). The most comprehensive study about Valie Export to date is the book by Anita Prammer,

Austria seem reluctant to support avant-garde filmmaking, Export literally has taken distribution of her work into her own hands, a move complementing the notion of independent film practice. Such action is, of course, political in its implication by refusing on the one hand to submit to the commercial dictates of the corporate motion picture structure, and on the other by defying as much as possible the censorship attached to state subsidies. Such courage is admirable, because it carries the promise of uncompromising and innovative thought and form.

Export's filmmaking is actually situated within a whole array of artistic endeavors: she photographs and draws, she sculpts in transformable materials, she does video installations and body performance pieces.[3] The underlying common denominator of this activity seems to be a passionate drive to eliminate the normal gaze, the iconocentricity of gaze, the prescription of "Visual Pleasure" (Laura Mulvey). Export's filmmaking rests also on an extensive body of knowledge in art history, semiotics, and feminist theory.[4] Not only does this analytic preoccupation evidence

---

Valie Export. Eine Multi-mediale Künstlerin, Frauenforschung, vol. 7 (Vienna: Wiener Frauenverlag, 1988). Two more books are currently in progress: Margret Eifler, *Image by Image: Towards a New Text* and Roswitha Mueller, *Screen Embodiments*.

3. Intermediale Aktionen (since 1967), Photography (since 1968), Video (Installationen, Skulptur, since 1970), Körpermaterial-Inter-Aktionen (since 1971), Zeichnungen (since 1971), Installationen (since 1971), and Plastik (since 1971).

4. Export's feminist viewpoint is stated quite succinctly in her foreword to *Kunst mit Eigen-Sinn: Aktuelle Kunst von Frauen, Texte und Dokumentation* (Vienna and Munich, 1985):

"'Art can be a medium for our self-determination, and this gives art new values. These values will change reality via the cultural process of semiotics, towards an accomodation to feminine requirements. The future of woman will be the history of woman (1973).'

These sentences, written by me more than ten years ago, have opened questions, challenges and prophesies, to which in the 80s massive answers and confirmation have been given. The present society is no longer one where women are isolated in the face of a discourse without answer. The subversive strategies and provocations of the 60s and 70s have transformed the profile of this society, and made its face more human. In the morass, a new sense has ascended like a periscope. Woman, as aquanaut of the symbolic order, has surfaced in the wings of the imperium and has abducted the power from the mythology of might. What she sees, is that which he hasn't recognized. The pole of the conquest melts; the Earth turns, balancing itself out, toward the pole of discovery. Image by image, another legibility of the world is produced.

The notion that is based in the familial sacrifice of social cohesion loses its pathos. The obligation of Angst as inheritance of religion loses its conviction. The home no longer remains the place of socialization; parents no longer remain the topic of self-realization.

In this connection, the liberation of woman from the status of sacrificial vic-

itself in her work, her theoretical writings, and her academic activity,[5] but it pervades – and critically informs – the subject matter of all of her films.

Her work is particularly suited for our efforts in "Film-Germanistik," since it not only contributes to, but participates in the preeminent issues of contemporary theoretical discourse. All her films can be read as carefully constructed visual texts,

---

tim is the revolutionary action of women in the new-construction of the society. As answer to the extermination of man and animal, women have developed an aggressive energy, an aesthetic of rebellion, of rage, but also of distance and serenity, which denude the the social bodies of the traces of colonialization of all types and degree. Society becomes naked – the naked woman reverses the mirror. Out of the subversive power of the past decade a movement has come about which no longer wants to dissolve the illusion of the association, but instead wants to float free of definition."

5. Valie Export holds an alternate-year full professorship for film and video at The University of Wisconsin, Milwaukee. Since 1991 she has held a tenured position at the Hochschule der Künste in Berlin. She also taught at the San Francisco Art Institute (1987) and was visiting professor in the Film Department of San Francisco State University (1988). PUBLICATIONS:

Weibel/Export: *Wien. Bildkompendium Wiener Aktionismus und Film* (Frankfurt/M.: Kohlkunstverlag, 1970) (Mitarbeit).

V.E.: *Zyklus zur Zivilisation, Fotomappe*, ed. Kalb (Vienna, 1972).

V.E.: "Women's Art ein Manifest (1972)," *Neues Forum* (January 1973).

V.E.: "Gertrude Stein/Virginia Woolf. Feminismus und Kunst I u. II," *Neues Forum* (March 1973).

V.E.: "Zur Geschichte der Frau in der Kunstgeschichte," in *Magna*, ed. Valie Export (Vienna: Galerie nächst St. Stephan, 1975).

V.E.: Works from 1968–1975. A Comprehension, Wien, 1975.

V.E.: "Gedichte," *Dimension* (1975).

V.E.: "Überlegungen zum Verhältnis Frau und Kreativität," in *Künstlerinnen International* (Berlin, 1977).

V.E.: "Zeichnungen," in *Arsenikblüten*, ed. Danielle Sarréa (Munich: Matthes and Seitz, 1980).

V.E.: "Feministischer Aktionismus," in *Frauen in der Kunst*, ed. Gislind Nabakowski, Helke Sander, Peter Gorsen, (Frankfurt/M., 1980).

V.E.: *Körpersplitter, Konfigurationen. Fotografien 1968–77*, Neue Texte, vol. 1 (Linz, 1980).

V.E.: *Kunst mit Eigen-Sinn*. Wien: Löcker, 1985.

V.E.: *Das Reale und sein Double: Der Körper*. Bern: Benteli, 1987.

V.E.: "The Real and Its Double: The Body," *Discourse* 11 (Fall/Winter 1988–89): 3–27.

V.E.: "Aspects of Feminist Actionism," *New German Critique* 47 (Spring/Summer 1989): 69–92.

TELEVISION DOCUMENTATIVE WORK:

Das bewaffnete Auge, script and presentation of a three-part series on international avant-garde film, ORF, Vienna 1982. *Table-Quotes*, a portrait of the writer Oswald Wiener, ORF, Vienna 1985. *Action-Art International*, an art-historical review of the neo-avantgardist movements of the fifties and sixties, ORF, Vienna 1989. *Aktionskunst International*, a documentation of pertinent examples and interviews dealing with contemporary actionism, ORF, Vienna, 1989.

demanding but also rewarding critical attention. Her primary concerns revolve around the dominance of normative discourse, which she deconstructs using the innovative mechanisms of a multimedial, avant-garde film style. Having studied art and art history and being well read, she concurs with the notion that representational realism has to be uprooted, that image and language as an instrument of domination cannot be tolerated, that communication may not be reduced to an agency of a regulatory code.

The origins of such a rejection of representation as instrumentality must be sought in the historical avant garde, particularly in its "literary" or "painterly" factions.[6] While painting developed the abstract tendencies of working with pure light as color, configurative design or expressive deformation of conventional imagery and material, literature developed the estrangement or distantiation principles of montage (documentary insert, dream sequences, slogan disruption, etc.). Both kinds of expression searched for forms of rupture to expose the hypocrisy of manipulated idealism, i.e., the false identity between sign and referent, truth and experience, value and product. The historic avant garde thus attempted a first reversal by searching for innovative expressions of intelligibility.

Only in the late 1950s did a new generation arise to continue the cause of the avant garde, and Export can be counted as a member of this group. It was to be the era of postmodernism, the era in which the early models were taken up as an underpinning of the ensuing concern with semiotics. If modernism may be compared to a still handmade collage, postmodernism appears as the result of cybernetics. Unfortunately, the centrifugal force of this artistic modernity was all too soon integrated, and thus neutralized, by market forces. Production and consumption became part of the new structure of pluralism, a process of creating and being absorbed in swift sequences of built-in obsolescence. International generations have since become addicted to the rapid "jump-cuts" of changing styles, to a lifestyle of mass-supplied novelties. The same is true in the

6. Substantive readings on the topic of the avant-garde: Peter Bürger, *Theorie der Avant-garde* (Frankfurt/M.: Suhrkamp, 1974). Karlheinz Barck et al., eds., *Künstlerische Avant-garde: Annäherungen an ein Unabgeschlossenes Kapitel* (Berlin [DDR], 1979). Karin Hirdina, "Der Kunstbegriff der Avant-garde," *Weimarer Beiträge* 32 (1986): 1461–1485. Peter Wollen, "The Two Avant-gardes," *Edinburgh Magazine* 7 (1976).

intellectual arena, where the brain became accustomed to the atomized ubiquity of (new) information. The recipient of all this information became drawn into the seductivity of the sign itself – and an employed programmer thereof. But in the midst of this pervasive economic process of desensitization, the artists of the neo-avant-garde kept sight of their actual interest, namely the deconstruction of fallacious homology. Theirs is the cybernetics of counter-discourse.

In view of this, Export's first feature-length film *Invisible Adversaries* (1977) is an especially poignant example on the avant-garde arrangement of a set of signs. Addressing the problem of "Ideologie-and Sprachkritik," she mirrors a chain of dominant language practices, creating a multilayered stratagem of variants on the impossibility of dialogue. The film takes as its object the investigation of codes that determine interhuman relationships, thereby foregrounding their means of signification. Of course, this intent aims at breaking the mechanisms of normed exchange. Export's film language wants to reverse these strangling closures of dominance and privilege with the processional, disjunctive, and investigative aperture of revelation. The film's substantive essence therefore is the exposure of the all-pervasive behavior of aggression. The invisible adversary is made visible.

The treatment of this rather existential subject does not border on semioclasm (Roland Barthes's term for the destruction of repressive connotation and denotation of dominant discourse): it is more a lucid and painful elegy lamenting the communicative animosity between nations, societal partners, human beings, lovers, and the sexes. The film moves through all these existing forms of dialogue to end in the resoluteness and defiance of monologue. It probes the discourse of relationships, their encodedness. In this sense the film is constructed not so much as the portrayal of a particular couple or as the particular experience of a female protagonist, but rather as the "condition humaine" of interaction. Only the aggregate of all discourses displays the filmmaker's statement of a total breakdown in communication, and it is the consciously chosen mix of material sign and social signified that makes *Invisible Adversaries* such a penetrating vision of the interhuman dilemma.

To focus specifically on the issue of communicative alienation in the film, it might be helpful to deduce from it at least eight different structures of discourse and cite those passages in the film text most relevant to each one:[7]

I. The Discourse of the Un-real

Export's first feature-length film *Invisible Adversaries* (1977) set in contemporary Vienna, can be called a most controversial feminist adaptation of the *Invasion of the Body Snatchers*. Anna, a Viennese photographer, discovers that extraterrestrial forces are colonizing the minds of her fellow citizens by raising the human aggression quotient. The outer world events become increasingly disjointed, but the inner world does, too, as Anna and her lover experience an increasingly deteriorating relationship.

At the outset of the film we are introduced to an outer-worldly force, called Hyksos, an invisible adversary taking on human form to destroy humankind. This idea of "bad spirits" forms the fictional glue of the whole film. Here are some incisive transcriptions:

Broadcast segments:

> Attention population: there is well-founded suspicion of an invisible adversary, a foreign, perhaps other-worldly power . . . an invisible adversary occupies the city and transforms people. . . . Hyksos are hardly distinguishable from real humans . . . anyone could already be a Hyksos . . . either he does not know it or it is already too late. . . . Beware of communication. . . . Hyksos are contagious. . . . You are alone. . . . The Hyksos recognize one another and destroy all who have not yet joined them. . . . The change comes about through radiation which permeates the brain of people. . . . The Hyksos occupy the earth through human beings. Their goal is to destroy the earth through increased aggression.
>
> In this new cosmos the Orient will be as responsible as the Occident if it allows itself to be duped by appearances. Never was lucidity won at such great cost. You, who squeezed the fish of Hyksos between layers of chalk, beware of the traps of the new Caesars. George Mathieu, 1961.

Anna calling Peter:

> Peter, I feel so awful. You know, that stuff with the Hyksos, the "foreign rulers." I had another experience. It seems like impacting energy that tries to change our feelings. . . . They slip into the body of humans and alter their minds from there, and through control of the mind they alter society.

7. Text as it appears in the subtitles of the film.

2. The Discourse of Heterosexuality

The focus of the film is placed on probing the relationship of man and woman. This probing follows stages with precise turning-point situations, analyzing the inevitable development of breakdown in today's heterosexuality. The paradoxical outset of sexual correspondence soon disintegrates into universal quarrels on partnership function (the satirical epitome being the quarrel scenes in the car). Export's portrayal makes it quite transparent that sexuality has become nothing else but routine mimicking of natural reproduction (scene: child "put on ice" in the refrigerator). The sexual relationship between Anna and Peter is depicted as an intimacy that ranges from infantile behavior to erotic sophistication (pillow talks of Mighty/Minnie Mouse to "The Gymno-plastics of Love"). The depiction of this heterosexual hypocrisy in their relationship is heightened by being attached at the next level to norms of obsolete role-play, where the woman cooks, listens and consoles, and the man supports financially, expounds, and protects. Therein lies the crux of the problem: the homomorphic structures of primitive society (Anna quotes Levi-Strauss) function in modernity only as ironic anachronisms. The dialogue of the couple turns to discord, accusation, violence, and separation.

Parting scene of Anna and Peter:

Anna: I don't understand. I used to photograph flowers and children, taking pictures of lovely things. But now my pictures often have ugly, destructive subjects. I even photographed my own excrement and don't know why.

Peter: I have noticed that, too. You have grown melancholic and so depressed.

Anna: And you have gotten so aggressive. All you have are ideas of destruction. I can't stand anymore the way we quarrel all the time, and the struggles with my own thoughts.

Peter: I can't stand your crazy thoughts anymore either. But maybe I am doing you an injustice, and it is me who is in a crazy world. At times I think you are an angel and I live in hell. What is abnormal about it, is that I want it that way. I even want to be alone in my hell. I don't want you to be part of this hell.

Anna: True, you always leave me alone.

Peter: I am not talking about that. Are you not listening? I can't stand these personal relations anymore, because they are a swamp. Love is nothing but a pain in the ass, friendship is the slimiest kind of cannibalism, this disgusting longing for love, for recognition sickens me. I don't want to need anyone. I still fight against this emotional plague.

Anna: I, however, believe the ability to love and to live are one and the same. Each organism needs warmth, energy, and love. I don't want to let this die in me. For me, concepts like humanity, with which I can identify, still exist.

Peter: Humanity disgusts me, even if it means you consider me dead. If I am dead it is because of this humanity. . . . Maybe there are secret laws of life I am transgressing. Maybe I am an evil element in life. Maybe that is the reason why we react to each other with aggression and suffering.

Anna: I know for sure I want to live without you.

Peter: I don't know whether I want to live without you. I only know we can't go on living together, because we are destroying each other despite our love.

3. The Discourse of Societal Order

Just as sexual role expectations make for an oppressive relationship, the social order will inflict injustice, arbitrariness, privilege, slavery. Society's power, however, does not only distinguish gender specifically, it bears at times on any of its citizens, Anna as well as Peter. The State of Law seems ultimately nothing but the backdoor to being a Police State. Anna's encounter with an angry shopkeeper illustrates this notion, when, exploding with rage, he tells her that she has parked her car illegally on private property and that he will call the police to restore law and order if she does not leave at once. Paralleling this, the next scene shows Peter, arguing unsuccessfully with a policeman also over a supposed parking violation. Export then follows the unfortunate fallout of these events, when the victims of the social order redirect their anger at those closest to them, continuing the process of victimization.

Peter: I fight against the privileges of officials and clerks, who think they can wallow in their power. And I don't mind paying for any opinions, even when it means a fine. My freedom of expression is worth that much.

Anna: But it won't get you anywhere to tell a policeman off. He is only an employee.

Peter: The way you talk shows the system of obedience we live under. In Austria to have one's own opinion probably counts as "insult" or "riot."

Anna: Well, stick to your opinion.

Peter: (addressing her now from the toilet):

I won't have other people drag me down. I have to stay receptive to experience. I can't spend my whole life looking at a lemon peel or sleeping with just one woman and one family. For one person it is drugs, for another the bottle, the third his family. He comes home from work every day and sucks his loved ones. He charges himself at night like a battery. It's admirable that there is a big Mother Battery like the family which can satisfy a person's needs all his life. But it wouldn't do for me.

Anna: The glorification of your personal anarchy is pure egotism.

Peter: You don't know what you are saying. . . .

Anna: You are mean and you demean everything.

Peter: I don't need to, everything is already deep in the mire. . . . I don't want to come to you and feel the same repulsion as outside. I might as well talk to a cop.

Anna: Don't compare me with a policeman.

Peter: If you defend them.

Anna: I don't.

Peter: But the system you keep talking about needs policemen.

Anna: But you are the worst cop. You oppress me so much, I can hardly breathe.

4. The Discourse of Cultural Politics

The film contains a lengthy statement on Austria's artistic history. The commentary is spoken by a woman, in all likelihood reflecting Export's personal views. It is an angry, disillusioned outcry against governmental abuse of and disrespect for the arts. As such, this lecture-like interlude heightens the perspectivist structure of the treatment of the issue of negative discourse; it functions as another segment in this filmic aggregate of antagonisms (most often accompanied visually by architectural examples or acts of demolition):

Vienna's history is oblivion and deceit. . . . The cultural climate of the Second Republic has intensified this continuum of corruption by its banality. . . . How does this Second Republic honor "Austria's Great Sons"? Mozart's rooms are now inhabited by Emperor Haile Selasse's ex-mistress. The Bulgarian Embassy resides in Ludwig Wittgenstein's house, the Republic and the city having no use for an unusual building built by the philosopher himself. It took massive protests at home and abroad to save it from demolition. For ten years, from 1902 to 1912, Otto Wagner fought to rebuild the Karlsplatz according to his plans, which were always rejected: "I want to give the church of St. Charles the framework it deserves . . . even if it costs me my life." It did. And the Opera House architects were so maligned that Edward von der Nüll hanged himself and his friend Siccard von Siccardsburg died of apoplexy. Emperor Franz Joseph's reign set the seal on Vienna's desecration. The Ringstrasse is a model of borrowed styles. The university and the museums are Renaissance style, of course, humanistic era; the parliament apes Greco-Roman style; every medieval town hall was Gothic, so the one built in 1880, meanwhile serving totally different purposes, is a Gothic lie to house other lies. From 1938-45 Austria produced revoltingly dishonest films, known typically as "Viennese films," and the elite of the Burg Theatre acted in them. After the war the same crew produced those popular rural and folklore films. The smooth transition from Nazi Austria to the Second Republic is typical of the hypocritical mentality of this country.

5. The Discourse of Feminism:

Primary concern of Export's visualizations is the social encodedness of the female body, as phallocratic imprint, as psycho-mutilated object or as heterosexual victim; the female body is always central issue for an iconoclastic break with biological, social, and cultural preconceptions. These sexual-feminist politics root in Export's notion that women's history is a history of oppression.

The question "When is a human being a woman," posed as the underlying question of Anna's search for herself and other women's experience, leads to militancy against phallocentrism. This battle is always fought artistically: Helke Sander, for example, seeing the women's question subordinated to the concept of the "natural" division of labor, turned to filmmaking to deal with the problem; Anna's friend in the video-recording session explains that she could survive the deceptive and empty modes of being a wife only by turning to writing about it; and Anna records her biographical experience as a photographer. In still another film sequence we see a video-overlay of a woman's body onto the woman's postures in the paintings by Veronese, Botticelli, Titian and Blake, pointing to the fact that the art-historical concepts of beauty demand grotesque gyrations by the imitating actress; the male image of woman does not correspond to female reality.

To be woman entails cognizance of role-victimization, defiance through self-expression, and ultimately self-determination through action. Export leads her character Anna through these stages of awareness, providing evidence of each phase of insight through the eye of Anna's camera. In one scene, for example, we see Anna developing an expressive photo of the female genitals as we hear the distorted orgasmic sounds of a male, which in all likelihood signals the penetration act of the Hyksos-power. In another scene, we see Anna first looking at photographs of children (the sound of a heartbeat underlining the affinity), then at a series of photos of car crashes (accentuated by the violence of their sound), and finally at pictures of social problems (pub brawls, a woman scrounging through garbage, and women reified as street-objects). In yet another scene we are given a sequence of shots of a murder case which ends with the dark-rimmed portrait of Anna: photography as projection, but also a register of woman's affliction.

Anna: It frightens me to see my latest pictures and the change in subject matter and their content. But if the subject were not there, I could not make these pictures, so they show me a change also in my environment. I feel a need to check up objectively, to see if something is changing outside, or just in me. Pictures pierce me like psychic meteors. They reflect a paranoid reality. Are the photos a defense mechanism against fear or do they produce fear? I don't want to protect myself against fear with methods associated with fear. Like a line becomes a circle.

6. The Discourse of Psychoanalysis

Is the pain of woman's reality, which comes to the surface in nightmarish dreams (Anna with skates everywhere but on a surface of ice, finally leaving bloody skating tracks on her skin), to be relieved in psychotherapy? Export's answer seems to be no. The dialogue between Anna and the psychoanalyst (Austrian, Freudian, male) is another construct of nonunderstanding, another form of systemized subjugation. Anna expresses her feelings of duality, of opposition, of difference, and the doctor responds by asking only about eyesight, her sleep patterns, and technical problems with her camera. Since none of these rather typically male, dismissive suggestions prove to be the cause, traditional Freudian description and modern medical prescription will solve the case indisputably.

Anna: I can see plainly that people don't act themselves. . . . Behind people I see other beings, as if they were double. . . . I only see shells of people, inside they are empty. They are sucked dry, occupied by strangers. I see craftsmen, but not people. Priests, conductors, but not people. Masters and slaves, but not people. I see a great battlefield, where humanity killed itself, I see mangled limbs. I am alone in my search for human beings. . . .

Doctor: What you tell me, I don't mind telling you, leads me to conclude that you are schizophrenic. Some of your symptoms are very indicative: the feeling of doubling, that you or other people are influenced, the feeling that you are hearing voices. We will combine treatments, first psychotherapy, like now, but also modern medicines that can certainly influence your symptoms beneficially. Do you agree with that? I don't think hospital treatment is needed or is likely to be needed anytime. Take what I prescribe regularly and come back in about one week.

7. The Discourse of Politics

Throughout the film we have references which point beyond the sufferings of the protagonist. We are exposed to newspaper headlines which make evident how widespread the psychic effects of hostility are and what devastating forms they can take. We are also repeatedly confronted with documentary footage of the terrors of war, epitomized in the film sequence "Weekly Death Show," where an ascending series of violent images and satirical commentary culminate in shocking pictures of war dead (there seems to be a linkage between the slumped-over bodies of shot hostages and the declining body-performance-gestures of "woman" in a previous segment). The beginning and end of the film, however, point most clearly to the rhetorical superstructures of conflict. News broadcasts make the generic design of negative discourse remarkably obvious. Their political subject matter internationalizes the ever-threatening dialogue. We hear nothing but combative diplomacy, war reporting, ideological war mongering on a global scale, transmitted via the ubiquitous collaboration of mass media.

News Reports (at end of film):

Israel-Austria: The Jerusalem cabinet has rejected the criticisms by Israeli newspapers raised against Austrian security forces in connection with the bomb attack on Tel Aviv Airport. . . . Kreisky remarked . . . that such unfounded criticism might endanger things . . . in this connection he mentioned the transit of Jewish emigrants from the USSR.

Lebanon: Syria has again intervened in the civil war by sending a force of 2,000 men. These troops crossed the border . . . this occupation was criticized by Socialist leader Djumblat and leading Palestinians. They said the siege was a welcome excuse for Syria to intervene in Lebanon.

Norway: In Oslo the talks between the foreign ministers of Britain and Iceland on the settlement of the so-called Cod War are due to be continued . . . it was announced that the two ministers could not agree despite certain progress.

Great Britain-Ireland: A new anti-terror law comes into force in both countries today. . . . The outlawed IRA has declared opposition . . . they threaten the murder of every British official travelling to collaborate with officials in Northern Ireland.

U.S.A.: By the early 80s the U.S.A. intends to have up to 1,000 so-called cruise-missiles in service. . . . As a result of this revolution in warfare, various critics fear that the balance of power between the adversaries has been disturbed.

8. The Discourse of Monologue

With the realization that there is only a dialogue of discord, Anna at first sees her situation as an existence reduced to loneliness, reduced to a crying soliloquy with her mirror image (such as the scene in which Anna turns away from the mirror, but the image remains in it).

Anna: My visual work is for me a monologue. . . . I tell myself, what I am suffering from, like a dialogue with an invisible partner, because I don't believe in the reality of my environment.

At the end Anna knows that the only discourse possible is counter-discourse. Words have lost their complementary function, so a period of silence has to commence with nothing but signifying actions. Thus, the last images rest on the activity of hands. The first tears up the fading picture of the atomic destruction of St. Stephan's Cathedral, defying the ultimate act of annihilation. The last image, a hand-in-glove (somewhat tongue-in-cheek), covers the names of the cast, denying any more thought of role.

By this point, it is clear that the text of this film is a mesh of carefully selected and interwoven sections of discursive reflection, an assemblage of interrelated thought. The script can truly be called a "Drehbuch" in the German sense of the word, a subject turned about in all its multiple facets. In an explanatory note on her filmmaking,[8] Export states that all sequences of a film are actually self-contained units, only decipherable by their semantic context. These units in themselves are determined by singular operatives such as image selection, image content, image creation, and montage; camera movement, optical effects, and interaction of the visual with the auditory.[9] Only read as a whole do they become the syntagmatic construct of a cultural code: Export's film is such a visual semiosis.

Experimental films, such as this one, consciously use a different aesthetics from that of mainstream narrative film, in which the montage techniques make the act of perceiving the film a part of the experience of it. Consciousness of the camera work, of diegetic and non-diegetic sound, of editing are all part of a speech act with the viewer. Film language of this sort speaks coherently, however not as mimetic expression, and establishes a reception process in which seeing and thinking become interdependent. The cinematic neo-avant garde, as represented by Export, does not pursue formal experimentation as an end in itself, but does speak through a highly reflexive strategy, a kind of politics of the signifier and the signified, making *Invisible Adversaries* an epistemological investigation of interpersonal relationships.

8. Export, *Eigen-Sinn*, 217.
9. There is homophonic congruence of the most diverse sounds: static, water drops, orgasm, mortar fire, car crashes, etc.

2 1

The Female Image as Critique in the Films of Valie Export

r a m o n a   c u r r y

Ramona Curry's discussion of Valie Export's
Syntagma (1983) examines
the relation of Export's film
both to the history of filmmaking by women since the early
1970s in the German-speaking
countries (above all in West
Germany) and to developments
in (predominantly Anglo-American) feminist film criticism during the same period. Curry sum-
marizes the feminist critique of the
cinematic representation of woman
(for male pleasure) begun by Mulvey, and its – partial – intersection
with the project of an avant-garde filmmaker like Export. But Curry
also notes that Export's experimental critique of the cinematic representation of the female body is perhaps less interested in deconstructing
male pleasure than exploring (or at least allowing) female pleasure in
viewing the representation of woman.
—THE EDITORS

From the opening of Valie Export's Syntagma (1983).
(Photo courtesy of Valie Export)

Introduction

Valie Export, a leading member of the Austrian avant garde
since the mid-1960s, is an extraordinarily talented and innovative creator. During the past twenty years, Export has produced

numerous performance pieces, which she calls "actions," as well as many short films and three feature films. Elements of her early performance work, which involved variously the human body, film and video, photography, architecture, landscape, and sketching and texts, are integrated into and further reflected on in her films.

Syntagma, an 18-minute experimental film that Export made in 1983, utilizes a number of materials and approaches to examine succinctly issues that Export's work has repeatedly addressed. Unlike Export's feature films, in particular her first feature *Invisible Adversaries* (*Unsichtbare Gegner*, 1976), *Syntagma* has not yet received broad attention in North America, despite the recognition it has won in Europe.[1] Yet *Syntagma* not only warrants but also rewards critical consideration, for it is a highly stimulating and important short film that can serve as a key to understanding the subjects and techniques of Export's work. The film is further worthy of attention for the contribution it makes to the ongoing international discourse in contemporary feminist film theory and practice about the representation of women.

Woman as Sign vs. Women as Characters

Syntagma introduces its concerns immediately in its title sequence and opening shots. These comprise a number of visual and aural elements in unusual combination and presentation: strips of film leader; a woman's hands gestering in sign language; a split image of a woman in a trench coat walking to and

1. *Invisible Adversaries* has been extensively discussed in the *Village Voice* and other New York, Chicago, and Toronto art scene journals as well as by Roswitha Mueller in the University of Wisconsin publication *SubStance* 37/38. Export has subsequently made two further feature-length films, *Menschenfrauen* (*Human Woman*, 1979) and *Die Praxis der Liebe* (*The Practice of Love*, 1984). *Invisible Adversaries, Syntagma,* and *The Practice of Love* are currently in distribution in the U.S. (Foreign Images, 1213 Maple Avenue, Evanston, IL 60202.)

Syntagma won the top awards at the West German Short Film Festival in Oberhausen in 1984 and at the Biboa Film Festival. The film was initially available in the U.S. only with *magnetic* soundtrack. This last technical detail accounts in part for the limited number of screenings the film has had in North America: while magnetic sound projectors are available at specialized media centers or rental houses, standard 16mm projectors in the U.S. play films with optical sound tracks only. In response to this dilemma, the feminist distribution company Foreign Images (1213 Maple Ave., Evanston, IL 60202), which also distributes *Invisible Adversaries,* has undertaken to have made and now distributes a print of *Syntagma* with optical sound track.

fro; and on the audio track, odd squeaking rhythmic sounds of rising pitch, which might be anything from synthesized music to distorted porpoise songs, and a woman's voice reading in Austrian-accented German a text which we see on a computer monitor screen. In English, this text, taken from radical British psychologist R. D. Laing's book *The Divided Self*, reads:

> My body clearly takes a position between me and the world. On the one hand, it is the core and center of my world, on the other an object in the world for others.

The structuring of these elements defines the film's primary subject: the construction of woman as sign in and through media. *Syntagma* addresses particularly the positioning of woman as object of desire. It is the female body that predominantly interests Export and that appears exclusively in *Syntagma*, as an object in social space circumscribed by its *mediation* – its presentation in film, on television, in photography, in texts, i.e., its *representation*.

Like much of Export's work, *Syntagma* offers a critique of the conventionally mediated female image by using multiple techniques of experimental film and performance to make the viewer aware of the processes of signification and its impact in film. I shall delve into this point in detail for several scenes of *Syntagma*. First, however, I wish to set the enterprise of representation of the female in perspective, by placing Export's work in the context of the many contemporary films by and about women.

Export works largely in an "experimental" cinematic mode, even when her films, such as the three feature films, have strong narrative lines. That is to say, her films draw on (and often invent) rather different styles and techniques from those by other women directors that utilize documentary or traditional narrative filmmaking conventions. In part, this is because Export's films are not "about" individual female characters or their experiences, as are many films by women directors with female protagonists, but rather are concerned with the very processes of representation, particularly of the female image. To put it another way, what is at issue in Export's work is not the "portrayal" but rather the *representation* of women.

The distinction is a central issue in contemporary feminist theory. Expanded "portrayals" of women – in the sense of positive, diverse, or complex models or roles for women, such as one might find in the work of Margarethe von Trotta, for example – express and address immediate concerns about the personal and political standing of women in the social world in comparison to their male counterparts. The more abstract issue of female "representation" is embedded in psychoanalytic and semiotic discourse. One must understand, then, at the outset that Export's films, while highly entertaining, undertake a somewhat different project than those of most narrative filmmakers, such as Doris Dörrie. (Among West German women filmmakers, I find the issue of how problematic representation of the female is most vividly formulated in the work of Helke Sander and Elfi Mikesch.)[2] A brief recapitulation of trends in the feminist film movement internationally will clarify this point.

Initially, in the late 1960s and early 1970s, the main interest among feminists who had begun making and analyzing film and video was to offer alternative *images* of women, different from those heretofore present in the dominant media. Filmmakers discovered or created as characters women from classes, races, and ages that had rarely been seen or heard in the media. These portrayals gave the female subjects "voice" and validated their life experiences as portrayed. Helga Reidemeister's film *Von Wegen Schicksal* (*This Is "Destiny?"* 1979) about a divorced welfare mother and Cristina Perincioli's fictionalized documentary *The Power of Men is the Patience of Women* (*Die Macht der Männer ist die Geduld der Frauen*, 1978) about shelters for abused women are examples from West Germany of such films.

Some of the alternative portrayals thus made visible strong, active, independent women previously invisible as roles in the media and in history more generally. Other alternative images of women emphasized the circumstances limiting the lives of their subjects while still others offered new, previously, and even yet tabooized images of women interacting with each other or their own bodies.

By the mid-1970s, a number of feminist critics had articulated models for the ideological – and psychoanalytic – constraints

2. Cf. for example, Sander's feature-length films *The All-Around Reduced Personality – REDUPERS* (1977), *The Subjective Factor* (1981), and *The Trouble with Love* (1983); and Mikesch's *I Often Think of Hawaii* (1978), *What Should We Do without Death* (1980) and the rather problematic *Seduction – Cruel Woman* (1985). (Sander's film *The All-Around Reduced Personality* is available in the German embassy collection administered by West Glen distributors in New York; *The Trouble with Love* is available from Foreign Images in Evanston, IL)

they saw imposed by dominant media formats or even by established conventions of independent media productions, such as *cinéma vérité*. Many critics argued that realist conventions, including those of *cinéma vérité*, create a fiction of the authenticity of the "pro-filmic" event (that which occurs before the camera) and mask the work of the filmmakers in constructing the film's world. Thus these realist conventions are seen as intrinsically incapable of representing women in any manner which might escape the ideological encoding – or evade the psychoanalytic mechanisms – of the dominant cinema.[3]

The issue of how women might be represented in keeping with feminist principles of women *speaking* and defining themselves was thus shown to be rather discouragingly complex. Even strong female roles in conventional narrative or documentary films were no true alternatives. It did not suffice for images of women to seem *different* from those previously created if the portraits were drawn with the same conventional means. Representation must be, if possible, differently structured or even eliminated. So, although early feminist film criticism had all along been alert to the interrelations and even indivisibility of content and form, the primary attention of those interested in restructuring images of women began to shift from content – the "portrayals" – to formal considerations of "representation" more generally.

The film avant garde, comparable in some ways to the equivalent movement in the visual arts more generally, had since its inception (roughly, as an institution, by the early 1920s in Europe) explored alternatives to and within representational practice. Thus it is not surprising that in the 1970s feminist critics (and a number of feminist filmmakers not already working in that mode) looked to the avant garde in an attempt to discover alternative *structures* with which to present/represent women.

Some strategies that might be considered attempts to that end are the following: the use of a woman's voice-over (often

3. Cf. especially the essay "Documentary, Realism and Women's Cinema," by Eileen McGarry in *Women & Film* 2, No. 7 (1975): 50–59; and the highly influential essay by Laura Mulvey, "Visual Pleasure and Narrative Cinema," *Screen* 16, no. 3 (Autumn 1975): 6–18; reprinted in *Women and the Cinema*, ed. Karyn Day and Gerald Peary (New York: Dutton, 1977). Further theorists who began early to address these issues are Julia Lesage, Claire Johnson, Pam Cook, Parveen Adams, and Elizabeth Cowie, among others. The film journal *Jump Cut* (P.O. Box 865, Berkeley, California 94701) has since its founding in 1974 dealt with questions of representation of women in the dominant cinema.

without human forms on the image); the use of printed or hand-written text set in counterpoint to sound and other image track; optical printing or other manipulation of the image (or sound) track to draw attention to its *construction* as artifact; camera work that works to create subjective (a particular woman's) or multiple points of view or which draws attention to *itself*, rather than the images of women the camera "captures" on film as the primary source of pleasure. Further means are the editing techniques or acting styles which disrupt or contradict expectations of narrative flow or conventional identification. All of these strategies can effect at least some critical distance to the ideology of conventional representation of women. Most of these elements are present to a high degree in the film work of Valie Export.

Critical Elements in *Syntagma*

This overview of developments in the last twenty years in feminist film theory and practice by no means implies any argument of intentionality or other attempt to subsume Export's unique contributions to general tendencies. Unlike in Darwinist theory, here ontogeny does not follow phylogeny: Export has been working at what I am implying is the "highest" evolutionary state of representational theory from her start as an artist in the mid-1960s. Nor does her work deal exclusively with approaches to the representation of women.

However, the preceding contextualization of some of the issues raised in and by Export's films offers a basis now for a closer analysis of *Syntagma*. The immediate experience of this highly cinematic 18-minute film is richly sensuous, not abstract. At the same time, *Syntagma* succinctly and cogently formulates many of the theoretical issues addressed above.

Visually, as all films, *Syntagma* consists of a sequence of images, here predominantly representations of parts of women's bodies: hands, feet, faces and torsos, clothed and unclothed, adorned and bare. These have been photographed and rephotographed in varying combinations, juxtaposed and layered. This not only creates but also comments on "*Syntagma*," sequences of signs which produce meaning.

The film's unusual title sequence establishes the construction of "*Syntagma*" as both a technique and subject of the film to come. The opening shot is of two strips of film leader, *running*

side-by-side downward across the screen, the magnified sprock-
et holes creating a rhythmic, digital pattern of light. Further
flashing digits appear in a gradually expanding gap between the
strips. These emerge as the fingers of a pair of hands, marked
with red nail polish as those of a woman. It is evident that the
image is drawn from diverse planes and has been constructed
through optical printing, yet the woman's hands effectively give
the illusion of forcing the strips of film leader apart, making
room to express themselves. This accomplished, they spell out
in sign language: "S-y-n-t-a-g-m-a."

The image cuts to a split screen showing a woman dressed in
an olive-drab raincoat, walking to and fro across a plaza. On the
audio track, a woman's voice reading the Laing quotation
speaks of the human – perhaps particularly female – dilemma of
both being and having body. An investigation of the multilayered production of meaning is thus established. The primary
site of the investigation is to be the female body, the woman in
the trench coat is at once investigator and object of research.

Fragments of women's faces and bodies appear throughout
Syntagma, many of the images drawn from Export's earlier performance and multimedia work, predominantly from three
series of projects Export called "body-material-interactions":
"From the Humanoid Sketchbook of Nature," "Body Configurations in Nature," and "Body Configurations in Architecture."[4]

The selection of images of women's bodies in *Syntagma* is, of
course, significant, for selection works on the paradigmatic axis
or dimension of language. Paradigmatic choice is reflected in
the framing and composition of the image: for example, the
presentation of relatively *young white women*'s legs and feet, these
predominantly in *close-up* shots or cropped photographs, rather
than as whole bodies; or, rather than men's legs, or old women's
legs, or a black woman's legs. I shall explore this point further
but first want to survey the range of images in *Syntagma*.

Women's feet, marked as such either – like the fingers in the
opening shot – with red polish or with high-heeled pumps, are a

4. Another source of image sequences in *Syntagma* is Export's 1973 project
"adjungierte Dislokationen" ("Adjuncted Dislocations"), for which she mount-
ed an 8mm camera on her chest and another on her back and filmed simultaneously the objects and environments she approached and those she left
behind. Several of the sound sources in *Syntagma* (for example, women count-
ing rhythmically in a sound loop, and an acoustically garbled account of body in
relation to environment) also draw on earlier performance work.

major motif. Often they appear mounting and descending stairs, often in multiple planes in one image (layered by techniques of front projection and optical printing) or framed by a television monitor within the film frame. Other images recur and are placed in shifting contexts that subtly alter their meanings. A television placed on a bed or table in a dim room frames up another monitor: a video screen through which authorities watch passengers in a subway station.

Most of the images, however, (and all of the human voices) are distinctly of the female body. These are repeatedly dissociated from conventional or "realistic" presentation and set in unexpected interaction with the material and spatial environment. A flesh-pink arm, then a woman's loins appear atop their black-and-white photographic likenesses. A woman's figure, then her rephotographed two-dimensional image ornaments a stone staircase, conjoining body, art, and architecture on one plane. The investigator sees herself in a rhythmically "jump-cut" sequence of car mirrors and later in a wall mirror, revealed as a projected film of herself. She sits alone in a room with pen and paper, a guitar, and a television monitor. The superimposition of an open text over the frame patterns the wallpaper with print. The camera zooms in to her image, now typing, on the monitor; a hand in close-up turns the pages of the superimposed text, reminding the viewer of the status and nature of the image.

Women reading and writing, looking and conscious of being looked at, duplicated and fragmented, moving and speaking in overlap and out of sync: these are the images being arrayed and investigated. Printed text, the spoken word, hand signals, computer and video screens put to private and public uses, mirrors, and projections: these "mediate" and give the signs their meanings. *Syntagma* makes clear that these organs of mediation function as more than surfaces or expressive context. The signification of the body is inherent in its formal enunciation. Following Derrida, the body signified always also serves as signifier.[5]

This crucial nuance in Export's work deserves further explication. Several shot sequences in *Syntagma* recall the paintings

5. Cf. Jacques Derrida, *Of Grammatology*, trans. Gayatri Chakravorty Spivak (Baltimore: Johns Hopkins Univ. Press, 1976), 7. See Kaja Silverman, *The Subject of Semiotics* (Oxford: Oxford Univ. Press, 1983), especially Chapter One, "From Sign to Subject, A Short History," for a lucid explication of theories of signification; pages 32–43 discuss Derrida's work in this context.

of surrealist artist Rene Magritte, in particular the two works *Ceci n'est pas une pipe* (1926) and the related work *Les Deux Mysteres* (1966), which Michel Foucault thoroughly analyzes in his essay, *Ceci n'est pas une pipe*. The former is a simple painting of a pipe, underneath it the handwritten statement in French, "This is not a pipe."[6]

One image in *Syntagma* evokes this Magritte painting particularly vividly: a hand with red-enameled fingernails carefully paints the German word "W-e-l-l-e," ("wave") in blue on a black and white photograph of an ocean wave. This subtly surrealistic composition addresses essentially the same concept as the Magritte painting, despite Export's apparently positive formulation: "This *is* a wave."

Foucault's discussion of the Magritte painting *This is not a Pipe* clarifies this point:

> Magritte's drawing . . . is as simple as a page borrowed from a botanical manual: a figure and the text that names it. . . . [W]hat lends the figure its strangeness is not the "contradiction" between the image and the text. . . . Contradiction could exist only between two statements, or within one and the same statement. Here there is clearly but one, and it cannot be contradictory because the subject of the proposition is a simple demonstrative. False, then, because its "referent" – obviously a pipe – does not verify it? But who would seriously contend that the collection of intersecting lines above the text is a pipe? . . . The statement is perfectly true, since it is quite apparent that the drawing representing the pipe is not the pipe itself. . . .
>
> What misleads us is the inevitability of connecting the text to the drawing . . . and the impossibility of defining a perspective that would let us say that the assertion is true, false, or contradictory. . . . The operation is a calligram . . . . First, it brings a text and a shape as close together as possible. It is composed of lines delimiting the form of an object while also arranging the sequence of letters. It lodges statements in the space of a shape, and makes the text *say* what the text *represents*. . . .
>
> The calligram is thus tautological. But in opposition to rhetoric. The latter toys with the fullness of language. It uses the possibility of repeating the same thing in different words, and profits from the

6. Michel Foucault, *This is not a Pipe*, trans. James Harkness (Berkeley: Univ. of California Press, 1983). See Brenda Longfellow, "Sex/Textual Politics: Tracing the Imaginary in the Films of Valie Export" in the Toronto publication *Borderlines* (Winter 1985–1986): 11–12, for a further semiotic analysis of Export's work drawing on Foucault.

extra richness of language that allows us to say different things with a single word. The essence of rhetoric is in allegory. The calligram uses that capacity of letters to signify both as linear elements that can be arranged in space and as signs that must unroll according to a unique chain of sound. As a sign, the letter permits us to fix words; as a line, it lets us give shape to things. Thus the calligram aspires playfully to efface the oldest oppositions of our alphabetical civilization: to show and to name; to shape and to say; to reproduce and to articulate; to imitate and to signify; to look and to read.[7]

The image in *Syntagma* of a woman's hands painting the word "wave" on a black and white photograph similarly explores and challenges the processes of meaning construction. Its effect, like that of the film as a whole, is that of the Magritte painting: exposure of the sign as arbitrary and the resultant distantiation and critique. But Export's film pushes the critique even further than does Foucault – or at least in a different direction. *Syntagma* deals specifically with *woman* as sign and with the function of the cinematic gaze in the *perception* of woman as sign. The film's choice of fragmented images of women's bodies – hands, breasts, thighs, lips, eyes, and most noticeably feet – has particular reference to psychoanalytic discussion of fetish object as substitute for the phallus. The ways in which cinematic representations of the female may function as fetish object have been a central and controversial issue in contemporary film theory.

Images in *Syntagma* have reference as well to early cinema history, in which the vocabulary of desire for the moving feminine representation was first established. The editing and reprinting of legs descending and ascending stairs recall most particularly what is probably the most famous image from Ferdinand Léger's 1924 *Ballet Méchanique,* the recurrent scene of a washerwoman ascending Parisian steps.

Recognized in this context of film theory and history, *Syntagma* succeeds as an evident deconstruction of the processes of signification of the body in media. But to what end is this detailed analysis put in *Syntagma? What* critique does it indeed effect?

The film's status as a critical text is not unproblematic, for its colorful, fluidly paced visuals and rhythmic sound track offer rich sensual pleasures. The images of slim, conventionally well-shaped and fashionably shod and stockinged feet stand as a paradigmatic choice: the legs might have been fat or those of an

7. Foucault, *This is not a Pipe,* 19–21.

old woman, the feet clad in shoddy house slippers. In intercutting sensuous images to a compelling rhythmic sound track, disrupted only occasionally and incompletely by a woman's voice, the film engages the viewer on a sensual as much as an intellectual level. What is remembered even after repeated viewings is the graceful turn of the black stockinged ankle, the bouncing breasts of the young blonde woman clad variously in black, red and bright blue as she moves to and fro towards and away from the camera down a corridor and through doorways. The film at times seems to be teasing the viewer sexually.

Does not this sensuous experience, in particular of the pleasurable representations of women's bodies, perpetuate rather than disrupt perceptions of the female body as object of desire? An analysis of the film cannot skirt the recurrent dilemma: what material realizations of female representation – visual, aural, technical – can in fact function critically? What, if any, pleasures in viewing can a text elicit without undercutting a purported feminist stance? Must the desire to undercut or deny conventional cinematic practices and uses of female representation perhaps not result in a feminist filmmaker's eschewing *any* imaging of the female body?

Implicit in this radical formulation is the concern with the functioning of the female form as fetish object. With specific reference to *Syntagma*, the question is the extent to which the film succeeds in deconstructing the fetishization of the female body. Certainly, while the film offers extensive material for such a critical response, it does not *require* a deconstructive, analytical reading. Nor perhaps could it do so, for, as some theorists argue, the fetishistic response to representations is neither avoidable nor intrinsically problematic, for it is a symbolic function not only of the male but also of the female psyche.[8]

This position recalls a further issue in the search for alternative film practice: that of *women's pleasure* in the representation of women's bodies and sexuality. The present general trend internationally for feminist filmmakers to turn to narrative forms may be understood as a response in part to a wish to satisfy not *men's* pleasure as conventionally defined and critiqued, but primarily *women's* pleasure in their own representation. Yet the gratification of pleasure presumes the use of recognizable sign systems.

8. Critical comments by Chuck Kleinhans and Mimi White have informed my brief discussion here of the fetishistic process in relation to *Syntagma*.

If, as many feminist theorists continue to argue, conventional representations of the female are by reason of psychoanalytic functioning and historical usage necessarily phallocentric, cinematic pleasures even created by women for women do not subvert but rather establish more firmly the female form as sign.[9]

Conclusion

In reference to Export's film *Syntagma*, the issue in essence is this: can a film, itself *Syntagma*, gain or retain critical distance to its own process? Or is "deconstruction" of signification rendered ultimately impossible by the necessarily signifying construction of the analytic text? In its 18-minute length, *Syntagma* adeptly formulates this hermeneutic dilemma, with all its implications for feminist theory and practice. Yet it proposes no resolution, unless it is possibly in the final two images of the film, following the ending credits, which are printed in small electronic letters on a computer screen. In the penultimate shot, as the attractive slim legs ascend the stairs, a less conventionally attractive, thicker pair of calves and feet, similarly shod, appear for the first time. It is this scene that most directly recalls the washerwoman in *Ballet Méchanique*. Can this newly introduced pair of legs be construed in critical *paradigmatic* relation to the others?

A possibly more convincing "counter-image" is offered in the final shot. A black and white photograph of a leg is matched by its more modeled facsimile, flesh-pink and distinctly hairy. Perhaps this assertion of a representational space for the "natural" (and thereby somehow the individual) is the most radical recasting of body signification that feminist filmmakers can attain. Whatever alternative representations *Syntagma* offers, their efficacy and impact depend clearly on the creation and maintenance of *literal* spaces for the viewing and critical reception of the film.[10]

Reprinted from "The Female Image as Critique in Valie Export's Syntagma,*" Schatzkammer 14.2 (1988): 70–79.*

9. For an alternative analysis of psychoanalytic mechanisms in the cinema viewing experience, see Gaylyn Studlar, "Visual Pleasure and the Masochistic Aesthetic," *Journal of Film and Video* 37 (Spring 1985): 5–26.

10. I am indebted to Klaus Phillips as organizer of the Hollins College conference, "Image of Women in Recent German Films," for the opportunity to rework and present this paper, and to conference participants, especially Sandra Frieden and Gretchen Elsner-Sommer, for their comments. Thanks are also due to Valie Export for facilitating access to the film and contributing through her cooperation and openness to the critical analysis of her work.

22

Interview with Valie Export

margret eifler and
sandra frieden

Valie Export is, as we have noted, an experimental filmmaker with roots in the Austrian avant garde, and she is quite conversant with film theory, having had much experience teaching and writing about film. Nonetheless, as she explains to Margret Eifler and Sandra Frieden in this interview, from her start as a performance artist in the late 1960s, the focus of her art has been the body, specifically the female body. Defining herself as a feminist, she discusses her understanding of feminism, as well as her understanding of political art, which is how she describes her own experimentation with cinematic signification. Not at all dogmatic about the rejection of narrative, Export is willing to use narrative in film to her own ends.
—THE EDITORS

The following interview was conducted in Houston by Margret Eifler and Sandra Frieden on 25 April 1987. Valie Export will appear in the text as V.E., and the interviewers will appear as I.

I.: We'd like to start by asking you what it is that you want to communicate when you make a film? What is it that you are concerned about and pay most attention to?

V.E.: First, to use the material like a painter, like a sculptor or a writer, to explore the possibilities of how the different forms of representation and different contents intersect. Second and also very important for me, to create some kind of political expression – a social commentary. This is to say that I try to create some new kind of cinematographic language, my own film language – as a writer or a poet would.

What I have in mind is the codification of language within discourse, a re-codification according to my own voice and thoughts. I want to experiment with codifications and other lan-

guages, for new future understandings. And I think that film is
quite a good medium for the development of a new discourse.

I.: What is the matter with the old kinds of discourse?

V.E.: The old kinds of discourse result from normed conditioning in old traditions. But when I create art, I always think
that it should go further. For example, there is something very
wrong with the codification through religion and gender socialization, the way behavior is prescribed through rules and so on.
But as an artist, I always think about what I can change or how
these codes could be broken through new content or structure.

I.: Are you breaking the codes or are you creating new ones?

V.E.: Both! If you create a new one you must break the old
one.

I.: Can you give us an example?

V.E.: I have been working on breaking the codification of the
human body, using the human body itself as some new kind of
codification. A very simple example is: I did performance work
earlier in which I was naked. But what I did had nothing to do
with showing a naked body in the context of voyeurism, or to
satisfy the male gaze. First the audience saw a naked woman.
They thought, perhaps this was a kind of voyeuristic or exhibi-
tionistic display. But what I did in these performances had no
relation to being naked in that way. So after a while the audience changed and looked at me as though I were not naked. It
was not important anymore to be naked or not to be naked. I
created a codification for the viewing of a naked female body,
not at all in the way the audience had always been accustomed.
I used the body without any connection or belonging to a class,
race, etc., through clothing. It was very important for me to
carry out my performances naked.

I.: Disassociation from the old to the new?

V.E.: Yes, I expressed something different with my body.

I.: What did you express differently, and how?

V.E.: I wanted to express myself first in an artistic way, to use
the body as a raw material and as an artistic material. And secondly, I was interested in socialization from a feminist point of
view. I always felt like a political artist and the female body is the
means to feminist art and feminist politics. And so I carried out
various action-performances. For example, one of my first such
body actions was in the sixties, and it was called "Touch Cinema." The theory behind it was, that you sit in a cinema hall and
see, for example, naked breasts on the screen. You are a voyeur,

you sit in the dark and are not seen. Nobody sees you, and you see the breasts; you pay for that, but you have nothing for it because you cannot really do anything. So I changed all this. I made a little box and put it on my breasts so that it was not a movie for the eyes – it was tactile. I went onto the street and said, this is a touch cinema. You can use the cinema. You can go into the cinema hall with your hands. You can touch the breasts, you have the real breasts. The body becomes the screen. It is free, but everybody sees you. You are not in the dark here. You are in public and will be seen by everybody. Thus I changed all that is related to the conventional cinematic apparatus, and did it outside on the street. My first goal had to do with traditional (film) theory; the second about breaking up the intimate sphere – after all, it was in the sixties, this sense of "my body belongs to me, my breasts belong to me," and so on. Furthermore, I don't allow myself to be defined any longer as "breasts," "womb," etc., which is to say, I am no longer identified according to female biology. This was also included in this performance piece. I called this the first real "woman's film," and the first "mobile film" because it was a social action on the streets.

I.: How did people react?

V.E.: It was funny. Most of them reacted very well, especially men, especially the fathers. Mothers were particularly afraid. They turned the children away and said, "No, no, no! This is not allowed." So mostly the fathers tried it first and said it was okay, that there was nothing wrong. They finally allowed their children to do it. And the movie was only twelve seconds long! It was strange how people reacted on the street. Some people told me to come to them after I was finished. And I explained that this had nothing to do with prostitution. It went further and further and ultimately the police stopped it. But, what was important was that I had used my body to explain something, I had explained through my body. It is theory, but expressed in an artistic performance, action related to film theory.

I.: You show this in the sequence from Invisible Adversaries where the photographer is using video and a female model, trying to get the woman's body lined up with classical paintings. You're dealing with art and aesthetics, but also with politics and the body. The superimpositions reveal the distortions and absurdity of what has been accepted (the old codification) of female beauty in art, but female beauty shaped to male desire.

V.E.: I wanted to break up the historical paintings and the historical determination through this body behavior, to reveal the ways in which the female body had been and still is forced to comply with male fantasy. In the 1970s, to break the codification of the representation of the female body was the one feminist and therefore also political project in the representation-history of woman. The breaking up of this codification, as it had been begun by me and others in the sixties and seventies, was carried on in the eighties. But, I did other body performances which were not related to feminism, but to material. I called this "context variation" or "semiotic analysis," an analysis by the body or through the body. You have one material and this material can be in different states – glass, for example. You have a glass window. You can look out of it. It is a border between inside and outside, it is transparent, nothing more. But then you have broken glass, and this is something quite different. I used the body to roll in broken glass.

I.: You rolled in broken glass? Didn't it hurt?

V.E.: No, it didn't hurt because I had very small pieces. Only thick glass stands up and punctures. But if you have very thin glass, there is no problem. And it wasn't meant to hurt. So I rolled in broken glass. The audience really knew it was broken glass, because the sound was so terrible, and they came to the performance space and said I should stop it, that I might hurt myself. Then I rolled on a normal glass plate, and there was silence. Through my body I explained the same material, but not in the same condition. This was also a body performance, using the body in an artistic way to analyze semantics through the body. This time, it was also related to feminism.

I.: Why is the body as a material so important?

V.E.: I think the body is the most important thing besides your spirit, your thinking. The body and the spirit are the only means you have to understand what is around you. The body is a medium of expression and was always a very important aesthetic mean in the arts. And the body is also a material through which you can know to which class you belong, to which gender you belong, and so on. The body has expressed all that through the centuries.

I.: But you don't think the old means of expression through body language were good ones, you think they should be changed.

V.E.: Of course! In Catholic religion, for example, the codification of the body was always a repressive discourse that repressed the women and not the men.

I.: This brings us back to film language. This anti-body discourse also becomes an anti-mimetic language. You want to go away from the normed, codified thinking, and also from the linear thinking, from the understandable and preconceived.

V.E.: Yes, this is a part of a new narrative and filmic language, to shift image and thought from one code to another.

I.: How do you relate to narrative plot? Do you feel that your films have to have it in order for you to be able to get a message across?

V.E.: Yes. I think a narrative is like a box to put all these little things in. If you had no narrative, for example, but wanted to show that somebody comes in, opens a door, and goes into a room: without a narrative, why should you do this? It doesn't mean anything, or you use it as formalism – and this is also okay. Of course, there are many films without narratives.

I.: It sets up a context?

V.E.: Yes. But I don't mean a normal narrative, rather a very simple one – for example, *The Children of a Lesser God*. This is a very simple narrative, but I like it. It gives a lot of space to put all the different psychological and physical expressions into a language of the body. But a film without a narrative also has a context.

I.: You do that with Practice of Love, *too: a simple narrative about a woman following up on a murder mystery, a narrative that mimics what a suspense/murder mystery would be. But it doesn't ever really go anywhere. You allow various plot elements to go off in their own directions.*

V.E.: Narrative for me is like the workings of your mind. You never think straight ahead. You think in many small pieces, and I think a movie should be able to make this visible. All these small pieces are related to each other, sooner or later. I might want to make a movie to be shown in a commercial cinema. Let's say I could film a particular gesture, and maybe twenty minutes later this gesture is repeated, and everybody is supposed to understand that it is related. This is very difficult because you do not remember this gesture after twenty minutes. So it must be more than this gesture, or it must have a very good story that will help everybody remember and make the connection. This is my goal, to make a movie in which everything is related, from one step to another step. For example, like Maya Deren's "parallel montage" principle, where every step is related or every movement is related, such as in an avant-garde film like Meshes of the Afternoon.

I.: Are you aiming toward commercial cinema?

V.E.: I want to have my work shown in theaters, not only in museums or festivals.

I.: You would provide enough for the audience, so that they could follow you?

V.E.: But I also think the audience must be educated. For example, in the sixties everybody complained about this quick-cutting and considered it terrible. But now all advertising and MTV are cut and edited that way. People can be educated to see; it is just a question of time. The state or society will not seek it out on their own, they have no interest. It is only a small group of intellectuals who seem to care.

I.: What do you start with when you make a film: do you get a certain idea that you want to express first, or visual images?

V.E.: Both. If I do a feature-length film, I usually have an idea of what I would like to express. Then I think about what kind of a story I could use, and parallel to that I have the images in my mind. Not all of them at once, but a good part of them.

I.: How did you proceed with Practice of Love?

V.E.: I wanted to focus on the topic of weapon sales and the production of weapons parts in Austria; and, on the other hand, I was interested in the narrative constellation of one woman and two men (it was just the opposite in the previous film). After that visualization and dramaturgical conception occurs, I write everything down on small pieces of paper. After a while, I put all these small papers down on the floor and start to shift them around. Then I have a vertical and a horizontal line in time, space and relations. This makes meetings and separations into which I sort the main characters and the others – the same with places and parts of the story, and even emotional patterns of each scene. And so, after a while, it all falls into place.

I.: Do you finally produce an actual script?

V.E.: Yes, including the camera-movement and all the scenes. Only with certain localities I'm not specific, because if the shooting requires a bar or a store, I don't know the actual locality beforehand, and so I leave shooting directions until we are there.

I.: Do you work on your filmscripting totally alone or do you have people who give you advice?

V.E.: I have a group of friends with whom I talk things over and over. And I can be sure that they give me their best advice.

Also, I have collaborated on the scripts for *Human Women* (*Menschenfrauen*) and *Invisible Adversaries* (*Unsichtbare Gegner*) with Peter Weibel. *The Practice of Love* I wrote alone, as I did with *Syntagma* and *A Perfect Couple*, or *Lust*.

I.: Do you also have discussions on projects you are working on with other women filmmakers?

V.E.: Not so much, since we don't have that many filmmakers in Austria, and those women filmmakers we have do not make films which correspond to my avant-garde style and artistic interests.

I.: Do you have any idea why Germany has so many women filmmakers and why more haven't come out of Austria?

V.E.: I think the women's movement was more effective in Germany. It had grown out of a very strong left movement which Austria never experienced. When I did my artistic work in the sixties, there were no other female artists around who worked with modern media (film, video, photography, performance). I was the first feminist artist/filmmaker after the war in Austria, and for years, the only one. My feminist concerns are in art, and also in theory, art theory, and feminist theory as it relates to society, art, and history. I also sought the roots of a feminist history, and I see my theoretical works as rewriting history. I have dealt with feminism since the 1960s. Beginning in 1972, I organized an art exhibit solely about art by women, but it couldn't be carried out until 1976 and was a symposium in the framework of the international language of art. This was a singular event at that time and was one of the first such exhibits in Europe. In 1984 I again initiated, organized, and set up an international art exhibition which gave an overview of the art production of women – again with symposia, film showings, performances, etc. And there was certainly no Austrian women's movement. But at that time in Germany, things went faster, more women participated, and also Germany instituted a law to subsidize young filmmakers much earlier than did Austria, and a lot of German women filmmakers took to subjects of social concern, such as abortion, or the social environment, etc. For example, Helke Sander started like that, and Ula Stöckl, and Helma Sanders-Brahms. They all came from the left movement which Austria didn't have.

I.: Could it also have something to do with Austria's cultural past?

V.E.: Austria's culture was always dominated by men. All

famous cultural aspects that we claim as ours have been produced by very strong men in the arts and sciences, so that one can really speak of a male-dominated cultural tradition controlling the museum directors, gallery owners, and critics. Today in our art schools we have only one female professor, and hardly any female professors in the universities.

I. What does feminism mean to you today?

V.E.: It seems something relatively simple. Women should become more conscious, they should try to do what they can do, all that they want to do.

I.: It is interesting that so many German women whose work American women would call "feminist" don't identify with feminism. Is that a problem for you?

V.E.: No, I am a feminist, and as a feminist, I expect every woman to learn how to become independent. It took me years to put it into practice.

I.: In this context, why did you have the woman professional in Practice of Love, *who seems quite enlightened, independent, and aware, act so weak and disgustingly submissive in her private life? Why this double standard?*

V.E.: Well, I actually wanted to show a normal woman. She has tried to understand men, and she tries to explain that she has a right to this understanding. Where are the actual heroes and heroines? She has her job, but she can't handle private life. I see such situations very often, and Helke Sander in *Trouble with Love* portrays the same thing. Feminism seems not to have taken root really, at least in the ..personal realm. Women are still quite disoriented.

I.: But the men in the film, the psychiatrist above all, appear to suffer from the same split.

V.E.: I think it reflects the feelings of the eighties. Both sexes are unsure nowadays. One cannot act any longer as in the sixties, nor as in the seventies. We should act according to the eighties, but how? There has been so much change, and not all of it worked out, so that everything is kind of floating. Maybe one should characterize the eighties as the "floating years." It is a transition phase. The sixties were very hard, the seventies worked on the problem, and now a kind of search for implementation has begun.

I.: Why isn't anybody showing what they think it should be?

V.E.: Well, first I prefer floating images, not determined ones.

And second, I think everybody is afraid to really show what that could be; it might turn out to be reactionary or simply carry the wrong message. I think that the nineties might even be more confused.

I.: Does this expression of floating contain something negative, or do you see it as being constructive?

V.E.: Floating images can, after a while, create a new code. Breakage, overturning, disassociation, all these moments of destruction are positive for me. Everything these days must be destroyed, deconstructed, de-coded, re-read, before it can be constructed anew.

I.: Do you read criticism on your own movies and if so, how do you evaluate it?

V.E.: Yes, I do read what is being written about me. Feuilletonistic critics are usually poor in perception, and they are quite uneducated in terms of film theory. I can't really respect their discussions. But if I read an in-depth study or a serious article, even if it is negative of me, I will pay attention and might even respond with a letter to the author, explaining my intent in the movie, pointing to what might not have been seen, or wrongly seen.

I. Do you like to have discussions with the audience?

V.E.: Sometimes, yes. I like it more if the audience is a little bit aggressive. When I did my performance work, I always had discussions afterwards, and they were very lively exchanges.

I. You also teach film, besides making films. What is important to you in teaching film?

V.E.: I take teaching film quite seriously, because I really want to pass on what I know about filmmaking, about images, about how to create a filmic image, about representation, about film theory. I also teach courses in art history, i.e., constructivism, surrealism, and I teach classes in performance, that means, directing and acting.

I.: How do students react to your teaching, to your information, to your thought-processes?

V.E.: Some are very good and understand very fast what I try to say, but most students have only very limited preparation in art history, and that makes it somewhat difficult, because they lack the basis from which to depart or to connect. And since my style of teaching can shift in any subject from art historical reference to music, to film techniques, to theoretical discourse, for many students it seems too unfamiliar too often.

I.: Do you bring in politics, or do they bring in politics?

V.E.: They don't and they are very surprised and interested if I raise political issues. I usually speak of my relationship to society, feminism (which actually touches on everything), or I speak of social issues that interest me. For example, in a recent video-class we did social advertising. That means students had to produce one-minute TV spots in a pro- or contra-fashion. Before shooting, we discussed possibilities: for example, if we were to make a floor commercial, shall we choose wood, which would mean cutting trees or shall we choose plastic, which could mean health hazards and pollution. Or we considered a possible advertisement for some of the big film supply companies, weighing their involvement in other enterprises, such as weapon sales, showing maybe a woman or a man buying their products, and on the other hand, showing what the money from this sale will go for. One student produced a very interesting spot on the cosmetic and pharmaceutical industries and their use of experiments on animals; others came up with quite humorous ideas, such as selling Jesus as a product and ending the spot with a number to call.

I.: At the Houston screening of Practice of Love *you said that in the future, you were headed more into looking at the medium itself, to working more with the technological aspects of film. What happens to the political then?*

V.E.: To use the medium in a very conscious way is also a political statement. Every painting also involves a political expression, either negative or positive. If you use the material in a way that it is not intended for, that makes it a political act. You do not always have to give a direct political message, it can be expressed in how you use the material. The consciousness of the audience can be sensitized by the medium itself. My performance art in the sixties and seventies, as all art expressions of that time, was highly political. I always pursue a political content.

I.: Women artists in this country seem to shy away from artistic expressions that involve a rather sophisticated knowledge of film techniques. You, however, seem very much at ease with such technological expertise. It is an integral part of your film language, while other women filmmakers concentrate more on people, on relationships, on the realistic level of portrayal. Is this maybe due to being part of the Austrian cultural scene?

V.E.: Yes, it is very Austrian, because Austria had a strong sci-

entific and artistic tradition. I grew up in a very avant-garde tradition, in a very experimental environment, and I felt very good
about these encounters. I saw here my artistic form, which at
the same time would express my political concerns. If you do
not use words in a conventional context, you have a political
message. So when I came into this avant-garde group, I got a
very good political feeling and it influenced me. I was the only
woman in the circle.

I.: *Could you elaborate on that?*

V.E.: Well, I did my performance work, but I was never asked
personally why I did what I did, rather my friends were asked to
explain my pieces; or at an art fair we once presented photographic pieces. I had worked just as hard as my male colleagues,
but I observed that my materials were always put underneath
the table. After two days I asked for the reason and was told that
it was too feminist. But that is when I realized that in the art
world, there is also something wrong, not only in the social
world. This was in the sixties.

I.: *Has it changed since?*

V.E.: Somewhat. But partly due to the fact that female artists
don't want to be called feminists any longer, because the market
won't buy feminist art. And in the eighties, everybody is more
interested in selling than in commitment. In the sixties and seventies we acted against the museums, we acted against the
gallery scene, we acted against the art market. We usually threw
away our performance pieces after the show, we didn't think of
selling them, we simply didn't want to be integrated in this kind
of an "establishment." We knew the establishment hated us. We
were a threat to them but, of course, this lasted only two to three
years in the late sixties. Then they became very clever, they
bought us after all and with it were back at determining how art
should look.

I.: *Do you think that governments providing money for filmmaking
are having an influence or are even censoring film?*

V.E.: Not yet. But it's starting. It would be regrettable if countries were to destroy their young film culture. More detrimental
to the art scene are the big companies and banks, who buy up
contemporary art. One such artist who let himself be bought up
by a very big bank is Josef Beuys; the contradiction here is that
this artist considered himself to be a very socially motivated and
involved artist, while the bank violates all his concerns with their

investment in South Africa or their transactions of weapon sales. Since the artist must have been aware of this, such action amounts to an unforgivable lie.

I.: Do filmmakers who are not producing within the commercial mainstream cinema make money?

V.E.: Not really. Although I have distributors in many countries, the audience is a relatively small one, because I make art films, avant-garde films, with themes that society doesn't like – or better put, themes that commercial society doesn't like. And although the distribution contracts guarantee a 50-70 percent return, the sums I receive are moderate. And I get paid for the directing and the script of the film and also for producing television specials. But I support myself by additional means: for one I founded my own production company for others to produce avant-garde films. Through my company I also have the copyright to my own films.

I.: What films of yours will now be available in the United States and through what outlet?

V.E.: *Invisible Adversaries* (16 mm), *Syntagma* (16 mm), and *Practice of Love* (35 mm) can be rented through "Foreign Images," (Gretchen Elsner-Sommer, 1213 Maple Avenue, Evanston, IL 60202, telephone 312/869-0543). The video-film *The Perfect Couple or Lust* is available through Maxie Cohen, 31 Greene Street, New York, New York 10013, telephone 212/966-6326, or as video-cassette from the VIDEO DATA BANK, 22 Warren Street, New York, NY 16007. *Menschenfrauen* (*Human Women*)unfortunately is still on 16 mm magnetic sound, and I still have to find a commercial distributor who will pay to have it put into optical sound. In the meantime, it can be ordered through the Austrian Cultural Institute in New York.

I.: Valie, we thank you very much for sharing so many of your thoughts and experiences with us.

Chronology for Volume I and II

German Film History

1895

Two months before Lumiere's first public performance in France, the Skladanovsky brothers showed their "Bioscop" in the Berlin Winter-garten – "bits of scenes shot and projected with apparatus they had built," as Siegfried Kracauer writes in *From Caligari to Hitler* (Princeton Univ. Press, 1947), p. 15; but, as Kracauer also informs us, the nickelo-deons and tent-theaters which sprung up in Germany around the turn of the century featured short films of French, Italian, and American origin; "until 1910 Germany had virtually no film industry of its own"

1913

Stellan Rye & Paul Wegener: *The Student of Prague*

1914 World War I begins

Henrik Galeen & Wegener: *The Golem*

1917 Russian Revolution

Wegener: *The Golem and the Dancer*

B. Weimar Republic: 1918–1933

1918 Kaiser Wilhelm II abdicates; Social Democrats (SPD) asked to form government: Weimar Republic – Germany's first attempt at democracy – proclaimed; Germany surrenders

1919 Versailles treaty: Germany given total blame for war, must pay heavy reparations to victorious powers

Robert Wiene: *The Cabinet of Dr. Caligari*
Ernst Lubitsch: *Passion* (*Madame du Barry*) *The Doll* (*Die Puppe*) *The Oyster Princess*

1919–23 Revolution and Counterrev-
olution in Germany: left-
wing Social Democrats
(Spartakus) form Commu-
nist Party (KPD); main-
stream Social Democrats in
the gov't. use antidemocrat-
ic, right-wing military (and
paramilitary) forces (*Freikorps*) to put down Spar-
takus uprising in Berlin,
other uprisings in Munich,
Hamburg, etc. Spartakus
founders Karl Liebknecht
and Rosa Luxemburg mur-
dered by the *Freikorps* in
Berlin on January 15, 1919.
Right-wing groups also try
to take over gov't.

1920 Kapp putsch

Wegener & Carl Boese: *The Golem –
How He Came into the World*
Lubitsch: *Anne Boleyn*

1921

Fritz Lang: *Destiny* (*Der müde Tod*)
Lubitsch: *Pharoah's Wife*

1922 Assasination of Rathenau
(gov't. minister, Jewish liberal) 1922

Friedrich Murnau: *Nosferatu*
Lang: *Dr. Mabuse, the Gambler.*

1923 Hitler's "beer hall" putsch in
Munich
Germany falling behind on
reparations, so French
troops occupy Ruhr (Ger-
man mining and industrial
region); one result: Ger-
man hyperinflation. At its
worst, $1.00 U.S. =
4,000,000,000,000 German
marks (*Reichsmark*)

Karl Grune: *The Street*
Lubitsch to Hollywood, where he di-
rected (among many other films):
Forbidden Paradise, 1924
The Student Prince, 1927
Design for Living, 1933
Ninotschka, 1939, with Greta Garbo
To Be or Not to Be, 1942 with Jack
Benny & Carole Lombard
Heaven Can Wait, 1943

1924 Dawes Plan ends inflation:
American banks refinance
reparations payments, make
loans – and invest in Germany; beginning of "Stabilized Period," period of relative prosperity (for some)
and (uneasy) social harmony

Murnau: *The Last Laugh* (*Der letzte
Mann*)

1925		E. A. Dupont: *Variety* G. W. Pabst: *The Joyless Street* (with Greta Garbo)
1926	Paragraph 218, outlawing abortion, reformed, made slightly more lenient	Lang: *Metropolis* (which nearly bankrupts Ufa; it is only saved by being bought in 1921 by right-wing media czar Hugenberg) Murnau: *Faust*
1927		Bruno Rahn: *Tragedy of the Street* (*Dirnentragodie*: literally, "Tragedy of a Whore") Murnau to Hollywood (directs *Sunrise*, 1927)
1928		Pabst: *Pandora's Box* (with Louise Brooks)
1929	Stock Market crash: American banks fail, call in loans, so Germany is hit hard, too (first in Europe)	Piel Jutzi: *Mother Krause's Journey to Happiness*
1930	Elections: Nazis go from 12 to 107 seats in *Reichstag* (Parliament)	Pabst: *The 3-Penny Opera* (*without* Bertolt Brecht's approval) Josef von Sternberg: *The Blue Angel* (with Marlene Dietrich)
1931	Activists Dr. Else Kienle and Dr. Friedrich Wolf arrested for having performed abortions; protests lead to massive popular campaign for the legalization of abortion, which however does not succeed	Leontine Sagan: *Girls in Uniform* (*Mädchen in Uniform*) Lang: *M* (with Peter Lorre)
1932	Nazis win 230 seats; Social Democrats and Communists on left continue fighting each other rather than uniting against the Nazis on the right	Slatan Dudow: *Kuhle Wampe* (script: Bertolt Brecht) Leni Riefenstahl: *The Blue Light*
1933		Lang: *The Testament of Mabuse*, which the National Socialists do not like; Lang is nonetheless asked by Goebbels to direct films for the Nazis; Lang, not so thrilled about

1933 *(continued)*

this offer (and also part Jewish), flees first to Paris, later to Hollywood, where he directs (among other films):
Fury, 1936 *Hangmen Also Die*, 1942 – (Brecht worked on an early version of screenplay)
Scarlet Street, 1946
The Big Heat, 1954

C. The "Third Reich": 1933–45

1933   Hitler becomes Chancellor; *Reichstag* (Parliament) burns; "emergency laws" passed that ban leftist parties; first concentration camps; *Reichstag* building not repaired (nor is parliament re-called as a serious legislative body); books by ethnic and political "undesirables" (Freud, Marx, Thomas Mann, etc.) burned

Hans Steinhoff: *Hitler-Youth Quex.*

1935   First "racial" laws passed

Steinhoff: *The Old and the Young King*
Leni Riefenstahl: *Triumph of the Will*

1936   Germany occupies Rhineland: breach of Versailles treaty

1937

Ufa becomes a state-owned monopoly
Gustav Ucicky: *The Broken Jug*
Detlef Sierck: *To New Shores*
   La Habanera. Detlef Sierck began as a director in the German theater during the 1920s. A leftist, he turned more and more to filmmaking during the Third Reich, since the film industry was at first less politicized than the theater, to the extent it still attempted to market films internationally. In 1937, however, Sierck and his wife, the actor Hilde Jary (who was Jewish) fled Germany, and by 1940 they were living in the U.S., where he "americanized" his name. As Douglas Sirk, he made films in the U.S., including:

1937 *(continued)*

Sleep My Love, 1948
Magnificent Obsession, 1954
All That Heaven Allows, 1956
Written on the Wind, 1957
Imitation of Life, 1959

1938   *Anschluß*: Austria annexed;
Munich agreement re Sude-
tenland;
so-called "Kristallnacht"
(night of the broken glass):
Jews attacked, Jewish busi-
nesses, synagogues vandal-
ized, burned

Riefenstahl: *Olympia* (Part II)

1939   Czechoslovakia under com-
plete German control
Hitler-Stalin Pact
Invasion of Poland: World
War II begins

1940   Denmark, Norway, France,
etc. fall to Germany

Hans Schweikart: *Fräulein von Barnhelm*
Veit Harlan: *Jew Süß*

1941   Germany attacks the Soviet
Union
Pearl Harbor

1942   Wannsee Conference: *Endlö-
sung* ("final solution") i.e.,
genocide, decided upon

1942–43 Battle of Stalingrad:
turning point of war

1943

Joseph von Baky: *Baron von Münch-
hausen*

1944   20 July plot to kill Hitler fails

1945   Yalta Conference: Churchill,
Stalin, Roosevelt agree on
boundaries of postwar
Europe
Hitler's suicide, Apr. 30
Soviets take Berlin, May 2
German surrender, May 7

premiere of Veit Harlan's *Kolberg*

D. Allied Occupation: 1945–49

1945	Potsdam Conference: division of Germany and Berlin into U.S., French, British, and Soviet Zones (Hiroshima 6 Aug.; Nagasaki 9 Aug.; Japan surrenders 14 Aug.)	In the three Western zones, under the initiative of the U.S., the state monopoly Ufa enjoyed under National Socialism is broken up; in the Soviet zone, Ufa is re-organized as "DEFA" (German Film Corporation), which would continue to control film production in the East German state (the German Democratic Republic, or the GDR) after its founding in 1949
1946	In Soviet Zone, Social Democrats and Communists (somewhat forcibly) united to form "Socialist Unity Party" (SED); Social Democrats in W. Berlin and Western Zones vote not to do so; Churchill coins term "Iron Curtain"	Wolfgang Staudte: *The Murderers are Among Us*, a DEFA-production
1947	U. S. announces Marshall Plan to rebuild (W.) Europe; Walter Lippmann coins term "Cold War"; "denazification" program in W. Zones gets de-emphasized	
1948	*Währungsreform*: currency of Western zones reorganized (basis of coming "*Wirtschaftswunder*" – "economic miracle"); in response to this, which they see as destabilization of the currency in their zone, Soviets blockade West Berlin; the U.S. responds with airlift ("*Luftbrücke*")	

E. The Two Postwar States: 1949–90

All films listed were made in FRG (West Germany) unless indicated as made in the GDR or Austria

1949	Founding of two German states: Federal Republic of Germany, or the FRG (W. Germany) and German Democratic Republic, or	Staudte: *The Subject* (based on the novel by Heinrich Mann) – DEFA (GDR)

GDR (E. Germany); Adenauer of Christian Democrats (CDU) first chancellor of FRG

1951

Peter Lorre: *The Lost Man* (*Der Verlorene*)

1952 Stalin suggests united, neutral Germany; skeptical Western powers refuse; GDR fortifies (seals off) its border, gets an army

Veit Harlan: *The Blue Hour*

1953 Stalin dies
"thaw" under Beria – opening to West on unifying Germany rejected by Dulles in U.S., then closed off by Soviet return to hard line under Malenkov
June 17: workers' uprising in E. Berlin put down by Soviet tanks
Ulbricht emerges as leader of party and government in GDR

1954 FRG gets an army, joins NATO

Helmut Käutner: *The Devil's General*

1955 Soviets and E. Europe (incl. GDR) form Warsaw Pact
Four powers – including Soviets – end occupation of Austria, leaving it united and neutral

Herbert Vesely: *Stop Running* (*nicht mehr fliehen* – FRG)
Staudte unable to make any more films with DEFA in the GDR

1956 Communist Party outlawed in FRG
Soviets crush Hungarian uprising

1957 Sputnik; Treaty of Rome: Common Market; Adenauer's Christian Democrats get absolute majority for his third term

Ottomar Dominick: *Jonas*
Harlan: *The Third Sex*

1958 Debate in FRG over owning atomic weapons

1959	Social Democrats approve "Godesberger Programm" – party distances itself from Marxism	Staudte: *Roses for the Prosecutor* Bernard Wicki: *The Bridge*
1960		Staudte: *Fairground* (*Kirmes*)
1961	August 13: after ever larger numbers of its citizens emigrate via W. Berlin, GDR erects Berlin Wall	At the Berlin Film Festival, the FRG's Minister of the Interior finds no German films worthy of the Federal Film Prize
1962	FRG: Spiegel-Affair: F.J. Strauß authorizes break-in, Adenauer stands behind him, causing new elections	26 young filmmakers, noted mostly for internationally recognized short films, sign the Oberhausen Manifesto: "The old film is dead. We believe in the new" usually considered birth of FRG's "New German. Cinema" Vesely: *The Bread of the Early Years*
1963	Kennedy in W. Berlin: "Ich bin ein Berliner" Adenauer resigns – precondition for Christian Democratic coalition with Free Democrats (FDP, the "Liberals") Erhard his successor	Konrad Wolf: *Divided Heaven* (*Der geteilte Himmel* – GDR)
1964	FRG already has more than one million "*Gastarbeiter*," or foreign workers after (dubious) "Gulf of Tonkin" incident, U. S. Congress gives Johnson free hand in Vietnam	
1965	Involvement of U. S. troops in Vietnam increases dramatically in FRG, end of "*Wirtschaftswunder*": two-year recession begins	"*Kuratorium junger deutscher Film*" founded in the FRG, making federally subsidized, interest-free loans to young filmmakers. Jean-Marie Straub & Danielle Huillet: *Not Reconciled*
1966	"*Große Koalition*" (Great Coalition) between Christian Democrats and Social Democrats; Christian Democrat – and ex-Nazi – Kiesinger becomes chancellor	Alexander Kluge: *Yesterday Girl* (*Abschied von gestern*) Volker Schlöndorff: *Young Törleß* *Yesterday Girl* wins the "Silver Lion" at the Venice Film Festival; *Not Reconciled* and *Young Törleß* win awards at the Cannes Festival

1967   Left-wing and student protesters in FRG form *"Außenparlamentarische Opposition"* (APO – extraparliamentary opposition) to oppose Kiesinger, the Social Democratic coalition with him, and FRG support for U. S. foreign policy, esp. in Vietnam; June 2: W. Berlin police shoot Benno Ohnesorg at student protest of visit of Shah of Iran – result: massive student demonstrations all over FRG

    Werner Herzog: *Signs of Life*
Konrad Wolf: *I Was 19* (GDR)

1968   High point of student movement in FRG (and internationally) – and beginning of decline: APO campaign against emergency laws (*Notstandsgesetze*) fails, factions begin to arise, e.g., "Rote Armee Faktion" (RAF, the "Red Army Faction," also called "Baader-Meinhof" gang); "Action Committee for the Liberation of Women" founded by feminists (including filmmaker Helke Sander) in FRG student movement
Soviet tanks move into Czechoslovakia

    Film Promotion Law (*"Filmforderungsgesetz"* or FFG) passed; in spite of the lobbying efforts of the young filmmakers, the new law subsidizes, not the new filmmakers, but the old commercial film industry in the FRG (the output of which consisted of approx. 50 percent sex films).
Ula Stockl: *The Cat Has 9 Lives*
May Spils: *Let's Get Down to Business, Darling* (*Zur Sache, Schätzchen*)

1969   FRG Elections: Social Democrats, in coalition w/ Free Democrats, form gov't.; Willi Brandt is chancellor

    Rainer Werner Fassbinder: *Love is Colder Than Death* and *Katzelmacher* (the first 2 of 41 feature-length films he will make over the next 13 years)
Werner Schroeter: *Eika Katappa*

1970   "Ostpolitik" (Eastern Policy): FRG regularizes relations w/ Soviets, Poland

    Rosa von Praunheim: *Not the Homosexual is Perverse, but the Situation in which He Lives*

1971   GDR's Ulbricht resigns, Honecker takes over
Four-Power Agreement: Soviets guarantee status of and transit to, rom W. Berlin

    13 young filmmakers, including Wim Wenders, form their own production and distribution company: the *"Filmverlag der Autoren"* (Film-Publishing-Co. of the Authors – or *auteurs*)

1971 *(continued)*

Brandt gets Nobel prize
inspired by French feminists,
feminists in FRG start campaign against Paragraph
218, i.e., they campaign for
legalization of abor-tion;
movement becomes massive

Fassbinder's *The Merchant of the 4 Sea-
sons* finally wins him critical acclaim
in the FRG
Christian Ziewer: *Dear Mother, I'm OK*
Schroeter: *The Death of Maria Mali-
bran*

1972   *Radikalenerlaß* ("Radicalism
Decree") becomes law in
the FRG; popularly known s
the *Berufsverbot* ("career
prohibition"), which led to
a type of blacklisting; on
the basis of this law, people
with a record of having
been involved in protest
demonstrations were often
denied civil service jobs
(which in the FRG include
almost all teaching jobs)
Palestinian "Black September" murders Israeli ath-
letes at Munich Olympics

Herzog: *Aguirre the Wrath of God*
Schlöndorff: *A Free Woman*
   (*Strohfeuer*)
Fassbinder: *The Bitter Tears of Petra
von Kant*
Wim Wenders: *The Scarlet Letter*
New York's Museum of Modern Art
begins its yearly show featuring
young German filmmakers

1973   "*Grundlagenvertrag*" (Basic
Treaty) between FRG and
GDR into effect; both states
admitted to U.N.; begin-
ning of international oil crisis

In West Berlin, Helke Sander and
Claudia von Alemann organize first
International Women's Film Semi-
nar
Wenders: *Alice in the Cities*
Fassbinder: *Ali, or Fear Eats the Soul*

1974   Guillaume scandal: Brandt
resigns; Schmidt (right-
wing of Social Democrats)
leads Social Democratic-
Free Democratic coalition
gov't

Helke Sander founds feminist film
journal, *Frauen und Film.*
Film/Television Agreement: agree-
ment between (public) television
networks and Film Promotion
Board in FRG turns networks into
main funders of "New German Cin-
ema"
Fassbinder's *Ali* wins the "Golden
Palm" at Cannes
Fassbinder: *Effi Briest*
Wenders: *The Wrong Move* (*Falsche
Bewegung*)
Herzog: *The Mystery of Kaspar Hauser*
   (*Jeder für sich und Gott gegen alle*)
Kluge: *Part-Time Work of a Domestic
Slave* (*Gelegenheitsarbeit einer Sklavin*)

1975 U. S. withdraws from Vietnam
RAF involved in bomb attack
on FRG embassy in Stock-
holm
Paragraph 218 liberalized
somewhat, but FRG wo-
men's movement looks
upon it as a defeat of their
efforts to decriminalize
abortion completely

Schlöndorff & Margarethe von Trotta: *The Lost Honor of Katharina Blum*;
this politically controversial film,
with Bernhard Sinkel's *Lina Braake*,
become the first commercial suc-
cesses of the "New German Cinema"
Peter Lilienthal: *The Country is Calm*
(*Es herrscht Ruhe im Land*)

1976 Brokdorf (FRG): demonstrations against proposed
nuclear power plant
U. Meinhof (RAF) dies in
prison (suicide?)

Newsweek proclaims "German Film
Boom"
Wenders: *Kings of the Road* (*Im Lauf
der Zeit*)
Herzog: *Heart of Glass*
Schlöndorff: *Coup de Grace* (*Der
Fangschuß*)
Stockl: *Erika's Passions*
Frank Beyer: *Jacob the Liar* (GDR)

1977 RAF actions in FRG: Ponto,
Buback murdered; then,
"*Deutscher Herbst*," the "German Autumn": Schleyer
kidnapped; Lufthansa jet
highjacked, stormed by GS-
9 unit; RAF old guard –
Baader, Raspe, Ensslin –
found dead in cells (sui-
cide?); Schleyer found dead

Helke Sander: *The All-Around Reduced
Personality* (or: *REDUPERS*)
Valie Export: *Invisible Adversaries*
(Austria)
Ulrike Ottinger: *Madame X*
Wenders: *The American Friend*
Herzog: *Stroszek*
Fassbinder: *Despair*
Hans Jürgen Syberberg: *Our Hitler*

1978 FRG: Anti-Terrorism Law

Time Magazine: "The New German
Cinema is the liveliest in Europe"
Wenders, disgusted with the film
scene in Germany, is lured to Hol-
lywood by Francis Coppola to make
Hammett
Kluge, Fassbinder, Schlöndorff,
Heinrich Böll, Edgar Reitz, et al.:
Germany in Autumn
von Trotta: *The 2nd Awakening of
Christa Klages*
Cristina Perincioli: *The Power of Men is
the Patience of Women* (*Die Macht der
Männer ist die Geduld der Frauen*)
Fassbinder: *In a Year with 13 Moons*
Reinhard Hauff: *Knife in the Head*
Carow: *Till Death Do You Part* (GDR)

1979 Thatcher becomes Prime
Minister in Britain
NATO warns Soviets that if it
does not remove SS-20 mis-
siles,
NATO will deploy Pershing
missiles in W. Europe; in
protest, new peace mvt. in
W. Europe starts
Soviet troops into Afghanistan

Manifesto of Women Film Workers;
among its demands: 50 percent of
ll film subsidies should be granted
to women filmmakers
Jutta Brückner: *Years of Hunger*
Helma Sanders-Brahms: *Germany,
Pale Mother*
Ottinger: *Ticket of No Return* (*Bildnis
einer Trinkerin*
Helga Reidemeister: *Von wegen Schick-
sal* (*What do you mean, Fate?*)
Heidi Genée: *1+1=3*
von Trotta: *Sisters – or the Balance of
Happiness*
Fassbinder: *The Marriage of Maria
Braun*
Schlöndorff: *The Tin Drum*
Kluge: *The Patriot*
Lilienthal: *David*
Schroeter: *The Kingdom of Naples*

1980 Reagan elected

The Tin Drum wins the Oscar for Best
Foreign Film; it and *Maria Braun*
are the first two German films to
earn more than $1 million apiece
in the US
Fassbinder: *Berlin Alexanderplatz*
Kluge, Schlöndorff, et al.: *The Candi-
date*
von Praunheim: *Red Love*
Lothar Lambert: *Nightmare Woman*
Konrad Wolf: *Solo Sunny* (GDR)

1981 Squatter demonstrations in
W. Berlin at high point: K.-
J. Rattay killed

von Trotta: *Marianne & Juliane* (*Die
bleierne Zeit*)
Sander: *The Subjective Factor*
Wolfgang Petersen: *The Boat*
Lothar Warnecke: *Apprehension* (*Die
Beunruhigung* – GDR)

1982 Free Democrats leave coalition w/Schmidt and Social
Democrats, form gov't with
Christian Democrats; Christian Democrat Kohl
becomes chancellor

von Trotta: *Sheer Madness* (*Heller
Wahn*)
Wenders's *Hammett* finally appears,
after four years in which various
scriptwriters, as well as Wenders
himself, had been fired (Wenders
was rehired)
Wenders: *The State of Things* (filmed
in Portugal and the U.S.), in part a
comment on his attempt at film
making in Hollywood

Herzog: *Fitzcarraldo* (filmed in South
America)
Fassbinder (born 1945) dies on 6
June 1982

1983 Kohl wins new elections, but
Greens get into Bundestag
more important house of
FRG parliament)
"*Heißer Herbst*" ("Hot
Autumn"): in spite of mas-
sive protests, Free Democra-
tic-Christian Democratic
majority in Bundestag votes
to accept deployment of
Pershing missiles
U.S. invades Grenada

Kluge, Schlöndorff, et al.: *War and
Peace*
Marianne Rosenbaum: *Peppermint
Peace*
Export: *Syntagma* (Austria)
Lambert: *Paso Doble, Fräulein Berlin*
Robert van Ackeren: *A Woman in
Flames (Die flambierte Frau)*
The "Achternbusch-Affair": at the
end of 1982, a conservative coalition had come to power in the
FRG; by mid-1983 the new Minister
of the Interior, Zimmermann,
gains notoriety by withdrawing
financial support for filmmaker
Herbert Achternbusch's *The Ghost*
because it "offended religious values"; West German filmmakers join
together in an ultimately unsuc-
cessful attempt to stop this attack
on their freedom of expression –
and the subsidy system; end of
"New German Cinema"?
Petersen: *The Never-Ending Story*
(filmed in Canada)

1984 Missile Deployment begins

Sander: *The Trouble with Love (Der
Beginn aller Schrecken ist Liebe)*
Ottinger: *The Mirror Image of Dorian
Gray in the Yellow Press (Dorian Gray
im Spiegel der Boulevard Presse)*
Export: *The Practice of Love* (Austria)
Stöckl: *Reason Asleep*
Elfi Mikesch & Monika Treut: *Seduc-
tion: The Cruel Woman*
Christa Mühl: *Pauline's Second Life*
(GDR)
Lambert: *Drama in Blonde*
Straub/Huillet: *Class Relations*
Edgar Reitz: *Heimat*
Schlöndorff: *Swann in Love* (filmed
in France)
Herzog: *Where the Green Ants Dream*
(filmed in Australia)
Wenders: *Paris, Texas* (filmed in the
US) wins at Cannes

1985	Gorbachev to power in USSR	Doris Dörrie: *Men* (breaks all German box office records since World War II) Kluge: *The Blind Director* (*Der Angriff der Gegenwart auf die übrige Zeit*) Percy Adlon: *Zuckerbaby*
1986	Reagan goes to Bitburg to honor German war dead – cemetery includes SS graves "Historian's Debate" in FRG over interpretation of the Holocaust nuclear accident at Chernobyl	Hauff: *Stammheim* Peter Timm: *Meier* von Trotta: *Rosa Luxemburg* Ottinger: *China* Ottinger, Export, Sander, et al.: *SevenWomen/Seven Sins*
1987		Wenders: *Wings of Desire* (*Himmel über Berlin*) Reidemeister: *Drehort Berlin* (*Shooting Location Berlin*) Adlon: *Bagdad Cafe* (*Out of Rosenheim*) von Praunheim: *Anita, Dances of Vice*
1988	Reagan and Gorbachev agree on INF treaty: Pershings & SS 20s, etc. to be removed from Europe	von Trotta: *3 Sisters* (filmed in Italy) Treut: *The Virgin Machine* Hark Bohm: *Jasmin* Thomas Brasch: *The Passenger* Sander: *The Germans and Their Men* (*Die Deutschen und ihre Männer*) Ottinger, *Johanna d'Arc of Mongolia* Dörrie: *Money* (*Geld*) Adlon *Rosalie Goes Shopping* Helke Misselwitz: *Winter Ade* (GDR) Heiner Carow: *Coming Out* (GDR)
1989	Christian Democrats lose elections in W. Berlin & Hessen by losing conservative voters to neo-fascist, anti-foreigner "Republican" party; leftist "redgreen" coalitions (Social Democrats & Greens) benefit from Christian Democratic losses and come to power	

Hungary cuts down its fences ("Iron Curtain"); GDR citizens escape from there to west, and then more try to flock to Hungary, then Prague; massive protests start in Leipzig, spread, led by dissidents who form umbrella group, New Forum

Gorbachev visits GDR; Honecker resigns

November 9: Berlin Wall opened

1990   Reunification on the fast track: in March elections in GDR, Christian Democrats beat Social Democrats, other parties, including New Forum, by promising quick reunification

1 July – yet another German currency reform: FRG and GDR merge monetary systems; FRG's D-Mark becomes currency in both states

Reunification official, October 3

Kohl and Christian Democrats win "all-German" elections in December

West German Greens lose representation in Bundestag; in East Greens in coalition w/New Forum do get enough votes to get into Bundestag

Michael Verhoeven's *The Nasty Girl* wins Silver Bear at Berlin Film Festival, wins acclaim at New York Film Festival

Filmography

Distribution information is provided for those films distributed in the U.S.[1] Addresses for the distributors are given after the filmography. Unless otherwise noted, films have English subtitles or, for silent films, English intertitles.

Alice in the Cities. German title: *Alice in den Städten.* Dir. Wim Wenders. 1973. 110 min. Video available from: Facets.

The All-Around Reduced Personality – REDUPERS. German title: *Die allseitig reduzierte Persönlichkeit – REDUPERS.* Dir. Helke Sander. 1977. 98 min. U.S. dist.: Cinema Guild.

The American Friend. German title: *Der amerikanische Freund.* Dir. Wim Wenders. 1977. 123 min. U.S. dist.: New Yorker Films.

Apprehension. German title: *Die Beunruhigung.* Dir. Lothar Warnecke. 1982. 102 min. DEFA (Berlin).

The Bitter Tears of Petra von Kant. German title: *Die bitteren Tränen der Petra von Kant.* Dir. Rainer Werner Fassbinder. 1972. 124 min. U.S. dist.: New Yorker Films.

The Cat Has Nine Lives. German title: *Neun Leben hat die Katze.* Dir. Ula Stöckl. 1968. 91 min. U.S. dist.: West Glen Films.

Class Relations. German title: *Klassenverhältnisse.* Dir. Jean-Marie Straub/Daniele Huillet. 1983. 126 min. U.S. dist.: New Yorker Films.

Effi Briest. German title: *Fontane Effi Briest.* Dir. Rainer Werner Fassbinder. 1974. 141 min. U.S. dist.: New Yorker Films.

Erika's Passions. German title: *Erikas Leidenschaften.* Dir. Ula Stöckl. 1976. 66 min. U.S. dist.: West Glen Films.

In a Year with 13 Moons. German title: *In einem Jahr mit 13 Monden.* Dir. Rainer Werner Fassbinder. 1978. 124 min. U.S. dist.: New Yorker Films.

1. For information about access to West German films not distributed in the U.S. contact the Goethe Haus in New York or one of the other Goethe Institutes in the U.S.: Boston, Chicago, Atlanta, Houston, Seattle, San Francisco, Los Angeles, etc. For information about distribution of films produced by DEFA ("Deutsche-Film-Aktiengesellschaft") in the former GDR (East Germany), contact the Bundesfilmarchiv, Fehrbellinerplatz 3, W-1000 Berlin 31.

Invisible Adversaries. German title: *Unsichtbare Gegner.* Dir. Valie Export. 1976. 112 min. US. dist.: Foreign Images.

Kings of the Road. German title: *Im Lauf der Zeit.* Dir. Wim Wenders. 1976. 176 min. Video available from: Facets.

Madame X. German title: *Madame X – eine absolute Herrscherin.* Dir. Ulrike Ottinger. 1977. 141 min. Autorenfilm Ulrike Ottinger/ Tabea Blumenschein.

The Mirror Image of Dorian Gray in the Yellow Press. German title: *Dorian Gray im Spiegel der Boulevardpresse.* Dir. Ulrike Ottinger. 1984. 150 min. Ulrike Ottinger Filmproduktion.

1+1=3. German title: *Eins + Eins = Drei.* Dir. Heidi Genee. 1979. 85 min. U.S. dist.: West Glen Films.

Paris, Texas. Dir. Wim Wenders. 1984. 148 min. U.S. dist.: Films, Inc.

Part-Time Work of a Domestic Slave. German title: *Gelegenheitsarbeit einer Sklavin.* Dir. Alexander Kluge. 1973. 91 min. Kairos-Film Munich.

Pauline's Second Life. German title: *Paulines zweites Leben.* Dir. Christa Mühl. 1984. DEFA (Berlin).

Persona. Dir. Ingmar Bergman. 1966. 81 min. U.S. dist.: Films Inc.

Reason Asleep. German title: *Der Schlaf der Vernunft.* Dir. Ula Stöckl.1984. 82 min. Ula Stöckl Filmproduktion/Common Film Produktion/ ZDF Mainz.

The Scarlet Letter. German title: *Der scharlachrote Buchstabe.* Dir. Wim Wenders. 1972. 90 min. Video available from: Facets.

The Second Awakening of Christa Klages. German title: *Das zweite Erwachen der Christa Klages.* Dir. Margarethe von Trotta. 1978. 88 min. Bioskop-Film Munich/WDR.

Sisters, or the Balance of Happiness. German title: *Schwestern - oder Die Balance des Glücks.* Dir. Margarethe von Trotta. 1979. 92 min. U.S. dist.: Krypton c/o Almi..

Solo Sunny. Dir. Konrad Wolf. 1980. 110 min. DEFA (Berlin).

Syntagma. Dir. Valie Export. 1983. 18 min. U.S. dist.: Foreign Images.

Ticket of No Return. German title: *Bildnis einer Trinkerin.* Dir. Ulrike Ottinger. 1979. 108 min. Autorenfilm.

Till Death Do You Part. German title: *Bis daß der Tod euch scheidet.* Dir. Heiner Carow. 1978. 100 min. DEFA (Berlin).

The Trouble with Love. German title: *Der Beginn aller Schrecken ist Liebe.* Dir. Helke Sander. 1983. 114 min. Provobis Film Hamburg.

U.S. Distributors

Budget Films, 4590 Santa Monica Blvd., Los Angeles, CA 90029.
(213) 660-0187 or 0080.

Cinema Guild, 1697 Broadway, Suite 802, New York, NY 10019.
(212) 246-5522.

Facets Multimedia, Inc., 1517 W. Fullerton Ave., Chicago, IL 60614.
(800) 331-6197. Video sales and rental.

Films Incorporated / Central, South, West , and Alaska:
5547 N. Ravenswood, Chicago, IL 60640-1199.
(800) 323-4222, ext. 42.

Films Incorporated / Northeast:
35 S. West St., Mt. Vernon, NY 10550.
(800) 223-6246.

Foreign Images, 1213 Maple Ave., Evanston, IL 60202.
(708) 869-0543.

International Films, Inc. Box 29035, Chicago, IL 60629.
(312) 436-8051.

Krypton c/o Almi Productions, 1900 Broadway, New York, NY 10023.
(212) 769-6400.

MOMA = Circulating Film Library, Museum of Modern Art,
11 W. 53 St., New York, NY 10019.
(212) 708-9530.

New Yorker Films, 16 W. 61 St., New York, NY 10023.
(212) 247-6110.

Trans-World Films, Inc., 332 S. Michigan Ave., Chicago, IL 60604.
(312) 922-1530.

West Glen Films, 1430 Broadway, New York, NY 10018-3396.
(212) 921-2800.

Bibliography for Volume I and II

Albrecht, Gerd. *Nationalsozialistische Filmpolitik*. Stuttgart: Ferdinand Enke Verlag, 1969.

Albrecht, Gerd, ed. *Der Film im 3. Reich*. Karlsruhe: DOKU, 1979.

Alford, C. Fred. "Nature and Narcissim." *New German Critique* 36 (1985).

Alloula, Malek. *The Oriental Harem*. Trans. Myrna Godzich and Wlad Godzich. Introd. Barbara Harlow. Minneapolis: Univ. Minnesota, 1986.

Altbach, Edith Hoshino, Jeanette Clausen, Dagmar Schultz, and Naomi Stephan, eds. *German Feminism: Readings in Politics and Literature*. Albany, N.Y.: SUNY, 1984.

Althusser, Louis. "Idéologie et appareils idéologiques d'état." *La Pense* 151 (June 1970). Also later published in *Positions 1964–1975*. Paris: Éditions sociales, 1976.

Andrew, J. Dudley. *Concepts in Film Theory*. New York: Oxford Univ., 1984.

Anger, Kenneth. *Hollywood Babylon*. San Francisco: Straight Arrow, 1975.

Atwell, Lee. *G. W. Pabst*. Boston: Twayne, 1977.

Aust, Stefan. *Der Baader Meinhof Komplex*. Hamburg: Hoffmann und Campe, 1986.

Baaker Schut, Pieter H. *Stammheim: Der Prozeß gegen die Rote Armee Faktion*. Kiel: Neuer Malik Verlag, 1986.

Bachmann, Ingeborg. "Undine geht." *Das dreißigste Jahr*. Munich: R. Piper, 1961.

Bächlin, Peter. *Der Film als Ware*. Frankfurt/M.: Fischer, 1975.

Bänsch, Dieter, ed. *Die fünfziger Jahre*. Tübingen: Günter Narr, 1985.

Baer, Harry. *Schlafen kann ich, wenn ich tot bin*. Köln: Kiepenheuer & Witsch, 1982.

Bakhtin, Mikhail. *Rabelais and His World*. Trans. Helene Iswolsky. Cambridge: M.I.T., 1968.

Bammer, Angelika. "Through a Daughter's Eyes: Helma Sanders-Brahms's *Germany, Pale Mother*." *New German Critique* 36 (1985).

Barck, Karlheinz et al., eds. *Künstlerische Avant-garde: Annäherungen an ein unabgeschlossenes Kapitel*. Berlin [DDR], 1979.

Barlow, John D. *Expressionist Film.* Boston: Twayne, 1982.

Bauer, Otto. *The Austrian Revolution.* Trans. H. J. Stenning. New York: Burt Franklin, 1970.

Becker, Gillian. *Hitler's Children.* Philadelphia and New York: Lippincott, 1977.

Bekh, Wolfgang Johannes. *Das dritte Weltgeschehen: bayerische Hellseher schauen in die Zukunft.* Pfaffenhofen: Ludwig, 1980.

Belotti, Elena Gianini. *Dalla Parte delle Bambine.* Milano: Gianciacomo Feltrinelli Editore, 1973.

Benjamin, Jessica. "Authority and the Family Revisited: Or, A World Without Fathers?" *New German Critique* 13 (Winter 1978).

Benjamin, Walter. "Theses on the Philosophy of History." In *Illuminations.*

————. *Illuminations.* Ed. Hannah Arendt. Trans. Harry Zohn. New York: Schocken, 1969 and 1978.

————. *Charles Baudelaire: A Lyric Poet in the Era of High Capitalism.* London: New Left, 1973.

Berens, E. M. *The Myths and Legends of Ancient Greece and Rome: Being a Popular Account of Greek and Roman Mythology.* London: Blackie and Son, 1880.

Berg-Ganschow, Uta. "Geschichte eines Nebenwiderspruchs." *Filme* 9 (June 1981).

————. "Die Puppe." In *Lubitsch,* ed. Hans Helmut Prinzler and Enno Patalas. Munich and Luzern: Stiftung Deutsche Kinemathek, 1984.

Bergman, Ingmar. *Persona* and *Shame.* Trans. K. Bradfield. London: Calder & Boyars, 1972.

Berning, Cornelia. *Vokabular des Nationalsozialismus.* Berlin: Walter de Gruyter, 1964.

Betancourt, Jeanne. *Women in Focus.* Dayton: Pflaum, 1974.

"Bischöfe fordern Jugendschutz–Gesetz." *Münchner Merkur.* (24 March 1950).

Bloch, Ernst. *Vom Hasard zur Katastrophe: Politische Aufsätze 1934–1939.* Frankfurt/M.: Suhrkamp, 1972.

Blum, Heiko R. "Gespräch mit Wim Wenders." *Filmkritik* (February 1972).

Boelcke, Willi A. *Kriegspropaganda 1939–1941.* Stuttgart: DVA, 1966.

Bond, Kirk. "Ernst Lubitsch." *Film Culture* 63/64 (1976).

Bovenschen, Silvia. "Is There a Feminine Aesthetic?" *New German Critique* 10 (1977).

————. "The Contemporary Witch, the Historical Witch and the Witch Myth." *New German Critique* 15 (1978).

————. *Die imaginierte Weiblichkeit. Exemplarische Untersuchungen zu kulturgeschichtlichen und literarischen Präsentationsformen des Weiblichen* Frankfurt/M.: Suhrkamp, 1978.

Brecht, Bertolt. *Der Dreigroschenprozeß. Versuche 1–12, Heft 3.* Berlin and Frankfurt: Suhrkamp, 1959.

Bridenthal, Renate, Atina Grossmann and Marion Kaplan, eds. *When Biology Became Destiny: Women in Weimar and Nazi Germany.* New York: Monthly Review, 1984.

Bridenthal, Renate, and Claudia Koonz. "Beyond *Kinder Küche Kirche*: Weimar Women in Politics and Work." In *When Biology Became Destiny: Women in Weimar and Nazi Germany,* ed. Renate Bridenthal, Atina Grossmann and Marion Kaplan. New York: Monthly Review, 1984.

Brinkmann, Richard. "Der angehaltene Moment. Requisiten – Genre – Tableau bei Fontane." *DVJS* 53 (1979).

Brooks, Louise. "On Making Pabst's *Lulu.*" In *Women and the Cinema,* ed. Karyn Kay and Gerald Peary. New York: E. P. Dutton, 1977.

Brooks, Peter. *The Melodramatic Imagination.* New Haven: Yale Univ. Press, 1976.

Brunet, Rene. Appendix. *The New German Constitution.* Trans. Joseph Gollomb. New York: Alfred A. Knopf, 1922.

Brückner, Jutta. "Recognizing Collective Gestures." Interview with Jutta Brückner. *Jump Cut* 27 (1982).

_____. "Sexualität als Arbeit im Pornofilm." *Argument* 141 (Sept./Oct. 1983).

_____. "Vom Erinnern, Vergessen, dem Leib und der Wut. Ein Kultur-Film-Projekt." *Frauen und Film* 35 (Oct. 1983).

_____. "Vom Pathos des Leibes oder: Der revolutionäre Exorzismus." *Ästhetik und Kommunikation: Intimität* 57/58 (1985).

_____. "Women Behind the Camera." In *Feminist Aesthetics,* ed. Gisela Ecker, trans. Harriet Anderson. Boston: Beacon, 1986.

Brüne, Klaus. Review of *Die Sünderin.* Reprinted in *Zwischen Gestern und Morgen. Westdeutscher Nachkriegsfilm 1946–1962.* Frankfurt: Deutsches Filmmuseum, 1989. Originally in *Katholischer film–Dienst.* (2 February 1951)

Bürger, Peter. *Theorie der Avant-garde.* Frankfurt/M.: Suhrkamp, 1974. Available in English as: *Theory of the Avant-garde.* Trans. Michael Shaw. Minneapolis: Univ. of Minnesota Press, 1984.

Butler, Judith. *Gender Trouble: Feminism and the Subversion of Identity.* New York: Routledge, 1990.

Canby, Vincent. "The Decline and Fall of Effi Briest." *New York Times,* 17 June 1977.

Carow, Heiner. "Bis daß der Tod euch scheidet." Interview mit Heiner Carow. *Progress. Pressebulletin Kino der DDR* 5 (1979).

Ciment, Michel, and Hubert Niogret. "Entretien avec Wim Wenders." *Positif* (September 1984).

Cixous, Hélène. "The Laugh of the Medusa." Trans. Keith Cohen and Paula Cohen. In *New French Feminisms.* Ed. Elaine Marks and Isabelle de Courtivron. New York: Schocken, 1980. 245–264. Originally published in English in *Signs* (Summer 1976). 875–93. "Le rire de la méduse." *L'arc.* 61 (1975). 39–54.

Codelli, Lorenzo. "Die bleierne Zeit." *Positif* 248 (November 1981).

Cook, Blanche Wiesen. "'Women Alone Stir My Imagination': Lesbianism and the Cultural Tradition." *Signs* 4.4 (1979).

Corrigan, Timothy. *New German Film: The Displaced Image.* Austin: Univ of Texas, 1983.

Craig, Gordon. *Germany 1866–1945.* New York: Oxford Univ., 1978.

Curry, Ramona. "The Female Image as Critique in the Films of Valie Export." *Schatzkammer* 14.2 (Fall 1988)

Dawson, Jan. *Alexander Kluge and the Occasional Work of a Female Slave.* Perth: Perth Film Festival Publication, 1975.

Dawson, Jan. *Wim Wenders.* New York: Zoetrope, 1976.

DDR Handbuch, 2 vols. Cologne: Wissenschaft und Politik, 1985.

Debord, Guy. *Society of the Spectacle.* Detroit: Black and Red, 1972.

de Jonge, Alex. *The Weimar Chronicle: Prelude to Hitler.* London: Paddington, 1978.

de Lauretis, Teresa. *Alice Doesn't: Feminism, Semiotics, Cinema.* Bloomington: Indiana Univ. Press, 1984.

————. *Technologies of Gender: Essays on Theory, Film, and Fiction.* Bloomington: Indiana Univ. Press, 1987.

Deleuze, Gilles. *Présentation de Sacher-Masoch; le froid et le cruel.* Paris: UGE 10/18, 1976. Available in English as: *Sacher-Masoch. An Interpretation.* Trans. Jean McNeil. London: Faber and Faber, 1971.

Delorme, Charlotte. "On the Film *Marianne and Juliane* by Margarethe von Trotta." *Journal of Film and Video* 37 (Spring 1985). This is Ellen Seiter's translation of "Zum Film 'Die bleierne Zeit' von Margarethe von Trotta." *Frauen und Film* 31 (February 1982).

Derrida, Jacques. *Of Grammatology.* Trans. Gayatri Chakravorty Spivak. Baltimore: Johns Hopkins Univ. Press, 1976.

Diamond, Elin. "Brechtian Theory/Feminist Theory: Toward a Gestic Feminist Criticism." *TDR/The Drama Review* 32 (1988).

DiCaprio, Lisa. "*Marianne and Juliane/The German Sisters*: Baader-Meinhof Fictionalized." *Jump Cut* 29 (February 1984).

Dieckmann, Katherine. "Wim Wenders: an Interview." *Film Quarterly* 38.2 (Winter 1984–85).

Doane, Mary Ann. "The Voice in Cinema: The Articulation of Body and Space." *Yale French Studies* 60 (1980).

————. "Film and the Masquerade: Theorizing the Female Spectator." *Screen* 23.3–4 (Sept./Oct. 1982).

————. "The ' Woman's Film': Possession and Address." In *Re-Vision: Essays in Feminist Film Criticism..*

————, et al., eds. *Re-Vision. Essays in Feminist Film Criticism.* The American Film Institute Monograph Series. Frederick, MD: Univ. Publications of America, 1984.

Douglas, Carol Anne. "German Feminists and the Right: Can It Happen Here?" *off our backs* 10.11 (December 1980).

Dukes, Ashley. *Jew Süss: a tragic comedy in 5 acts* . London: Martin Secker, 1929.

Eco, Umberto. "The Frames of Comic 'Freedom.'" In *Carnival!,* ed. Thomas A. Sebeok. Berlin, New York, and Amsterdam: Mouton, 1984.

Eifler, Margret. "Valie Export: Feministische Filmautorin." In *Österreich in Amerikanischer Sicht,* ed. Luise Caputo-Mayr. New York: Austrian Institute, 1990.

Eisenführ, Juliane. *Die Sünderin. Geschichte und Analyse eines Kinoskandals.* Universität Osnabrück, 1982. Unpublished master's thesis.

Eisner, Lotte H. *The Haunted Screen.* Berkeley: Univ. of California, 1969.

Elsaesser, Thomas. "A Cinema of Vicious Circles." In *Fassbinder,* ed. Tony Rayns. London: British Film Institute, 1976.

———. *"Lili Marleen*: Fascism and the Film Industry." *October* 21 (Summer 1982).

———. "Social Mobility and the Fantastic: German Silent Cinema." *Wide Angle* 5.2 (1982).

———. "Mother Courage and Divided Daughter." *Monthly Film Bulletin* 50 (July 1983).

———. "Achternbusch and the German Avant-Garde." *Discourse* 6 (Fall 1983).

———. "Film History and Visual Pleasure: Weimar Cinema." In *Cinema Histories, Cinema Practices,* ed. Patricia Mellencamp and Philip Rosen. Frederick, MD: Univ. Publications of America, 1984.

———. "American Grafitti und Neuer Deutscher Film: Filmemacher zwischen Avantgarde und Postmoderne." In *Postmoderne. Zeichen eines kulturellen Wandels,* ed. Andreas Huyssen and Klaus R. Scherpe. Reinbek: Rowohlt, 1986.

———. "Tales of Sound and Fury: Observations on the Family Melodrama." In *Home is Where the Heart is: Studies in Melodrama and the Women's Film,* ed. Christine Gledhill. London: BFI, 1987.

———. *New German Cinema: A History.* New Brunswick: Rutgers Univ. Press, 1989.

Elwenspoek, Curt. *Joseph Süß Oppenheimer, der große Finanzier und galante Abenteurer des 18. Jahrhunderts.* Stuttgart: Süddeutsches Verlagshaus, 1926.

Ettinger, Elzbieta. *Rosa Luxemburg: A Life.* Boston: Beacon, 1981.

Evans, Richard. *The Feminist Movement in Germany 1894–1933.* Beverly Hills: Sage, 1976.

Export, Valie. *Zyklus Zur Zivilisation, Fotomappe.* Ed. Kurt Kalb. Vienna: Kurt Kalb, 1972.

———. "Women's Art Ein Manifest (1972)." *Neues Forum* (January 1973).

———. "Gertrude Stein/Virginia Woolf. Feminismus und Kunst I u. II." *Neues Forum* (1973)

_____. "Zur Geschichte der Frau in der Kunstgeschichte." In *Magna,* ed. Valie Export. Vienna: Galerie nächst St. Stephan, 1975.

_____. *Works from 1968–1975. A Comprehension.* Vienna: Valie Export,.1975.

_____. "Gedichte." *Dimension* (1975).

_____. "Überlegungen Zum Verhältnis Frau und Kreativität." In *Künstlerinnen International.* Berlin, 1977.

_____. "Zeichnungen." In *Arsenikblüten,* ed. Danielle Sarréa. Munich: Matthes and Seitz, 1980.

_____. "Feministischer Aktionismus," In *Frauen in der Kunst,* ed. Gislind Nabakowski, Helke Sander, Peter Gorsen. Frankfurt/M., 1980.

_____. *Körpersplitter, Konfigurationen. Fotografien 1968–77.* Neue Texte. Vol 1. Linz, 1980.

_____. *Kunst mit Eigen-Sinn: Aktuelle Kunst von Frauen, Texte und Dokumentation.* Vienna and Munich, 1985.

_____. "The Real and Its Double: The Body." *Discourse* 11 (Fall/Winter 1988–89).

_____. "Aspects of Feminist Actionism." *New German Critique* 47 (Spring/Summer 1989).

Faderman, Lillian. *Surpassing the Love of Men: Romantic Friendship and Love Between Women from the Renaissance to the Present.* New York: Morrow, 1981.

Faderman, Lillian, and Brigitte Eriksson. *Lesbian Feminism in Turn-of-the-Century Germany.* Tallahassee, FL: Naiad, 1979.

Fassbinder, Rainer Werner. "Six Films by Douglas Sirk." Trans. Thomas Elsaesser. In *Douglas Sirk,* ed. Laura Mulvey and John Halliday. Edinburgh: Edinburgh Film Festival, 1972.

_____. *In a Year of 13 Moons.* Trans. Joyce Rheuban. *October* 21 (Summer 1982).

Fehrenbach, Heide. *Cinema in Democratizing Germany. The Reconstruction of Mass Culture and National Identity in the West, 1945–1960.* Rutgers University, 1990. Unpublished dissertation.

_____. "The Fight for the Christian West: German Film Control, the Churches, and the Reconstruction of Civil Society in the Early Bonn Republic." *German Studies Review* 14.1 (February 1991).

Feuchtwanger, Lion. *Jud Süß. Schauspiel in drei Akten.* Munich: Georg Müller, 1918.

_____. *Jud Süß.* Munich: Drei Masken Verlag, 1925.

"Film and Feminism in Germany Today." Special Section in *Jump Cut* 27 (1982)

Fischetti, Renate "Écriture Féminine in the New German Cinema: Ulrike Ottinger's *Portrait of a Woman Drinker.*" *Women in German Yearbook* 4 (1988).

_____. *Das neue Kino – Filme von Frauen. Acht Porträts von Deutschen Regisseurinnen.* tende: Dülmen–Hiddingsel, 1992.

Fisk, Otis H. *Germany's Constitutions of 1871 and 1919.* Cincinnati: Court Index, 1924.

Fontane, Theodor. *Effi Briest.* Trans. Douglas Parmee. Middlesex: Penguin, 1967.

Foucault, Michel. *This is not a Pipe.* Trans. James Harkness. Berkeley: Univ. of California, 1983.

Franck, Barbara. *Ich schaue in den Spiegel und sehe meine Mutter.* Hamburg: Hoffmann und Campe, 1979.

Franklin, James. *New German Cinema.* Boston: Twayne, 1983.

Frenzel, Elisabeth, *Stoffe der Weltliteratur: ein Lexikon dichtungsgeschichtlicher Längsschnitte,* 2nd ed. Stuttgart: Kröner, 1963.

Freud, Sigmund. "The Psycho-Analytic View of Psychogenic Disturbance of Vision (1910)." In *The Standard Edition of the Complete Psychological Works of Sigmund Freud,* vol. XI, ed. James Strachey. London Hogarth, 1964.

Frevert, Ute. *Women in German History. From Bourgeois Emancipation to Sexual Liberation.* Providence/Oxford: Berg, 1989.

Frieden, Sandra. *Autobiography: Self Into Form. German Language Autobiographical Writings of the 1970s.* Frankfurt/M.: Lang, 1983.

Friedländer, Saul. *Reflections of Nazism: An Essay on Kitsch and Death.* New York: Harper and Row, 1985.

Friedman, Régine Mihal. *L'image et son juif.* Paris: Payot, 1983.

Fromm, Erich. *The Anatomy of Human Destructiveness.* New York: Holt, Rinehart and Winston, 1973.

"German Film Women." *Jump Cut* 29 (1984).

"Germany's Danse Macabre." *New German Critique* 12 (Fall 1977).

Giese, Fritz. *Girlkultur. Vergleiche zwischen amerikanischem und europäischem Lebensgefühl.* Munich: Delphin-Verlag, 1920.

Gleber, Anke. "Das Fräulein von Tellheim: Die ideologische Funktion der Frau in der nationalsozialistischen Lessing-Adaption." *German Quarterly* 59 (1986).

Gledhill, Christine. "The Melodramatic Field: An Investigation." In *Home is Where the Heart is: Studies in Melodrama and the Women's Film,* ed. Christine Gledhill. London: BFI, 1987.

Glucksmann, André. "Der alte und der neue Faschismus." In *Neuer Faschismus, Neue Demokratie,* ed. Michel Foucault. Berlin: Wagenbach Verlag, 1972.

Grafe, Frieda, and Enno Patalas. *Im Off. Filmartikel.* Munich: Hanser, 1977.

Gransow, Volker. *Kulturpolitik in der DDR.* Berlin: Volker Spiess, 1975.

Greer, Germaine. *Sex and Destiny: The Politics of Human Fertility.* New York: Harper and Row, 1984.

Grimm, Jacob, and Wilhelm Grimm. "The Twelve Brothers." In *Grimm's Tales for Young and Old,* trans. Ralph Manheim. New York: Doubleday, 1983.

Grunberger, Bela. *Narcissim: Psychoanalytic Essays.* Trans. Joyce S. Diamanti. New York: International Univ.Press, 1979.

H., F. "Die Männer dieser Generation." *Filmreport* 5–6 (1976).

Habermas, Jürgen. "Modernity: An Incomplete Project." In *The Anti-Aesthetic: Essays on Postmodern Culture,* ed. Hal Foster. Port Townsend, WA: Bay, 1983.

Hake, Sabine."Gold, Love, and Adventure: Postmodern Piracy of *Madame X.*" *Discourse* 11 (Winter 1988).

Hamilton, Edith. *Mythology.* Boston: Little, Brown, 1942.

Hamon, Philippe. "Pour un statut sémiotique du personnage." In *Poétique du récit.* Paris: Seuil, 1977.

Hansen, Miriam. "Cooperative Auteur Cinema and Oppositional Public Sphere." *New German Critique* 24–25 (Fall/Winter 1981–82).

_____. "Silent Cinema: Whose Public Sphere?" *New German Critique* 29 (Spring/Summer 1983).

_____. "Visual Pleasure, Fetishism, and the Problem of Feminine/Feminist Discourse: Ulrike Ottinger's *Ticket of No Return.*" *New German Critique* 31 (Winter 1984).

_____. "Messages in a Bottle?" *Screen* 28.2 (1987).

Harlan, Veit. *Im Schatten meiner Filme. Autobiographie.* Gütersloh, 1966.

Harlan, Veit, and Werner Krauß. *Das Schauspiel meines Lebens, einem Freund erzählt.* Ed. Hans Weigel. Stuttgart, 1958.

Harrigan, Renny. "The German Women's Movement and Ours." *Jump Cut* 27 (1982).

Harris, Adrienne and Robert Sklar. "Marianne and Juliane." *Cinéaste* 12.3 (1983).

Haskell, Molly. *From Reverence to Rape.* New York: Penguin, 1974.

Hauff, Wilhelm. "Jud Süß." In *Gesammelte Werke.* Leipzig: Bonn Verlag, 1907.

Hausen, Karin. "Mother's Day in the Weimar Republic." Trans. Miriam Frank with Erika Busse Grossmann. Ed. Marion Kaplan with Ellen Weinstock. In *When Biology Became Destiny: Women in Weimar and Nazi Germany,* ed. Renate Bridenthal, Atina Grossmann, and Marion Kaplan. New York: Monthly Review, 1984.

Heath, Stephen. "Narrative Space." In *Questions of Cinema.* Bloomington: Univ. of Indiana Press, 1981. Also in *Narrative, Apparatus, Ideology,* ed. Philip Rosen. New York: Columbia Univ. Press, 1986.

Hiller, Eva. "mütter und töchter: zu 'deutschland, bleiche mutter,' (helma sanders-brahms), 'hungerjahre' (jutta brückner), 'daughter rite' (michelle citron)." *Frauen und Film* 24 (1980).

Hitler, Adolf. *Mein Kampf.* Munich: Zentralverlag der NSDAP, 1927.

Hippler, Fritz. *Betrachtungen zum Filmschaffen.* Berlin: Max Hesse Verlag, 1942.

_____. *Die Verstrickung.* Düsseldorf: Verlag Mehrwissen, 1982.

Hirdina, Karin. "Der Kunstbegriff der Avant-garde." *Weimarer Beiträge* 32 (1986).

Hollstein, Dorothea. *"Jud Süß" und die Deutschen. Antisemitisches Vorurteil im nationalsozialistischen Spielfilm. Materialien.* Frankfurt/M. and Bern: Ullstein, 1983.

Horkheimer, Max, and Theodor W. Adorno. "Excursus II: Juliette or Enlightenment and Morality." In *Dialectic of Enlightenment* [1944], trans. John Cumming. New York: Continuum, 1987.

Huillet, Danièle. "Das Feuer im Innern des Berges." Interview with Helge Heberle and Monika Funke Stern. *Frauen und Film* 32 (June 1982).

Hull, David Stewart. *Film in the Third Reich,* Berkeley: Univ. of California Press, 1969. Also available in the more recent edition: New York: Simon and Schuster, 1973.

Hutcheon, Linda. *A Poetics of Postmodernism: History, Theory, Fiction.* London: Routledge, 1988.

Huyssen, Andreas. "Technology and Sexuality in Fritz Lang's Metropolis." *New German Critique* 24–25 (Fall/Winter 1981–82).

―――. "Mass Culture as Woman: Modernism's Other." In *Studies in Entertainment. Critical Approaches to Mass Culture,* ed. Tania Modleski. Bloomington: Indiana University Press, 1989.

Hyams, Barbara. "Is the Apolitical Woman at Peace?: A Reading of the Fairy Tale in *Germany, Pale Mother." Wide Angle* 10.3 (1988).

Irigaray, Luce. "Demystifications." In *New French Feminisms,* ed. Elaine Marks and Isabelle Courtivron. New York: Schocken, 1980.

Iser, Wolfgang. "Die Apellstruktur des Textes." In *Rezeptionsästhetik,* ed. Rainer Warning. Munich: Wilhelm Fink, 1975.

―――. "Indeterminacy and the Reader's Response in Prose Fiction." In *Aspects of Narrative,* ed. J. Hillis Miller. New York: Columbia Univ. Press, 1971.

Jacobs, Monica. "Civil Rights and Women's Rights in the Federal Republic of Germany Today." *New German Critique* 13 (Winter 1978).

Jansen, Peter W. "Exil würde ich noch nicht sagen." *Cinema* (Zurich) 2 (1978).

Johnson, Catherine. "The Imaginary & *The Bitter Tears of Petra von Kant." Wide Angle* 3 (1980).

Johnston, Claire. "Women's Cinema as Counter-Cinema," In *Notes on Women's Cinema..*

―――, ed. *Notes on Women's Cinema.* London: Society for Education in Film and Television, 1973.

Johnston, Sheila. "The German Sisters." *Films & Filming* 334 (July 1982).

―――. "A Star is Born: Fassbinder and the New German Cinema." *New German Critique* 24–25 (Fall/Winter 1981–82).

Jürschik, Rudolf. "Erkundungen. Filmbilder – Heldentypus – Alltag." *Film und Fernsehen* 4 (1981).

―――. "Streitbare Spielfilme – sozialistisches Lebensgefühl," pt. 1. *Film und Fernsehen* 9 (1979); pt. 2. *Film und Fernsehen* 11 (1979).

Kaes, Anton. *From Hitler to Heimat: The Return of History as Film.* Cambridge: Harvard Univ. Press, 1989.

Kafka, Franz. *Amerika.* Frankfurt: Fischer, 1973.

————. "The Judgement." In *The Basic Kafka.* Intro. Erich Heller. New York: Washington Square, 1979.

————. *Tagebücher 1910–1923.* New York: Schocken, 1949.

Kann, Robert A. *A History of the Habsburg Empire 1526–1918.* Los Angeles: Univ. of California Press, 1974.

Kaplan, E. Ann. *Women and Film: Both Sides of the Camera.* London and New York: Methuen, 1983.

————. "Discourses of Terrorism, Feminism, and the Family in von Trotta's *Marianne and Juliane.*" *Persistence of Vision* 2 (Fall 1985).

————. "The Search for the Mother/Land in Sanders-Brahms's *Germany, Pale Mother.*" In *German Film and Literature: Adaptations and Transformations,* ed. Eric Rentschler. New York: Methuen, 1986.

Karesek, Helmuth. "Niemandsland Amerika." *Der Spiegel* 38 (27 Feb. 1984).

————. "In kitschigem Rosa," *Der Spiegel* 15 (7 April 1986).

Katz, Jonathan. *Gay American History.* New York: Avon, 1976.

Kay, Karyn. "Part-Time Work of a Domestic Slave, or Putting the Screws to Screwball Comedy." In *Women and the Cinema,* ed. Karyn Kay and Gerald Peary. New York: E.P. Dutton, 1978.

Kiernan, Joanna. "Films by Valie Export." *Millennium* 16, 17, 18 (Fall, Winter 1986–87).

Klein, Michael. "Peter Handke: *Die linkshändige Frau:* Fiktion eines Märchens." In *Studien zur Literatur des 19. und 20. Jahrhunderts in Österreich.* Ed. Johann Holzner, Michael Klein and Wolfgang Wiesmüller. Innsbruck: Kowatsch, 1981.

Koch, Gertrud. "Der höhere Befehl der Frau ist ihr niederer Instinkt. Frauenhaß und Männer-Mythos in Filmen über Preußen." In *Preussen im Film,* ed. Axel Marquardt and Heinz Rathsack. Reinbek: Rowohlt, 1981.

————. "Why Women Go to the Movies." *Jump Cut* 27 (1982).

————. "Die Internationale tanzt," *Konkret* 4 (1984).

————. "Exchanging the Gaze: Revisioning Feminist Film Theory." *New German Critique* 34 (Winter 1985).

Knode, Helen. "At long last, love: Wim Wenders." *East Village Eye* (November 1984).

Kokula, Ilse. "Die urnischen Damen treffen sich vielfach in Konditoreien." *Courage* 7 (July 1980).

Koonz, Claudia. *Mothers in the Fatherland: Women, the Family and Nazi Politics.* New York: St. Martin's, 1987.

Kosta, Barbara. "*Deutschland, bleiche Mutter:* An addendum to history." Berkeley, Univ. of California, 1983. Unpublished essay.

Kracauer, Siegfried. *Schriften.* Ed. Karsten Witte. Frankfurt/M.: Suhrkamp, 1971.

_____. *From Caligari to Hitler.* Princeton: Princeton Univ. Press, 1947 and 1974.

Kraushaar, Wolfgang. "Notizen zu einer Chronologie der Studenten-bewegung." In *Was wir wurden, was wir wollten,* by Peter Mosler. Reinbek: Rowohlt, 1977.

Kuhn, Anna K. "Rainer Werner Fassbinder: The Alienated Vision." In *New German Filmmakers: From Oberhausen Through the 1970s,* ed. Klaus Phillips. New York: Ungar, 1984.

Kuhn, Annette. *Women's Pictures.* London: Routledge and Keagan Paul, 1982.

_____, ed. *Frauen in der deutschen Nachkriegszeit. Frauenarbeit. 1945–1949. Quellen und Materialien,* vol. 1. Düsseldorf: Pädagogisch-er Verlag Schwann–Bagel, 1984.

_____, ed. *Frauen in der deutschen Nachkriegszeit. Frauenpolitik. 1945–1949. Quellen und Materialien,* vol. 2. Düsseldorf: Pädagogisch-er Verlag Schwann–Bagel, 1986.

Lacan, Jacques. *Le séminaire.* Paris: Seuil, 1973.

_____. *Feminine Sexuality.* Ed. Juliet Mitchell and Jacqueline Rose. New York: Norton, 1982.

Lachman, Edward, Peter Lehman, and Robin Wood. "Wim Wenders: An Interview." *Wide Angle* 2 (1976).

Langer, Ingrid. "Die Mohrinnen hatten ihre Schuldigkeit getan: Staatlich-moralische Aufrüstung der Familien." In *Die fünfziger Jahre,* ed. Dieter Bänsch. Tübingen: Günter Narr, 1985.

Laplanche, Jean and J. B. Pontalis. *The Language of Psycho-Analysis.* Trans. Donald Nicholson-Smith. New York: Norton, 1973.

Leiser, Erwin. *Nazi Cinema.* New York: Macmillan, 1974.

Lemke, Christiane. "Social Change and Women's Issues in the GDR: Problems of Leadership Positions." In *Studies in GDR Culture and Society* 2. Washington, D.C.: Univ. Press of America, 1982.

Lennox, Sara. "Women in Brecht's Works." *New German Critique* 14 (1978).

Lenssen, Claudia. "When love goes right, nothing goes wrong. . . ." *Frauen und Film* 12 (1977).

_____. "Mit glasigem Blick." *Frauen und Film* 22 (1979).

_____. "Die schwere Arbeit der Erinnerung." *Frauen und Film* 29 (1981).

Lenssen, Claudia, Helen Fehervary and Judith Mayne. "From Hitler to Hepburn: A Discussion of Women's Film Production and Reception." *New German Critique* 24–25 (Fall/Winter 1981–82).

Lesage, Julia. "Feminist Film Criticism: Theory and Practice." *Women and Film* 5/6 (1974).

Lenz, Ilse. "Die öde Wildnis einer Schminkerin." *Frauen und Film* 22 (1979).

Limmer, Wolfgang. *Rainer Werner Fassbinder: Filmemacher.* Reinbek bei Hamburg: Rowohlt, 1981.

Linhart, Paula. "Zur Praxis des Filmjugendschutzes." In *Jugend–Film–Fernsehen* 3.4 (1959).

Longfellow, Brenda. "Sex/Textual Politics: Tracing the Imaginary in the Films of Valie Export." *Borderlines* (Winter 1985–1986).

Love, Myra. "Christa Wolf and Feminism: Breaking the Patriarchal Connection." *New German Critique* 16 (Winter 1979).

Luft, Herbert G. "G. W. Pabst: His Films and His Life Mirror the Tumult of 20th Century Europe." *Films in Review* 15.2 (February 1964).

Lukács, Georg. "The Marxism of Rosa Luxemburg." In *History and Class Consciousness*, trans. Rodney Livingston. Cambridge: MIT, l972.

Lukasz, Gudrun, and Christel Strobel, eds. *Der Frauenfilm*. Munich: Heyne Verlag, 1985.

Luxemburg, Rosa. "The Russian Revolution." In *The Russian Revolution: Leninism or Marxism?*, trans. Bertram D. Wolfe. Ann Arbor: Univ. of Michigan Press, l961.

_____. *Selected Political Writings*. Ed. Dick Howard. New York: Monthly Review, l971.

_____. *Briefe an Leon Jogiches*. Trans. Mechthild Fricke Hochfield and Barbara Hoffmann. Frankfurt/M.: Europäische Verlagsanstalt, 1971.

_____. *Comrade and Lover: Rosa Luxemburg's Letters to Leo Jogiches*. Translated and ed. Elzbieta Ettinger. Cambridge: MIT, 1981.

Maaß, Joachim. "Film *Die Beunruhigung*." *Neue Berliner Illustrierte* 7 (1982).

_____. "Frauenrollen in DEFA-Filmen." *Neue Berliner Illustrierte* 37 (1982).

Maetzig, Kurt, Konrad Wolf, Lothar Warneke and Ruth Herlinghaus. "Discussion." *Film und Fernsehen* 7 (1980).

Mann, Erika and Klaus Mann. *Escape to Life*. Boston: Houghton Mifflin, 1939.

Manvell, Roger, and Heinrich Fraenkel. *The German Cinema*. New York: Praeger, 1971.

Marcuse, Herbert. *Eros and Civilization*. New York: Vintage, 1962.

Marks, Elaine. "Lesbian Intertextuality." In *Homosexualities and French Literature*, ed. George Stambolian and Elaine Marks. Ithaca, NY: Cornell Univ. Press, 1979.

Mason, Tim. "Women in Germany, 1925–1940: Family, Welfare and Work. Part II." *History Workshop* 2 (1976).

Masson, Alain, and Hubert Niogret. "Entretien avec Wim Wenders." *Positif* (October 1977).

May, Rollo. *The Meaning of Anxiety*. New York: Norton, 1977.

Mayne, Judith. "Fassbinder and Spectatorship." *New German Critique* 12 (Fall 1977).

_____. "Female Narration, Women's Cinema: Helke Sander's *The

All-Around Reduced Personality – REDUPERS." *New German Critique* 24–25 (Fall/Winter 1981–82).

McCormick, Richard W.. "The Politics of the Personal: West German Literature and Cinema in the Wake of the Student Movement" Ph.D. diss., Univ. of California, Berkeley, 1986.

_____. *Politics of the Self: Feminism and the Postmodern in West German Literature and Film.* Princeton: Princeton Univ. Press, 1991.

McGarry, Eileen. "Documentary, Realism and Women's Cinema." *Women & Film* 2.7 (1975).

McRobbie, Angela. Introduction to "Interview with Ulrike Ottinger," by Erica Carter. Trans. Martin Chalmers. *Screen* 4 (Winter/Spring 1982).

Metz, Christian "The Imaginary Signifier." Trans. Ben Brewster, *Screen* 16.2 (Summer 1975).

_____. *Le signifiant imaginaire.* Paris: 10/18 UGE, 1977.

_____. *Psychoanalysis and the Cinema: The Imaginary Signifier.* Bloomington: Indiana Univ. Press, 1982.

_____. "Story/Discourse: Notes on Two Kinds of Voyeurisms." In *Movies and Methods, Vol. II: An Anthology,* ed. Bill Nichols. Berkeley: Univ. of California Press, 1985.

Meyer, Sibylle and Eva Schulze. *Von Liebe sprach damals keiner. Familienalltag in der Nachkriegszeit.* Munich: C.H. Beck, 1985.

Mihan, Hans-Rainer. "Sabine, Sunny, Nina und der Zuschauer. Gedanken zum Gegenwartsspielfilm der DEFA." *Film und Fernsehen* 8 (1982).

Mittman, Elizabeth. "History and Subjectivity: Differences in German and French Feminisms." University of Minnesota, 1986. Unpublished essay.

Möhrmann, Renate. *Die Frau mit der Kamera: Filmemacherinnen in der Bundesrepublik Deutschland. Situation, Perspektiven. 10 exemplarische Lebensläufe.* Munich: Hanser, 1980.

_____. "Ich sehe was, was du nicht siehst . . . Überlegungen zu den Darstellungs- und Wahrnehmungsformen weiblicher Kinofiguren im westdeutschen Frauenfilm." Univ. of Texas, Austin. March, 1986. Unpublished essay.

Moeller, A.J.K. "The Woman as Survivor: The Development of the Female Figure in Heinrich Böll's Fiction." *DAI* 40A, no. 3 (1979).

Moeller, H-B. "West German Women's Cinema: The Case of Margarethe von Trotta." *Film Criticism* 9.2 (Winter 1984–85).

Moeller, Robert. "Protecting Mother's Work: From Production to Reproduction in Postwar West Germany." *Journal of Social History* 22.3 (Spring 1989).

Mommsen, Hans. "Suche nach der 'verlorenen Geschichte'?" *Historikerstreit. Die Dokumentation der Kontroverse um die Einzigartigkeit der nationalsozialistischen Judenvernichtung.* Munich: Piper, 1987.

Monaco, James. *How to Read a Film.* New York: Oxford, 1981.

Monaghan, Patricia. *The Book of Goddesses and Heroines.* New York: Dutton, 1984.

Moreck, Curt. *Sittengeschichte des Kinos.* Dresden: Paul Aretz, 1926.

Morgner, Irmtraud. *Amanda. Ein Hexenroman.* Darmstadt und Neuwied: Luchterhand, 1983.

Mosse, George L. *Nazi Culture.* New York: Schocken, 1981.

Mouton, Jan. "The Absent Mother Makes an Appearance in the Films of West German Women Directors." *Women in German Yearbook* 4 (1988).

Müller, André. "Das Kino könnte der Engel sein." *Der Spiegel* (19 October 1987).

Mueller, Roswitha. Interview with Ulrike Ottinger, *Discourse* 4 (1981/82).

———. "The Uncanny in the Eyes of a Woman: Valie Export's *Invisible Adversaries.*" *SubStance* 37/38 (1983).

———. "The Mirror and the Vamp." *New German Critique* 34 (Winter 1985).

Münzberg, Olav. "Schaudern vor der 'bleichen Mutter.'" *Medium* 10 (1980).

Mulvey, Laura. "Feminism, Film and the Avant-Garde." *Framework* 10 (Spring 1979).

———. "Visual Pleasure and Narrative Cinema." *Screen* 16.3 (Autumn 1975). Reprinted in *Women and the Cinema,* ed. Karyn Kay and Gerald Peary. New York: Dutton, 1977; and also reprinted in *Film Theory and Criticism,* 3rd. ed., ed. Gerald Mast and Marshall Cohen, New York: Oxford Univ. Press, 1985.

Nettl, J.P. *Rosa Luxemburg.* London: Oxford Univ. Press, 1966.

Netzeband, Günter. Interview with Hans Dieter Mäde. *Film und Fernsehen* 5 (1978).

Neus, Chrisel. *Die Kopfgeburten der Arbeiterbewegung oder Die Genossin Luxemburg bringt alles durcheinander.* Hamburg/Zurich: Rasch und Rühring, l985.

New German Critique 40 (Winter 1987). "Special Issue on Weimar Film Theory."

Newton, Judith. "History as Usual? Feminism and the 'New Historicism,'" in *The New Historicism,* ed. H. Aram Veeser. New York: Routledge, 1989.

Nichols, Bill. Introduction to "Visual Pleasure and Narrative Cinema," by Laura Mulvey. In *Movies and Methods: An Anthology,* vol.II, ed. Bill Nichols. Berkeley: Univ. of California, 1985.

Owens, Craig. "The Discourse of Others: Feminists and Postmodernism." In *The Anti- Aesthetic,* ed. Hal Foster. Port Townsend, WA: Bay, 1983.

Ottinger, Ulrike. *Madame X – eine absolute Herrscherin. Drehbuch.* Berlin/Basel: Stroemfeld/ Roter Stern, 1979.

———. "Der Zwang zum Genrekino. Von der Gefährdung des Autoren-Kinos." *Courage* 4 (1983).

Pardo, Herbert, and Siegfried Schiffner. *"Jud Süß:" Historisches und juristisches Material zum Fall Veit Harlan.* Hamburg: Auerbach, 1949.

Penley, Constance. *The Future of an Illusion: Film, Feminism, and Psychoanalysis.* Minneapolis: Univ. of Minnesota Press, 1989.

Perlmutter, Ruth. "Visible Narrative, Visible Woman: A Study of Under-narratives." *Millenium Film Journal* (Spring 1980).

Petro, Patrice. *Joyless Streets: Women and Melodramatic Representation in Weimar Germany.* Princeton: Princeton Univ. Press, 1989.

Pflaum, Hans Günther and Hans Helmut Prinzler. *Cinema in the Federal Republic of Germany.* Bonn: Internationes, 1983.

Phillips, Klaus, ed. *New German Filmmakers. From Oberhausen Through the 1970s.* New York: Ungar, 1984.

Piccone, Paul. "The Crisis of One-Dimensionality." *Telos* 35 (Spring 1978).

Pipolo, Tony. "Bewitched by the Holy Whore." *October* 21 (Summer 1982).

Plat, Wolfgang. *Die Familie in der DDR.* Frankfurt/M: S. Fischer, 1972.

Plummer, Thomas G., ed. *Film and Politics in the Weimar Republic.* Minneapolis: Univ. of Minnesota Press, 1982.

Pore, Renate. *A Conflict of Interest: Women in German Social Democracy, 1919–1933.* Westport, CT: Greenwood, 1981.

Potamkin, Harry Alan. "Pabst and the Social Film." *Hound and Horn* 6.2 (Jan.-Mar. 1933).

Prammer, Anita. *Valie Export. Eine Multi-mediale Künstlerin.* Frauenforschung, vol. 7. Vienna: Wiener Frauenverlag, 1988.

Prokop, Ulrike. *Weiblicher Lebenszusammenhang.* Frankfurt/M.: Suhrkamp, 1976.

Ramm, Klaus. *Reduktion als Erzählprinzip bei Kafka.* Frankfurt/M.: Athenaum, 1971.

Rawlinson, Arthur-Richard. *Scenario and dialogues of "Jew Süß" from the novel by L. Feuchtwanger.* London: Methuen, 1935.

Regel, Helmut. "Historische Stoffe als Propagandaträger." In *Der Spielfilm im III. Reich.* Oberhausen, 1966.

Reich, Wilhelm. *The Function of the Orgasm.* New York: Orgone Institute, 1942.

Reich, Wilhelm. *Mass Psychology of Fascism.* New York: Orgone Institute, l946.

Reichwaldau, Franz. "Das ideale Kino." *Die Weltbühne.* 16.19 (1920).

Reitlinger, Gerald. *The Final Solution.* London, 1971.

Rentmeister, Cillie. "Frauen, Körper, Kunst: Mikrophysik der patriarchalischen Macht." *Ästhetik und Kommunikation* 37 (1979).

Rentschler, Eric. "American Friends and the New German Cinema." *New German Critique* 24–25 (Fall/Winter 1981–82).

————. *West German Film in the Course of Time.* Bedford Hills, NY: Redgrave, 1984.

————, ed. *West German Filmmakers on Film: Visions and Voices.* New York: Holmes and Meier, 1988.

Reschke, Karin. "Frau Ottingers (Kunst)gewerbe." *Frauen und Film* 22 (1979).

Rheuban, Joyce, ed. *The Marriage of Maria Braun*. New Brunswick, NJ: Rutgers Univ. Press, 1986.

Rich, Adrienne. *On Lies, Secrets and Silence*. New York: Norton, 1979.

Rich, B. Ruby. "The Crisis Of Naming in Feminist Film Criticism." *Jump Cut* 19 (December 1978)

―――――. "In the Name of Feminist Film Criticism." *Heresies* 9 (Spring 1980). Also reprinted in *Movies and Methods*, ed. Bill Nichols. Berkeley: Univ. of California Press, 1985.

―――――. "*Mädchen in Uniform*: From Repressive Tolerance to Erotic Liberation." *Jump Cut* 24–25 (1981).

―――――. "She Says, He Says: The Power of the Narrator in Modernist Film Politics." *Discourse* 6 (1983).

Rotha, Paul. *The Film Till Now*. 2d ed. New York: Funk and Wagnalls, 1951.

Rother, Hans-Jörg. "Kino neuer Ideen im Meinungsstreit. Gedanken zu DEFA-Filmen aus den Jahren 1979/80." *Prisma. Kino- und Fernseh-Almanach* 12 (1981).

Rubin, Gayle. "The Traffic in Women: Notes On the 'Political Economy' of Sex." In *Toward Anthropology of Women*, ed. Rayna R. Reiter. New York: Monthly Review, 1975.

Ruhl, Klaus-Jörg, ed. *Frauen in der Nachkriegszeit, 1945–1963. Dokumente.* Munich: Deutscher Taschenbuch Verlag, 1988.

Ruppelt, Georg. *Schiller im nationalsozialistischen Deutschland: Der Versuch einer Gleichschaltung*. Stuttgart: Metzler, 1979.

Russo, Vito. *The Celluloid Closet: Homosexuality in the Movies*. New York: Harper and Row/Colophon, 1981.

Said, Edward. *Orientalism*. New York: Random House, 1979.

Sander, Helke. "Sexism in den Massenmedien." *Frauen und Film* 1 (1974).

―――――. "Feminism and Film." Trans. Ramona Curry. *Jump Cut* 27 (1982).

Sander, Helke, and Ula Stöckl. "Die Herren machen das selber, daß ihnen die arme Frau Feind wird: Ablehnungsgeschichten." *Frauen und Film* 23 (April 1980).

Sanders, Marion K. *Dorothy Thompson: A Legend in Her Time*. Boston: Houghton Mifflin, 1973.

Sanders-Brahms, Helma. *Deutschland, bleiche Mutter. Film-Erzählung.* Reinbek bei Hamburg: Rowohlt, 1980.

Sandford, John. *The New German Cinema*. New York: DeCapo, 1980.

Schanze, Helmut. "*Fontane Effi Briest*: Bemerkungen zu einem Drehbuch von Rainer Werner Fassbinder." In *Literatur in den Massenmedien – Demontage von Dichtung?*, ed. Friedrich Knilli, Knut Hickethier, and Wolf Dieter Lützen. Munich and Vienna: Carl Hanser Verlag, 1976.

Schenk, Ralph. "Zwischen Tag und Traum." *Film und Fernsehen* 13 (1985).

Schlüpmann, Heide, and Karola Gramann. "Momente erotischer Utopie – ästhetisierte Verdrängung: Zu *Mädchen in Uniform* and *Anna und Elisabeth.*" *Frauen und Film* 28 (1981).

Schlüpmann, Heide, and Karola Gramann. *Hungerjahre, medienpraktisch.* Ed. Gemeinschaftswerk der Evangelischen Publizistik, 1983.

Schlungbaum, Barbara, and Claudia Hoff. "Eindruck – Ausdruck. Tabea talks." *Frauen und Film* 26 (1980).

Schneider, Michael. "Väter und Söhne, posthum. Das beschädigte Verhältnis zweier Generationen." In *Den Kopf verkehrt aufgesetzt* . Darmstadt: Luchterhand, 1981.

_____. "Fathers and Sons Retrospectively: The Damaged Relationship between Two Generations." Trans. Jamie Owen Daniel. *New German Critique* 31 (1984).

Scholar, Nancy. "*Mädchen in Uniform.*" In *Sexual Stratagems: The World of Women in Film*, ed. Patricia Erens. New York: Horizon, 1979.

Scholar, Nancy and Sharon Smith. *Women Who Make Movies.* New York: Hopkinson and Blake, 1975.

Schröder-Krassnow, Sabine. "The Changing View of Abortion: A Study of Friedrich Wolf's *Cyankali* and Arnold Zweig's *Junge Frau von 1914.*" *Studies in Twentieth Century Literature* 1 (1981).

Schütte, Wolfram. "Arbeit, Gerechtigkeit, Liebe." *Frankfurter Rundschau* (24 Feb. 1984).

Schulte-Sasse, Linda. "The Never Was as History." Ph. D. diss., Univ. of Minnesota, 1985.

Schuster, Peter-Klaus. *Theodor Fontane: Effi Briest—Ein Leben nach christlichen Bildern.* Studien zur deutschen Literatur, vol. 55. Tübingen: Max Niemeyer, 1979.

Seiter, Ellen. "The Political is Personal: Margarethe von Trotta's *Marianne and Juliane.*" *Journal of Film and Video* 37 (Spring 1985).

_____ "Women's History, Women's Melodrama: *Deutschland, bleiche Mutter.*" *German Quarterly* 59 (1986).

Seldon, Caroline. "Lesbians and Film: Some Thoughts." In *Gays and Film*, ed. Richard Dyer. London: British Film Institute, 1977.

Shaffer, Harry G. *Women in the Two Germanies.* New York: Pergamon, 1981.

Sichtermann, Barbara. "Über Schönheit, Demokratie und Tod." *Ästhetik und Kommunikation : Sex und Lust* 7 (1981).

Silberman, Marc. "Cine-Feminists in West Berlin." *Quarterly Review of Film Studies* 5.2 (Spring 1981).

_____. An interview with Jutta Brückner, Cristina Perincioli and Helga Reidemeister, "Conversing together finally." *Jump Cut* 27 (July 1982).

_____. "The Ideology of Re-Presenting the Classics: Filming *Der Zer-*

brochene Krug in the Third Reich." *German Quarterly* 57 (1984).

———. "Ula Stöckl: How Women See Themselves." In *New German Filmmakers From Oberhausen Through the 1970s*, ed. Klaus Phillips. New York: Ungar, 1984.

Silverman, Kaja. *The Subject of Semiotics* . New York: Oxford Univ. Press, 1983.

———. "Helke Sander and the Will to Change." *Discourse* 6 (1983).

———. "Dis-Embodying the Female Voice." In *Re-Vision. Essays in Feminist Film Criticism*, ed. Mary Ann Doane et al. Frederick, MD: Univ. Publications of America, 1984.

Sontag, Susan. "Notes on 'Camp.'" In *Against Interpretation*. New York: Farrar, Strauss and Giroux, 1967.

Snitow, Ann Barr. "The Front Line: Notes on Sex in Novels by Women, 1969–1979." In *Women: Sex and Sexuality*, ed. Catherine R. Stimpson and Ethel Spector Person. Chicago: Univ. of Chicago Press, 1980.

"*Solo Sunny*: Kritische Diskussion." *Film und Fernsehen* 6 (1980).

Sparrow, Norbert. "'*I let the Audience Feel and Think*' – An Interview with Rainer Werner Fassbinder." *Cineaste* 8 (1977).

Steakley, James D. *The Homosexual Emancipation Movement in Germany*. New York: Arno, 1975.

Steinborn, Bion and Carola Hilmes. "'Frieden' hat für uns Deutsche einen amerikanischen Geschmack." Reihe: Der unbekannte deutsche Film. *Filmfaust* 39 (1984).

Stephan, Cora. "Der widerspenstigen Zähmung." *Der Spiegel* 15 (7 April1986).

Stern, Selma. *Jud Süß, ein Beitrag zur deutschen und zur jüdischen Geschichte*. Berlin: Akademie Verlag, 1929.

Stöckl, Ula. "Die herren machen das selber, daß ihnen die arme frau feind wird ablehnungsgeschichten." *Frauen und Film* 23 (1980).

———. "The Medea Myth in Contemporary Cinema." *Film Criticism* 10.1 (Fall 1985).

Strempel, Gesine. "Nicht einfach nur klauen mit einem Tonband und einem Fotoapparat. Gespräch mit der Filmemacherin Ulrike Ottinger." *Courage* 3 (1979).

Studlar, Gaylyn. "Visual Pleasure and the Masochistic Aesthetic." *Journal of Film and Video* 37 (Spring 1985).

Taubin, Amy. "Von Trotta, Wanting it All," *The Voice* (12 May 1987).

Thalmann, Rita. *Frausein im dritten Reich*. Karlsruhe: DOKU, 1979.

Theweleit, Klaus. *Männerphantasien*. 2 vols. Frankfurt/M.: Roter Stern, 1977–78.

———. *Male Fantasies. Vol. 1. Women, Floods, Bodies, History*. Trans. Erica Carter and Chris Turner in collaboration with Stephen Conway. Theory of History and Literature. Vol. 22. Minneapolis: Univ. of Minnesota, 1987.

———. *Male Fantasies. Vol. 2. Male bodies: Psychoanalyzing the White Terroe*. Trans. Erica Carter and Chris Turner in collaboration with

Stephen Conway. Theory of History and Literature. Vol. 23. Minneapolis: University of Minnesota Press, 1989.

Thomas, Paul. "Fassbinder: The Poetry of the Inarticulate." *Film Quarterly* 30 (Winter 1976).

Thompson, E. P. "History Turns on A New Hinge." *The Nation* 29 (January 1990).

Thomsen, Christian Braad. "Interview with Fassbinder (Berlin, 1974)." In *Fassbinder,* ed. Tony Rayns. London: British Film Institute, 1976.

Thomsen, Christian Braad. "Five Interviews with Fassbinder." In *Fassbinder,* ed. Tony Rayns. London: British Film Institute, 1980.

Thurm, Brigitte. "Rückhaltlos und verletzbar." *Film und Fernsehen* 2 (1980).

Treut, Monika. "Ein Nachtrag zu Ulrike Ottinger's Film *Madame X.*" *Frauen und Film* 28 (1981).

Truffaut, Francois. *Hitchcock.* London: Granada, 1978. Also available from New York: Simon and Schuster, 1984.

Todorov, Tzvetan. *The Fantastic. A Structural Approach to a Literary Genre.* Cleveland and London: Press of Case Western Reserve Univ., 1973.

Tröger, Annemarie. "Between Rape and Prostitution. Survival Strategies and Chances of Emancipation for Berlin Women after World War II," trans. Joan Reutershan. In *Women in Culture and Politics: A Century of Change,* ed. J. Friedlander, B. Wiesen Cook, et al. Bloomington: Indiana University Press, 1986.

Trotta, Margarethe von. *Die bleierne Zeit: ein Film von Margarethe von Trotta.* Ed. Hans Jürgen Weber and Ingeborg Weber. Frankfurt/M.: Fischer Taschenbuch, 1981.

Tyler, Parker. *Screening the Sexes.* New York: Holt, Rinehart and Winston, 1972.

Viertel, Salka. *The Kindness of Strangers.* New York: Holt, 1969.

Virmaux, Alain and Odette Virmaux, eds. *Colette au cinéma.* Paris: Librairie Ernest Flammarion, 1975.

Vogel, Angela. "Familie." In *Die Bundesrepublik Deutschland. Band 2: Gesellschaft,* ed. Wolfgang Benz. Frankfurt/M.: Fischer, 1985.

Waniek, Erdmann. "Beim zweiten Lesen: der Beginn von Fontanes *Effi Briest* als verdinglichtes *tableau vivant.*" *German Quarterly* 55 (March 1982).

Warneke, Lothar. Interview. *Progress. Pressebulletin Kino der DDR* 2 (1982).

Weber-Kellermann, Ingeborg. *Die deutsche Familie: Versuch einer Sozialgeschichte.* Frankfurt/M.: Hanser, 1984.

Weibel, Peter and Valie Export. *Wien. Bildkompendium Wiener Aktionismus und Film.* Frankfurt/M.: Kohlkunstverlag, 1970.

Weinberg, Herman G. *The Lubitsch Touch.* New York: Dover, 1977.

Weinstock, Jane. "Sexual Difference and the Moving Image." In *Difference: On Representation and Sexuality.* New York: New Museum of Contemporary Art, 1984.

Welch, David. *Propaganda and the German Cinema, 1933–1945*. Oxford: Clarendon, 1983.

Whalen, Robert Weldon. *Bitter Wounds. German Victims of the Great War, 1914–1939*. Ithaca: Cornell University Press, 1984.

Wiegand, Wilfried. "Interview with Rainer Werner Fassbinder." In *Fassbinder*. Trans. Ruth McCormick. New York: Tanam, 1981.

Wiggerhaus, Renate. *Frauen unterm Nationalsozialismus*. Wuppertal: Hammer, 1984.

Wilde, Oscar. "Preface," *The Picture of Dorian Gray*. New York: Ward Lock, 1891.

Wilson, Elizabeth. "Psychoanalysis: Psychic Law and Order." *Feminist Review* 8 (1981).

Windmöller, Eva, and Thomas Höpker. *Leben in der DDR*. Hamburg: Gruner + Jahr, n.d.

Winsloe, Christa. *Das Mädchen Manuela: Der Roman von "Mädchen in Uniform."* Leipzig: E.P. Tal, 1933.

_____. *Gestern und Heute (Ritter Nérestan): Schauspiel in 3 Akten*. Vienna: Georg Marton Verlag, 1930.

_____. *Girls in Uniform: A Play in Three Acts*. Trans. Barbara Burnham. Boston: Little, Brown, 1933.

_____. *The Child Manuela: The Novel of "Mädchen in Uniform."* Trans. Agnes Niel Scott. London: Chapman and Hall , 1934.

Wischnewski, Klaus et al. "Gespräch zwischen Klaus Wischnewski, Konrad Wolf und Wolfgang Kohlhaase." *Film und Fernsehen* 1 (1980).

Witte, Karsten. "Die Filmkomödie im Dritten Reich." In *Die deutsche Literatur im Dritten Reich*, ed. Horst Denkler and Karl Prümm. Stuttgart: Reclam, 1976.

_____. "Dame and Dandy. Ulrike Ottinger's Filme." In *Im Kino. Texte von Sehen & Hören*. Frankfurt/M.: Fischer, 1985.

_____. "How Nazi Cinema Mobilizes the Classics: Schweikart's *Das Fräulein von Barnhelm* (1940)." In *German Film and Literature: Adaptations and Transformations*, ed. Eric Rentschler. New York: Methuen, 1986.

Wolf, Christa. *The Quest for Christa T.* Trans. Christopher Middleton. New York: Delta, 1970.

_____. "The Reader and the Writer." In *The Reader and the Writer: Essays, Sketches, Memories*, trans. Joan Becker. New York: International Publishers, 1977.

_____. *Kein Ort Nirgends*. Darmstadt/Neuwied: Luchterhand, 1979. (English version, *No Place on Earth*. Trans. Jan van Heurck. New York: Farrar Straus Giroux, 1982.)

_____. *Cassandra*. Trans. Jan van Heurck. New York: Farrar Straus Giroux, 1984.

Wolf, Dieter. "Die Kunst, miteinander zu reden. 'Bis daß der Tod euch scheidet' im Gespräch." *Film und Fernsehen* 11 (1979).

Wolf, Konrad. "Es ist etwas im Gange. Spiegel-Interview mit dem DDR-Filmregisseur Konrad Wolf." *Der Spiegel* 15 (1980).

Wolf, Renate. "Tabea Blumenschein und Ulrike Ottinger." *Zeitmagazin* 14 (25 Mar. 1977).

Wollen, Peter. "The Two Avant-gardes." *Edinburgh Magazine* 7 (1976).

Wulf, Joseph. *Theater und Film im Dritten Reich.* Gütersloh, 1964.

Zimmermann, Manfred. *Joseph Süß Oppenheimer: ein Finanzmann des 18. Jahrhunderts.* Stuttgart: Riegersche Verlagsbuchhandlung, 1874.

Notes on Contributors

Gisela E. Bahr is Professor of German Emerita at Miami University of Ohio. In addition to studies on Bertolt Brecht, she has written and/or lectured frequently on GDR literature, culture, and society, especially women. As a filmmaker by hobby, she has made several GDR documentaries.

Barton Byg teaches German and film at the University of Massachusetts-Amherst. He pursued graduate study at Washington University (St. Louis) and at the Free University of Berlin. In addition to a general survey of GDR film history, he is presently completing a book on the cinema of Danièle Huillet and Jean-Marie Straub.

Ramona Curry teaches media studies in the Department of English at the University of Illinois at Urbana-Champaign. Between earning academic degrees, she worked as program coordinator of the Goethe Institute in Chicago and made independent films. She is presently completing a book-length feminist analysis of the star image of Mae West.

Margret Eifler is Professor of German Studies at Rice University. Her research and teaching trace cultural issues from a sociohistorical perspective. She has published several books and numerous articles on contemporary novelists, modern novel theory, feminism, and the New German Film.

Sandra Frieden is the author of *Autobiography: Self into Form. German Language Autobiographical Writings of the 1970s* (Frankfurt: Lang, 1983) and has published articles on contemporary German literature, film, and film pedagogy. She has taught German film at the University of Houston since 1982.

Kathe Geist has a doctorate in art history and specializes in cinema. She is the author of *The Cinema of Wim Wenders: From Paris, France to "Paris, Texas."*

Sabine Hake is Associate Professor of German at the University of Pittsburgh. She is the author of *Passions and Deceptions: The Early Films of*

Ernst Lubitsch (Princeton: Princeton Univ. Press, 1992). Her other work on Weimar culture includes articles on Lang, Chaplin, Sander, von Unruh, and Kracauer, and a book-length study of early German film theory.

Miriam Hansen is Professor of English and Director of the Film Studies Center at the University of Chicago as well as coeditor of *New German Critique*. Her most recent book is *Babel and Babylon: Spectatorship in American Silent Film* (Cambridge: Harvard Univ. Press, 1991). She has published on a wide variety of topics in German film history and film theory, from female moviegoing in the silent era to Alexander Kluge, and is currently writing a book on the Frankfurt School's debates on film and mass culture.

Sheila Kay Johnson received her Ph.D. from McGill University, Montreal (1979). She is presently the Coordinator of the German Program at the University of Texas, San Antonio. She is the author of *Oskar Maria Graf: Critical Reception* and *Frauen und Humor* (in progress) as well as various essays on O.M. Graf, R.W. Faßbinder, Ula Stöckl, István Szabó, G.W. Pabst, Christa Wolf, and Irmtraud Morgner. Her present research concerns Humor and *Karikaturistinnen..*

Anna K. Kuhn is Professor of German at the University of California, Davis. Her main fields of interest are twentieth-century literature and culture, women's studies, and film studies. She has published on modern German drama, GDR literature, and Christa Wolf. Her work on film includes articles on Max Ophuls, Rainer Werner Fassbinder, and Margarethe von Trotta. She is the co-editor of *Playing for Stakes: German Language Drama in Social Context*, forthcoming from Berg Publishers (Winter 1993).

Richard W. McCormick is the author of *Politics of the Self: Feminism and the Postmodern in West German Literature and Film* (Princeton: Princeton Univ. Press, 1991). He is Associate Professor in the Department of German at the University of Minnesota, where he teaches courses on German film and literature. He has published articles on West German cinema and on Weimar cinema.

Jan Mouton is Associate Professor in the Department of Modern Languages and Literatures at Loyola University of Chicago, where she teaches courses on European film. She has published in *Literature/Film Quarterly, Jump Cut, Women in German Yearbook,* and *Germanic Review.* Currenty she is working on a book on European women filmmakers.

Renate Möhrmann is Professor at the Institute for Theater, Film, and Television of the University of Cologne. Her publications on women filmmakers in the Federal Republic of Germany, on women on the stage, and on the theater history of Berlin include *Die andere Frau* (1977), *Die Frau mit der Kamera* (1980), *Berlin-Theater der Jahrhundertwende* (1986), *Die Schauspielerin. Zur Geschichte der weiblichen Bühnenkunst* (1989), and *Theaterwissenschaft heute. Eine Einführung* (1990).

Roswitha Mueller, Associate Professor of German and Film Studies at the University of Wisconsin, Milwaukee, is the author of *Bertolt Brecht and the Theory of Media* and coeditor of *Discourse,* a journal for theoretical studies in media and culture. She also coedits a series of monographs on International Women Filmmakers.

Jeffrey M. Peck is Associate Professor of Germanics and Comparative Literature at the University of Washington. Among his theoretical interests are anthropology and ethnographic theory in relation to literary and cultural studies, specifically personal narratives of minorities and refugees in dominant cultures. He is currently completing a book of interviews and video documentary on German Jews who returned to East and West Berlin.

Ruth Perlmutter has been Professor of film history at the University of the Arts and Tyler School of Art since 1975. She lectures widely on many topics and has published extensively. Her most recent research concerning feminism and German films includes articles on *Petra Von Kant* in *The Minnesota Review, The Malady of Death* in *The Journal of Dureassian Studies,* and Edgar Reitz's *Heimat* in *Wide Angle.*

Vibeke Rützou Petersen is Associate Professor of German and Director of Women's Studies at Drake University, where she teaches film, German, and Women's Studies. She has published on sociopolitical and literary issues of West Germany, on Doris Dörrie, and on Anna Seghers and is currently writing a book-length study on Vicki Baum, women, and Weimar consciousness.

Klaus Phillips, founding director of the annual Hollins Colloquia on German film and editor of *New German Filmmakers. From Oberhausen through the 1970s,* is Associate Professor of German and Film at Hollins College.

B. Ruby Rich is a cultural critic who contributes regularly to the *Village Voice, Mirabella, Sight and Sound,* and numerous other popular and scholarly journals. An Adjunct Visiting Professor (spring semesters) at the University of California, Berkeley, she recently was honored with a residency as Distinguished Visitor at the John D. and Catherine T. MacArthur Foundation in Chicago. For a decade, she served as Executive Director of the Film Program at the New York State Council on the Arts. She is currently preparing a volume of her collected essays for publication.

Marc Silberman teaches at the University of Wisconsin-Madison in the German Department and the Communication Arts Department. He has published on twentieth-century Germany literature and on German Cinema. He is the editor of the Brecht Yearbook and is completing a manuscript on history and the German cinema.

Laurie Melissa Vogelsang is completing a dissertation on German canon formation in the eighteenth century at Yale University, where she has also worked to incorporate film into the second-year language program.

Gabriele Weinberger teaches German, Film, and Women's Studies at Lenoir-Rhyne College in Hickory, North Carolina. She has taught Film and German Studies at Cornell University and does research in Film and Women's Studies.

Index

Möhrmann, Renate, II: 251
Monaco, James, I: **94**
montage, I: **67, 101, 149, 169, 214,
218, 232, 244, 254, 272;** II: 23, 39,
63, 66, 82–83, 243, 280, 286–287.
See also collage; episode
Mörike, Eduard, II: 176
mother tongue, I: **90.** *See also* language
Mühl, Christa, I: **136, 140**
Müller-Westernhagen, Marius, I: **74**
Mulvey, Laura, I: **89, 115, 189, 194,
197, 213–214, 220, 242;** II: 117,
121, 130–131, 242, 260, 305
Mumm, Karin, II: 273
Murnau, F. W., II: 126
music, I: **33, 52, 68, 101, 104, 108;** II:
176, 179, 199, 229, 281
Musil, Robert, II: 6
mute, I: **23–33, 82, 124.** *See also*
silence
myth, I: **6, 64–65, 93–110, 163, 171,
194, 202;** II: 18, 223, 266–268. *See
also* folklore

narcissism, I: **37, 55, 64, 69–71, 174,
194, 199, 203;** II: 21, 77
female, I: **198–200, 203**
National Socialism. *See* Third Reich
Nazi. *See* Third Reich
Negri, Pola, II: 22
Neilsen, Asta, II: 22, 45
Nemec, Jan, II: 237
Newton, Judith, I: **xiii;** II: xviii
Night and Fog. See Resnais, Alain
nightmare. *See* dream

Oberhausen Manifesto, I: **1**
oedipal, I: **7, 209, 213–214, 223;** II:
26, 34, 260, 263
pre-oedipal, I: **117, 185;** II: 17–18,
41
Oppenheimer, Joseph Süss, II: 122
oppression, I: **xiv, xvi, 37, 79, 104,
120, 194, 212–213, 228, 232, 238,
248–250;** II: xiv, xvi, 56, 69, 73,
173, 183, 212, 233, 238, 242–246,
250–251, 254, 257, 267
Organization of Women Working in
Film, I: **3**
Oswalda, Ossi, II: 15, 21–22, 27
Ottinger, Ulrike, I: **2, 4, 191, 225;** II:
171, 293
Madame X, I: **7, 75, 179–188,
192–193**

Ticket of No Return, I: **189–204**
*The Mirror Image of Dorian Gray in
the Yellow Press,* I: **7, 167–168**

Pabst, G. W., II: 91
Joyless Street, II: 3, 43–59
painting, I: **167, 193–194, 213, 244,
263, 267, 269;** II: 21, 229
pantomime, I: **25, 48**
parataxis, I: **170.** *See also* episode
parody. *See* humor
Patalas, Enno, II: 19
Penley, Constance, I: **xv;** II: xv
perspective. *See* point of view
Petro, Patrice, I: **xiii;** II: xiii, 3
phallic mother/woman, I: **184, 186;**
II: 67
photography, I: **193, 196–197, 220,
242, 247, 251, 256–257, 262,
263–264, 269, 273;** II: 21, 95, 245,
249, 254–255, 257, 262–263, 267,
284, 286–287, 297, 303
Piccone, Paul, II: 260
Pieck, Wilhelm, II: 167
Pipolo, Tony, II: 216
pleasure, I: **8, 55–56, 58, 177, 184,
188, 211–213, 228, 260, 264–265;**
II: 13, 25–26, 34, 130–131, 223,
235–236, 247, 251
erotic, II: 24
female/woman's, I: **89;** II: 13
male, I: **255;** II: 242, 249
"pleasure principle," I: **61;** II: 29
seeking, I: **62**
viewing/visual, I: **xiv, 26, 55–56, 58,
189, 194, 197, 199–201, 209,
214–215, 220, 221–223;** II: xiv,
13–14, 17, 21, 24, 32, 121–122,
129, 247
point of view, I: **27, 55, 58, 60–61, 78,
145, 164, 170, 192, 222, 260, 268;**
II: 8, 14, 26, 39, 77, 80, 129, 196,
224, 231, 237, 275, 281, 300
female/woman's, II: 185
male, II: 34
narrative, II: 38
political. *See also* representation, politics of
pornography, I: **226, 228, 233, 236;**
II: 298
postmodern, I: **175, 188, 244**
Prague Film Academy, II: 230
Praunheim, Rosa von, I: **225, 232**
pre-oedipal. *See* oedipal
Prokop, Ulrike, II: 298